Benjamin Weiß

Deductive Verification of Object-Oriented Software

Dynamic Frames, Dynamic Logic and Predicate Abstraction

Deductive Verification of Object-Oriented Software

Dynamic Frames, Dynamic Logic
and Predicate Abstraction

by
Benjamin Weiß

 Scientific Publishing

Dissertation, Karlsruher Institut für Technologie
Fakultät für Informatik
Tag der mündlichen Prüfung: 1. Dezember 2010

Impressum

Karlsruher Institut für Technologie (KIT)
KIT Scientific Publishing
Straße am Forum 2
D-76131 Karlsruhe
www.ksp.kit.edu

KIT – Universität des Landes Baden-Württemberg und nationales
Forschungszentrum in der Helmholtz-Gemeinschaft

KIT Scientific Publishing 2011
Print on Demand

ISBN 978-3-86644-623-6

Deductive Verification of Object-Oriented Software

Dynamic Frames, Dynamic Logic and Predicate Abstraction

zur Erlangung des akademischen Grades eines

Doktors der Naturwissenschaften

von der Fakultät für Informatik
des Karlsruher Instituts für Technologie
genehmigte

Dissertation

von

Benjamin Weiß

aus Heidelberg

Tag der mündlichen Prüfung: 1. Dezember 2010

Erster Gutachter: Prof. Dr. Peter H. Schmitt,
                      Karlsruher Institut für Technologie

Zweiter Gutachter: Prof. Dr. Arnd Poetzsch-Heffter,
                      Technische Universität Kaiserslautern

Acknowledgements

First of all, I would like to express my gratitude to my *Doktorvater* Prof. Dr. Peter H. Schmitt for giving me the opportunity to undertake this project, for his scientific guidance, for his continued support of my work, and for the trust he placed in me.

I am thankful to Prof. Dr. Arnd Poetzsch-Heffter for agreeing to be the second reviewer of this thesis, and for fulfilling his role with commitment. Thanks also go to Prof. Dr. Ralf Reussner and to Juniorprof. Dr. Mana Taghdiri for being examiners in the thesis defense.

I am highly grateful to my former and current colleagues Dr. Christian Engel, David Faragó, Mattias Ulbrich and Dr. Frank Werner for the inspiring discussions, the teamwork, the excellent working atmosphere, and the joint breaks from computer science. The same applies to our new group member Christoph Scheben, and to the members of the other verification-related research groups at the Institute for Theoretical Computer Science: Thorsten Bormer, Daniel Bruns, Dr. Stephan Falke, Aboubakr Achraf El Ghazi, Christoph Gladisch, Florian Merz, Dr. Hendrik Post, Dr. Carsten Sinz, and Dr. Olga Tveretina. Many thanks also go to our administrators Lilian Beckert, Bernd Giesinger and Elke Sauer.

This work is deeply rooted in the KeY project, and it would not have been possible without the great work of many KeY people. I would like to sincerely thank the leaders of KeY—Prof. Dr. Bernhard Beckert, Prof. Dr. Reiner Hähnle and Prof. Dr. Peter H. Schmitt—as well as all past and present members of the project, and in particular Dr. Wolfgang Ahrendt, Dr. Richard Bubel, Dr. Vladimir Klebanov, Dr. Wojciech Mostowski, Dr. Andreas Roth, Dr. Philipp Rümmer and Dr. Steffen Schlager.

Special thanks go to my friends and family.

I gratefully acknowledge the financial support of my work by the Deutsche Forschungsgemeinschaft (DFG), the Karlsruhe Institute of Technology (KIT), and the European Cooperation in Science and Technology (COST).

Karlsruhe, December 2010
Benjamin Weiß

Zusammenfassung (German Summary)

Diese Arbeit entstand im Rahmen des Forschungsprojekts *KeY*. Kernbereich des KeY-Projekts ist die deduktive Verifikation objektorientierter Software, also die Überprüfung der Korrektheit objektorientierter Programme mittels logischen Schließens. Das Ergebnis einer erfolgreichen deduktiven Verifikation ist ein formaler Beweis für die Korrektheit des untersuchten Programms. Das im Rahmen des KeY-Projekts entwickelte KeY-System erlaubt die deduktive Verifikation von Programmen, die in einer sequentiellen Teilmenge der Programmiersprache Java geschrieben sind.

Die Bedeutung des Begriffs *Korrektheit* ergibt sich aus einer formalen *Spezifikation*, die das gewünschte Verhalten eines konkreten Programms oder Programmteils beschreibt. Bei der *vertragsbasierten* Spezifikation (engl.: *design by contract*) werden die Methoden des Programms mit sogenannten *Verträgen* versehen, die mit Hilfe von *Vor-* und *Nachbedingungen* das Ein-/Ausgabeverhalten der Methoden beschreiben. Zusätzlich werden *Objektinvarianten* angegeben, die festlegen, wann sich ein Objekt zur Laufzeit in einem "gültigen" Zustand befindet. Eine Art De-facto-Standard für die vertragsbasierte Spezifikation von *Java*-Programmen – und die bevorzugte Eingabesprache des KeY-Systems – ist die *Java Modeling Language (JML)*.

Ein zentrales Ziel bei der Verifikation objektorientierter Programme ist die *Modularität* der Verifikation: Einzelne Programmteile (z.B. Methoden) sollen unabhängig von ihrem Programmkontext verifiziert werden, und eine einmal bewiesene Korrektheitsaussage soll bei Erweiterung des Programms erhalten bleiben. Hierzu muss bereits die Spezifikation geeignet formuliert werden. Insbesondere verwendet man in öffentlich sichtbaren Spezifikationen nicht die internen Datenstrukturen des spezifizierten Programmteils, sondern führt sogenannte *abstrakte Variablen* ein (die in zwei unterschiedlichen Ausprägungen auch als *Modell-* und *Geistervariablen* bekannt sind). Abstrakte Variablen existieren nur auf der Ebene der Spezifikation, und ihre Beziehung zu den konkreten Datenstrukturen wird als Implementierungsgeheimnis behandelt.

Das Konzept der abstrakten Variablen ist zwar im Prinzip seit den 1970er Jahren bekannt, aber im Detail mit einigen Schwierigkeiten verbunden, deren Lösung bis heute Forschungsgegenstand ist. Interessant ist insbesondere das Zusammenspiel von abstrakten Variablen mit Aussagen über die Speicherstellen, die von einem Programmteil höchstens geändert werden dürfen (engl.: *modifies clau-*

ses). Solche Aussagen sind für die modulare Verifikation unverzichtbar. Auch hier dürfen in einer abstrakten Spezifikation nicht direkt die von der Implementierung intern verwendeten Speicherstellen benutzt werden. Umgekehrt hängen die Werte abstrakter Variablen von konkreten Speicherstellen ab, die im Allgemeinen ebenfalls nicht alle öffentlich sind. Das Kernproblem ist letztlich, unerwünschte *Alias*-Effekte zwischen konkreten und/oder abstrakten Variablen auszuschließen, ohne dabei alle beteiligten Speicherstellen explizit zu kennen. Eine ähnliche Problematik ist mit Objektinvarianten verbunden, deren Gültigkeit in einem Programmzustand typischerweise ebenfalls von nicht-öffentlichen Speicherstellen abhängt.

Ältere Lösungsansätze für diesen Problemkreis sind entweder nicht modular, oder sie basieren auf teils drastischen Einschränkungen der erlaubten Programme. *Besitzbasierte* Ansätze (engl.: *ownership*) erlauben eine effiziente Behandlung vieler typischer Fälle, sind aber für nicht-hierarchische Objektstrukturen weniger geeignet. Ein vor wenigen Jahren vorgeschlagener Ansatz ohne derartige Einschränkungen ist die Verwendung sogenannter *dynamischer Rahmen* (engl.: *dynamic frames*): abstrakte Variablen, deren Werte selbst Mengen von Speicherstellen sind. Die für eine Methode oder eine abstrakte Variable relevanten Speicherbereiche und ihre dynamische Veränderung zur Laufzeit werden hier mit Hilfe von Vor- und Nachbedingungen und mengentheoretischen Operatoren explizit spezifiziert. Trotz ihrer Einfachheit und Allgemeinheit hat diese Technik bisher noch keinen Einzug in verbreitete vertragsbasierte Spezifikationssprachen wie JML gefunden.

Dynamische Logik ist ein etablierter Ansatz zur deduktiven Programmverifikation. Dynamische Logik erweitert Prädikatenlogik erster Stufe um modale Operatoren, die ausführbare Programmfragmente enthalten. Eine konkrete Variante der dynamischen Logik, bei der die Programmfragmente in *Java* geschrieben sind, ist die Grundlage der Verifikation im KeY-System. Eine zentrale Neuerung dieser Variante der dynamischen Logik ist das Konzept der *expliziten Zustandsaktualisierungen* (engl.: *updates*), mit deren Hilfe Zustandsübergänge des Programms syntaktisch in einer programmiersprachenunabhängigen Form dargestellt werden. Dies erlaubt es, die deduktive Programmverifikation als eine *symbolische Ausführung* des Programms zu fassen.

Auf dynamischer Logik basierende Verifikationsverfahren bieten bisher keine Unterstützung für Ansätze wie dynamische Rahmen, und erreichen daher das Ziel der Modularität nur in begrenztem Umfang. In der dynamischen Logik des KeY-Systems ist eine Unterstützung von dynamischen Rahmen nicht unmittelbar möglich, da die der Logik zugrundeliegende Modellierung des Halden-Speichers mit sogenannten *nichtrigiden Funktionssymbolen* es zwar erlaubt, in logischen Formeln über die *Werte* von Speicherstellen in Programmzuständen zu sprechen, nicht aber über die Speicherstellen als solche.

Ein weiteres Ziel bei der deduktiven Verifikation objektorientierter Programme ist die weitestmögliche *Automatisierung* des Verifikationsvorgangs. Neben Interaktionen zum Schlussfolgern auf prädikatenlogischer Ebene ist Benutzerinteraktion in einer Verifikationsumgebung wie dem KeY-System vor allem zur Behandlung von Schleifen in Programmen erforderlich. Schleifen können bei der symbolischen Ausführung des Programms im Allgemeinen nicht automatisch behandelt werden, sondern es müssen *Schleifeninvarianten* angegeben werden, also prädikatenlogische Formeln über den Variablen des Programms, die zu Beginn eines jeden Durchlaufs der Schleife gelten.

Andererseits existieren außerhalb des Gebiets der deduktiven Verifikation Techniken zur *automatischen* statischen Analyse von Schleifen. Diese basieren mehrheitlich auf der sogenannten *abstrakten Interpretation*, d.h. der Berechnung eines Fixpunkts durch wiederholte, approximative, symbolische Ausführung der Schleife. In der Verwendung symbolischer Ausführung ähnelt abstrakte Interpretation der Verifikation in KeY. Eine besonders eng verwandte Variante der abstrakten Interpretation ist die sogenannte *prädikatenbasierte Abstraktion* (engl.: *predicate abstraction*). Hier ist die symbolische Ausführung nicht approximativ, sondern die für die Terminierung der Fixpunktberechnung nötige Approximation wird durch explizite Abstraktionsschritte eingeführt, bei denen mittels automatischem Theorembeweisens eine gültige boolesche Kombination einer Menge von vorgegebenen Prädikaten über den Variablen des Programms ermittelt wird.

In dieser Arbeit wird die deduktive Verifikation objektorientierter Software basierend auf dynamischer Logik verbunden mit der Spezifikation durch dynamische Rahmen einerseits, und mit der Technik der prädikatenbasierten Abstraktion andererseits. Es wird also zum einen die *Modularität* und zum anderen die *Automatisierung* der Verifikation mit dynamischer Logik verbessert. Im Einzelnen sind die Beiträge der Arbeit:

- Eine vertragsbasierte Spezifikationssprache für Java wird vorgeschlagen, die auf JML basiert und das Konzept der dynamischen Rahmen integriert. Im Gegensatz zu gewöhnlichem JML erlaubt diese Sprache das Schreiben modular verifizierbarer Spezifikationen für nichttriviale Java-Programme.

- Eine dynamische Logik mit expliziten Zustandsaktualisierungen für Java wird definiert. Die Logik basiert auf der traditionell im KeY-System verwendeten Logik, weicht aber in der fundamentalen Frage der Modellierung des Halden-Speichers von dieser ab. Anstelle von nichtrigiden Funktionssymbolen wird hier die sogenannte *Theorie der Reihungen* (engl.: *theory of arrays*) verwendet und um spezialisierte Operatoren erweitert, die zum modularen Schlussfolgern über Java-Programme nützlich sind. Der Kalkül der Logik wird an die veränderte Speichermodellierung angepasst, und die Korrektheit wesentlicher Regeln wird nachgewiesen. Insbesondere ergeben sich vorteilhafte Auswirkungen auf die *Schleifeninvariantenregel* zum Behandeln von Schleifen mit Hilfe von Schleifeninvarianten.

- Ein System von Beweisverpflichtungen wird definiert, welche die Korrektheit eines Programms in Bezug auf eine Spezifikation in der eingeführten Spezifikationssprache in der eingeführten dynamischen Logik formalisieren. Dank der veränderten Speichermodellierung können dynamische Rahmen unterstützt werden. Ergänzend zu den Beweisverpflichtungen werden vertragsbasierte Kalkül-Regeln definiert, mit denen sich z.B. ein Methodenaufruf während der symbolischen Ausführung mit Hilfe eines Vertrags modular behandeln lässt. Es wird nachgewiesen, dass diese Regeln korrekt sind, sofern die zu dem Vertrag gehörenden Beweisverpflichtungen erfüllt sind.

- Ein Ansatz zur Integration von prädikatenbasierter Abstraktion in dynamische Logik wird vorgestellt. Die Integration erlaubt es in manchen Fällen, die für die Verifikation einer Schleife notwendigen Schleifeninvarianten automatisch zu ermitteln. Die Fixpunktberechnung zum Finden einer Schleifeninvariante ist dabei nahtlos in den eigentlichen Verifikationsprozess integriert; die symbolische Ausführung ist gleichzeitig deduktives Beweisen und abstrakte Interpretation. Dadurch wird vermieden, die umfangreiche Semantik der Programmiersprache redundant sowohl im Verifikationssystem als auch in einem separaten abstrakten Interpretierer modellieren zu müssen.

- Die vorgeschlagenen Ansätze sind im KeY-System implementiert und an kleineren Beispielen erprobt worden.

Contents

III. Loop Invariant Generation   163

7. Background on Abstract Interpretation   165

8. Predicate Abstraction in Java Dynamic Logic   185

List of Figures

List of Tables

1. Introduction

1.1. Software Verification

Computer software plays a central role in modern society. The reliability of software systems is important economically, and it is downright essential for safety-critical systems such as those in the areas of automotive, aeronautical or medical applications. At the same time, software flaws ("bugs") are still considered to be virtually inevitable; in all but the most safety-critical areas, it is generally accepted that shipped software products do contain bugs. This is in contrast to disciplines like electrical or mechanical engineering, which are older and more mature than computer science, and where faulty products are viewed as exceptions rather than the norm.

This thesis is about improving the quality of software systems through *formal methods*, i.e., techniques for describing, designing, developing and analysing software systems with mathematical rigour. Although formal methods are not a "silver bullet" that magically solves all problems of software reliability, they can be expected to continuously gain importance in the future, complementing and in some cases replacing traditional software engineering techniques.

More precisely, this thesis is about *software verification* on the source code level: the goal is to ensure in a rigorous way that pieces of software written in a real-world programming language are correct. In contrast, examples for formal methods that are more oriented towards abstract design rather than source code are modelling languages such as *Z* [Spivey, 1992], *B* and *Event-B* [Abrial, 1996; Hallerstede, 2009], *Alloy* [Jackson, 2002], and *Abstract State Machines* [Börger and Stärk, 2003].

The meaning of the notion of *correctness* is defined for an individual program by a formal *specification* that describes the intended behaviour of the program in a formal language. The description may cover the entire functional behaviour of the code, or it may be concerned with specific properties only. A widely used variety of rather specific formal specification—although not always thought of as such—are the *types* of mainstream programming languages: the type of a variable restricts the intended values that should be stored in the variable at run-time. As stated by Pierce [2002], "type systems are the most popular and best established lightweight formal methods".

A slightly less lightweight, but also widely popular kind of formal specification are *assertions*, i.e., Boolean expressions in the programming language (or formulas in a more expressive language) that should always be satisfied when program execution reaches a particular point in the code. The idea of attaching formulas to program points was first introduced by Floyd [1967]. Assertions allow expressing more complex properties than usual type systems. As an example for their popularity, Hoare [2003a] estimated that at the time there were about a quarter of a million assertions in the code of Microsoft Office.

Design by contract is an extension of the assertion mechanism of standard programming languages. Here, the procedures of an object-oriented program are specified through *pre- and postconditions*, and its classes through *object invariants*. Building on earlier work such as that of Hoare [1969, 1972], the term "design by contract" was coined by Meyer [1992, 2000] when designing the *Eiffel* programming language, which features built-in support for design-by-contract specifications. Procedure and class specifications are viewed as *contracts* between client and implementer of the procedure or class, defining mutual responsibilities and facilitating modularisation of the program.

Techniques for *verifying* software with respect to a specification can be divided into *static* and *dynamic* techniques. Static techniques operate on the source code without actually executing it; an example is the type checking done by a compiler. In contrast, dynamic techniques are based on executing the program for concrete input values, i.e., on *testing* the program. Testing may or may not be considered to be a (lightweight) formal method. It is today the primary means for establishing software reliability, and industry is accustomed to spending massive efforts on it. Even though testing will undoubtedly remain important in the future, its reach is hardly satisfactory: for all but the most trivial software systems, the state space is so large that exhaustive testing is utterly infeasible. Thus, as Dijkstra [1972] famously put it, "program testing can be used to show the presence of bugs, but never to show their absence".

Assertions and design-by-contract specifications are today usually used for dynamic run-time checks, which can serve as *test oracles* that indicate whether a test run has been successful or not. This thesis is about instead verifying such specifications *statically*. More precisely, it is concerned with fully-fledged, heavyweight static verification, where the goal is to indeed show the absence of bugs in a program. Static verification techniques (beyond simple type checking) can be useful also in more lightweight flavours, where the goal is to just find bugs earlier and more cheaply than through extensive testing. Heavyweight static verification is an undecidable problem. This may be taken as an indication of how challenging a problem it is, but it does not imply that handling the practically relevant instances is impossible. A vision in the area of static verification, put forward as a "grand challenge" for computer science research by Hoare [2003b,c], is to devise a "verifying compiler" that checks the correctness of assertions much like compilers perform type checking already today.

The form of static verification embraced in this thesis is *deductive verification*. Deductive verification, which was pioneered by Hoare [1969], is arguably the most formal verification technique of all: a program is verified by constructing a *logical proof* of its correctness. Two other broad approaches to static software verification, where logic may or may not play a role but where typically no formal proofs are created, are *abstract interpretation* [Cousot and Cousot, 1977] and *symbolic software model checking* [Henzinger et al., 2003; Clarke et al., 2004; Ball et al., 2006]. Abstract interpretation emphasises the role of approximation for achieving automation. It also plays a role in this thesis, although the focus is on deductive verification. The idea of software model checking grew out of classical model checking, where properties of finite-state systems are checked by explicit state exploration. For checking source code, symbolic software model checkers may use automatic abstraction techniques, much like in abstract interpretation. The boundaries between deductive verification, abstract interpretation and symbolic software model checking are not sharp, the reasons for the differentiation being to some extent historical.

An important point to note is that even deductive verification, aiming at soundly proving the absence of bugs in a program, is not about gaining *absolute certainty* that a program works as intended. Absolute certainty is impossible to achieve, for example because there is always a gap between the formal specification of a program and the human intention on what the program is really supposed to do. The goal of deductive verification is a dramatic, but still only gradual, increase in trust in the correctness of a piece of software. As a corollary, and as argued in more detail by Beckert and Klebanov [2006], it is useful but not necessary for a verification system to itself be strictly verified in some way; trust in its functioning may also be gained by other means, such as, only seemingly paradoxically, by means of testing.

1.2. KeY

The research underlying this thesis has been carried out as a part of the *KeY project* [Beckert et al., 2007]. The KeY project started in 1998 at the University of Karlsruhe, and is today a joint effort between the Karlsruhe Institute of Technology, Chalmers University of Technology in Gothenburg, and the University of Koblenz. Its central topic is deductive verification of object-oriented software.

The main software product of the KeY project is the *KeY system*, a verification tool for proving the correctness of programs written in the *Java* language [Gosling et al., 2000]. More precisely, KeY supports the full *Java Card* language in version 2.2.1 [Java Card 2003], which is roughly a subset of sequential Java 1.4 with some smart card specific extensions, and it supports a few Java features beyond Java Card. On the side of specification, KeY accepts (customised versions of) the *Java Modeling Language (JML)* [Leavens et al., 2006a] and the *Object Constraint Language* [OCL 2006], in addition to its own input format.

Given a Java program with an accompanying specification, KeY first translates it into *proof obligations*, which are formulas whose logical validity corresponds to correctness of the program with respect to the specification. The logic used for this purpose is a *dynamic logic* [Pratt, 1976; Harel et al., 2000], i.e., an extension of first-order predicate logic with modal operators that contain executable program fragments of some programming language. In the dynamic logic of KeY, which we refer to as *JavaDL* here, these program fragments are written in Java. As programs directly appear in dynamic logic formulas, the pre-processing step of generating the proof obligations is relatively small. The rest of the verification process is deductive: at its core, KeY is a theorem prover for dynamic logic. It allows both for interactive proving using a special-purpose graphical user interface, and for automatic proving with the help of automated proof search strategies. The final outcome of a successful verification attempt is a proof for the logical validity of a proof obligation.

An important novel feature of JavaDL, as opposed to other versions of dynamic logic, is its concept of state *updates* [Beckert, 2001; Rümmer, 2006]. Updates are an explicit, syntactic representation of state changes, which is independent of the programming language being verified. With the help of updates, programs in formulas are handled in the JavaDL calculus by performing a *symbolic execution* of the program, where the verification process resembles executing the program, using symbolic instead of concrete values for the variables of the program.

Symbolic execution ultimately removes programs from formulas, thereby reducing the verification problem to the problem of proving the logical validity of formulas in first-order predicate logic with built-in theories. These remaining tasks are usually also handled within KeY itself. As an alternative, KeY allows sending such verification problems to external *satisfiability modulo theories (SMT) solvers* such as *Simplify* [Detlefs et al., 2005] or *Z3* [de Moura and Bjørner, 2008]. These are then used as trusted "black boxes" that can automatically determine the validity of some first-order formulas, thereby sacrificing some traceability for sometimes better automation and performance than offered by KeY itself.

Where SMT solvers are useful but non-essential add-ons in KeY, there are a number of verification tools that use SMT solvers as their primary foundation, namely most tools that follow the paradigm of *verification condition generation*: the program and its specification are first translated into first-order formulas called *verification conditions*, which are then passed to an SMT solver. Symbolic execution in KeY is related to verification condition generation, but differs in that it may be intertwined with other forms of reasoning. Also, it is a deductive, rule-based process, while verification condition generation usually is not. Tools based on verification condition generation often compile the source code to an *intermediate language* before generating the verification condition. This multi-step architecture is beneficial in that it facilitates modularisation of the verification system, but the compilation is another non-deductive, black-box step. No explicit proofs for the correctness of the verified program are created. For these reasons, even though such tools may be considered deductive because of their use of logic and SMT solvers, they are so to a lesser degree than KeY.

Examples of verifiers for object-oriented programs based on verification condition generation are *ESC/Java* [Flanagan et al., 2002], its successor *ESC/Java2* [Cok and Kiniry, 2005], *Spec#* [Barnett et al., 2005, 2010], and a number of offsprings of Spec# [Leino, 2008; Smans et al., 2008] that also use its backend *Boogie* [Barnett et al., 2006] for generating verification conditions. In the spirit of the "verifying compiler", these tools are fully automatic, in the sense that when executed, they run to termination without any interaction in between. Ideally, this architecture should spare their users the need to understand their internals. However, full automation of functional software verification is today way beyond the state of the art. Thus, in practice, one does need to interact with these tools: the interaction consists of guiding the tool along by writing auxiliary source code annotations [Beckert et al., 2009a]. If the employed SMT solver—dealing heuristically with instances of an undecidable problem—is unable to prove a valid verification condition, verifying a correct program may fail; a human verification expert may be able to solve this problem by adding appropriate annotations. *JACK* [Burdy et al., 2003] and *Krakatoa* [Marché et al., 2004] are Java verifiers based on verification condition generation that are unusual in that they target interactive provers for higher-order logic (in particular *Coq*) for proving the verification conditions, in addition to SMT solvers.

Two tools for deductively verifying object-oriented programs that like KeY do not follow the verification condition generation approach are *KIV* [Reif, 1995; Stenzel, 2004] and *Jive* [Meyer and Poetzsch-Heffter, 2000; Darvas and Müller, 2007b]. Both use logics where programs are directly embedded into formulas, and both allow constructing proofs for such formulas interactively. KIV, like KeY, uses a dynamic logic, and performs the entire verification within one prover. Jive uses a Hoare logic (which is similar to, but more restricted than dynamic logic), and employs a separate, generic prover (*Isabelle/HOL*) or an SMT solver for proving program-independent properties.

According to estimates of Klebanov [2009], the KeY system consists of roughly 124 000 lines of Java code, not counting comments; its calculus comprises about 1725 rules, of which about 1300 are symbolic execution rules that formalise the semantics of Java; approximately 30 person years have been spent on its development. The system includes several add-on functionalities that build on its theorem proving core, such as automatic *generation of test cases* [Engel and Hähnle, 2007; Beckert and Gladisch, 2007] and *symbolic debugging* [Baum, 2007; Hähnle et al., 2010]. The current release version is KeY 1.4, and the current developer version KeY 1.5. Case studies of verification with KeY have, amongst others, targeted parts of a flight management system developed by Thales Avionics [Hunt et al., 2006], the *Demoney* electronic purse application provided by Trusted Logic S.A. [Beckert et al., 2007, Chapter 14], a Java implementation of the *Schorr-Waite* graph marking algorithm [Beckert et al., 2007, Chapter 15], a Java Card implementation of the *Mondex* electronic purse [Schmitt and Tonin, 2007], and an implementation of the *Java Card API* [Mostowski, 2007].

1.3. Problems and Contributions

An important goal in deductive verification of object-oriented software is *modularity* of the verification: parts of the program (e.g., methods) should be verified independently from the rest of the program, and a proof that has been completed once should not have to be redone when the program is extended later. To this end, already the specification must be formulated in a modular way. In particular, public interface specifications must not use internal data structures of the specified program part. Instead, one can introduce so-called *abstract variables* [Hoare, 1972], which in two different forms are also known as *model* and *ghost* variables. Abstract variables exist only on the level of the specification, and their relationship with the concrete data structures of the program is treated as an implementational secret to be hidden from the rest of the program.

Even though the basic concept of abstract variables has been known since the 1970s, some aspects of it are still a challenge for current research. A particularly interesting area is the relationship between abstract variables and specifications about the memory locations that may at most be modified by a program part (so-called *modifies clauses*). Such specifications are necessary for modular verification. Here, too, an abstract specification must not directly mention the memory locations used in a particular implementation. Conversely, the values of abstract variables depend on concrete memory locations, which in general are also not all publicly visible. Ultimately, the problem is to prevent unwanted *aliasing* between concrete and/or abstract variables, without knowing all involved locations explicitly. A similar problem occurs for object invariants, whose validity in a program state typically also depends on the values of private memory locations.

Older approaches for solving these issues are either non-modular, or they are based on sometimes drastic restrictions on what a programmer may write in a program. Approaches based on object *ownership* [Clarke et al., 1998; Müller, 2002] allow for an efficient treatment of many typical cases, but they are ill-suited for non-hierarchical object structures. Kassios [2006a] proposed an approach without such limitations, namely the use of so-called *dynamic frames*. Dynamic frames are abstract variables whose values themselves are sets of memory locations. The set of memory locations that are relevant for a method or for an abstract variable, and how this set changes dynamically at run-time, are then specified explicitly through pre- and postconditions and set-theoretic operators. Even though it is both simple and general, the approach of dynamic frames has not yet found its way into widespread specification languages such as JML.

Verification techniques based on dynamic logic so far support neither dynamic frames nor alternative approaches such as ownership, and thus achieve the goal of modularity only partially. In JavaDL, handling dynamic frames is not directly possible, because the underlying logical model of *heap memory*, based on so-called *non-rigid functions*, allows talking in logical formulas about the *values* stored at memory locations, but not about the locations as such.

Another goal in deductive verification is *automating* the verification process as far as possible. Besides interactions on the level of first-order reasoning, human intervention is required mainly for handling *loops* in programs. Symbolic execution (or verification condition generation) in general cannot handle loops automatically, but rather expects that *loop invariants* are provided interactively, i.e., first-order formulas that are valid at the beginning of each loop iteration. Finding a sufficiently strong loop invariant for verifying a property at hand can be a difficult task.

On the other hand, outside of the area of deductive program verification there are techniques for statically analysing loops in an automatic way. These are predominantly based on abstract interpretation. In abstract interpretation, loops are handled in a way that can be seen as repeated symbolic, approximative execution of the loop body until stabilisation at a fixed point. In its use of symbolic execution, abstract interpretation resembles the verification process in KeY. A form of abstract interpretation particularly closely related to deductive verification is *predicate abstraction* [Graf and Saïdi, 1997]. Here, the symbolic execution is itself not approximative, and the necessary approximation is instead introduced through explicit abstraction steps, where automated theorem proving is used to determine a valid Boolean combination of formulas from a predetermined set of so-called *loop predicates*.

This thesis combines deductive verification of object-oriented software based on dynamic logic with dynamic frames on one hand, and with predicate abstraction on the other hand. It thus aims at improving the *modularity* and the *automation* of verification with dynamic logic. In more detail, its main contributions are the following:

- A design-by-contract *specification language* for Java is presented, which is based on JML and which integrates the essence of the theory of dynamic frames. In contrast to ordinary JML, the language allows writing modularly verifiable specifications for non-trivial Java programs.

- A *dynamic logic* with updates for Java is defined. The logic is based on JavaDL as it is traditionally used in KeY, but differs in the fundamental question of how to logically model the program's heap memory. Instead of non-rigid function symbols, it uses the *theory of arrays* of McCarthy [1963] and extends it with specialised operators that are useful for modular reasoning about Java programs. The JavaDL calculus is adapted to the changed heap modelling, and the soundness of core rules is formally proven. In particular, the change in heap modelling has positive effects on the *loop invariant rule* for handling loops with the help of loop invariants.

- A system of *proof obligations* is defined, which use the introduced logic to capture the correctness of Java programs with respect to specifications written in the introduced specification language. The changed heap modelling allows for supporting dynamic frames. The proof obligations are complemented by contract-based *calculus rules*, which for example allow reasoning about a method call during symbolic execution modularly with the help of a contract for the called method. It is proven that these rules are sound, provided that the proof obligations belonging to the employed contract are logically valid. Parts of this material and of the underlying logical foundation have been published as [Schmitt et al., 2011, 2010].

- An approach for *integrating predicate abstraction* into dynamic logic is presented. The integration sometimes allows determining the necessary loop invariants for a loop automatically. The fixed-point computation for determining the loop invariant is deeply integrated into the verification process itself: the resulting symbolic execution process is deductive verification and abstract interpretation at the same time. This avoids having to redundantly encode knowledge about the semantics of the programming language and about the involved logical theories both in the deductive verification system and in a separate abstract interpretation system that generates loop invariants for the deductive system. These contributions have largely been published as [Weiß, 2009, 2011], and include some additional ideas published in [Bubel et al., 2009].

- The proposed techniques have been implemented in the KeY system and tested on moderately sized examples.

1.4. Outline

The thesis is divided into three parts, where Part I is about *specification*, Part II about the modular *verification* of specifications, and Part III about improving automation of the verification by *generating loop invariants*.

Part I begins with a review of JML, and thereby of the state of the art in design-by-contract specification for Java, in Chapter 2. Chapter 3 then presents the new specification language based on JML and on dynamic frames.

As the first chapter of Part II, Chapter 4 discusses several possibilities for modelling heap memory in program logics. This provides motivation for Chapter 5, which defines the dynamic logic based on JavaDL that uses a different way of modelling the heap. Proof obligations and contract rules for verifying specifications in the language of Chapter 3 in this logic are presented in Chapter 6.

Part III first provides background on the theory of abstract interpretation in Chapter 7, before introducing the approach for integrating predicate abstraction into dynamic logic in Chapter 8.

The thesis ends with conclusions in Chapter 9.

Part I.

Specification

2. Background on JML

The *Java Modeling Language* (*JML*) [Leavens et al., 2006a, 2008] is a language for writing formal specifications about Java programs. Its authors classify it as a *behavioural interface specification language* [Hatcliff et al., 2009], i.e., a language for specifying the functional behaviour of the interfaces of program modules (such as, in an object-oriented setting, methods and classes). Using a metaphor proposed by Meyer [1992], one can also call it a *design by contract* language: its specifications can naturally be understood as "legal contracts" between the clients and the implementers of each module, where the responsibility for overall correctness is split between the contracting parties. Some other examples for this general type of specification language are Larch [Guttag et al., 1993], Eiffel [Meyer, 2000], SPARK [Barnes, 2003], Spec# [Barnett et al., 2005] and OCL [OCL 2006]. In the area of design-by-contract style specification for Java, JML can today be considered the de facto standard, and it is supported by a large number of tools (refer to Burdy et al. [2005] for a slightly outdated overview of JML tools).

The KeY tool accepts JML as one of its input formats, and translates it into its verification logic JavaDL. Alternatively, specifications can be written in JavaDL directly, but using JML usually means better readability and less verbosity, and requires less special knowledge. The present chapter serves as an introduction to the parts of JML relevant for this thesis, and, by this example, to the basics of design-by-contract style specification for object-oriented software in general. Particular emphasis is placed on the difficult issue of *data abstraction* in specifications. i.e., the question how classes and interfaces can be specified in an abstract way, without referring to the concrete data structures used in any particular implementation of the specified functionality. These issues motivate the extensions to JML proposed in Chapter 3, and the changes in the definition of JavaDL in Chapter 5, compared to the traditional definition of this logic as given by Beckert [2001]; Beckert et al. [2007]. Just as the definition of JML [Leavens et al., 2008] is written in natural language rather than in some formal notation, both the present chapter and Chapter 3 have a less formal nature than later chapters of this thesis. Formalisations of parts of JML are explored by Leavens et al. [2006b] and by Bruns [2009].

Outline We start with a look at JML's expression sub-language in Section 2.1. Section 2.2 then introduces what is arguably JML's most elementary specification

13

feature, namely basic *method contracts* consisting of *pre- and postconditions*, *modifies clauses*, and sometimes *diverges clauses*. Besides method contracts, a second main feature of design by contract specification for object-oriented software in general and of JML in particular is that of *object invariants*, which are the topic of Section 2.3. In Section 2.4 we take a look at the interplay between *subtyping* and *inheritance* on one hand and JML specifications on the other hand. Section 2.5 deals with the question of *data abstraction* in specifications, and presents JML's answers to this question, namely *ghost fields*, *model fields*, *data groups*, and *pure methods* with *depends clauses*. We conclude in Section 2.6.

2.1. Expressions

JML is a specification language dedicated to specifying Java programs. As such, it aims to provide a flat learning curve for experienced Java programmers new to formal specification, and strives to be as close to the Java language as possible. Its expressions are mostly just Java expressions, which for pre- and postconditions and invariants are of type **boolean**. The only restriction compared to Java expressions is that JML expressions must not have side-effects on the program state, in order to give them a logical, rather than imperative, character. This means that Java expressions like i++ or calls to state-changing methods are not legal JML expressions.

On the other hand, JML features a number of extensions over the expressions allowed in Java. Two important such extensions are the universal quantifier **\forall** and the existential quantifier **\exists**. An expression (**\forall** T x; b1; b2), where T is a type, where x is a variable identifier bound in b1 and b2, and where b1 and b2 are **boolean** expressions, means that for all instances x of type T for which the expression b1 holds, expression b2 must also hold. Analogously, an expression (**\exists** T x; b1; b2) means that *there is* an instance of type T such that *both* b1 and b2 hold. One can also write (**\forall** T x; b) and (**\exists** T x; b) to abbreviate the expressions (**\forall** T x; **true**; b) and (**\exists** T x; **true**; b), respectively.

Some other extensions are only available in method postconditions. Here, the method's return value, if applicable, can be referred to using the keyword **\result**. The value that an expression e had in the pre-state before method execution (but after assigning values to its formal parameters) can be denoted as **\old**(e). For an expression e of a reference type, **\fresh**(e) is a **boolean** expression which is true if and only if the object to which e evaluates was not yet created in the pre-state.

JML also features a meta-type **\TYPE** whose instances are the types themselves, and a few operators for this type. Firstly, for every type T, **\type**(T) is an expression of type **\TYPE** evaluating to T. Also, for every expression e, **\typeof**(e) is an expression of type **\TYPE** which evaluates to the dynamic type of the value of e. Thus, for example, "**\typeof**(3+4) == **\type**(Object)" is a JML expression that always evaluates to false.

A problem with using Java expressions directly for specification is that in Java, expressions do not have a defined value in every state; sometimes, trying to evaluate an expression instead results in an exception being thrown. For example, evaluating the expression x/y in a state where the sub-expression y has the value 0 will trigger an exception of type java.lang.ArithmeticException. Because of this, Java's **boolean** expressions used in JML to formulate, for example, pre- and postconditions and invariants, are essentially *three-valued* formulas, which in every state evaluate to either "true", "false", or "undefined" (if an exception is thrown).

In specifications, we may nevertheless want to stay within the world of classical two-valued logic, which is generally easier to handle in verification tools. A common approach to achieve this, which used to be employed by JML, is known as *underspecification* [Gries and Schneider, 1995]. Here, we use fixed, but unknown ("underspecified") regular values instead of a dedicated "undefined" value. This works largely well, because "good" specifications avoid cases of undefinedness anyway. For example, specifications may use Java's short-cut evaluation of the operators || and && to avoid throwing exceptions: in "y == 0 || x/y == 3", the value (or lack thereof) of x/0 is irrelevant, because the subexpression x/y is never evaluated in a state where y has the value 0.

However, if the person writing the specification makes a mistake, specifications can be insufficiently guarded against undefinedness, and in these cases simple underspecification can lead to unexpected results. For example, the expression "x/y == 3 || y == 0" throws an exception in Java if y has the value 0, but evaluates to true with underspecification. Another example is "x/0 == x/0", which always throws an exception in Java, but which is always true if underspecification is used: the value of x/0 may be unknown, but it is the same on both sides of the equality operator.

After these discrepancies between the underspecification semantics of JML and the semantics of Java had been criticised by Chalin [2007a], JML switched to an approach called *strong validity* [Chalin, 2007b]. Here, a top-level pre- or postcondition or invariant evaluates to true if it logically evaluates to true *and* if it would not throw an exception in Java; it evaluates to false otherwise. In other words, Java's three-valued semantics is used, but at the top level of a specification expression, the value "undefined" is converted into the value "false". For example, a top-level expression "x/0 == x/0" and its negation "!(x/0 == x/0)" both always evaluate to false: in both cases, the subexpression x/0 is "undefined", making the overall expression "undefined" also, which is then converted into the value "false". Short-circuit evaluation is respected, so "**true** || x/0 == x/0" is always true, while "x/0 == x/0 || **true**" is always false. Note that even though—in contrast to the underspecification approach—a third truth value is involved, this does not imply that a verification system supporting JML must necessarily use many-valued logic; see for example the work by Darvas et al. [2008].

2.2. Method Contracts

JML specifications can be written directly into Java source code files, where they appear as comments that start with the character "@" to distinguish them from other, non-JML comments. A first example for a Java class annotated with JML is shown in Figure 2.1.

Those comments that precede method declarations in Figure 2.1 specify *method contracts* (sometimes called just *contracts*, or *specification cases* in JML) for the respective method. As a first approximation, we can see method contracts as lists consisting of an arbitrary number of *preconditions* and *postconditions* for the method. A method can be annotated with multiple contracts, separated by the **also** keyword. For example, method **get** in line 27 has two contracts, one starting with "**public normal_behaviour**" and one starting with "**public exceptional_behaviour**".

As demonstrated by these occurrences of the keyword **public**, Java's *visibility* system extends also to JML specifications. Specification elements, such as contracts, may refer only to fields and methods of higher (more public) visibility than the specification element itself. However, a field or method may be marked as **spec_protected** or **spec_public** (as in lines 2 and 4 of Figure 2.1) to increase its visibility in JML specifications, without changing it on the level of Java. Beyond this syntactical requirement, visibilities do not carry semantical meaning. They may however influence the behaviour of a modular verifier (Chapter 6).

The elements of method contracts that we consider in this section are *pre- and postconditions* (Subsection 2.2.1), *modifies clauses* (Subsection 2.2.2), and *diverges clauses* (Subsection 2.2.3). Another element occurring as a part of method contracts, the *depends clause*, is introduced later in Section 2.5.

2.2.1. Pre- and Postconditions

Method preconditions are declared with the keyword **requires**, followed by a **boolean** JML expression. Postconditions are declared with the keyword **ensures**. Their meaning is that if all the preconditions of a contract hold before method execution and if the method terminates normally—i.e., it terminates not by throw-

—— Java + JML ——————————————————————————————

```
1  public class ArrayList {
2      private /*@spec_public nullable@*/ Object[] array
3                                        = new Object[10];
4      private /*@spec_public@*/ int size = 0;
5
6      /*@ private invariant array != null;
7        @ private invariant 0 <= size && size <= array.length;
8        @ private invariant (\forall int i; 0 <= i && i < size;
9        @                                   array[i] != null);
10       @ private invariant \typeof(array) == \type(Object[]);
11       @*/
12
13      /*@ public normal_behaviour
14        @   ensures \result == size;
15        @*/
16      public /*@pure@*/ int size() {
17          return size;
18      }
19
20      /*@ public normal_behaviour
21        @   requires 0 <= index && index < size;
22        @   ensures \result == array[index];
23        @ also public exceptional_behaviour
24        @   requires index < 0 || size <= index;
25        @   signals_only IndexOutOfBoundsException;
26        @*/
27      public /*@pure@*/ Object get(int index) {
28          if(index < 0 || size <= index) {
29              throw new IndexOutOfBoundsException();
30          } else {
31              return array[index];
32          }
33      }
34
35      /*@ public normal_behaviour
36        @   assignable array, array[*];
37        @   ensures size == \old(size) + 1 && array[size - 1] == o;
38        @   ensures (\forall int i; 0 <= i && i < size - 1;
39        @                           array[i] == \old(array[i]));
40        @*/
41      public void add(Object o) {...}
42  }
```

—————————————————————————————— Java + JML ——

Figure 2.1.: Java class `ArrayList` with JML specifications

ing an exception—then all the postconditions declared with **ensures** must hold afterwards. For example, lines 21 and 22 of Figure 2.1 state that if the method `get` is called with an argument `index` that lies between 0 and `size`, and if the method terminates normally, then its return value is the object contained in the array `array` at position `index`.

Postconditions for the case of *exceptional* termination (i.e., termination by throwing an exception) are specified using clauses of the form "**signals(E e) b**", where E is some subtype of class `java.lang.Exception`, where e is a variable identifier bound in b, and where b is a boolean JML expression. The meaning of such a **signals** clause is the following: if the method terminates by throwing an exception e of type E (and if the preconditions held on method entry), then b must evaluate to true in the post-state.

The keyword **normal_behaviour** at the beginning of a contract is essentially "syntactic sugar" for a postcondition "**signals(Exception e) false**": it means that the method must not throw any exception if the contract's preconditions hold. Conversely, the keyword **exceptional_behaviour** is syntactic sugar for "**ensures false**", meaning that the method must not terminate *normally*. Another abbreviation are clauses of the form "**signals_only** $E_1, \ldots, E_n$", which can be spelled out as

signals(Exception e) e **instanceof** E_1 || ... || e **instanceof** E_n;

For example, the second contract of method `get` in Figure 2.1 states that if the method is called in a state where the argument `index` is out of bounds, then the method may terminate only by throwing an exception of the type `java.lang.IndexOutOfBoundsException` (or of a subtype). Like **requires** and **ensures** clauses, multiple **signals** clauses are connected by conjunction, so if a method terminates by throwing an exception of type E, then *all* signals clauses about E or about any of its supertypes apply.

Note that JML specifications can only talk about the method's post-state in case of normal termination, or in case of termination by throwing an object whose type is a subtype of `java.lang.Exception`. The possibility that an object could be thrown that is of some other subtype of `java.lang.Throwable`, in particular a subtype of `java.lang.Error`, is silently ignored. The rationale behind this is that such events typically represent "external" problems, which are not directly caused by the program itself. Two examples are `java.lang.OutOfMemoryError` and `java.lang.UnknownError`. As we consider these errors to be out of the program's control, we do not demand that the program guarantees that they do not occur, or that any conditions hold afterwards if they do occur.

Yet another abbreviation supported by JML is the keyword **non_null**. Affixing this e.g. to a method parameter x or to a method return type means to add to all contracts of the method an implicit precondition "**requires x != null**" or an implicit postcondition "**\result != null**", respectively. Moreover, as proposed by Chalin and Rioux [2006], **non_null** has become the default in JML: now the **non_null** modifier is always implicitly present, unless something is explicitly labelled as **nullable**. Thus, both contracts of method **get** in Figure 2.1 have an invisible postcondition "**\result != null**", and the contract of method **add** has an invisible precondition "**o != null**".

2.2.2. Modifies Clauses

If a method contract is to be useful for modular verification, where method calls are dealt with only by looking at the called method's contract instead of its implementation, it must constrain *what* part of the state may be changed by the method in addition to just *how* it is changed. This act of constraining is often referred to as *framing*, the part of the state that may be changed as the *frame* of the method, and the whole issue of framing as the *frame problem* [Borgida et al., 1995].

In principle, framing can be done with a postcondition that just lists all the unchanged memory locations, and uses something like the **\old** operator to state that their current values are the same as their values in the pre-state. However, doing so is at best cumbersome due to the typically high number of unchanged locations, and at worst impossible if, in a modular setting, the program context is not entirely available. One solution to this problem is to allow universal quantification over memory locations. Another common solution, which is employed in JML, is to extend method contracts with *modifies clauses* [Guttag et al., 1993]. A modifies clause is a list of the (typically few) locations that may be modified, implying that all the others may not be modified.

In JML, modifies clauses are also called *assignable clauses*. This difference in nomenclature hints at a subtle semantical difference: when defining the precise meaning of modifies clauses, there is a choice on whether *temporary modifications* to locations not in the modifies clause are to be allowed or not. If, as above, modifies clauses are viewed as being essentially postconditions that frame the overall effect of the method, then any temporary modification that is undone before method termination can have no effect on the validity of the modifies clause. However, as the name *assignable* clause suggests, JML imposes a stricter policy: a method satisfies its assignable clause only if every single assignment executed during its execution is covered by the assignable clause. In a concurrent setting, this interpretation is advantageous, because then, modifies clauses also constrain the intermediate states of execution, which allows them to be used for reasoning about non-interference between threads. On the other hand, for sequential programs the classical, more semantic, interpretation is completely sufficient, and in this thesis we stick with it.

Modifies clauses are declared in JML with the keyword **assignable**. The expression after this keyword is not a normal expression, but a list of so-called "store ref expressions" denoting sets of memory locations. The overall modifies clause evaluates to the union of these individual sets. The store ref expression o.f, where f is some field defined for the type of expression o, denotes the singleton location set consisting of the field f of the object which is the value of o (and not, as in a normal expression, the *value* of this location). Similarly, the store ref expression a[i] denotes the singleton set containing the ith component of array a. A range of array components, or all components of an array, can be denoted as a[i..j] or a[*], respectively. By o.* we can refer to the set of all fields of a single object o. There are also the keywords **\nothing** and **\everything**, standing for the border cases of an empty set of locations and the set of all locations in the program, respectively.

We see an example for a modifies clause in line 36 of Figure 2.1. If the contract's precondition holds when calling method **add** (i.e., if the method's argument is different from **null**), then the method may modify only the field **array** of the receiver object **this**, and the array components of the array pointed to by **this.array**. Note that modifies clauses are always evaluated in the pre-state, so the modifies clause refers to the array which is pointed to by **this.array** at the beginning of the execution, which may be a different one than at the end of the method. Another important thing to note is that modifies clauses only constrain changes to locations on the heap (i.e., object fields and array components), but never changes to local variables: these variables are internal to a method, and any changes to them can be neither relevant nor visible to any of the method's callers anyway. Modifies clauses also never constrain the allocation of new objects, or assignments to locations belonging to newly allocated objects. Thus, method **add** is free to allocate a new array object and assign to its components (e.g., if the old array is filled up completely), even though these locations are not (and cannot be) mentioned in the modifies clause.

Specifying that a method has *no* side effects is an important border case of modifies clauses. Such methods are called *pure*, and JML has a special keyword **pure** which can be attached to method declarations in order to designate a method as pure. Examples for pure methods are **size** and **get** in Figure 2.1. The meaning of the **pure** modifier is essentially the same as adding an implicit **assignable \nothing** to all contracts of the method (and using **diverges false** for all contracts, see Subsection 2.2.3 below). It also determines whether a method may be used in specifications or not.

As JML's modifies clauses implicitly allow the allocation and initialisation of new objects, its pure methods are free to create, modify and even return a newly allocated object. This definition of purity is known as *weak purity*, as opposed to *strong purity*, where pure methods must not have an effect on the heap at all. The more liberal approach of weak purity is useful in practice: for example, imagine a method that is to return a pair of integers, which it can do by creating, initialising and returning an object of a class `Pair`, while being otherwise free from side effects. However, weak purity complicates the semantics of expressions. It is for example debatable whether the specification expression `newObject() == newObject()`, where the weakly pure method `newObject` creates and returns a fresh object, should be considered as always true (because the entire expression is evaluated in the same state and so both method calls return the same object), or as always false (because, as in Java, the post-state of the first method call is the pre-state of the second, and so the second call will allocate a different object), or neither. It can also be argued that such an expression should not be permitted in specifications at all [Darvas and Leino, 2007; Darvas, 2009].

2.2.3. Diverges Clauses

JML allows one to specify when a method must terminate (either normally or by throwing an exception) using so-called *diverges clauses*. A diverges clause is declared in a contract using the keyword **diverges**, followed by a **boolean** expression. The meaning of a diverges clause **diverges b** is that the method may refrain from terminating (may "diverge") only if b held in the pre-state. In contrast to other clauses in contracts, the default used in case of a missing diverges clause is not the most liberal possibility, but rather the most strict one, namely "**diverges false**", which says that the method must terminate under all circumstances (provided that the contract's preconditions held in the pre-state). Leavens et al. [2008] do not define how multiple **diverges** clauses are to be understood; however, the natural way seems to be combining them disjunctively, i.e., multiple **diverges** clauses allow the method to diverge if at least one of the conditions holds in the pre-state.

2.3. Object Invariants

An *object invariant* (sometimes called *class invariant* or just *invariant*) is a consistency property on the data of the objects of some class that we want to hold "always" during program execution. Where method contracts constrain the behaviour of individual methods, object invariants are intended to constrain the behaviour of a class as a whole. The concept of object invariants goes back to Hoare [1972]. In JML, object invariants are declared with the keyword **invariant**. Examples are the invariants of class `ArrayList` in lines 6–10 of Figure 2.1: for the objects of this class, we want the array `this.array` to always be different from `null`; we want the value of the location `this.size` to always be between 0 and the array's length; we want the array components between these bounds to be different from **null**; and finally, we want the dynamic type of the array to always be exactly **Object[]**, not a subtype: otherwise, method **add** might trigger a **java.lang.ArrayStoreException**, because the type of its argument might not be compatible with the type of the array.

Like method parameters and return values, field declarations of a reference type can be annotated with **non_null** and **nullable** to specify whether **null** values are allowed or not. For a **non_null** field f, an object invariant "**this.f != null**" is implicitly added to the specification. And like before, **non_null** is the default that is used when neither annotation is given explicitly. Thus, the invariant in line 6 of Figure 2.1 would not be necessary if we had not used **nullable** for the declaration in line 2. The reason for the use of **nullable** is that on variables of a reference array type, the effect of **non_null** goes beyond demanding that the pointer to the array is not **null**: it also demands that all *components* of the array be different from **null**. But since this is too strict for the example, where some of the array components *should* be allowed to be **null**, we use **nullable** to suppress the default, and spell out the appropriate invariants explicitly.

Above we stated that, in a correct program, invariants hold "always". As the quotation marks suggest, this is not entirely the truth: as soon as invariants mention more than one field, requiring them to hold absolutely always is too strict for practical purposes. For example, imagine a class that declares a field x of type **int** and a field **negative** of type **boolean**, where we want **negative** to be true exactly when x is negative. We can specify this in a natural way with an invariant "**negative == (x<0)**". Since the two fields cannot be updated both at the same time, this invariant must sometimes get violated when the value of x changes, at least for the short moment before a subsequent assignment to **negative**.

Another complication with invariants is that—in contrast to method contracts, which confine a single method (or, at most, a hierarchy of overriding methods, Section 2.4)—they are effectively *global* properties: for an invariant to hold anything near to "always" for some object *o*, it must be respected not only by all methods called on *o*, or even only by all methods defined for the class of *o*. Rather, it must be respected by all methods in the entire program. This may be surprising at first, because object invariants (as introduced above) are usually intended as constraints on a single class or on its objects, not on the entire program. One might hope that methods outside the class of *o* have no way of violating an invariant on *o*. But—unless special measures are taken—this is wrong. For example, the invariant could mention **public** fields, which can be assigned to anywhere in the program; or, more subtly, it could depend on other objects that can be manipulated directly, circumventing *o*. In Figure 2.1, if a method outside **ArrayList** were to obtain a reference to the array object referenced by the field **array** of some **ArrayList** object, it could modify this array directly, and thereby break the invariant in line 8.

Because of these issues, the exact semantics of object invariants is much less straightforward than it appears on first sight, and getting it "right" is a target of active research (see for example the work of Poetzsch-Heffter [1997]; Barnett et al. [2004]; Leino and Müller [2004]; Roth [2006]; Müller et al. [2006]). JML's current answer, as defined by Leavens et al. [2008], is its *visible state semantics*. Essentially (we omit **static** methods, **static** invariants, and finalisers for the sake of simplicity), this requires an invariant to hold for an object *o* in all states that are *visible* for *o*. A state is called *visible* for an object *o* if it occurs either (i) at the end of a constructor call on *o*, or (ii) at the beginning or at the end of a method call on *o*, or (iii) whenever neither such call is in progress. In other words, the invariants of *o* must hold always, except in situations where a method or constructor call on *o* is currently in progress, and where also we are neither in the post-state of a constructor call on *o* nor in pre- or post-state of a method call on *o*.

Returning to the above example, the visible state semantics solves the problem that the fields which the invariant "**negative == (x < 0)**" depends on cannot be updated simultaneously, because it permits a method to temporarily violate the invariant for its **this** object, as long as no other methods are called on **this** before the invariant is re-established. In cases where such a method call is necessary, one can annotate the called method with the keyword **helper**. It is then exempt from the visible state semantics, i.e., the receiver object's invariants do not have to hold in its pre- or post-state. The disadvantage of doing so is that **helper** methods may not rely on the invariant for satisfying their contracts. In contrast, non-**helper** methods are only required to satisfy their contracts for pre-states where the receiver's invariants hold. For example, method **get** in Figure 2.1 relies on the value of **array** being different from **null** as guaranteed by the invariant, and would not satisfy its **normal_behaviour** contract if it were a **helper** method.

2.4. Subtyping and Inheritance

A core element of object-orientation is the dynamic dispatch of method calls, where the method implementation to be executed is determined at run-time based on the dynamic type of the receiver object. Ideally, the caller does not have to know what this dynamic type is, because the objects of any subtypes of the receiver's static type can be used as if they were objects of the static type itself. This principle, which demands that subtypes conform to the behaviour of their supertypes when accessed using methods declared in a supertype, is known as *behavioural subtyping* [Liskov and Wing, 1994].

In formal specification, behavioural subtyping typically means that a method which overrides another method has a precondition that is implied by the overridden method's precondition, and, conversely, a postcondition that implies the overridden method's postcondition. If all subtypes are behavioural subtypes, then this enables modular reasoning about a dynamically bound method call using only the contract found in the static type of the receiver: if the precondition of this contract holds, then this implies that the precondition of any overriding method must also hold; and the postcondition found in the static type is guaranteed to also be established by any overriding method. For this reason, JML globally enforces behavioural subtyping, even though this limits the programmers' freedom to (mis-)use the subtyping mechanism of Java.

Behavioural subtyping is enforced in JML by inheriting method contracts to all subclasses: a method must always satisfy the contracts declared for any methods that it overrides. Subclasses are free to introduce additional contracts. We can see multiple contracts for the same method as syntactic sugar for a single, larger contract [Raghavan and Leavens, 2000]. With this view, adding contracts for an overriding method corresponds to weakening the precondition and strengthening the postcondition of the overall method contract, as above.

Object invariants, too, are inherited, and additional invariants may be introduced in subclasses. Note that the interplay between invariants and inheritance is not unproblematic for modular verification. For example, according to the visible state semantics, when calling a method on an object, the invariants of this object have to hold. In this situation, the invariant acts as a precondition for the method call. Adding invariants in a subtype corresponds to strengthening this precondition, which violates the principle that a behavioural subtype may only *weaken* method preconditions. Approaches for the modular verification of programs with invariants have to face these issues, in addition to those hinted at in Section 2.3 above. We return to this subject in Chapter 3.

2.5. Data Abstraction

Abstraction, i.e, the process of simplifying away unnecessary details while keeping something's essence, is a fundamental concept in computer science. In software development, abstraction is crucial because software systems are usually too complex to be conceived or understood by a human mind in their entirety at any point in time. Abstraction allows us to focus on some aspects of a system, while (temporarily) blocking out others. For abstraction from program structures, we can distinguish between *control abstraction*, which abstracts from control flow, and *data abstraction*, which abstracts from data structures.

A module interface is an example of abstraction: it provides a simplified outside view on the module's behaviour, freeing its clients from having to consider its internals and protecting them from being affected by changes to the internals, as long as the interface itself is not changed. This is known as the *principle of information hiding* [Parnas, 1972]. Design by contract specifications can be a part of such interfaces; in particular, a method contract can be seen as a description of the externally visible behaviour of a method, abstracting from how this behaviour is achieved. However, if such contracts are formulated directly over the internal data structures used in the method's implementation, then this abstraction is brittle, and the principle of information hiding is violated. For example, the contracts in Figure 2.1 are unsatisfactory in this regard, because they expose the internal data structures of `ArrayList` with the help of the **spec_public** modifier. If these internals are changed, then the specification is also affected. What is missing is some form of data abstraction in the specifications.

Where abstraction is the process of going from a detailed to a simple model, the notion of *refinement* refers to the other way round, i.e., going from an abstraction to a more detailed model. This process is common during software development, as the program being developed evolves from a vague idea to a running implementation. Various formalisations for such a refinement process exist, where the program is first specified formally on an abstract level using some form of "abstract variables"; where these are then refined into a representation on "concrete" variables in one or multiple refinement steps; and where the correctness of these steps is verified formally. Such techniques are for example described by Hoare [1972]; Morgan [1990]; Abrial [1996]; Hallerstede [2009].

Even without a formal concept of refinement, the phenomenon of refinement still occurs frequently in object-oriented software development. A typical case is adding new subclasses for existing classes or interfaces. For example, instead of providing class `ArrayList` in Figure 2.1 directly, we might have started with a Java interface `List`, which would then be implemented by `ArrayList`. We might also want to add other classes that use different implementation techniques than an array, such as a class `LinkedList`. In order to specify the abstract `List` interface independently of such future refinements, we again need data abstraction in specifications. And unlike the situation above, where we only aimed at specifying `ArrayList` itself in an abstract way, here using **spec_public** is not even an (albeit unsatisfactory) option: in a Java interface such as `List`, there are not yet any internal data structures which could be exposed to the outside world.

For data abstraction, JML features *ghost fields* (Subsection 2.5.1), as well as *model fields* and *data groups* (Subsection 2.5.2). Also, pure methods can be used for data abstraction in specifications, especially when combined with *depends clauses* (Subsection 2.5.3).

2.5.1. Ghost Fields

Ghost fields and *ghost variables* are fields and local variables that are declared, read and written solely in specifications. They are not visible to a regular compiler, and do not exist in the compiled program. Still, their semantics is exactly the same as that of ordinary fields and variables. In JML, ghost fields and variables are declared with the keyword **ghost**, and they are assigned to using the keyword **set**. An example is given in Figure 2.2, where the class **ArrayList** of Figure 2.1 is split up into a Java interface **List** and into a separate class **ArrayList** which implements the interface using an array. The behaviour of the interface is specified abstractly using a ghost field **contents**. The declaration of **contents** in line 2 uses the JML keyword **instance**; without it, a ghost field declaration in an interface creates a **static** field. This mirrors the behaviour of Java itself, where interfaces are not allowed to contain non-**static** fields at all, and where thus all field declarations in interfaces are assumed **static** by default.

Abstract specifications can often be formulated naturally using basic mathematical concepts such as sets or relations. For example, the desired behaviour of the **List** interface is similar to the behaviour of a finite mathematical sequence. Specification languages usually provide some form of mathematical vocabulary to facilitate writing such specifications. JML is no exception, but—in pursuit of its goal to stay as close to Java as possible—it does not introduce the mathematical notions into the language directly as additional primitive types. Rather, it comes with a library of so-called *model classes*, which try to sneak the mathematical concepts in through the back door by modelling them as ordinary Java classes. One such class, **JMLObjectSequence**, is used in Figure 2.2 as the type of the ghost field **contents**. The intuition behind this is to think of **contents** as a sequence of Java objects, and verification tools may attempt to map model classes like **JMLObjectSequence** directly to the mathematical concepts that they represent [Leavens et al., 2005; Darvas and Müller, 2007a]. Still, the elements of model classes are first and foremost Java objects. This implies, for example, that the **equals** method should be used for comparing two such elements instead of the regular equality operator "==", as in line 31. Otherwise, the *references* to the objects are compared, which is rarely intended.

The specification of the **List** interface in Figure 2.2 has the same structure as the **public** specification of **ArrayList** in Figure 2.1. Instead of **size** and **array**, it uses calls to pure methods on the **contents** object, where method **int_size** returns the length of the sequence, and where method **get** retrieves an element out of the sequence.

The implementing class **ArrayList** in Figure 2.2 works exactly as in Figure 2.1. However, for satisfying its inherited contracts, which talk about the ghost field **contents** instead of the concrete data, all changes to the list must be applied to the sequence stored in the ghost field, too. The constructor initialises the ghost field to an empty sequence, and the **add** method appends its argument to the end of the sequence. Note that the expressions occurring in **set** statements are no exception to the rule that JML expressions must not have side effects; **set**

```
     ── Java + JML ──────────────────────────────────────
 1  public interface List {
 2      //@ public ghost instance JMLObjectSequence contents;
 3
 4      /*@ public normal_behaviour
 5        @   ensures \result == contents.int_size();
 6        @*/
 7      public /*@pure@*/ int size();
 8
 9      /*@ public normal_behaviour
10        @   requires 0 <= index && index < contents.int_size();
11        @   ensures \result == contents.get(index);
12        @ also ...
13        @*/
14      public /*@pure@*/ Object get(int index);
15
16      /*@ public normal_behaviour
17        @   assignable \everything; //imprecise
18        @   ensures contents.int_size() == \old(contents.int_size())+1;
19        @   ensures ...
20        @*/
21       public void add(Object o);
22  }
23
24  public class ArrayList implements List {
25      private /*@nullable@*/ Object[] array = new Object[10];
26      private int size = 0;
27
28      public ArrayList() {/*@set contents = new JMLObjectSequence();@*/}
29
30      /*@ /*first four invariants as in Figure 2.1*/
31        @ private invariant contents.equals(
32        @                   JMLObjectSequence.convertFrom(array, size));
33        @*/
34
35      public int size() {...}
36      public Object get(int index) {...}
37      public void add(Object o) {
38          ...
39          //@ set contents = contents.insertBack(o);
40      }
41  }
     ────────────────────────────────────── Java + JML ──
```

Figure 2.2.: Java interface List specified using ghost fields, and class ArrayList implementing the interface

statements only modify the ghost field on the left hand side of the assignment. This fits with the use of class `JMLObjectSequence`, because the objects of this class are *immutable* in the sense that all their methods are pure. A method like `insertBack`, which is used in line 39 of Figure 2.2, returns a new object that incorporates the changes, instead of changing the original object itself.

The connection which is maintained between the abstract and the concrete representation of the data is recorded as an additional object invariant, which we can see in line 31 of Figure 2.2. It uses the `convertFrom` method of the class `JMLObjectSequence` as a convenient way to construct a sequence out of the first `size` elements of the array. The correctness of the methods `size` and `get` depends on this invariant, because the inherited contracts are formulated using the ghost field, while the methods read and return the actual data just as in Figure 2.1. The invariant bridges this gap. Invariants in such a role are known as *gluing invariants* in other contexts [Hallerstede, 2009].

An open problem in Figure 2.2 is the modifies clause of method `add` in line 17. Obviously, any implementation of `add` has to modify `contents`. However, it needs the license to modify more than just `contents`, namely, the concrete data structures used to implement the list. In order to specify this, we would need to enumerate the concrete data structures of all subclasses of `List` in the modifies clause of `add` within the interface. But this is not an option, because it would contradict the idea behind using an interface and an abstract specification in the first place. The specification in Figure 2.2 circumvents the problem by resorting to a trivial modifies clause of `\everything`. This makes the contract satisfiable by overriding methods in subclasses, but it also makes the contract effectively useless for modular reasoning about calls to `add`, because such a call must then be assumed to have an unknown effect on the entire program state. This shows that in the presence of data abstraction, framing becomes a difficult problem, which ghost fields alone cannot solve. One possible solution is to use *data groups*. These are connected to the concept of *model fields*, and the two notions are discussed together in Subsection 2.5.2 below.

2.5.2. Model Fields and Data Groups

Like ghost fields, *model fields* [Leino and Nelson, 2002; Cheon et al., 2005] are declared just as Java fields, but inside specifications. Reading a model field is done using the same notation as for reading a regular Java field or a ghost field, too. But at this point the similarity ends; despite being called "fields", model fields are in many ways more closely related to pure methods than to Java fields. Where a Java field or a ghost field represents an independent memory location (one per object), which has its own state that can be manipulated by assigning to the field, both pure methods and model fields *depend* on the state of memory locations, instead of being locations themselves. Just like the value returned by a pure method is determined by a method body, the value of a model field is determined by a *represents clause* (also known as an *abstraction function*). In JML, model fields are declared with the keyword **model**, and represents clauses with the keyword **represents**. A variation of the List and ArrayList types from Figure 2.2, where the specification uses a model field and a represents clause instead of a ghost field and **set** assignments, is shown in Figure 2.3.

The List interface in Figure 2.3 is unchanged over Figure 2.2, except that the keyword **ghost** is replaced by **model**, and except that the modifies clause of add now uses contents instead of \everything. Ignoring the modifies clause for the moment, we notice the represents clause for contents in line 26. The symbol = separates the model field to be defined and its defining expression. Here, the defining expression again uses the convertFrom method to construct a JMLObjectSequence from the array. Where in Figure 2.2 this relation between contents and the array was an object invariant, which was maintained by explicit **set** assignments (and which was sometimes broken in intermediate states, in accordance with the visible state semantics), here contents by definition adjusts itself immediately and automatically whenever the right hand side of the represents clause changes. This again mirrors the behaviour of (pure) methods, whose return value also immediately changes whenever a location is modified on which the return value of the method depends.

Represents clauses that use the = symbol are said to be in *functional form*. There is also a *relational form* of represents clauses, which allows us to define abstraction *relations* instead of only abstraction functions. The JML keyword for relational represents clauses is \such_that. It is followed by a **boolean** expression which describes the possible values of the model field. The functional form can be reduced to the relational form. For example, the represents clause in line 26 of Figure 2.3 can equivalently be written as

```
private represents contents
  \such_that contents == JMLObjectSequence.convertFrom(array,size);
```

In Subsection 2.5.1, we observed that objects of model classes should usually be compared with the equals method. Yet, here using "==" (either explicitly as above, or hidden in the functional form of the represents clause) works as intended. The represents clause—unlike the invariant in Figure 2.2—holds by definition, and never needs to be actively established by the program. This gives us the freedom to assume the stronger proposition that the objects are even identical, instead of just being equal with respect to equals. Note that the remark on *weak purity* of pure methods in Subsection 2.2.2 directly extends to model fields, too. In fact, contents is only weakly pure, because—as defined by the represents clause—it allocates and returns a fresh object of type JMLObjectSequence.

```
——— Java + JML ————————————————————————————————
 1  public interface List {
 2      //@ public model instance JMLObjectSequence contents;
 3
 4      //@ ...
 5      public /*@pure@*/ int size();
 6
 7      //@ ...
 8      public /*@pure@*/ Object get(int index);
 9
10      /*@ public normal_behaviour
11        @    assignable contents;
12        @    ensures ...
13        @*/
14       public void add(Object o);
15  }
16
17  public class ArrayList implements List {
18      private /*@nullable@*/ Object[] array = new Object[10];
19          //@ in contents;
20          //@ maps array[*] \into contents;
21
22      private int size = 0; //@ in contents;
23
24      //@ /*four invariants as in Figure 2.1*/
25
26      /*@ private represents contents
27        @      = JMLObjectSequence.convertFrom(array, size);
28        @*/
29
30      public int size() {...}
31      public Object get(int index) {...}
32      public void add(Object o) {...}
33  }
—————————————————————————————————————————— Java + JML ———
```

Figure 2.3.: Java interface `List` specified using model fields and data groups, and class `ArrayList` implementing the interface

Another intricacy that we observe "along the way", without being overly concerned with it here, is the question of what happens if the value of the model field cannot be chosen in every state such that the represents clause is satisfied. An extreme case is a represents clause "**represents** x **\such_that false**", which is obviously impossible to satisfy in any state at all. More subtly, a represents clause "**represents** x **\such_that** y == 3", where y is a Java field, is also problematic, because a satisfying value for x can be found only in states where y happens to contain the value 3. There is no "official" answer for how to understand such represents clauses in the JML documentation [Leavens et al., 2008]. The simplest approach is to just consider represents clauses to be assumptions that hold in all states by definition, to accept the fact that then an inconsistent represents clause makes the entire specification trivially satisfied, and to consider the person writing the represents clause responsible for avoiding such a situation. Other, more involved solutions are explored by Breunesse and Poll [2003], Leino and Müller [2006] and Leino [2008].

In line 11 of Figure 2.3, the model field **contents** is used in the modifies clause of method **add**. Without further explanation, this would seem to be nonsensical. After all, the model field is not a location that the program could assign to, and thus **this.contents** should not be considered a legal store-ref expression. The foundation for allowing the use of model fields in modifies clauses is the concept of *data groups* [Leino, 1998]. A data group is a name referring to a set of memory locations. In JML, model fields always have two faces: in addition to their regular meaning, they are also data groups. In every state, a model field can be evaluated both to a value, as we have seen before, and to a set of locations. When used in a normal expression, a model field stands for its value, whereas at the top level of a modifies clause, it stands for its set of locations. Thus, the modifies clause in line 11 of Figure 2.3 refers to the locations in the data group interpretation of **contents**, and it allows the **add** method to modify these locations.

Like the value of a model field is defined via a represents clause, its data group interpretation is defined by declaring locations to be part of the data group with the keyword **in**. As an example, the JML annotations in lines 19 and 22 of Figure 2.3 make the locations **this.array** and **this.size** part of the data group of **this.contents**. The **in** annotation must be placed directly after the declaration of the field to be added. This kind of inclusion, where a field of an object becomes part of a data group of the *same* object, is known as *static inclusion*. In addition, there are *dynamic inclusions*, where a field of an object becomes part of the data group of some *other* object. These are declared using the keywords **maps** and **\into**. For example, adding the location **this.contents** in line 19 of Figure 2.3 is not enough; the *components* of the array pointed to by **this.contents** must be included as well, which is achieved by the annotation in line 20. Dynamic data group inclusions make data groups depend on the state: if the **array** field is changed, then the locations denoted by **contents** also change, because **array[*]** afterwards denotes a different set of locations than before.

In situations where only the data group aspect of a model field is desired, the regular value can simply be ignored. The type of such a model field, which is used only as a data group, does not matter. For documenting the intention that only the data group is relevant, it is however customary to use the type `JMLDataGroup`, which is another member of JML's model class library (which also contains `JMLObjectSequence`). We can use such a model field to resolve the problem with the modifies clause for `add` in Figure 2.2, without switching from ghost fields to model fields completely: we declare a model field "`model JMLDataGroup footprint`" in addition to the ghost field `contents`, and use `footprint` in the modifies clause of the `add` method. The `ArrayList` class then needs to declare the data group inclusions for `footprint` as for `contents` in Figure 2.3, but no represents clause is necessary.

2.5.3. Pure Methods and Depends Clauses

As we have seen in Subsection 2.5.2, model fields are in many ways similar to pure methods. This correctly suggests that like model fields, we can also use pure methods to achieve data abstraction in specifications. Using pure methods has the appeal that, unlike model fields, methods are a native concept of the programming language, and the necessary methods may already be present in the program anyway. An example for this is again the `List` interface from Figures 2.2 and 2.3, which can also be specified using its own pure methods `size` and `get` as shown in Figure 2.4.

The calls to methods of class `JMLObjectSequence` have been replaced by calls to `size` and `get` in Figure 2.4. The fact that these pure methods are now themselves the basic building blocks of the specification is emphasised by their self-referential postconditions in lines 6 and 13, which are trivially satisfied by any implementation. The modifies clause of `add` is as problematic here as it is in the approach based on ghost fields, because like ghost fields, pure methods do not provide a means to abstract over sets of locations. This is solved in Figure 2.4 with the help of a model field `footprint` that is used only in its role as a data group.

For modular reasoning about specifications that use pure methods, it is usually necessary to limit the *dependencies* of these pure methods, that is, the memory locations that may influence the result of a method invocation. An example is the code in Figure 2.5. The precondition of m tells us that before the call to m, the list is not empty. We expect that the list is still not empty in line 9, and that thus the precondition of the first contract of method `get` is satisfied. However, without looking into all implementations of `size` (thereby sacrificing modularity of reasoning) and concluding that they do not depend on x, we cannot be sure that the intervening change to x does not affect the result of `size`. This demonstrates a general problem when using pure methods in specifications [Leavens et al., 2007, Challenge 3]: without further measures, any change to the heap can affect the value returned by a pure method in an unknown way.

```
 ── Java + JML ──────────────────────────────────
 1  public interface List {
 2      //@ public model instance JMLDataGroup footprint;
 3
 4      /*@ public normal_behaviour
 5        @    accessible footprint;
 6        @    ensures \result == size();
 7        @*/
 8      public /*@pure@*/ int size();
 9
10      /*@ public normal_behaviour
11        @    requires 0 <= index && index < size();
12        @    accessible footprint;
13        @    ensures \result == get(index);
14        @ also ...
15        @*/
16      public /*@pure@*/ Object get(int index);
17
18      /*@ public normal_behaviour
19        @    assignable footprint;
20        @    ensures size() == \old(size()) + 1;
21        @    ensures get(size() - 1) == o;
22        @    ensures ...
23        @*/
24       public void add(Object o) {...}
25  }
26
27  public class ArrayList implements List {
28      private /*@nullable@*/ Object[] array = new Object[10];
29          //@ in footprint;
30          //@ maps array[*] into footprint;
31
32      private int size = 0; //@ in footprint;
33
34      //@ /*four invariants as in Figure 2.1*/
35
36      public int size() {...}
37      public Object get(int index) {...}
38      public void add(Object o) {...}
39  }
 ─────────────────────────────────── Java + JML ──
```

Figure 2.4.: Java interface `List` specified using pure methods and data groups, and class `ArrayList` implementing the interface

```
——— Java + JML ————————————————————————————————————
 1   public class Client {
 2       public int x;
 3
 4       /*@ normal_behaviour
 5         @    requires 0 < list.size();
 6         @*/
 7       void m(List list) {
 8           x++;
 9           Object o = list.get(0);
10           ...
11       }
12   }
                                                    ——— Java + JML ———
```

Figure 2.5.: Client code that uses the `List` interface of Figure 2.4

JML provides a (partial) solution to this problem, namely *depends clauses*, also known as *accessible clauses*. Depends clauses are a dual concept to modifies clauses. Where a modifies clause is used to specify which locations a method may modify (which locations a method may *write* to), a depends clause is used to specify which locations a method's result may depend on (which locations a method may *read* from). In JML, depends clauses are declared within method contracts using the keyword **accessible**. Lines 5 and 12 of Figure 2.4 give depends clauses for `size` and `get`. These use the already introduced data group `footprint`, because the locations to be read by `size` and `get` are the same as those that are to be modified by `add`. The method bodies in class `ArrayList` (which are still those shown in Figure 2.1) satisfy these depends clauses.

In the example shown in Figure 2.5, the depends clause of `size` reduces the problem of determining that the change to `this.x` does not affect the result of `list.size()` to the problem of determining that `this.x` is not an element of the data group `list.footprint`. This would be easy if only *static* data group inclusions were permitted: then, we could conclude from the lack of an **in** clause next to the declaration of `x` in line 2 of Figure 2.5 that `x` is not part of any data group. In the presence of dynamic data group inclusions, it is more difficult, because there could always be a **maps** ... **\into** clause in some subclass of `List` that effectively puts `this.x` into `list.footprint` for some program states. We return to this problem in Chapter 3.

Note that even though we have not considered these dependency issues in Subsections 2.5.1 and 2.5.2, they are nevertheless present in all variations of the specification of `List`. In the previous approaches, the dependencies of the pure methods declared in `JMLObjectSequence` are relevant, as well as the contents of the involved data group.

As an aside, the usefulness of depends clauses goes well beyond reasoning about pure methods in the context of data abstraction. For example, a second (related) application of depends clauses is in the specification of *object immutability* [Haack et al., 2007]: an immutable object is an object that does not change, so all its methods must be pure. Additionally, one typically expects the return values of these pure methods to remain the same from state to state. This can be specified with depends clauses which express that the methods do not depend on any mutable state outside of the immutable object. Also, the problem of *secure information flow* [Sabelfeld and Myers, 2003] is in its basic form just a minor generalisation of the verification of depends clauses, where one is interested not only in the dependencies of the method return value, but in the dependencies of any number of locations.

2.6. Conclusion

In this chapter, we have reviewed the basic concepts of design by contract specification for object-oriented programs, on the example of the Java Modeling Language (JML). The main components of such specifications are method contracts and object invariants. Both contracts and invariants are inherited to subclasses, enforcing behavioural subtyping and facilitating modular reasoning about program correctness. To allow for information hiding in specifications, and for refinement in the sense of adding new subclasses to existing classes and interfaces without having to change the supertype's specification, data abstraction mechanisms are necessary. In this area, JML offers ghost fields, model fields, data groups, and the use of pure methods together with depends clauses.

By far not all features of JML have been covered in this chapter. Omitted features include simple in-code *assertions*, *loop invariants*, **static** object invariants, *history constraints*, *model programs*, and others. Also note that JML is constantly evolving. This chapter is based on the state described in the newest version of the reference manual available at the time of writing [Leavens et al., 2008].

We have touched on a few problems with the current state of JML that we investigate more deeply in Chapter 3, concerning the semantics of object invariants and the mechanism of data groups.

3. Dynamic Frames in JML

In Chapter 2, we have reviewed design by contract specification with the Java Modeling Language (JML). For modular static verification, where the goal is to check the correctness of individual program parts locally—that is, without considering the program as a whole—the demands both on specifications and on the specification language itself are higher than, e.g., for run-time checking of specifications. JML aims to satisfy the additional demands of modular verification, but in its current state, it falls short of this goal. The main shortcomings are in two related areas: *object invariants* on one hand, and *data groups* on the other hand. In the present chapter, we investigate a solution for these issues, based on an approach for framing in the presence of data abstraction proposed by Kassios [2006a,b, 2010], called *dynamic frames*. Compared with alternative solutions, the advantages of this approach are its simplicity and generality. We define a variant of JML that incorporates central ideas of dynamic frames, which we call JML*.

Outline   The necessity for modifying the specification language is justified in Section 3.1. We sketch Kassios' theory of dynamic frames in Section 3.2, before transforming JML into its dynamic frames based variation JML* in Section 3.3. A detailed example for the use of JML* is presented in Section 3.4, and a discussion of how the changes to the language solve the previously identified problems is contained in Section 3.5. There is a substantial amount of related work, which we examine in Section 3.6, before concluding in Section 3.7.

3.1. Motivation

JML's modularity problems are in the visible state semantics for object invariants (Subsection 3.1.1), and in the mechanism of data groups, especially in the concept of dynamic data group inclusions (Subsection 3.1.2).

3.1.1. Issues with Object Invariants

As we have seen in Chapter 2, the visible state semantics of JML requires that the invariants of an object o must hold in a state s if s is a post-state of a constructor call on o, if s is a pre- or post-state of a method call on o, or if no call on o is in progress. This allows invariants to be broken temporarily, as long as a method is in the process of being executed on the object for which the invariant is broken. We have also seen that whether a method is considered to be correct with respect to its method contracts depends on the specified invariants: a method must behave according to its contracts only when certain invariants hold in the method's pre-state. For example, we regard method `get` in Figure 2.1 as correct, because the implementation may assume that (in addition to at least one precondition) the invariants of the receiver object hold upon method entry, and because under this condition no `NullPointerException` or `IndexOutOfBoundsException` can occur.

It is not unusual for a method to have to rely on the invariants of *other* objects as well. For example, every time a method m calls a (non-**helper**) method on some object *o* other than **this**, this call is allowed by the visible state semantics only if the invariants of *o* hold at the time of the call. This is typically only the case if the invariants of *o* held already when entering m. According to Leavens et al. [2008], method m is indeed allowed to rely on the invariants of *o* being satisfied in its pre-state, but only if no call on *o* is in progress at the time. If a call on *o* *is* in progress, then the pre-state of m is "invisible" for *o*, and thus the invariants of *o* may be violated in this state.

The problem with this definition is that the set of methods which are already in the process of being executed when entering m is not a property of m itself. Rather, it is a property of a particular call to m, or of the possible calls to m which can occur in the program as a whole. A modular checker attempting to verify m independently of the rest of the program is not able to know which other methods are already on the call stack when entering m. Thus, the only invariants it can safely assume to hold in the beginning are the invariants of the receiver object itself. This is clearly not enough. For example, it is not enough to establish that the call to a method on *o* in the body of m is admissible.

A second problem with object invariants is that any modification of the heap can potentially break an invariant anywhere in the program. For example, the unshown body of method `add` in Figure 2.1 needs to modify the array. Since any invariant in the program might potentially depend on this array (via *aliasing*, i.e., by using another reference to the same array object, which might also be obtained via a quantifier), we can only assure ourselves that this modification does not break an invariant for any object which is in a "visible" state by considering all invariants and all objects in the entire program.

A third problem occurs in the interplay of invariants with inheritance. As mentioned in Chapter 2, adding object invariants in a subtype implies strengthening the effective preconditions of the methods inherited from its supertypes. Such a strengthening is usually forbidden in behavioural subtyping for good reasons: it breaks the ability to use an object of a subtype as if it was an object of a supertype.

As a fourth and final problem with object invariants, the visible state semantics requires that all invariants of an object hold at the end of a constructor call which initialises this object. This implies that if a constructor of a class C is executed on an object of a subclass D (via an explicit or implicit **super** call in a constructor of D), then all invariants of D must hold already in the post-state of this constructor call in class C, even though the enclosing constructor call in class D is still in progress. As the additional invariants of D typically constrain fields introduced in D, it is unreasonable to expect that the constructor of C is able to establish these invariants. This aspect of the visible state semantics thus leads to classifying programs as incorrect that probably should be considered correct.

Overall, these issues render the visible state semantics plainly unusable for modular verification. This fact is well-known in the JML community [Leavens, 2006; Leavens et al., 2008]. According to Leavens [2006], the expected future solution is to include in JML some methodology that restricts how invariants may be used and how programs may be written. Two concrete such methodologies, which we take a look at in Section 3.6, are the *relevant invariant semantics* of Müller et al. [2006] and the *Boogie methodology* of Barnett et al. [2004]; Leino and Müller [2004]. Both are based on *ownership types* [Clarke et al., 1998; Müller, 2002] as a means to control aliasing. Dynamic frames allow for a different third possibility, which we investigate in Section 3.3.

3.1.2. Issues with Data Groups

Data groups enable a specification to provide modifies and depends clauses, while leaving a certain amount of freedom to implementations about the actual locations that can be modified or read. However, when reasoning about such specifications, data groups raise the problem of how we can determine which locations are in a given data group and which ones are not. In a basic version of the data group mechanism where there are only *static* data group inclusions [Leino, 1998], we can determine a field's data group memberships by checking the **in** clauses at its declaration. This is so simple because there is no way a field can become part of a data group other than an **in** clause at its declaration, and because the inclusion does not depend on the state: for every object of the class, the field becomes part of a data group of this very same object.

In the presence of dynamic data structures, where objects use other, dynamically allocated objects to implement their functionality, it is necessary to allow a data group of one object to contain locations of other objects. Such *dynamic inclusions* into data groups are realised in JML via **maps ... \into** clauses. Unfortunately, they complicate modular reasoning about data groups significantly: without further measures, we cannot determine locally whether a given location may be part of a given data group, because an applicable dynamic inclusion might occur in any subclass of the class or interface that declares the model field, and because its meaning is state-dependent. We have seen an example for this problem in Chapter 2, where in the context of the client code in Figure 2.5 it is unknown which locations are in the data group of the `List` object and which ones are not. Similar to the solutions for object invariants, an approach for solving this is to impose global restrictions on how dynamic inclusions may be used in programs. Such an approach has for example been proposed by Leino et al. [2002]. As defined by Leavens et al. [2008], JML currently features dynamic inclusions, but no such restrictions. Thus, its version of data groups is unsuitable for modular verification.

A second, lesser issue is the question of how to specify dependencies for model fields. We have seen in Chapter 2 how dependencies of pure methods can be specified via depends clauses, but there is no equivalent mechanism for model fields in JML. A natural solution is to consider the data group associated with a model field as a built-in depends clause for the model field, i.e., to demand that the contents of the data group must be a superset of the locations on which the represents clause depends. Data groups even evolved out of a notion of dependencies [Leino, 1995; Leino and Nelson, 2002], which is closely related to the depends clauses of JML. The JML reference manual [Leavens et al., 2008] *recommends* that one "should always" put the dependencies of a represents clause into the corresponding data group, but does not state any consequences if this recommendation is ignored. This appears to be merely an oversight, though.

Finally, a drawback of data groups which is of a rather aesthetic nature is their coupling to model fields. This forces us to declare a model field of a dummy type such as `JMLDataGroup` when only a data group is needed, as in Figure 2.4. It also prevents us from using a "ghost" data group, where the data group contents are manipulated via **set** assignments instead of via **in** and **maps** ...**into** clauses.

The more serious problem of dynamic inclusions mentioned above can be solved by enforcing a set of restrictions, such as the one proposed by Leino et al. [2002]. Dynamic frames allow for an alternative solution, which also avoids the other, minor downsides of JML's data groups. We explore this solution in Section 3.3.

3.2. Dynamic Frames

Kassios [2006a] proposes a theory for solving the frame problem in the presence of data abstraction, which he calls *dynamic frames*. The essence of the dynamic frames approach is to elevate the ubiquitous location sets (data groups) to *first-class citizens* of the specification language: specification expressions are enabled to talk about such location sets directly. In particular, this allows us to explicitly specify that two such sets do not overlap, or that a particular concrete location is not part of a particular set. This is an important property, which is called the absence of *abstract aliasing* [Leino and Nelson, 2002; Kassios, 2006a]. For example, this property is what is missing in the program of Figure 2.5, where knowing that the location `this.x` is not a member of the set `list.footprint` would allow us to conclude that the call to `list.get` satisfies the precondition of its `normal_behaviour` contract.

Using JML terminology, what is called a *dynamic frame* in the theory of dynamic frames is a model field of a type "set of locations", without an additional attached data group. A dynamic frame is thus similar to a model field of type `JMLDataGroup` in regular JML. However, it has no value other than the set of locations, and it stands for this set of locations in any expression, not just in special contexts (namely, in modifies and depends clauses). A dynamic frame is "dynamic" in the sense that the set of locations to which it evaluates can change during program execution, just like the value of any other model field can change.

Specifications may constrain the values of dynamic frames with elementary set operations such as set membership, set union, and set intersection. Another operator on dynamic frames defined by Kassios [2006a] is the *modification operator* Δ, which can be applied to a dynamic frame f within a postcondition, where Δf means that at most the values of the locations in f have been changed compared to the pre-state. This is similar to the *modifies clauses* in JML. Conversely, the *framing operator* **frames** plays the role of *depends clauses*: for a dynamic frame f and a model field v, the expression f **frames** v is true in a state s if any state change (starting in s) that preserves the values of the locations in the evaluation of f in s also preserves the value of v. As dynamic frames are themselves model fields, they may also occur on the right hand side of **frames**. It is even common for a dynamic frame to "frame itself": f **frames** f means that if the values of the *locations* in the value of f are not changed, then the value of f *itself* also remains the same.

The so-called *swinging pivots operator* Λ can be applied to a dynamic frame f within a postcondition. The meaning of Λf is that if there are any locations in the set f in the post-state that have not been there in the pre-state, then these must belong to objects that have been freshly allocated in between. This operator is useful for preserving the absence of abstract aliasing. For example, if for some method execution we know that (i) the dynamic frames f and g do not contain any unallocated locations in the pre-state, that (ii) f and g are disjoint in the pre-state, that (iii) g frames itself in the pre-state (g **frames** g), that (iv) only the values of the locations in f may be different in the post-state (Δf), and that (v) the modification respects Λf, then we can conclude that f and g are still disjoint in the post-state. The reasoning behind this is as follows. Δf and the disjointness of f and g together imply that the values of the locations in g are not changed. Combined with g **frames** g, this implies that the location set g itself

41

also remains the same. The set f may change, but Λf guarantees that if this change adds to f any additional locations, then these locations were previously unallocated. As the set g is unchanged and did not contain any unallocated locations in the pre-state, the locations added to f cannot be members of g, and so the sets must still be disjoint. We see a concrete application of this chain of reasoning in Section 3.4.

Object invariants are modelled in the examples of Kassios [2006a] with the help of a Boolean model field *inv*. Program-specific axioms are used to define *inv* to be true for an object whenever the desired invariant properties hold for the object. Instead of a global protocol for when invariants have to hold—such as JML's visible state semantics—specifications use *inv* to state explicitly where the invariants of which object are expected to be satisfied. Typically, **this**.*inv* is part of both the precondition and the postcondition of a method. Reducing invariants to model fields in this way allows giving dependencies for invariants, using the same mechanisms as for other model fields.

A disadvantage of the dynamic frames approach is that specifications based on dynamic frames can be more verbose than others. On the other hand, the core advantage of the approach is that it enables modular verification without imposing any global, methodological restrictions. For example, properties akin to Λf are hard-coded into the methodology in some other approaches [Leino and Nelson, 2002; Leino et al., 2002], while dynamic frames allow choosing whether to use them or not on a case by case basis.

The dynamic frames theory is formulated in an abstract higher-order setting. Concrete implementations of dynamic frames have been devised by Smans et al. [2008] and Leino [2008]. In Section 3.3, we develop another concrete version of dynamic frames, in the framework of JML.

3.3. JML*

In this section we define a variant of JML, called *JML**, that makes use of dynamic frames. The basic idea is to decouple location sets (data groups) from model fields, and to make them first-class elements of the language. To this end, we start from a JML version where data groups and data group inclusions are omitted. This implies that it is no longer allowed to use arbitrary model fields as top level operators of modifies or depends clauses, because there are no associated data groups that would give meaning to such modifies and depends clauses.

As the next step towards JML*, we introduce a type `\locset` into the specification language. This type is a *primitive* type like **int** or **boolean**, not a subtype of `java.lang.Object` like JMLObjectSet and JML's other model classes. Semantically, expressions of type `\locset` stand for sets of memory locations. These expressions replace JML's "store ref expressions" as the expressions that are used to write modifies and depends clauses. The primary difference between "store ref expressions" and **\locset** expressions is that **\locset** is a proper type. This for example allows us to declare model and ghost fields of this type. We use the name *dynamic frames* for such model and ghost fields.

The singleton set consisting of the (Java or ghost) field **f** of the object **o** can be denoted in JML* as **\singleton(o.f)**, and the singleton set consisting of the **i**th component of the array **a** as **\singleton(a[i])**. Like in JML, the set consisting of a range of array components and the set consisting of all components of an array are written as **a[i..j]** and **a[*]**, and the set of all fields of an object is written as **o.***. The keywords **\nothing** and **\everything** are also present in JML*. In addition, JML* features the following basic set operations on expressions of type **\locset**, with the standard mathematical meaning: the set intersection **\intersect**, the set difference **\set_minus**, the set union **\set_union**, the subset relation **\subset**, and the disjointness relation **\disjoint**. (The more obvious syntax **\union** for unifying sets is unavailable for a technical reason: as defined by Gosling et al. [2000], the character sequence "\u" is in Java a "Unicode escape sequence", and the four characters following this sequence must be hexadecimal digits encoding a single Unicode character. This holds even inside comments, where the JML* keywords occur.)

The original JML store ref notations **o.f** and **a[i]** can still be used as shorthands for the singleton sets **\singleton(o.f)** and **\singleton(a[i])** in JML*, but only in syntactical contexts where understanding them as representing the *value* of **o.f** or **a[i]** does not make the overall expression syntactically valid. For example, on the top level of a modifies clause, the expression **o.f** is equivalent to **\singleton(o.f)** if **f** is a Java or ghost field of type **int**, but it denotes the value of the field if the field is of type **\locset**. As another familiar shorthand, a comma separated list $s_1, \ldots, s_n$ can be used to abbreviate the union of the **\locset** expressions s_i where this does not lead to syntactical ambiguity.

JML* extends JML's **\fresh** operator so that it can be applied to location sets, in addition to applying it to objects. An expression **\fresh(s)**, where **s** is an expression of type **\locset**, is satisfied in a postcondition if and only if all the locations in the post-state interpretation of **s** belong to an object that was not yet allocated in the pre-state. Postconditions in JML* may also contain **boolean** expressions of the form **\new_elems_fresh(s)**, where **s** is of type **\locset**. This is an abbreviation for **\fresh(\set_minus(s, \old(s)))**: the expression is satisfied if and only if all locations in the post-state value of **s** are either fresh (in the sense of **\fresh**) or were already contained in **s** in the pre-state. The **\new_elems_fresh** operator is the "swinging pivots operator" Λ from Section 3.2.

We do not introduce versions of the modification operator Δ or of the framing operator **frames** from Section 3.2. Instead, such properties are expressed in JML* with modifies and depends clauses, just like in JML. While depends clauses for pure methods are already part of ordinary JML, we generalise the mechanism of depends clauses to model fields here. A depends clause for a model field is declared inside a class, using the syntax "**accessible** m: s;", where m is a model field (defined for the class containing the depends clause) and where s is an expression of type **\locset**. Such a depends clause means that m may depend at most on the locations in s (in other words, s **frames** m must hold), provided that the invariants of the **this** object hold in the current state. This is a contract that all represents clauses for m must satisfy (in the current class or interface and in its subclasses), just like a depends clause for a pure method is a contractual obligation on all implementations of the method.

JML* does not use the visible state semantics, or any other global protocol, to define which object invariants have to hold at what moments during program execution. Instead, the concept of object invariants is reduced to the concept of model fields. JML* features a built-in model field **\inv** of type **boolean**, which is defined in **java.lang.Object** and inherited to all its subtypes. Invariant declarations are syntactic sugar for represents clauses on **\inv**: together, the declarations "**invariant** e_1; ...; **invariant** e_n;" of a given class C (including the invariant declarations inherited from its supertypes) stand for the represents clause "**private represents \inv** = e_1 && ... && e_n;", which defines the meaning of **\inv** for objects whose dynamic type is the class C.

The model field **\inv** can be used freely in specification expressions. The expression o.**\inv** states that the invariants of object o are expected to be true. By default, all method contracts (except those for constructors) contain an implicit precondition **requires this.\inv**, as well as implicit postconditions **ensures this.\inv** and **signals**(Exception) **this.\inv**. These defaults correspond to the expected "standard" case, where a method relies on the invariants of **this** holding on method entry, and guarantees to preserve these invariants both in case of normal and in case of exceptional termination. They can be turned off by annotating the method with the **helper** keyword. If a method requires the invariants of any other objects to hold, or takes care to preserve them, then this must be specified with explicit pre- and postconditions.

When a method contract is attached to a constructor, the subject of this *constructor contract* is in JML only the body of the constructor as it appears in the class. That is, it does not include the process of *allocating* the new object. In contrast, in JML* constructor contracts apply to the object allocation and initialisation as a whole, i.e., to an allocation statement of the form **new** C(...). They do not constrain the behaviour of nested constructor invocations via **this**(...); or **super**(...); statements. Thus, for example, a constructor postcondition

\fresh(this) is always false in JML, because **this** is already allocated when entering the constructor; but it is always true in JML*. By default, constructor contracts have the same implicit postconditions for \inv as contracts for regular methods, but not the implicit precondition **this.\inv**. Since the **this** object does not exist in the pre-state of the **new** C(...); statement, referring to **this** in a constructor precondition is not even syntactically allowed in JML*. As usual, the **helper** keyword turns off the default postconditions.

According to Leavens et al. [2008], the range of a quantifier over a reference type "may include references to objects that are not constructed by the program". Adding an operator \created to JML, which would allow us to distinguish in specifications between objects that are already allocated (\created(o)) and those that are not (!\created(o)) has been discussed in the JML community, but at the time of writing, this has not found its way into the reference manual. In JML*, there is no such operator, and quantification on reference types always ranges only over objects that have so far been created by the program. For example, the expression (\exists C o; true) is satisfied in a state only if an object of class C has been allocated previously. Also, we demand that in every program state, a model field of a reference type evaluates to an object that is allocated in this state (or to **null**); if a represents clause demands otherwise, then it is equivalent to a represents clause of **false**. Together, these properties of JML* ensure that it is impossible to obtain a reference to a non-allocated object in a JML* expression, just like this is impossible in a Java expression.

Analogously to the definition for reference types, quantification for the type **\locset** ranges only over location sets where all members of the set belong to allocated objects, and model fields of type **\locset** always evaluate to such sets. Also, **\everything** evaluates to the set of all *allocated* locations. As there is no JML* expression denoting an unallocated object, there also is no other way of constructing an expression which denotes a set that contains unallocated locations. In Section 3.4, we encounter an example for why it is useful that dynamic frames in JML* never contain unallocated locations.

3.4. Example

A version of the List interface from Chapter 2, this time specified in JML*, is shown in Figure 3.1. It includes an additional pure method **contains**, with an unsurprising method contract. As in Figure 2.4, the specification of the interface is based on the pure methods **get** and **size**. It is also based on a dynamic frame **footprint**, which abstracts from the memory locations that represent the list in possible subclasses. Like the data group in Figure 2.4, this dynamic frame is used in the modifies clause of the **add** method, and in the depends clauses of the pure

—— Java + JML* ————————————————————————————

```
1   public interface List {
2       //@ public model instance \locset footprint;
3       //@ public accessible \inv: footprint;
4       //@ public accessible footprint: footprint;
5
6       //@ public invariant 0 <= size();
7
8       /*@ public normal_behaviour
9         @    accessible footprint;
10        @    ensures \result == size();
11        @*/
12      public /*@pure@*/ int size();
13
14      /*@ public normal_behaviour
15        @    requires 0 <= index && index < size();
16        @    accessible footprint;
17        @    ensures \result == get(index);
18        @ also public exceptional_behaviour
19        @    requires index < 0 || size() <= index;
20        @    signals_only IndexOutOfBoundsException;
21        @*/
22      public /*@pure@*/ Object get(int index);
23
24      /*@ normal_behaviour
25        @    accessible footprint;
26        @    ensures \result == (\exists int i; 0 <= i && i < size();
27        @                                        get(i) == o);
28        @*/
29      public /*@pure@*/ boolean contains(Object o);
30
31      /*@ public normal_behaviour
32        @    assignable footprint;
33        @    ensures size() == \old(size()) + 1 && get(size() - 1) == o;
34        @    ensures (\forall int i; 0 <= i && i < size() - 1;
35        @                            get(i) == \old(get(i)));
36        @    ensures \new_elems_fresh(footprint);
37        @*/
38      public void add(Object o);
39  }
```

————————————————————————————————— Java + JML* ——

Figure 3.1.: Java interface `List` specified in JML* using pure methods and a dynamic frame `footprint`

methods of `List`. In lines 3 and 4 of Figure 3.1, depends clauses are additionally given for the model fields `\inv` and `footprint`: their values, too, may depend at most on the locations in `footprint`.

As none of the methods of `List` are annotated with the **helper** keyword, all given contracts contain implicit pre- and postconditions which assert that `this.\inv` is true before and after method execution. No other objects have to satisfy their invariants before calling the methods of the interface. In particular, the contracts allow calling method `add` with an argument o for which `o.\inv` does not hold at the time of the call. This reflects the intention that the list is only supposed to store *references* to these objects, without ever having to call methods on them, and without being concerned with their invariants in any way.

The additional postcondition for `add` in line 36 demands that even though the set `footprint` may change, all locations that are added to it must be fresh. This grants an implementation of `add` the license to discard old data structures in `footprint` and to add fresh ones as needed, but not, for example, to make the locations of the parameter object o a part of `footprint`. For the other methods of `List`, there is no need for a postcondition which describes their effect on `footprint`. Roughly, this is because these methods are pure, and thus we expect that they cannot affect `footprint` at all. This expectation is correct, but the precise justification for this is more complex than it may seem at first sight, because pure methods *are* allowed to allocate and initialise new objects, and because without further knowledge, such a state change *might* affect the interpretation of a model field such as `footprint`. Fortunately, JML* guarantees that dynamic frames like `footprint` never contain any unallocated locations. We know from the depends clause in line 4 that `footprint` "frames itself", i.e., that a change to locations that are not in the value of `footprint` cannot affect the value of `footprint`. Thus, any change to previously unallocated locations in a pure method is guaranteed to leave the value of `footprint` untouched.

Figure 3.2 shows a class `Client` which uses the `List` interface. Compared with the client class in Figure 2.5, we have only inserted the additional precondition in line 5: when entering m, the invariants of `list` must hold, and there must not be abstract aliasing between `list.footprint` and the fields of the **this** object. Unlike in Chapter 2, we are now able to conclude that the call to `list.get` in the body of m satisfies the precondition of the applicable **normal_behaviour** contract, by using only the code and specifications in Figures 3.1 and 3.2.

We reach this conclusion as follows. Since `list.\inv` holds in the pre-state of m, the precondition of `size` is satisfied in this state. The disjointness of `list.footprint` and `this.*` implies that `this.x` is not currently an element of `list.footprint`. Thus, the depends clause of `size` guarantees that changing `this.x` does not affect `size`. Therefore, `0 < list.size()` still holds after the change to `this.x` in line 9 of Figure 3.2. Analogously, the depends clause for `\inv`

———— Java + JML* ——————————————————————————

```
1  public class Client {
2      public int x;
3
4      /*@ normal_behaviour
5        @   requires list.\inv && \disjoint(list.footprint, this.*);
6        @   requires 0 < list.size();
7        @*/
8      void m(List list) {
9          x++;
10         Object o = list.get(0);
11     }
12 }
```

————————————————————————————————————— Java + JML* ——

Figure 3.2.: Client code using the `List` interface of Figure 3.1

———— Java + JML* ——————————————————————————

```
1  public class ArrayList implements List {
2      private /*@nullable@*/ Object[] array = new Object[10];
3      private int size = 0;
4
5      //@ private represents footprint = array, array[*], size;
6
7      /*@ private invariant array != null;
8        @ private invariant 0 <= size && size <= array.length;
9        @ private invariant (\forall int i; 0 <= i && i < size;
10       @                                    array[i] != null);
11       @ private invariant \typeof(array) == \type(Object[]);
12       @*/
13
14     /*@ public normal_behaviour
15       @   ensures size() == 0 && \fresh(footprint);
16       @*/
17     public /*@pure@*/ ArrayList() {}
18
19     public int size() {...}
20     public Object get(int index) {...}
21     public boolean contains(Object o) {...}
22     public void add(Object o) {...}
23 }
```

————————————————————————————————————— Java + JML* ——

Figure 3.3.: Java class `ArrayList` implementing the `List` interface of Figure 3.1

in `List` guarantees that `list.\inv` still holds after the change. Altogether, we have established that `list.\inv && 0 < list.size()` holds in line 10 of Figure 3.2, which implies that precondition of the first contract of `get` must hold, too. This property holds independently of the concrete implementations of `List` that may occur as the dynamic type of `list`, as long as all these implementations satisfy the specifications given in the interface.

A particular implementation of the `List` interface is shown in Figure 3.3. The contents of the dynamic frame `footprint` are defined for objects of dynamic type `ArrayList` via the represents clause in line 5. This represents clause fulfils the same role as the **in** and **maps**...**\into** clauses in Figure 2.4. The represents clause satisfies the depends clause for `footprint` in Figure 3.1, because all locations that its right hand side depends on are themselves part of the right hand side. If we would omit `array` in the represents clause, then the depends clause would be violated: the location **this**.`array` would then not be a member of the value of **this**.`footprint`, but changing the value of this location would still affect the value of the expression **this**.`array[*]` and thereby the value of **this**.`footprint`.

The **invariant** declarations of `ArrayList`—including the one inherited from `List`—together define a represents clause for **\inv**. This represents clause satisfies the depends clause for **\inv** specified in Figure 3.1, because it only accesses locations that are part of `footprint` as defined in the applicable represents clause for `footprint`. We do not consider `array.length` to be a location here, because it is unmodifiable.

Line 15 of Figure 3.3 gives a postcondition **\fresh**(`footprint`) for the constructor of `ArrayList`. This postcondition is satisfied by the empty implementation of the constructor: the **this** object is in JML* considered to be fresh in the postcondition of a constructor, and consequently the locations **this**.`array` and **this**.`size` are also fresh. By the represents clause of `footprint`, its other members are the locations of the array which is stored in `array`. This array is freshly allocated by the constructor via the field initialiser in line 2 (which we consider to be a part of the constructor body, even though it syntactically appears elsewhere).

Figure 3.4 shows a class `Set` that forms a layer above `List` and `ArrayList`. It uses a `List` object to implement a set of objects. Much like `List`, the public interface of `Set` is described using a dynamic frame `footprint`, which frames both itself and **\inv**. Internally, `footprint` is defined to consist of the fields of the **this** object, and of the `footprint` of the nested `list` object which is used to implement the set. Objects of class `Set` maintain the invariant that the invariant of the `list` object holds, that the `footprint` of `list` does not overlap with the fields of **this**, and that `list` is free from duplicates (the latter invariant is not spelled out in Figure 3.4).

```
──── Java + JML* ──────────────────────────────────
 1  public class Set {
 2      //@ public model \locset footprint;
 3      //@ public accessible \inv: footprint;
 4      //@ public accessible footprint: footprint;
 5
 6      private List list = new ArrayList();
 7
 8      //@ private represents footprint = this.*, list.footprint;
 9
10      /*@ private invariant list.\inv;
11        @ private invariant \disjoint(list.footprint, this.*);
12        @ private invariant (*list contains no duplicates*);
13        @*/
14
15      /*@ public normal_behaviour
16        @    ensures (\forall Object x; !contains(x));
17        @    ensures \fresh(footprint);
18        @*/
19      public /*@pure@*/ Set() {}
20
21      /*@ public normal_behaviour
22        @    accessible footprint;
23        @    ensures \result == contains(o);
24        @*/
25      public /*@pure@*/ boolean contains(Object o) {
26          return list.contains(o);
27      }
28
29      /*@ public normal_behaviour
30        @    assignable footprint;
31        @    ensures (\forall Object x; contains(x)
32        @                == (\old(contains(x)) || o == x));
33        @    ensures \new_elems_fresh(footprint);
34        @*/
35      public void addToSet(Object o) {
36          if(!list.contains(o)) {
37              list.add(o);
38          }
39      }
40  }
──────────────────────────────────── Java + JML* ──
```

Figure 3.4.: Java class Set built on top of the List interface of Figure 3.1

The constructor of the `Set` class establishes the invariants by assigning to `list` a fresh object of class `ArrayList`. In particular, the initial disjointness of `list.footprint` and **this.*** is implied by the postcondition **\fresh**(footprint) of the constructor of `ArrayList` and by the fact that the `Set` object already exists at the time when the constructor of `ArrayList` is called. The pure method `contains` is used to specify the functionality of the set. It depends only on the locations in the `Set` object's `footprint`.

The most interesting method of `Set` is `addToSet`. Using the specification of `List`, we can deduce that `addToSet` indeed satisfies its contract. Roughly, this deduction goes as follows. Since the `contains` method of `List` is pure, the call to `list.contains` in line 36 of Figure 3.4 does not change the state of allocated objects, in particular it does not change the values of the fields of **this** and the values of the locations in **this.list.footprint**. If the call to `contains` yields **true**, then nothing further happens. The invariant of the `Set` object then follows from the fact that it held before the call to `addToSet`, and from the fact that the model fields and pure methods of `List` that occur in the invariant all have contracts which state that they may depend only on the locations in **this.list.footprint**, whose values are unchanged. The **ensures** postconditions also follow rather directly.

If the call to `contains` yields **false**, then method `add` is called on **this.list**, which may change the values of the locations in **this.list.footprint**. Without further knowledge about this dynamic frame, it could be any set of locations— the `add` method could even change the `list` field of the **this** object, making the postcondition of `addToSet` refer to a *different* `List` object than the one that `add` has been called on. Fortunately, the invariant of `Set` tells us that the set of changed locations is disjoint from the fields of **this**, which rules out this scenario. This allows us to conclude from the postcondition of `add` that both the invariant of **this** and the postcondition of `addToSet` are satisfied after the call to `add`. In particular, the postcondition **\new_elems_fresh**(footprint) of `add` ensures that the disjointness of **this.list.footprint** and **this.*** is preserved. This follows by the kind of reasoning with the help of the "swinging pivots operator" that we have seen in Section 3.2.

As a last step before closing the consideration of the example, we add to `List` and `ArrayList` the method `concatenate` shown in Figure 3.5. The figure does not give a complete specification for `concatenate`, but the intention is that the argument list should be appended to the end of the receiver list. The contract requires that the dynamic frames of the two lists are disjoint initially, but does not demand that this disjointness is preserved. Rather, it allows locations of `l.footprint` to be absorbed into **this.footprint**. This admits efficient implementations of `concatenate`, which reuse existing data structures instead of copying them. An example is the implementation in `ArrayList` shown in Fig-

```
—— Java + JML* ————————————————————————————
public interface List {
    ...
    /*@ public normal_behaviour
      @    requires l.\inv && \disjoint(footprint, l.footprint);
      @    assignable footprint;
      @    ensures \new_elems_fresh(\set_minus(footprint, l.footprint));
      @*/
    void concatenate(List l);
}

public class ArrayList implements List {
    ...
    public void concatenate(List l) {
        if(size == 0 && l instanceof ArrayList) {
            array = ((ArrayList)l).array;
            size = ((ArrayList)l).size;
        } else {
            ...
        }
    }
}
—————————————————————————————————————— Java + JML* ——
```

Figure 3.5.: Additional method `concatenate` for the `List` interface from Figure 3.1 and for its `ArrayList` implementation from Figure 3.3

ure 3.5, which "swallows" the array of the second list if the first list is empty. A `LinkedList` implementation of `List` could easily reuse the nodes of the argument list. The price for allowing such implementations is that a client cannot assume that the two lists are still independent after a call to `concatenate`.

3.5. Discussion

In this section, we analyse how the modularity problems of JML that we identified in Section 3.1 are addressed in JML*. Comparisons with related work are drawn in Section 3.6 below.

A general first observation is that like in JML, "correctness" is in JML* still a *global* property. That is, the judgement on whether a method is "correct" or "incorrect" with respect to its contracts is made in the context of a particular program. For example, consider a program consisting of the classes `List`, `Client` and `ArrayList` of Figures 3.1, 3.2 and 3.3, where the contracts for `get` in Figure 3.1 are omitted. Method `m` of class `Client` is still correct in this context even without the contracts for `get`, because the only available implementation of `get` does not throw an exception for the call in line 10 of Figure 3.2, and thus the **normal_behaviour** property of m is always satisfied. It may however be incorrect in the context of a program which contains another (itself correct) implementation of `List`, where `get` does throw an exception.

Modularity of verification means that when verifying a part of the program (in particular, a method), we use the context of this part only in a limited way. Adhering to the principle of information hiding, we refrain from making use of properties which may hold in the current context but which are expected to change. This has the desirable consequence that such changes do not invalidate previously performed verifications. Typical "expected" changes in the object-oriented world are adding new classes (possibly subclasses of existing classes), as well as changing invisible fields, represents clauses and method bodies of existing classes. A method may be correct with respect to its contracts in a particular context, but not be verifiable in a modular fashion. An example is method m in the context described above, where there is no contract for method `get`. JML* improves upon standard JML by providing better facilities to write modularly verifiable specifications (such as those in Section 3.4), not by making the notion of correctness itself modular.

One main problem with the visible state semantics that we have seen in Section 3.1 is that only the invariants of the **this** object can safely be assumed to hold on method entry, not those of any other objects. JML* does not have this problem, because here, specifications control explicitly which object invariants are supposed to hold when invoking a particular method. In the verification of a method, those invariants which are mentioned in the precondition may be used as assumptions, no matter which other method calls may or may not already be on the call stack when entering the method.

It is still the case in JML* that any modification of heap state might break any object invariant. However, unlike in JML, there is no need for a verification system to check after every assignment that this does not happen, because in general JML* allows any invariant to be broken. The validity of an object invariant must be checked only on demand, such as in cases where the invariant is needed to conclude that an occurring method call satisfies its precondition.

Strengthening invariants in subclasses does not negate the advantages of behavioural subtyping in JML*, because the invariants occur in preconditions only as occurrences of the model field `\inv`. Modularly verifiable specifications treat the `\inv` field of objects other than **this** as a "black box": their correctness may depend on the fact that `\inv` implies any publicly visible invariants, but they may never assume that the represents clause of `\inv` does not contain any other, invisible conjuncts. Thus, establishing that `\inv` holds for an object other than **this** is possible only via mentions of `\inv` in method contracts, and via public depends clauses provided for \inv. Strengthening the representation of \inv in a subclass does not invalidate such reasoning, because it affects only "invisible" properties of \inv.

In contrast to other objects, for **this** even a modular verifier may use the precise meaning of \inv (and of other model fields). For example, the correctness of add in Figure 3.3 relies on the precise definition of **this**.\inv. If a method and an associated contract are inherited to a subclass, we have to consider the correctness of the method with respect to the contract separately for both classes, because the representation of any model fields occurring in the contract (in particular the representation of \inv) may be different in the subclass than in the superclass.

As constructor contracts in JML* apply to whole allocation statements "**new** C(...)", they only need to be verified for the case where the dynamic type of the receiver is exactly C, i.e., the class in which the constructor is declared. This solves the last mentioned problem with invariants in JML, where a superclass constructor running on an instance of a subclass is obliged, but probably unable, to establish the invariants declared in the subclass. The downside of this solution is that it costs some degree of modularity: nested constructor calls with **this**(...); or **super**(...); statements are not covered by contracts, so reasoning about such calls can only be done in a non-modular fashion. This downside can be considered acceptable, because hiding the internals of a superclass from a subclass is less important in object-orientation than hiding these internals from unrelated classes: subclasses have rather extensive access to the internals of their superclasses anyway.

On the side of data groups, the problems identified in Section 3.1 are all solved in JML*. The concept of location sets is decoupled from the notion of model fields. This, for example, makes it possible to use ghost dynamic frames just as well as model ones, similar to how model and ghost could be used interchangeably in the examples of Chapter 2. Specifications can determine the dependencies of a model field in a way analogous to the way for pure methods that already exists in JML. The absence of abstract aliasing can be specified explicitly in contracts and invariants, using operators such as \disjoint and \new_elems_fresh. Such contracts enable modular reasoning about the specified methods, without having to be concerned about possible dynamic data group inclusions in unknown subclasses. It must only be ensured that all subclasses adhere to the method contracts and model field depends clauses declared in their supertypes.

3.6. Related Work

JML* is intimately related to the dynamic frames based version of the Spec# specification language [Barnett et al., 2005] which has been proposed by Smans et al. [2008], and which inspired the design of JML*. The main difference between the language of Smans et al. [2008] and ours is that their language does not support model fields. Instead, its specifications are wholly based on pure methods, including pure methods of a type "set of locations". The advantage of this approach is its uniformity: we have seen that model fields are inherently similar to pure methods, so collapsing the two notions into one is worth consideration. However, doing so decreases the expressivity of the language, because unlike represents clauses, the bodies of pure methods are (usually) not allowed to contain specification-only features such as quantifiers. Furthermore, Smans et al. [2008] restrict the body of every pure method to be only a single return statement. This rather drastic restriction on pure methods seems to be motivated not by considerations on the level of the specification language, but by limitations of the verification of these specifications in the Spec# system. As an extension of their language, Smans et al. [2008] propose the inclusion of extensive defaults, where a dynamic frame `footprint` is present in all classes implicitly, and is used as the default for all modifies and depends clauses. Such defaults could be adopted in JML* as well.

Another relative of JML* is the *Dafny* language of Leino [2008]. Dafny is a simple theoretical language which supports writing both specifications and implementations. For data abstraction, Dafny specifications rely on ghost fields, and on so-called *functions*, which can be seen as a crossover between model fields and pure methods: like the value of a model field, the value of a function is defined by a single expression, instead of by a whole method body; like a pure method, a function can have an arbitrary number of parameters. Dafny insists that all functions are *strongly* pure. In typical Dafny specifications, dynamic frames occur in the form of ghost fields of a type "set of objects", where each object stands for all locations belonging to the object. This is coarser, but simpler than reasoning with arbitrary sets of locations. Much like the handling of object invariants in the work of Smans et al. [2008] and in JML*, Dafny specifications encode invariants by introducing a Boolean function `Valid` that is defined as needed, and that is used in pre- and postconditions symbolically.

This approach to object invariants traces back to the specification language of the *ESC/Modula-3* tool [Detlefs et al., 1998], a predecessor of ESC/Java [Flanagan et al., 2002] and of Spec#. Leino and Nelson [2002] discuss framing and data abstraction in the context of ESC/Modula-3. The key feature of their approach is that of *abstraction dependencies*, which serve to declare the dependencies of a model field (an "abstract variable"), in a way which is similar to the depends clauses in JML*. A distinction is made between *static dependencies*, where a model field depends on a field of the same **this** object, and *dynamic dependencies*, where a model field depends on a field of some other object that itself is referenced by a field of **this**. This distinction corresponds to the one between static and dynamic inclusions for data groups. A field that is used as an intermediary to define a dynamic dependency is called a *pivot field*. For example, the `array` field in Figure 2.3 would be considered a pivot field, because the model field `contents` depends on the components of the array via a dynamic dependency mediated by `array`.

Leino and Nelson [2002] enable modularity of reasoning by globally enforcing an extensive and non-trivial set of programming restrictions. One such restriction is that a pivot field may only ever be changed in a program by setting it either to `null` or to a freshly allocated object. This drastic limitation is called the *swinging pivots restriction*. This is the story behind the nomenclature of the *swinging pivots operator* Λ in the dynamic frames approach, which serves to enforce a similar (but semantic, rather than syntactic) property locally for a method. By not imposing such restrictions globally, dynamic frames can handle cases that the approach of Leino and Nelson [2002] cannot, such as method `concatenate` of Figure 3.5.

Data groups evolved out of the abstraction dependencies of ESC/Modula-3, and remain closely related to them. While the first version of data groups [Leino, 1998] features only static inclusions, Leino et al. [2002] describe a variation which also allows dynamic inclusions. Modularity is maintained despite the introduction of dynamic dependencies by enforcing a set of programming restrictions which is similar to that of Leino and Nelson [2002]. In particular, this set includes the swinging pivots restriction.

Müller et al. [2003] describe a version of JML which features abstraction dependencies in place of data groups. Instead of the restrictions of Leino and Nelson [2002] or those of Leino et al. [2002], they use *ownership types* [Clarke et al., 1998]—more precisely, the *universe types* of Müller [2002]—to solve the modularity issues that go along with dynamic dependencies. Roughly, the idea of *ownership* is to structure the domain of objects which occur at run-time into a tree of disjoint *contexts*, where the objects of each context have a common *owner object* belonging to the parent context. The only exception is the root context, whose objects do not have an owner. An ownership *type system* can guarantee statically that at run-time every object is *encapsulated* in its context, i.e., that it is only ever referenced from within its context or from its owner object (with the possible exception of *read-only* references, which cannot be used for writing to locations of the object).

Ownership can prevent unwanted aliasing, including abstract aliasing. For example, we can consider an object of class `ArrayList` in Figure 2.3 to "own" the array object referenced by its `array` field. An ownership type system can guarantee that no other object outside of the array's context is able to obtain a reference to the array. If in addition we know that the dependencies of `contents` include only fields of the `List` object and fields of objects owned by the `List` object, and that the `Client` object in Figure 2.5 is not owned by the `List` object, then we can draw the desired conclusion that updating x does not interfere with `contents`. In the dynamic frames specification in Figure 3.2, this absence of abstract aliasing is instead expressed as the precondition in line 5. The dynamic frames counterpart of an ownership tree is a nesting of "footprints" as in Figures 3.3 and 3.4, where the locations of the array are part of the `ArrayList` object's `footprint`, which in turn is a subset of the `Set` object's `footprint`. Unlike ownership types, the dynamic frames approach does not insist on having only such strictly hierarchical structures. For example, the implementation of `concatenate` of Figure 3.5 is not admissible in usual ownership type systems, because it lets the **this** object obtain a (non-read-only) reference to an array which is owned by the `l` object.

Compared to a reduction of object invariants to model fields, the advantage of a global protocol for invariants—such as JML's visible state semantics—is that it leads to shorter specifications, because the interaction between methods and invariants is present in specifications implicitly, instead of having to be coded into method contracts manually. Müller et al. [2006] use ownership types to define an invariant semantics, called the *relevant invariant semantics*, which avoids the modularity problems of the visible state semantics. Here, the only locations that an invariant may mention are those of **this** and those of objects in the ownership tree which is rooted in **this**. Assignments to fields of objects other than **this** are prohibited. An invariant is required to hold for an object *o* in a state if this state is a pre- or post-state of a method call, and if *o* is *relevant* for this call. An object is called *relevant* for a method call if it belongs to the context of the receiver object, or to one of its sub-contexts. A modular verifier can now safely assume the invariants of all relevant objects to hold in a method's pre-state, but must ensure in the post-state only the invariants of **this**, because the global restrictions on invariant dependencies and on assignments guarantee that the invariants of other relevant objects cannot be broken anyway. Again, the main limitation of the approach is that the ownership concept only fits for hierarchical object structures.

Müller et al. [2006] also define a more flexible variation of the relevant invariant semantics, called the *visibility technique*. Here, an invariant may additionally depend on fields of objects in the same context as **this**, provided that the invariant is *visible* in the class where the field is declared. Assignments are allowed not only for fields of **this**, but for all objects in the context of **this**. The definition of when invariants have to hold is the same as in the basic version of the approach, but verification now has to ensure that a method's post-state satisfies not only the invariants of the receiver object, but also the visible invariants of all objects in the same context as the receiver object. Even though this is more flexible than the basic version of the relevant invariant semantics, it is still based on global restrictions and thus cannot handle all cases.

Another ownership based approach to object invariants is the *Spec# methodology* of Barnett et al. [2004], also known as the *Boogie methodology*. Here, invariants are encoded with a ghost field st, instead of the model field used elsewhere. The st field is manipulated via two special statements: "pack o" sets st to "valid" for the object o, whereas "unpack o" sets it to "invalid". Before every "pack o", all objects owned by o must already be packed, and the invariants of o itself must hold. Before every "unpack o", the owner of o (if any) must already be unpacked. As in the basic version of the relevant invariant semantics, invariants may depend only on locations of **this** and locations of objects below **this** in the ownership hierarchy. Modifying a field of an object is allowed only if the object is unpacked. Altogether, the methodology guarantees that the invariants of an object and of all its owned objects hold whenever the object is packed. The methodology also addresses the frame problem: roughly speaking, it gives each method the license to modify the state of objects below the receiver in the ownership hierarchy, without having to declare this in a modifies clause. Leino and Müller [2004] extend the Spec# methodology with a concept of *visibility based* invariants similar to the visibility technique of Müller et al. [2006]. In later work, Leino and Müller [2006] furthermore extend the methodology to support model fields; the general idea is to reduce model fields to ghost fields that are updated automatically by **pack** statements.

The authors of Spec# report that the Spec# methodology proved too restrictive for some programs they encountered [Barnett et al., 2010], a problem which presumably could be remedied by dynamic frames. On the other hand, the *VCC* project—a spin-off of the Spec# project which aims at functional verification of system-level C code—turned back to an ownership based approach, after reportedly encountering limiting performance problems with an approach based on dynamic frames [Cohen et al., 2009].

Separation logic [Reynolds, 2002] is similar to dynamic frames in that it makes disjointness properties of location sets expressible in specifications. Such properties are however not formulated directly as set theory here. Rather, they are blended with other specifications, using special "separating" versions of logical connectives. For example, where in dynamic frames we write something like a.x > 0 && b.x > 0 && \disjoint(a.x, b.x), in separation logic we write a.x > 0 * b.x > 0, where the use of the *separating conjunction* * means that in addition to a.x and b.x both being positive, it must also hold that the location sets on which the two expressions depend are disjoint. Instead of explicit modifies clauses and depends clauses (or corresponding operators Δ and **frames**), in separation logic framing information is inferred from a method's precondition: only locations mentioned by the precondition may be read or written by the method. Overall, this leads to specifications that tend to be shorter, but perhaps less clear, than dynamic frames specifications. Separation logic provides a specialised framework for reasoning about such specifications, as an extension of Hoare logic.

Parkinson and Bierman [2005] extend separation logic with a mechanism for data abstraction. Their *abstract predicates* are similar to JML's model fields and pure methods, and to the *functions* in Dafny. There are examples which cannot be handled by this approach, but which can be handled by dynamic frames [Kassios, 2006a]. Distefano and Parkinson [2008] describe a Java verifier *jStar* based on separation logic with abstract predicates.

Implicit dynamic frames [Smans et al., 2009a] is an approach inspired both by dynamic frames and by separation logic. Instead of using location sets explicitly in the specification language, the technique centres around a concept of *permissions*: a method may read or write a location only if it has acquired the permission to do so, and these permissions are passed around between method calls by mentioning them in pre- and postconditions. Disjointness of location sets is expressed using the operators of separation logic. In contrast to special-purpose verifiers for separation logic, Smans et al. [2009a] describe a verifier based on an encoding into *Boogie* [Barnett et al., 2006] and thereby on more traditional first-order theorem proving (modulo theories). As a more efficient alternative, Smans et al. [2009b] propose a verifier for implicit dynamic frames that does not use Boogie, and that instead generates its own encoding into first-order logic using a form of *symbolic execution*.

Specifications in *regional logic* [Banerjee et al., 2008b] are closely related to dynamic frames specifications, more so than specifications in the implicit dynamic frames approach. Here, modifies and depends clauses are expressed with the help of *regions*, which are expressions that evaluate to sets of object references. Ghost fields are used to abstract from concrete sets of objects, much like dynamic frames ghost fields as they are used, for example, in Dafny. Regional logic is an extension of Hoare logic for reasoning about such specifications. As an alternative, Banerjee et al. [2008a] report on experiments where regional logic specifications were instead translated into Boogie and verified using the Boogie tool.

Parkinson [2007] makes the case that class invariants may be obsolete as a fundamental concept in specifying object-oriented programs, pointing out the restrictions of the existing modular global invariant protocols such as those of Barnett et al. [2004] and of Müller et al. [2006], and arguing that a concept like the abstract predicates of Parkinson and Bierman [2005] can provide a more flexible foundation for expressing consistency properties of object structures. By and large, dynamic frames based approaches such as JML* follow this argument, as they reduce invariants to concepts similar to abstract predicates, such as model fields or Dafny's functions.

In response to Parkinson [2007], a defence of invariants as independent entities controlled by a global invariant protocol has been put forward by Summers et al.

[2009]. Roughly, their arguments are the following: (i) invariants are useful as a way of thinking, and lead to good software design; (ii) verification based on an invariant protocol can be easier for the verification tool than verification without one, because the protocol ensures certain properties already on the meta-level; (iii) an invariant protocol leads to shorter specifications; and (iv) an invariant protocol can guarantee that a method preserves the invariants of objects other than the receiver, without these objects being mentioned directly in the method's specification.

It can be argued that points (i) and (iv) are addressed in JML*, even though it does not use an invariant protocol. Like JML, but unlike the other dynamic frames based specification languages mentioned in this section, JML* still features invariants as a built-in language concept, and still has invariants constrain the behaviour of all methods by default. Even though this is merely syntactic sugar, it nevertheless still encourages thinking in terms of invariants, and thus addresses issue (i). Like the other dynamic frames based languages, JML* allows us to give depends clauses for invariants. Such depends clauses guarantee the preservation of an object's invariants by all methods which do not modify the dependencies of this invariant, without having to specify this explicitly for the preserving methods. This addresses issue (iv). It seems that points (ii) and (iii) are indeed inherent advantages of having a global invariant protocol, and giving up these advantages is the price to pay for the increased flexibility and reduced methodological complexity that come with avoiding such a protocol. Point (iii) can be solved at least partially by fixing a more extensive set of defaults than the one used in this chapter, such as the one proposed by Smans et al. [2008].

In the context of the KeY project, previous work on object invariants and on modularity has been done by Roth [2006]. Here, the semantics of invariants is based on the notion *observed state correctness*. Roth [2006] defines several variations of observed state correctness. In the most basic version, all methods are required to preserve *all* invariants in the program. One of the possible refinements is to allow for a decision during verification on which invariants are to be assumed when entering a particular method, and which ones are to be ensured at the end. This is similar to JML*, where when writing specifications we have to decide which invariants are part of which pre- and postconditions. In JML* these decisions are documented within the specification itself, whereas in the approach of Roth [2006] the bookkeeping of invariants is instead done during verification, either manually or with the help of the verification system.

All variations of observed state correctness treat invariants as being implicitly universally quantified over **this**. Such a universal quantification effectively turns an invariant into a **static** invariant, which does not belong to a particular object any more. While this interpretation simplifies the definition of a semantics for invariants, it is too coarse. For every invariant and every method entry or exit point, it only leaves us two choices: either we require the invariant to hold for *all* objects of its class, or we do not require that it holds for any object at all. For example, we have seen that method `get` of class `ArrayList` in Figure 2.1 satisfies its contract only if the invariants of `this` hold upon method entry. Thus, in the observed state semantics, we are forced to assume that the invariants of *all* `ArrayList` objects hold when entering m. This assumption then prevents us from modularly verifying the correctness of a program where method `get` is called on an object that does satisfy its invariant, while the invariant of some *other*, irrelevant `ArrayList` object is broken temporarily.

To achieve modularity, Roth [2005, 2006] uses a flexible notion of encapsulation based on a reachability predicate, and a notion of depends clauses for invariants similar to the one in JML*. Instead of strictly enforcing behavioural subtyping, Roth [2006] introduces a concept of *extension contracts* which allow constraining the admissible extensions of a given program in a flexible way. This approach could be combined with JML*. Roth [2006, Section 10.4] touches on the issue of data abstraction, but does not cover the interplay between data abstraction and framing, which is mentioned as future work.

3.7. Conclusion

In the first section of this chapter, we have examined several known problems with the current version of the Java Modeling Language, which render its modular static verification impossible. As a solution to these issues, we have altered JML into JML*, which incorporates central ideas from the theory of *dynamic frames* of Kassios [2006a]. JML* is similar to languages of Smans et al. [2008] and of Leino [2008], which also use dynamic frames. At its core is the introduction of a type `\locset`, replacing the concept of *data groups* and elevating sets of memory locations to first-class citizens of the language. Compared with existing techniques for modular specification of object-oriented programs based on global restrictions and/or ownership, the dynamic frames approach allows for a remarkably simple and uniform treatment of model fields, pure methods, and invariants. This conceptual simplicity is not only an advantage for the *authors* of a specification language or a verification system, but also for *practitioners*, who need to be able to grasp the exact meaning of the specifications they write.

The cost for this simplicity is that specifications based on dynamic frames can be more verbose, and—more crucially—that the verification of such specifications can be more difficult and computationally expensive. This is because properties that in other approaches are ensured by an (efficient) ownership type system, or by a once-and-forall proof on the meta level, are in the dynamic frames approach typically verified on a case by case basis, using (more heavyweight, less efficient) theorem proving. An interesting line of future work may be to investigate combinations of dynamic frames and ownership based approaches, where dynamic frames serve as the thinking model and fundamental framework, and where the verification of common special cases is made more efficient through the use of ownership techniques.

A minor drawback of JML* is that it does not facilitate modular verification *within* a class hierarchy: we expect to handle nested constructor calls by inlining, and to have to reverify an inherited method in the context of the subclass. Thus, changing a superclass leads to new proof obligations in its subclasses. This is a consequence of the decision to model invariants via a single model field for all classes. An alternative is to use "type-indexed" invariants, where for every object, one considers the validity of the invariants declared in every supertype of the object's type separately. Such an approach is used in the Spec# methodology [Barnett et al., 2004], allowing for additional modularity within class hierarchies at the cost of additional complexity.

This concludes Part I on *specification*. We meet JML* again in Chapter 6, where we see a concrete approach for the *verification* of JML* specifications. The logic underlying this approach to verification is defined in Chapter 5, after a discussion of the issue of heap modelling in Chapter 4.

Part II.

Verification

4. Modelling Heap Memory

Chapter 5 defines a variation of the dynamic logic JavaDL [Beckert, 2001; Beckert et al., 2007] that underlies the KeY system. This variation is suitable for verifying dynamic frames specifications, such as those written in JML* (Chapter 3). In keeping with the distinction between JML and JML*, we call this logic JavaDL* to distinguish it from traditional JavaDL. The primary difference between the two logics is in the logical modelling of Java's *heap memory*: JavaDL is based on an encoding using *non-rigid functions* [Beckert and Platzer, 2006], whereas JavaDL* models the heap using the *theory of arrays* [McCarthy, 1963]. The present chapter is a prelude to Chapter 5, and serves to motivate and explain this difference in heap modelling.

Outline   Section 4.1 is a review of the functioning of heap memory in Java. Section 4.2 sketches three different logical models of the heap, where the first is the model of classical JavaDL, the third is the one used in JavaDL* (Chapter 5), and the second is an in-between. We compare the three models and conclude in Section 4.3.

4.1. The Java Heap

A main difference between simple "while languages" and realistic imperative programming languages is that the latter allow the dynamic allocation of pieces of memory at run-time. These areas of memory are then read and written via dynamically determined *memory addresses*, also called *references* or *pointers*. This step of indirection leads to the phenomenon of *aliasing*, where two syntactically different expressions can evaluate to the same reference at run-time, such that two memory accesses using the two syntactically different expressions nevertheless affect the same piece of memory. In contrast, (local) *program variables* are accessed directly via static names known already at compile time, and are thus not subject to aliasing. The area of physical memory used for the dynamically allocated data is usually called the *heap*.

A low-level view of the heap is to understand the addresses as natural numbers, and the states of the heap as functions that map natural numbers to values. This view more or less directly corresponds to the reality of typical hardware: the computer's memory is a linear sequence of *memory locations*, where the sequence number of each location is its address, and where in a state each of these locations contains some value.

Programming languages such as C or Java structure the heap into pieces of memory which semantically belong together, called *structs* or *objects*. The individual locations inside of a struct or object can be talked about using *fields* (also known as *attributes* or *member variables*). In the above hardware-oriented view, an object is an interval of successive memory locations, and a field is an offset that must be added to the start address of such an interval to get the address of a particular location inside the interval. For example, given an expression o of an object type, a field f, and a state s, the expression o.f accesses a location whose address is determined by evaluating o in s and adding the statically known offset number denoted by f.

In a language like C, this low-level view where addresses are numbers is exposed to the programmer. Addresses can be manipulated using arithmetical operations (*pointer arithmetic*) and subsequently be used for accessing the heap, circumventing the language's type system. In contrast, a stricter language like Java guarantees that the structuring of the heap into objects is always maintained. For example, in Java an expression of some object type always actually holds a reference to a suitable object (or *null*), and two non-identical objects never overlap in memory.

Because of these guarantees, we can understand the Java heap more abstractly as a set of locations, where a location is a pair of an object (in the sense of an object *reference*) and a field. A state of the heap is a mapping from locations to values. This is visualised in Figure 4.1. Boxes represent locations; their order is immaterial. A state assigns values to the locations, which in the figure are written inside the boxes. In the shown state, the location $(o, \mathtt{f})$ contains the value 27. The expressions o1 and o2 both evaluate to o. This implies that both o1.f and o2.f speak about the location $(o, \mathtt{f})$, which is an example of aliasing. The location $(o, \mathtt{h})$ contains a reference to the object o'. Thus, the expression o1.h.i accesses the location $(o', \mathtt{i})$.

Java *arrays* are a special case of objects. Their components are accessed via dynamically determined natural numbers instead of via statically known fields. Nevertheless, they behave much like ordinary objects. We omit them in this chapter in order to simplify the presentation. For the same reason we do not consider **static** fields in this chapter.

4.2. Logical Models of the Heap

Many formalisms for reasoning about programs, such as *Hoare logic* [Hoare, 1969], *weakest preconditions* [Dijkstra, 1975], or *dynamic logic* [Pratt, 1976; Harel et al.,

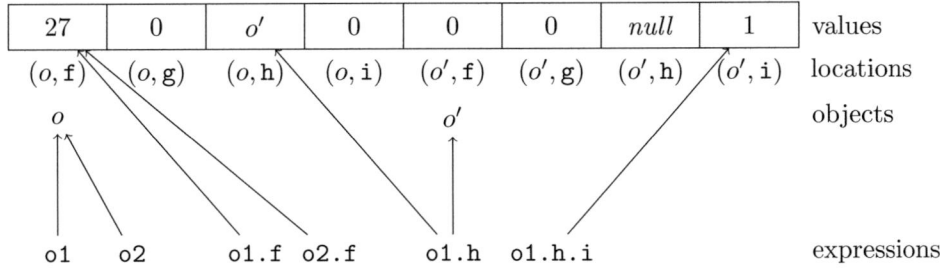

Figure 4.1.: Visualisation of the Java heap

2000], were originally formulated for languages with program variables but without a heap. Program variables can be modelled in a first-order logic based setting either as logical variables or as constant symbols, whose interpretation is changed by program assignments. Modelling the heap is not as straightforward, and there are several approaches for doing so. In this section, we consider three such approaches: modelling fields as *non-rigid* function symbols (Subsection 4.2.1), modelling the heap as a binary non-rigid function symbol (Subsection 4.2.2), and modelling the heap as a program variable (Subsection 4.2.3).

4.2.1. Fields as Non-Rigid Functions

One approach to heap modelling based on typed first-order logic is to represent a field f of a type A declared in a class C as a function symbol $f : C \rightarrow A$, which maps objects of type C to values of type A. A heap access expression $o.f$ is viewed as a term $f(o)$, where the function symbol f is applied to the subterm o. A *state* of the heap is a first-order structure which interprets all the function symbols f as mathematical functions. Executing an assignment $o.f = x;$ in a state s leads to a modified state s' which is identical to s, except that the interpretation of the function symbol f is modified such that it maps the value of o in s to the value of x in s. As the interpretation of such function symbols f can change from one state to another, we call them *non-rigid* function symbols to distinguish them from *rigid* function symbols whose interpretation is the same in all states, such as arithmetic operators. This technique of modelling heap memory is used in JavaDL [Beckert, 2001; Beckert et al., 2007], as well as in its bare-essentials version *ODL* [Beckert and Platzer, 2006]. It is also used in the theory of *Abstract State Machines* (*ASMs*) [Börger and Stärk, 2003] and in the *JACK* verifier [Burdy et al., 2003].

Besides non-rigid symbols that represent fields, it is useful to allow for another kind of non-rigid symbols that do not stand for locations and that cannot be assigned to, but whose interpretation can instead change as a consequence of the change of memory locations [Bubel, 2007; Bubel et al., 2008]. For example, it may be convenient to have a unary predicate symbol *nonNullFields*, where *nonNullFields*(o) is defined to hold in a state if and only if all locations belonging to the object which is the value of o contain non-*null* values. As the value of o is in fact just an object *reference*, the value of *nonNullFields*(o) can change between states even if o refers to the same object in both states: the value *implicitly* depends on the locations belonging to the object referred to by o. Another example is a reachability predicate *reach*, where *reach*(o1, o2) is defined to hold in a state if there is a chain of references from o1 to o2, and whose evaluation thus depends on the fields of the objects in the chain.

The semantics of non-rigid symbols like *nonNullFields* and *reach* is fundamentally different from the semantics of non-rigid symbols that represent fields. We use the name *location dependent symbols* for the former, and the name *location symbols* for the latter. To illustrate the difference, let f be a location symbol. If g is also a location symbol (but different from f), then the assignment o.f = x; cannot affect the value of the expression o.g, because the expressions o.f and o.g access different memory locations. If however g is a location dependent symbol, then it is possible that the value of o.g is affected by the assignment, because it might depend on the modified location. In essence, this difference is the same as that between ghost fields and model fields in JML (Chapter 2).

Bubel [2007]; Bubel et al. [2008] propose an approach to syntactically express restrictions on the dependencies of location dependent symbols. In this approach, a description of the locations that a location dependent symbol may depend on is included in its declaration and in all of its occurrences, enclosed in square brackets. For example, one might write something like *reach*[*for C c; c.f*](o1, o2) to indicate reachability of o2 from o1 via all locations that are formed by objects of class *C* and the field f. When reasoning about this proposition in a theorem prover such as KeY, we can exploit that its validity depends at most on the mentioned locations, and that it is thus guaranteed that an assignment to any *other* location cannot affect it.

The dependency mechanism of Bubel [2007]; Bubel et al. [2008] is reminiscent of the depends clauses in JML*. Nevertheless, it is designed for reasoning about recursively defined predicates such as *reach*, and cannot without adaptations be used for reasoning about specifications that use data groups or dynamic frames. Two main limitations are that it requires deciding on the precise dependencies of a symbol up front when introducing the symbol, and that it features no way of introducing symbolic names for sets of locations.

Extending and adapting the technique of Bubel [2007]; Bubel et al. [2008] to make it usable for verifying abstract specifications has been investigated [Beckert et al., 2009b; Krenický, 2009]. In the investigated approach, a location dependent symbol carries *two* semantical interpretations, namely its regular value and the set of locations it depends on. This is much like a model field with an associated data group in JML. The set of locations on which a symbol can depend no longer needs to be declared already when introducing the symbol, but can be specified freely using formulas and set theoretical operators, like in the dynamic frames approach. But some limitations remain. For example, it is still not possible to give dependencies for a set of locations itself. Overall, we found that the investigated approach leads to a specialised, non-trivial logic that includes many non-standard concepts in its core definitions. The underlying difficulty is that the ability to syntactically talk about locations and about sets of locations is crucial for data abstraction, and that this is cumbersome to make possible in a logic where the heap is modelled using non-rigid functions: here, fields are syntactical function symbols, which only allows terms and formulas to talk about their *values*, not about the fields *as such*.

4.2.2. The Heap as a Binary Non-Rigid Function

Another approach to modelling the heap is representing the fields not as syntactical function symbols, but as semantical values of a type *Field* introduced for this purpose. Of course, there must nevertheless be a way to syntactically refer to these values. To this end, we can introduce a constant symbol $f : Field$ for every field f of the program. We do not need to fix the exact interpretation of f, or the domain of the type *Field*, but we do need to define that the values of two such constant symbols f and g are always different. We can, for example, achieve this by introducing an axiom $f \neq g$ for every such pair. Some existing tools and languages feature a mechanism for declaring constant symbols as *unique* [Barnett et al., 2006] or (equivalently) as *distinct* [Ranise and Tinelli, 2006], which conveniently allows defining this kind of property without resorting to a quadratic number of axioms.

The heap can then be represented as a non-rigid function symbol $heap : Object$, $Field \rightarrow Any$ that maps locations to values. Typing becomes an issue here, because the desired type of a term $heap(o, f)$ is the type of the field declaration that gave rise to the function symbol f, but this type got lost in translation. A simple solution is to resort to an essentially untyped heap where the result type of $heap$ is Any, which is a supertype of all types of the program. An alternative solution, which allows keeping all type information at the cost of higher complexity, is to use a polymorphic type system. The latter solution is for example used by Leino and Rümmer [2010].

A heap access expression $o.f$ is now seen as a term $heap(o, f)$, and an assignment $o.f = x;$ is understood as changing the interpretation of the function symbol $heap$ at the position given by o and f to the value of x. In contrast to a modelling of fields as non-rigid function symbols, here fields are first-class citizens of the logic on par with object references, meaning that terms and formulas can refer to them explicitly. This makes it straightforward to syntactically talk about locations and sets of locations. Function symbols of a type "set of locations" can be defined, and these can serve to encode specification concepts such as data groups or dynamic frames.

Using the terminology of Subsection 4.2.1, the non-rigid function symbol *heap* is a *location symbol*. When modelling the heap as a single location symbol as in the present subsection, there is no need for any other location symbols besides *heap*. Yet, the need for *location dependent symbols* as a separate category of non-rigid symbols remains: symbols such as *nonNullFields* or *reach*—or symbols intended to represent JML model fields—need to depend on the interpretation of *heap*. But *heap*, being a binary function symbol, cannot be used as an argument to these symbols in first-order logic.

4.2.3. The Heap as a Program Variable

As we have seen in Section 4.1, states of the heap are functions that map locations to values. In the approach of Subsection 4.2.2, these heap states occur as interpretations of the function symbol *heap*. Alternatively, we can model them as instances of an algebraic data type *Heap*, which allows them to be stored in a mere program variable $\mathtt{heap} : Heap$ instead of in a binary location function symbol $heap : Object, Field \rightarrow Any$. This kind of approach is for example used in the *Jive* verifier [Poetzsch-Heffter, 1997; Poetzsch-Heffter and Müller, 1999], in the *KIV* verifier [Stenzel, 2004], in the *Spec# methodology* [Barnett et al., 2004], in the dynamic frames based verifier of Smans et al. [2008], and in the *Dafny* verifier of Leino [2008]. It was also employed in earlier versions of the *Krakatoa* verifier [Marché et al., 2004].

A common choice as the data type for representing heap states are the arrays of the *theory of arrays* [McCarthy, 1963; Ranise and Tinelli, 2006], where locations are used as array indices. A function symbol $select : Heap, Object, Field \rightarrow Any$ serves to retrieve an element out of a heap array at a specified position, and a function symbol $store : Heap, Object, Field, Any \rightarrow Heap$ serves to write into a heap array at a specified position. The two function symbols are connected by the axiom

$$\forall Heap\ h;\ \forall Object\ o, o';\ \forall Field\ f, f';\ \forall Any\ x;$$
$$select\big(store(h, o, f, x), o', f'\big)$$
$$\doteq if(o \doteq o' \wedge f \doteq f')\,then(x)\,else\big(select(h, o', f')\big),$$

which resolves possible aliasing with the help of an if-then-else term.

In this approach, an expression $\mathtt{o.f}$ is viewed as a term $select(\mathtt{heap}, \mathtt{o}, \mathtt{f})$, and an assignment $\mathtt{o.f = x;}$ as changing the interpretation of the program variable

heap such that the value of x is written into the position in the array that is designated by the terms o and f.

The approach does not make use of non-rigid function symbols, relying only on program variables and on rigid symbols. The effect of a *location dependent symbol* can be achieved by including **heap** as an explicit argument to a *rigid* function or predicate symbol, as in *nonNullFields*(**heap**, o) or in *reach*(**heap**, o1, o2). Quantification over heap arrays can be used to express as a formula that the interpretation of such a symbol depends only on certain locations. For example, the formula below states that *reach* depends only on the locations $(c, \mathbf{f})$, where c is of class C and $\mathbf{f}$ a field (as in the example of Subsection 4.2.1):

$$\forall Heap\ h_1, h_2;\ (\forall C\ c;\ select(h_1, c, \mathbf{f}) \doteq select(h_2, c, \mathbf{f})$$
$$\rightarrow \forall Object\ o_1, o_2;\ (reach(h_1, o_1, o_2) \leftrightarrow reach(h_2, o_1, o_2)))$$

The formula demands that if all such locations $(c, \mathbf{f})$ contain the same value in h_1 as they do in h_2, then the interpretation of *reach* must also be the same for h_1 and h_2.

4.3. Conclusion

We have looked at three possibilities for modelling heap memory in a setting based on first-order logic. All three are *abstract* in the sense that they use objects and fields (locations) as indices into the heap, not integer addresses. This abstraction is an advantage of Java-like programming languages, as opposed to more low-level languages such as C. They differ in how fields and the heap are manifested in the logic's signature. In the first approach (which we refer to as *A1* in the remainder of this section), every field becomes a *non-rigid* function that maps objects to values. In the second approach (*A2*), fields are constants of a type *Field*, and the heap is a non-rigid function that maps objects and fields to values. In the third approach (*A3*), fields are again constants of type *Field*, but the heap is a program variable that holds a data structure which maps objects and fields to values.

When going from A1 to A3, the size of the terms representing field access expressions o.f increases continuously: f(o) only has one subterm, *heap*(o, f) has two, and *select*(**heap**, o, f) has three subterms. Because these terms occur in large numbers when verifying object-oriented programs, choosing an approach that makes them small means an advantage in efficiency.

On the other hand, expressivity increases from A1 to A3. The step from A1 to A2 turns locations into first-class values, which for example enables quantification over locations, and function symbols that stand for locations or for sets of locations. Going from A2 to A3 furthermore turns heap arrays into first-class values.

In both cases, increasing the expressivity by changing the heap model leads to a simpler and more standard formalism than retrofitting the same expressivity onto an originally less expressive heap model. In particular, the step from A2 to A3 removes the need for a special concept of *location dependent symbols* built into the logic.

In a *typed* verification logic, the issue of typing heap access terms is an exception to the rule that the logic becomes simpler by going from A1 to A2 and A3: this typing is straightforward in A1, where the type A of a field f and the type C containing the declaration of f can be used as directly as the signature of the corresponding function symbol $f : C \to A$, but it is more complicated in A2 and in A3. One solution is to use a type system with support for polymorphism [Leino and Rümmer, 2010]. Here we can, for example, use a polymorphic type *Field* α parametrised by the declared type of the field, and let the constant symbol representing the field f be of the instantiated type *Field A*. A simpler alternative (used above) is to enforce only a weaker typing discipline, which allows any value to be stored in any location, and which allows a location to be constructed by combining any object with any field, even if the particular field is not defined for the object in the program. This means less protection against the verification system itself being faulty, but does not matter if the verification system works correctly and thus produces only terms that would be legal also in a system with stronger type checks.

The three approaches are not the only possibilities. For example, the *Krakatoa* tool originally used a variant of A3 [Marché et al., 2004], but then switched to an approach based on a per-field array [Marché and Paulin-Mohring, 2005]. Here, there is a type *Field*, but unlike in A2 and A3, its values are not the fields themselves, but rather one-dimensional arrays (in the sense of the theory of arrays) mapping objects to values. Java fields are represented as program variables (as opposed to rigid constants) of type *Field*. A heap access expression $o.f$ is understood as the term $select(f, o)$, where we read from the array stored in the program variable f at the index denoted by o. Marché and Paulin-Mohring [2005] report that inefficiency in the handling of aliasing was the reason for the switch in heap modelling: it took up too much time during verification to repeatedly determine that two locations $o.f$ and $o.g$ (where f and g are not the same symbol) are different, and that thus assigning to one of them does not affect the value stored in the other. Like A1, their new approach allows neither quantification over locations nor function symbols that stand for location sets.

The definition of JavaDL* in Chapter 5 uses A3 instead of A1. This difference compared to traditional JavaDL allows JavaDL* to be used for the verification of JML* specifications, which is the topic of Chapter 6.

5. Java Dynamic Logic with an Explicit Heap

Dynamic logic [Pratt, 1976; Harel et al., 2000] is a verification logic where programs of some programming language are embedded into logical formulas. An instance of dynamic logic where the programming language is *Java* has been defined by Beckert [2001]; Beckert et al. [2007]. We refer to this logic as JavaDL in this thesis. A central feature of JavaDL—and a unique extension to classical dynamic logic as defined by Harel et al. [2000]—is its representation of state changes as so-called *updates* [Beckert, 2001; Rümmer, 2006]. The handling of Java programs in the JavaDL calculus is closely linked to the concept of updates. JavaDL and its updates are the theoretical foundation of the KeY system.

In exact terms, the programming language supported by JavaDL is not Java but *Java Card*, a Java dialect for smart cards [Java Card 2003]. Java Card extends a subset of sequential Java with smart card specific features, such as a *transaction* mechanism. These additional features of Java Card are supported by KeY [Mostowski, 2005], but we are not concerned with them in this thesis. Instead, we consider the programming language of JavaDL to be only the intersection between Java Card and Java (version 1.4, as defined by Gosling et al. [2000]). Compared with full Java, the Java Card subset lacks features like concurrency, floating point arithmetic, and dynamic class loading, but retains the essentials of object-orientation. A core version of JavaDL for a simpler, artificial object-oriented language is the *object-oriented dynamic logic (ODL)* of Beckert and Platzer [2006]. A different dynamic logic for Java is used in the *KIV* verifier [Stenzel, 2004].

As motivated in Chapter 4, the present chapter introduces a variation of JavaDL where heap memory is modelled as a single program variable, whose values are arrays in the sense of the *theory of arrays* [McCarthy, 1963]. We refer to this variation of JavaDL as *JavaDL**. The changes affect the logic's syntax, semantics and calculus. They enable the formulation and verification of JavaDL* proof obligations that capture the correctness of JML* specifications (Chapter 6).

Outline Section 5.1 provides an introduction to dynamic logic as a framework for program verification, and to the notion of updates as an extension of this framework. The syntax and the semantics of JavaDL* are formally defined in

Sections 5.2 and 5.3, respectively. Section 5.4 is concerned with the JavaDL*
calculus. Example proofs in Section 5.5 illustrate the functioning of the calculus,
and Section 5.6 contains conclusions.

5.1. Dynamic Logic with Updates

Dynamic logic extends classical first-order predicate logic by modal operators $[p]$
(called *box modality*) and $\langle p \rangle$ (called *diamond modality*) for every program p of
the considered programming language. A dynamic logic formula $[p]post$ holds
in a program state if the program p either does not terminate when started in
this state, or if it terminates in a state where the formula *post* holds (*partial
correctness*). Provided that p is deterministic, the formula $\langle p \rangle post$ holds in a
state if $[p]post$ holds, and if additionally p does indeed terminate when started in
this state (*total correctness*).

Dynamic logic can be seen as a generalisation of *Hoare logic* [Hoare, 1969]. A
formula *pre* $\rightarrow$ $[p]post$, where *pre* and *post* are first-order formulas (i.e., where
they do not contain modal operators), has the same meaning as the *Hoare triple*
$\{pre\}p\{post\}$: if p is executed in a state satisfying *pre*, and if the execution
terminates, then the final state must satisfy the postcondition *post*. A Hoare-style
logic is for example used in the *Jive* verifier [Poetzsch-Heffter and Müller, 1999].
In contrast to Hoare logic, dynamic logic is closed under all logical operators,
including the modal operators $[p]$ and $\langle p \rangle$.

In instances of dynamic logic such as JavaDL, the semantics of the programming language is formalised as a set of *calculus rules*. These rules are used
during verification to incrementally shorten and finally eliminate the occurring
modal operators, thereby reducing a formula of dynamic logic to a formula of
first-order logic. This process is related to the *verification condition generation*
in other verifiers (for example, in *ESC/Java2* [Cok and Kiniry, 2005], in *Boogie*
[Barnett et al., 2006], in *JACK* [Barthe et al., 2007] and in *Why* [Filliâtre and
Marché, 2007]), where a first-order formula called the *verification condition* is
first generated from a program and its specification, and then passed on to an
SMT solver. In dynamic logic, both generating verification conditions and first-
order reasoning happen within one dynamic logic theorem prover, and can be
intertwined during the overall verification process.

A popular approach to automatically transforming programs and specifications
to first-order verification conditions is the *weakest preconditions* predicate transformer of Dijkstra [1975]. Given a program p and a postcondition formula *post*,
it constructs a formula $wp(p, post)$ which is the *weakest precondition* of p with
respect to *post*: if $wp(p, post)$ holds before p, then *post* holds afterwards; and
all other formulas with this property are "stronger" than $wp(p, post)$, i.e., they

logically imply $wp(p, post)$. In particular, $wp(p, post)$ is trivially implied by the *strongest* such formula, namely *false*. All of the above-mentioned verifiers (ES-C/Java2, Boogie, JACK and Why) use weakest preconditions for generating their verification conditions.

For an assignment $\mathsf{a} = t$, the weakest precondition with respect to a postcondition *post* can be constructed as $wp(\mathsf{a} = t, post) = post[t/\mathsf{a}]$, where the notation $post[t/\mathsf{a}]$ stands for the result of substituting in *post* all occurrences of a by t. For example, $wp(\mathsf{a} = \mathsf{a} + 1, \mathsf{a} \doteq 3) = (\mathsf{a} + 1 \doteq 3)$: if the variable a is to have the value 3 after the assignment, then before the assignment the term $\mathsf{a} + 1$ must have been equal to 3. The weakest precondition of the sequential composition $p_1 ; p_2$ of programs p_1 and p_2 can be computed as $wp(p_1 ; p_2, post) = wp(p_1, wp(p_2, post))$. That is, the *wp* transformer is first applied to p_2 and *post*, and then the result of this application is used as the postcondition to be established by p_1.

The weakest precondition approach can be used in dynamic logic in a natural way. In fact, the dynamic logic formula $\langle p \rangle post$ *is* the weakest precondition of p with respect to *post*, albeit not in a first-order form. It can be rewritten to a first-order form by starting from the back and applying assignments to the postcondition as substitutions, as above. For example, a formula $\langle \mathsf{a} = t; \mathsf{b} = t' \rangle post$ can first be transformed into $\langle \mathsf{a} = t \rangle post[t'/\mathsf{b}]$ and then into $(post[t'/\mathsf{b}])[t/\mathsf{a}]$.

A less popular alternative to weakest preconditions is the *strongest postconditions* predicate transformer [Floyd, 1967]. Given a precondition formula *pre* and a program p, it constructs a formula $sp(pre, p)$ that is guaranteed to hold after running p in a state satisfying *pre*, and that implies all other formulas with this property. In particular, $sp(pre, p)$ trivially implies the *weakest* formula with this property, namely *true*. The dynamic logic calculus for Java programs in the KIV tool is based on a variation of strongest postconditions.

The strongest postcondition of an assignment $\mathsf{a} = t$ can be derived as $sp(pre, \mathsf{a} = t) = \exists a'; (pre[a'/\mathsf{a}] \wedge \mathsf{a} \doteq t[a'/\mathsf{a}])$: there must be some "previous value" a' of a, such that *pre* holds when using a' for a, and such that the new value of a is the previous value of t. Alternatively, we can define $sp(pre, \mathsf{a} = t) = (pre[a'/\mathsf{a}] \wedge \mathsf{a} \doteq t[a'/\mathsf{a}])$, where a' is fresh function symbol; this corresponds to a Skolemisation of the existential quantifier. As an example, we have $sp(\mathsf{a} \doteq 2, \mathsf{a} = \mathsf{a} + 1) = (a' \doteq 2 \wedge \mathsf{a} \doteq a' + 1)$. Sequential composition $p_1 ; p_2$ can be handled by first applying sp to p_1 and then to p_2: $sp(pre, p_1 ; p_2) = sp(sp(pre, p_1), p_2)$.

The weakest precondition transformation produces smaller verification conditions than the strongest postcondition transformation. For *wp*, an assignment amounts to a mere substitution in the postcondition, whereas *sp* needs to introduce an existentially quantified symbol a' to denote the pre-assignment value of the changed variable. On the other hand, an advantage of the strongest postconditions approach is that it processes programs in a *forward* manner, which is closer to human understanding of programs than the backwards procedure of weakest preconditions. As a forward procedure follows the natural control flow of the program, it can be viewed as *symbolic execution* [King, 1976] of the program, where terms serve as symbolic values for the program variables.

JavaDL extends traditional dynamic logic with another syntactical category besides terms, formulas and programs, namely *updates* [Beckert, 2001; Rümmer, 2006]. Like programs, updates denote state changes. For example, an update a := *t* assigns the value of the term *t* to the variable a. If *u* is an update and *post* is a JavaDL formula, then $\{u\}post$ is also a JavaDL formula, which holds in a state if executing *u* in this state produces a state that satisfies *post*. The difference between updates and programs is that updates are a simpler and more restricted concept. For example, updates always terminate, and the expressions occurring in updates never have side effects. This difference is more pronounced for a realistic language like Java than for a simple theoretical language.

Updates allow the calculus of JavaDL to handle Java programs by doing a *forward symbolic execution* of the program even though ultimately computing *weakest preconditions*, avoiding the existential quantifier of strongest postconditions. This works by stepwise turning all program assignments into updates, starting from the first statement in the program, and in the end applying the resulting updates to the postcondition as a substitution. For example, symbolic execution in JavaDL transforms the formula $\langle \texttt{a = } t\texttt{; b = } t'\rangle post$ to the formula $\{\texttt{a} := t\}\langle \texttt{b = } t'\rangle post$, where the first program-level assignment has been replaced by an equivalent update. We can read this update as a symbolic description of the state that the remaining program b = t' is started in. Symbolic execution then continues with this second assignment, leading to the formula $\{\texttt{a} := t\}\{\texttt{b} := t'\}post$. Now that the program has disappeared, the updates are applied to the postcondition as substitutions, yielding first $\{\texttt{a} := t\}post[t'/\texttt{b}]$ and finally $(post[t'/\texttt{b}])[t/\texttt{a}]$. This is the weakest precondition of the program with respect to *post*, as in the example above.

In a setting such as JavaDL, where the heap is modelled using a non-rigid function symbol for every field (Chapter 4), there is a second, independent argument for the usefulness of updates: here, computing either *wp* or *sp* for a heap assignment o.f = *t* immediately leads to case distinctions because of possible aliasing. When dealing with an assignment a = *t* to a *program variable* a, we can just substitute *t* (when using *wp*) or a' (when using *sp*) for a, as above. But when dealing with an assignment to a *heap location* f(o), we need to replace all occurrences of terms f(o'), where o' is a term that can be syntactically different from o, *if* it is the case that o and o' stand for the same semantical value. Because in general this cannot be determined syntactically, case distinctions must be introduced, for example in the form of if-then-else terms. The use of updates delays this introduction of case distinctions until the program has been dealt with completely and the update is applied to the postcondition. In some cases, eagerly simplifying the occurring updates during symbolic execution even allows avoiding some of the case distinctions entirely. For example, simplifying the formula $\{\mathtt{f(o)} := 1\}\{\mathtt{f(o)} := 2\}\langle p\rangle post$ to the equivalent formula $\{\mathtt{f(o)} := 2\}\langle p\rangle post$ eliminates one of the two updates without a case split.

If—as in JavaDL*—the heap is modelled as a single program variable `heap` holding an array, then computing a weakest precondition or strongest postcondition for a heap assignment `o.f` = t is unproblematic, because we can substitute something for `heap` without a case distinction. The handling of aliasing is delegated to the theory of arrays, which introduces an if-then-else term when evaluating an application of *select* to an application of *store*. Simplifying nested *store* terms has the same effect as simplifying updates in a heap modelling based on non-rigid functions. For example, we can simplify the term $store\big(store(\mathtt{heap}, \mathtt{o}, \mathtt{f}, 1), \mathtt{o}, \mathtt{f}, 2\big)$ to the equivalent term $store(\mathtt{heap}, \mathtt{o}, \mathtt{f}, 2)$ without a case distinction, in analogy to the example with updates above.

Thus, in JavaDL*, updates lose the responsibility for handling aliasing to the theory of arrays, and the second argument for their usefulness no longer applies. Nevertheless, the first argument remains valid: updates enable computing weakest preconditions by forward symbolic execution of programs. In this role, they are as central in JavaDL* as they are in JavaDL.

5.2. Syntax

The syntax of JavaDL* is based on the notion of *signatures*. A JavaDL* signature is basically a signature of typed first-order logic with subtyping, together with a Java program *Prg*. We distinguish in signatures between *logical variables*, which can be quantified, and *program variables*, which can occur in programs. As a new feature compared to JavaDL, JavaDL* allows marking function symbols as *unique*. For constant symbols, this means that the interpretations of all constant symbols marked in this way must be pairwise different. The exact definition of the semantics of uniqueness is given in Section 5.3.

Definition 5.1 (Signatures)**.** *A signature Σ is a tuple $(\mathcal{T}, \preceq, \mathcal{V}, \mathcal{PV}, \mathcal{F}, \mathcal{F}^{Unique},$ $\mathcal{P}, \alpha, Prg)$ consisting of*
  - *a set $\mathcal{T}$ of* types,
  - *a partial order $\preceq$ on $\mathcal{T}$, called the* subtype relation,
  - *a set $\mathcal{V}$ of* (logical) variables,
  - *a set $\mathcal{PV}$ of* program variables,
  - *a set $\mathcal{F}$ of* function symbols,
  - *a set $\mathcal{F}^{Unique} \subseteq \mathcal{F}$ of* unique *function symbols*,
  - *a set $\mathcal{P}$ of* predicate symbols,

- a static typing function α such that $\alpha(v) \in \mathcal{T}$ for all $v \in \mathcal{V} \cup \mathcal{PV}$, such that $\alpha(f) \in \mathcal{T}^* \times \mathcal{T}$ for all $f \in \mathcal{F}$, and such that $\alpha(p) \in \mathcal{T}^*$ for all $p \in \mathcal{P}$ (where $\mathcal{T}^*$ denotes the set of arbitrarily long tuples of elements of $\mathcal{T}$), and
- a program Prg in the intersection between Java and Java Card, i.e., a set of Java classes and interfaces.

We use the notation $v : A$ for $\alpha(v) = A$, the notation $f : A_1, \ldots, A_n \to A$ for $\alpha(f) = ((A_1, \ldots, A_n), A)$, the notation $f : A$ for $\alpha(f) = ((), A)$, and the notation $p : A_1, \ldots, A_n$ for $\alpha(p) = (A_1, \ldots, A_n)$. Function symbols f with $f : A$ for some $A \in \mathcal{T}$ are also called constant symbols.

Let $\mathcal{F}^{NU} = \mathcal{F} \setminus \mathcal{F}^{Unique}$. We require that the following types, program variables, function symbols, and predicate symbols are present in every signature:

- $Any, Boolean, Int, Null, LocSet, Field, Heap \in \mathcal{T}$
- all reference types of Prg also appear as types in $\mathcal{T}$; in particular, $Object \in \mathcal{T}$
- all local variables $\mathtt{a}$ of Prg with Java type T also appear as program variables $\mathtt{a} : A \in \mathcal{PV}$, where $A = T$ if T is a reference type, $A = Boolean$ if $T = \mathtt{boolean}$, and $A = Int$ if $T \in \{\mathtt{byte}, \mathtt{short}, \mathtt{int}\}$
- $\mathtt{heap} : Heap \in \mathcal{PV}$
- $cast_A : Any \to A \in \mathcal{F}^{NU}$ (for every type $A \in \mathcal{T}$)
- $TRUE, FALSE : Boolean \in \mathcal{F}^{NU}$
- $select_A : Heap, Object, Field \to A \in \mathcal{F}^{NU}$ (for every type $A \in \mathcal{T}$)
- $store : Heap, Object, Field, Any \to Heap \in \mathcal{F}^{NU}$
- $create : Heap, Object \to Heap \in \mathcal{F}^{NU}$
- $anon : Heap, LocSet, Heap \to Heap \in \mathcal{F}^{NU}$
- all Java fields $\mathtt{f}$ of Prg also appear as constant symbols $\mathtt{f} : Field \in \mathcal{F}^{Unique}$
- $arr : Int \to Field \in \mathcal{F}^{Unique}$
- $created : Field \in \mathcal{F}^{Unique}$
- $\mathtt{length} : Object \to Int \in \mathcal{F}^{NU}$
- $\dot{\emptyset}, allLocs : LocSet \in \mathcal{F}^{NU}$
- $singleton : Object, Field \to LocSet \in \mathcal{F}^{NU}$
- $\dot{\cup}, \dot{\cap}, \dot{\setminus} : LocSet, LocSet \to LocSet \in \mathcal{F}^{NU}$
- $allFields : Object \to LocSet \in \mathcal{F}^{NU}$
- $arrayRange : Object, Int, Int \to LocSet \in \mathcal{F}^{NU}$
- $unusedLocs : Heap \to LocSet \in \mathcal{F}^{NU}$
- $\mathtt{null} : Null \in \mathcal{F}^{NU}$
- $exactInstance_A : Any \in \mathcal{P}$ (for every type $A \in \mathcal{T}$)
- $\doteq : Any, Any \in \mathcal{P}$
- $wellFormed : Heap \in \mathcal{P}$
- $\dot{\in} : Object, Field, LocSet \in \mathcal{P}$,
- $\dot{\subseteq}, disjoint : LocSet, LocSet \in \mathcal{P}$

We also require that $Boolean, Int, Object, LocSet \preceq Any$; that for all $C \in \mathcal{T}$

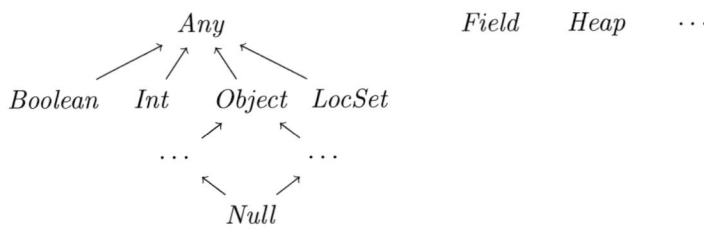

Figure 5.1.: Structure of JavaDL* type hierarchies

with $C \preceq Object$ we have $Null \preceq C$; that for all types A, A' of Prg we have $A' \preceq A$ if and only if A' is a subtype of A in Prg; and that the types explicitly mentioned in this definition are otherwise unrelated wrt. $\preceq$ both to each other and to other types. Finally, we demand that $\mathcal{T}$ is finite, and that $\mathcal{V}$, $\mathcal{PV}$, $\mathcal{F}^{NU}$ and $\mathcal{P}$ each contain an infinite number of symbols of every typing.

For illustration, the structure of the type hierarchies allowed by Definition 5.1 is visualised in Figure 5.1. Individual type hierarchies differ in the subtypes of *Object*, and in possible additional types that are unrelated to the fixed types.

Program variables can be seen as *non-rigid* constant symbols, i.e., as nullary function symbols whose interpretation can be changed by programs. In contrast to JavaDL, non-rigid function symbols with an arity greater than zero are not used for modelling the heap in JavaDL*, and are left out in Definition 5.1 for this reason: we will see in Section 5.3 that the function symbols in $\mathcal{F}$ are all rigid.

As evidenced in the requirement that the local variables of *Prg* are also program variables in $\mathcal{PV}$, we identify the Java type **boolean** with the JavaDL* type *Boolean* $\in \mathcal{T}$, and map the Java integer types **byte**, **short** and **int** to the type *Int* $\in \mathcal{T}$. Note that Java Card does not support the other primitive types of Java, namely **char**, **long**, **float** and **double**. The type *Int* represents the mathematical integers $\mathbb{Z}$.

Mapping the finite-width integer types of Java to an unbounded type such as *Int* does *not* necessarily mean that integer overflows are ignored [Schlager, 2007; Beckert et al., 2007]. However, we do ignore them in this thesis for the sake of simplicity. The implementation in the KeY system allows choosing between (i) ignoring integer overflows, (ii) checking that no integer overflows can occur, and (iii) using the actual modulo semantics of Java integers. The latter option is realised by mapping the arithmetical operators of Java to function symbols that accept arguments of type *Int* and return a value of type *Int*, but that nevertheless perform modular arithmetic.

Besides the built-in types and the pivotal built-in program variable **heap** : *Heap*, Definition 5.1 also stipulates that a number of function and predicate symbols are present in every JavaDL* signature. These symbols are assigned a pre-defined semantics in Section 5.3, and we discuss their meaning there. Some other pre-defined symbols are implicitly assumed to be present without being mentioned in Definition 5.1, in particular operators for integer arithmetic, and the predicate symbols $\leq$ and $<$. These have their canonical meaning, which is unchanged compared to JavaDL [Beckert et al., 2007]. In the following, we assume a fixed signature $\Sigma = (\mathcal{T}, \preceq, \mathcal{V}, \mathcal{PV}, \mathcal{F}, \mathcal{F}^{Unique}, \mathcal{P}, \alpha, Prg)$.

Like in JavaDL, the programs p occurring in modal operators $\langle p \rangle$ and $[p]$ in JavaDL* formulas are written in Java, or, more precisely, in the intersection between Java and Java Card. Thus, for full formal rigour, the definitions of JavaDL* would have to include definitions of the syntax and semantics of this subset of Java. However, this is as far beyond the scope of this thesis as it is beyond the scope of the definition of JavaDL given by Beckert et al. [2007]. Instead, Definition 5.2 below defines the admissible programs p rather informally, by referring to the *Java language specification* [Gosling et al., 2000].

Definition 5.2 (Legal program fragments). *A legal program fragment p in the context of Prg is a sequence of Java statements, where there are local variables $a_1, \ldots, a_n \in \mathcal{PV}$ of Java types $T_1, \ldots, T_n$ such that extending Prg with an additional class*

```
class C {
    static void m(T₁ a₁, ..., Tₙ aₙ) { p }
}
```

yields again a legal program according to the rules of Gosling et al. [2000], except that

- *p may refer to fields, methods and classes that are not visible in C, and*
- *p may contain method frames in addition to normal Java statements. A method frame is a statement of the form*

$$\texttt{method-frame(result=}r\texttt{, this=}t\texttt{)} : \{ \ body \ \},$$

where r is a local variable, t is an expression free from side effects and from method calls, and where body is a legal program fragment in the context of Prg. Inside body (but outside of any nested method frames that might be contained in body), the keyword **this** *evaluates to the value of t, and the meaning of a* **return** *statement is to assign the returned value to r and to then exit the method frame.*

The parameter declarations $T_1 \ a_1, \ldots, T_n \ a_n$ of m bind *free* occurrences of the program variables $a_1, \ldots a_n$ in p, i.e., occurrences not bound by a declaration within p itself. For example, in the legal program fragment "`int a = b;`" there is a free occurrence of the program variable $b \in \mathcal{PV}$. Program fragments that contain *method frames* typically do not occur in proof obligations, but only as intermediate states of symbolic execution (Section 5.4).

Having defined JavaDL* signatures and legal program fragments, we are ready to define the syntax of JavaDL* terms, formulas, and updates.

Definition 5.3 (Syntax). *The sets $Term_\Sigma^A$ of terms of type A, Fma_Σ of formulas and Upd_Σ of updates are defined by the following grammar:*

$$Term_\Sigma^A ::= x \mid \mathtt{a} \mid f(Term_\Sigma^{B_1'}, \ldots, Term_\Sigma^{B_n'}) \mid$$
$$\quad if(Fma_\Sigma)then(Term_\Sigma^A)else(Term_\Sigma^A) \mid \{Upd_\Sigma\}Term_\Sigma^A$$

$$Fma_\Sigma ::= true \mid false \mid p(Term_\Sigma^{B_1'}, \ldots, Term_\Sigma^{B_n'}) \mid \neg Fma_\Sigma \mid Fma_\Sigma \wedge Fma_\Sigma \mid$$
$$\quad Fma_\Sigma \vee Fma_\Sigma \mid Fma_\Sigma \rightarrow Fma_\Sigma \mid Fma_\Sigma \leftrightarrow Fma_\Sigma \mid$$
$$\quad \forall A\, x; Fma_\Sigma \mid \exists A\, x; Fma_\Sigma \mid [p]Fma_\Sigma \mid \langle p \rangle Fma_\Sigma \mid \{Upd_\Sigma\}Fma_\Sigma$$

$$Upd_\Sigma ::= \mathtt{a} := Term_\Sigma^{A'} \mid Upd_\Sigma \parallel Upd_\Sigma \mid \{Upd_\Sigma\}Upd_\Sigma$$

for any variable $x : A \in \mathcal{V}$, any program variable $\mathtt{a} : A \in \mathcal{PV}$, any function symbol $f : B_1, \ldots, B_n \rightarrow A \in \mathcal{F}$ and predicate symbol $p : B_1, \ldots, B_n$ where $B_1' \preceq B_1$, $\ldots$, $B_n' \preceq B_n$, any legal program fragment p in the context of Prg, and any type $A' \in \mathcal{T}$ with $A' \preceq A$. The set $Term_\Sigma$ of (arbitrarily typed) terms is defined as $Term_\Sigma = \bigcup_{A \in \mathcal{T}} Term_\Sigma^A$.

As syntactic sugar, we use infix notation for the binary symbols $\dot{\cup}$, $\dot{\cap}$, $\dot{\backslash}$, $\dot{=}$, and $\dot{\subseteq}$. Furthermore, we use the notation $(A)t$ for the term $cast_A(t)$, the notation $o.\mathtt{f}$ for $select_A(\mathtt{heap}, o, \mathtt{f})$ where $\mathtt{f} : Field \in \mathcal{F}^{Unique}$, the notation $a[i]$ for $select_A(\mathtt{heap}, a, arr(i))$, the notation $a.\mathtt{length}$ for $\mathtt{length}(a)$, the notation $\{(o, f)\}$ for $singleton(o, f)$, the notation $t_1 \not\eqcirc t_2$ for $\neg(t_1 \dot{=} t_2)$, the notation $(o, f) \dot{\in} s$ for $\dot{\in}(o, f, s)$, the notation $(o, f) \dot{\notin} s$ for $\neg(o, f) \dot{\in} s$, and the notation $QA\, x_1, \ldots, x_n; \varphi$ for $QA\, x_1; \ldots; QA\, x_n; \varphi$, where $Q \in \{\forall, \exists\}$.

Apart from the syntactic sugar for built-in symbols, Definition 5.3 is largely as in JavaDL. Updates u can be prefixed to terms, to formulas and to updates, enclosed in curly braces. Intuitively, an *elementary update* $\mathtt{a} := t$ assigns the value of the term t to the program variable $\mathtt{a}$. A *parallel update* $u_1 \parallel u_2$ executes the sub-updates u_1 and u_2 in parallel. The precise definition of the semantics of updates is given in Section 5.3 below.

In JavaDL, elementary updates are more generally of the form $f(t_1, \ldots, t_n) := t$, where f is a non-rigid symbol with arity n (more precisely, f must be a *location symbol*, not a *location dependent symbol*; see Chapter 4 for an explanation of the difference). As JavaDL* does not have general non-rigid function symbols, its elementary updates are always of the simpler form $\mathtt{a} := t$, where the left hand side is a program variable. JavaDL also features *quantified updates*. For example, the quantified update *for A x;* $\big(f(x) := g(x)\big)$ changes the interpretation of $f(x)$ for all x of type A in parallel. Quantified updates are not useful without general non-rigid function symbols: an update like *for A x;* $\big(\mathsf{a} := g(x)\big)$ attempts to assign to the variable a many different values at once (a "clash"), and it is equivalent to a non-quantified update $\mathsf{a} := g(x_0)$, where x_0 is chosen according to the clash resolution rules for quantified updates [Rümmer, 2006]. JavaDL* therefore does not include quantified updates.

5.3. Semantics

The semantics of JavaDL* terms, formulas and updates is based on the notion of *Kripke structures* as defined below.

Definition 5.4 (Kripke structures). *A Kripke structure* $\mathcal{K}$ *is a tuple* $(\mathcal{D}, \delta, I, \mathcal{S}, \rho)$ *consisting of*

- *a set* $\mathcal{D}$ *of semantical values, called the* domain,
- *a dynamic typing function* $\delta : \mathcal{D} \to \mathcal{T}$, *which gives rise to the subdomains* $\mathcal{D}^A = \{x \in \mathcal{D} \mid \delta(x) \preceq A\}$ *for all types* $A \in \mathcal{T}$,
- *an interpretation function* I *mapping every function symbol* $f : A_1, \ldots, A_n \to A \in \mathcal{F}$ *to a function* $I(f) : \mathcal{D}^{A_1}, \ldots, \mathcal{D}^{A_n} \to \mathcal{D}^A$ *and every predicate symbol* $p : A_1, \ldots, A_n \in \mathcal{P}$ *to a relation* $I(p) \subseteq \mathcal{D}^{A_1} \times \cdots \times \mathcal{D}^{A_n}$,
- *a set* $\mathcal{S}$ *of* states, *which are functions* $s \in \mathcal{S}$ *mapping every program variable* $\mathsf{a} : A \in \mathcal{PV}$ *to a value* $s(\mathsf{a}) \in \mathcal{D}^A$, *and*
- *a function* ρ *that associates with every legal program fragment* p *a transition relation* $\rho(p) \subseteq \mathcal{S}^2$ *such that* $(s_1, s_2) \in \rho(p)$ *if and only if* p, *when started in* s_1, *terminates normally (i.e., not by throwing an exception) in* s_2 *[Gosling et al., 2000]. We consider Java programs to be deterministic, so for all legal program fragments* p *and all* $s_1 \in \mathcal{S}$, *there is at most one* s_2 *such that* $(s_1, s_2) \in \rho(p)$.

We require that every Kripke structure satisfies the following:
- $\mathcal{S}$ *is the set of all functions mapping program variables to properly typed values (it is therefore completely determined by* $\mathcal{D}$ *and* δ*)*
- $\mathcal{D}^{Boolean} = \{tt, ff\}$
- $\mathcal{D}^{Int} = \mathbb{Z}$
- $\mathcal{D}^{Null} = \{null\}$
- $\mathcal{D}^{LocSet} = 2^{\mathcal{D}^{Object} \times \mathcal{D}^{Field}}$
- $\mathcal{D}^{Heap} = \mathcal{D}^{Object} \times \mathcal{D}^{Field} \to \mathcal{D}^{Any}$
- *for every interface or abstract class* $C \in \mathcal{T}$, *the set* $\{x \in \mathcal{D} \mid \delta(x) = C\}$ *is empty*
- *for every* $C \in \mathcal{T}$ *with* $C \preceq Object$, $C \neq Null$ *which is not an interface or an abstract class, and every* $n \in \mathbb{N}$, *the set* $\{x \in \mathcal{D} \mid \delta(x) = C, I(\mathtt{length})(x) =$

$n\}$ *is infinite*

- *for all* $f, g \in \mathcal{F}^{Unique}$ *with* $f \neq g$, *the function* $I(f)$ *is injective, and the ranges of the functions* $I(f)$ *and* $I(g)$ *are disjoint*

- $I(cast_A)(x) = \begin{cases} x & \text{if } x \in \mathcal{D}^A \\ null & \text{if } x \notin \mathcal{D}^A \text{ and } A \preceq Object \\ \emptyset & \text{if } x \notin \mathcal{D}^A \text{ and } A = LocSet \\ f\!f & \text{if } x \notin \mathcal{D}^A \text{ and } A = Boolean \end{cases}$

- $I(TRUE) = tt$, $I(FALSE) = f\!f$

- $I(select_A)(h, o, f) = I(cast_A)(h(o, f))$ *for all* $h \in \mathcal{D}^{Heap}$, $o \in \mathcal{D}^{Object}$, $f \in \mathcal{D}^{Field}$

- $I(store)(h, o, f, x)(o', f') = \begin{cases} x & \text{if } o = o', f = f' \text{ and } f \neq I(created) \\ h(o', f') & \text{otherwise} \end{cases}$
  for all $h \in \mathcal{D}^{Heap}$, $o, o' \in \mathcal{D}^{Object}$, $f, f' \in \mathcal{D}^{Field}$, $x \in \mathcal{D}^{Any}$

- $I(create)(h, o)(o', f) = \begin{cases} tt & \text{if } o = o', o \neq null \text{ and } f = I(created) \\ h(o', f) & \text{otherwise} \end{cases}$
  for all $h \in \mathcal{D}^{Heap}$, $o, o' \in \mathcal{D}^{Object}$, $f \in \mathcal{D}^{Field}$

- $I(anon)(h, s, h')(o, f) = \begin{cases} h'(o, f) & \text{if } \big((o, f) \in s \text{ and } f \neq I(created)\big) \\ & \text{or } (o, f) \in I(unusedLocs)(h) \\ h(o, f) & \text{otherwise} \end{cases}$
  for all $h, h' \in \mathcal{D}^{Heap}$, $s \in \mathcal{D}^{LocSet}$, $o \in \mathcal{D}^{Object}$, $f \in \mathcal{D}^{Field}$

- $I(\texttt{length})(o) \in \mathbb{N}$ *for all* $o \in \mathcal{D}^{Object}$

- $I(\dot{\emptyset}) = \emptyset$, $I(allLocs) = \mathcal{D}^{Object} \times \mathcal{D}^{Field}$

- $I(singleton)(o, f) = \{(o, f)\}$

- $I(\dot{\cup}) = \cup$, $I(\dot{\cap}) = \cap$, $I(\dot{\backslash}) = \backslash$

- $I(allFields)(o) = \{(o, f) \mid f \in \mathcal{D}^{Field}\}$

- $I(arrayRange)(o, i, j) = \{(o, I(arr)(x)) \mid x \in \mathbb{Z}, i \leq x, x \leq j\}$

- $I(unusedLocs)(h) = \{(o, f) \in I(allLocs) \mid o \neq null, h(o, I(created)) \neq tt\}$

- $I(\texttt{null}) = null$

- $I(exactInstance_A) = \{x \in \mathcal{D} \mid \delta(x) = A\}$

- $I(\doteq) = \{(x, x) \in \mathcal{D}^2\}$

- $I(wellFormed) = \{h \in \mathcal{D}^{Heap} \mid \text{for all } o \in \mathcal{D}^{Object}, f \in \mathcal{D}^{Field}:$
  $\quad \text{if } h(o, f) \in \mathcal{D}^{Object},$
  $\quad\quad \text{then } h(o, f) = null$
  $\quad\quad \text{or } h(h(o, f), I(created)) = tt;$
  $\quad \text{if } h(o, f) \in \mathcal{D}^{LocSet},$
  $\quad\quad \text{then } h(o, f) \cap I(unusedLocs)(h) = \emptyset;$
  $\quad \text{and there are only finitely many } o \in \mathcal{D}^{Object}$
  $\quad\quad \text{for which } h(o, I(created)) = tt\}$

- $I(\dot{\in}) = \{(o, f, s) \in \mathcal{D}^{Object} \times \mathcal{D}^{Field} \times \mathcal{D}^{LocSet} \mid (o, f) \in s\}$

- $I(\dot{\subseteq}) = \left\{ (s_1, s_2) \in (\mathcal{D}^{LocSet})^2 \mid s_1 \subseteq s_2 \right\}$
- $I(disjoint) = \left\{ (s_1, s_2) \in (\mathcal{D}^{LocSet})^2 \mid s_1 \cap s_2 = \emptyset \right\}$

We do not give a formalisation of the semantics of Java here. Instead, the function ρ serves as a black box that captures the behaviour of the legal program fragments p. As in JavaDL, we explicitly formalise this behaviour only on the level of the calculus, in the form of symbolic execution rules (Section 5.4).

The domains of the built-in types *Boolean*, *Int*, *Null*, *LocSet* and *Heap* are hard-coded into Definition 5.4. In particular, $\mathcal{D}^{LocSet}$ consists of all sets of locations (i.e., subsets of $\mathcal{D}^{Object} \times \mathcal{D}^{Field}$), and $\mathcal{D}^{Heap}$ consists of all functions mapping locations to values in $\mathcal{D}^{Any}$.

The domains of the subtypes of *Object* are sets of unspecified values. We often refer to these values as *objects*, but note that they are objects in the sense of *object references*, not in the sense of data structures containing field values. This is as in Java itself, where the value of an expression of a subtype of *Object* is always an object *reference*.

All states of a Kripke structure $\mathcal{K}$ share a common domain $\mathcal{D}$. This is sometimes referred to as the *constant domain assumption*. It simplifies, for example, reasoning about quantifiers in the presence of modal operators and updates. On the other hand, the Java programs appearing in formulas may allocate new objects (i.e., elements of $\mathcal{D}^{Object}$) that did not exist previously. This apparent contradiction is resolved with the help of the special field *created* introduced in Definition 5.1: given a heap array $h \in \mathcal{D}^{Heap}$ and an object $o \in \mathcal{D}^{Object}$, the object o is considered "created" in h in the sense of Java if and only if *created* is set to true for this object in h, i.e., if $h(o, I(created)) = tt$. An allocation statement in a program is understood as choosing a previously non-created object in $\mathcal{D}^{Object}$, and setting its *created* field to true in the heap. Similar solutions are, for example, also used in JavaDL and in *Spec#* [Barnett et al., 2004]. The alternative of abandoning the constant domain assumption has been investigated by Ahrendt et al. [2009].

The components of *Java arrays* are modelled in JavaDL* with the help of the function symbol $arr : Int \rightarrow Field \in \mathcal{F}^{Unique}$. Given an integer $i \in \mathbb{Z}$, the function $I(arr)$ returns a field $I(arr)(i) \in \mathcal{D}^{Field}$ representing the array component at index i. This allows treating array components in the same way as object fields. As the length of a Java array is determined at the time of its creation and never changes afterwards, we choose to model the `length` field of Java not as a constant symbol `length : Field` $\in \mathcal{F}^{Unique}$, but rather as a function symbol `length : Object` $\rightarrow Int \in \mathcal{F}^{NU}$. The function $I(\texttt{length})$ associates an unchangeable length $I(\texttt{length})(o) \in \mathbb{N}$ with every object $o \in \mathcal{D}^{Object}$ (where the set $\mathbb{N}$ of natural numbers includes 0). Array creation is understood as choosing a non-created array object of the desired length, and setting its *created* field to true. The advantage of this choice is that accessing the length of an array as length(a) is simpler than accessing it as *select*(heap, a, length). In particular, the term length(a) is independent of the heap.

Note that I(length) gives a length for all objects, even though we are interested in this length only for array objects. Relatedly, in JavaDL* any object can be combined with any field to get a legal location, although most of these locations do not exist on the level of Java, and are thus never used by Java programs or by JML/JML* specifications.

As interfaces and abstract classes cannot have direct instances in Java, Definition 5.4 demands that there are no values $x \in \mathcal{D}$ where $\delta(x)$ is an interface or an abstract class. Note that for all such types A, the domain $\mathcal{D}^A$ nevertheless includes at least the value *null*. For all other reference types, the definition requires that there is an infinite reservoir of objects of every length. Together with the *wellFormed* predicate (see below), this guarantees that there is always a suitable object left that can be created by a program p.

The domain D^{Field} is an unspecified set of values. The interpretation of the function symbols representing Java fields is restricted only by their status as *unique* function symbols. Definition 5.4 demands that the function $I(f)$ which is the interpretation of a unique function symbol f is injective; in particular, this implies that for $i_1, i_2 \in \mathbb{Z}$, we have $I(arr)(i_1) = I(arr)(i_2)$ if and only if $i_1 = i_2$. The definition also demands that for two unique function symbols f and g, the ranges of the functions $I(f)$ and $I(g)$ are disjoint. In the border case where f and g are *constant* symbols, this comes down to $I(f) \neq I(g)$.

The function symbols $cast_A : Any \rightarrow A$ resemble type casts in Java: for arguments in $\mathcal{D}^A$, the interpretation $I(cast_A)$ of $cast_A$ behaves like the identity function. For other arguments, a cast operation in Java would throw an exception. In JavaDL*, such a "failed" cast instead behaves as follows: if A is a subtype of *Object*, then Definition 5.4 demands that the cast returns *null*; if A is *LocSet*, then it demands that the cast returns $\emptyset$; if A is *Boolean*, then it demands that the cast returns *ff*; otherwise, Definition 5.4 does not demand anything, so the cast returns a fixed but unknown value of type A. The cast symbols are also present in JavaDL, but there, the behaviour of a failed cast is unspecified for all result types. Fixing *null*, $\emptyset$ and *ff* as the values of failed casts to reference types, to *LocSet* and to *Boolean* may seem arbitrary. The rationale behind this decision is explained in Subsection 5.4.4.

The heap arrays of JavaDL*—i.e., the functions in $\mathcal{D}^{Heap}$—allow storing an arbitrary value in any location. Nevertheless, when reading a particular location, the result is usually expected to be of a particular type A. The JavaDL* solution is to "cast" the value found in the heap to the desired type A, in the sense of the function symbol $cast_A$. For convenience, this cast operation is built right into the JavaDL* version of the *select* function symbol: there is a separate instance *select$_A$* : *Heap, Object, Field* $\rightarrow$ *A* for every type *A*, and applying its interpretation $I(select_A)$ to a heap array $h \in \mathcal{D}^{Heap}$, to an object $o \in \mathcal{D}^{Object}$ and to a field $f \in \mathcal{D}^{Field}$ is the same as reading $h(o, f)$ and casting the result to *A*. Note that if $h(o, f)$ is not an element of $\mathcal{D}^A$, then the value returned by this cast is *different* from $h(o, f)$, i.e., it is *not* the value actually stored in h at location (o, f). If no cast is desired, then *select$_{Any}$* can be used. As $I(cast_{Any})(x) = x$ for all $x \in \mathcal{D}^{Any}$, we have $I(select_{Any})(h, o, f) = h(o, f)$ for all $h \in \mathcal{D}^{Heap}$, $o \in \mathcal{D}^{Object}$ and $f \in \mathcal{D}^{Field}$.

The function symbol *store* : *Heap, Object, Field, Any* $\rightarrow$ *Heap* is almost as in the standard theory of arrays. However, it does not allow changing the *created* field; we have $I(store)(h, o, I(created), x) = h$, i.e., attempting to change *created* with the help of *store* has no effect at all. For changing *created*, there is the separate function symbol *create* : *Heap, Object* $\rightarrow$ *Heap*. Applying $I(create)$ to a heap array $h \in \mathcal{D}^{Heap}$ and an object $o \in \mathcal{D}^{Object} \setminus \{null\}$ yields a heap array $I(create)(h, o)$ with $I(create)(h, o)(o, I(created)) = tt$, no matter whether the object o is already "created" in the original heap array h or not. There is no need for supporting to change *created* in the other direction, because programs only allocate objects but never delete them (we do not consider garbage collection), and there are advantages to *not* supporting it (see Subsection 5.4.4 and Lemma 6.2).

Besides *create*, JavaDL* features another custom extension to the theory of arrays, namely the function symbol *anon* : *Heap, LocSet, Heap* $\rightarrow$ *Heap*. This function symbol is tailor-made for expressing a partially unknown state change, where the locations of a particular location set (a *modifies clause*) may be changed, and where new objects may be created and their locations changed, but where *other* locations are guaranteed to remain unchanged. A need for expressing such state changes occurs when reasoning about loops with the help of loop invariants (Section 5.4), and when reasoning about method calls with the help of method contracts (Chapter 6). In the context of JavaDL, this kind of state change is usually called an *anonymisation* [Beckert et al., 2007; Engel et al., 2009]; hence the name *anon*. Anonymisation is related to the `havoc` statement in the Boogie language [Barnett et al., 2006].

As fixed in Definition 5.4, applying the function $I(anon)$ to an "original" heap array $h \in \mathcal{D}^{Heap}$, to a location set $s \in \mathcal{D}^{LocSet}$ and to an "anonymous" heap array $h' \in \mathcal{D}^{Heap}$ yields a heap array $I(anon)(h, s, h') \in \mathcal{D}^{Heap}$ that is identical to h in some locations and to h' in others. The values of the locations in s are taken from h'; the only exception is the *created* field, similar to the definition of $I(store)$. The values of "unused" locations, i.e., locations belonging to objects that are not "created" in h, are also taken from h'. The values of all other locations are taken from h. Intuitively, they are not affected by the "anonymisation".

Definition 5.4 gives the standard set theoretical operators on *LocSet* (that is, the function symbols $\emptyset$, *allLocs*, *singleton*, $\dot{\cup}$, $\dot{\cap}$, $\backslash$, $\dot{\in}$, $\dot{\subseteq}$ and *disjoint*) their expected meaning. For the function symbol *allFields* : *Object* → *LocSet*, applying its interpretation $I(\text{allFields})$ to an object $o \in \mathcal{D}^{Object}$ yields the set of all locations belonging to the object o. For the function symbol *arrayRange* : *Object, Int, Int* → *LocSet*, the set $I(\text{arrayRange})(o, i, j)$ is the set of all array components belonging to o and to an index between i and j, inclusive. For the function symbol *unusedLocs* : *Heap* → *LocSet*, its interpretation $I(\text{unusedLocs})$ returns the set of all locations belonging to objects that are not "created" in the passed heap array. Locations of the *null* object are never considered "unused".

The predicate symbol $exactInstance_A$: *Any* characterises values x whose dynamic type $\delta(x)$ is A. The heap arrays h characterised by the predicate symbol *wellFormed* : *Heap* have three properties: firstly, all objects stored in h must be either the *null* object or be "created" in h; secondly, all location sets stored in h must contain only locations belonging to objects that are "created" or belonging to *null* (storing location sets in heap arrays happens through JML* ghost fields of type \locset; see Chapters 2, 3 and 6); and finally, only finitely many objects may be "created" in h. These well-formedness properties are maintained by every terminating Java program, because such a program can never obtain a reference to a non-created object (much less store it in the heap), cannot deallocate a created object, and can never allocate an infinite number of objects.

Having defined Kripke structures, we move on to defining the semantics of JavaDL* terms, formulas and updates.

Definition 5.5 (Semantics). *Given a Kripke structure $\mathcal{K} = (\mathcal{D}, \delta, I, \mathcal{S}, \rho)$, a state $s \in \mathcal{S}$ and a variable assignment $\beta : \mathcal{V} \to \mathcal{D}$ (where for $x : A \in \mathcal{V}$ we have $\beta(x) \in \mathcal{D}^A$), we evaluate every term $t \in Term_\Sigma^A$ to a value $val_{\mathcal{K},s,\beta}(t) \in \mathcal{D}^A$, every formula $\varphi \in Fma_\Sigma$ to a truth value $val_{\mathcal{K},s,\beta}(\varphi) \in \{tt, ff\}$, and every update $u \in Upd_\Sigma$ to a state transformer $val_{\mathcal{K},s,\beta}(u) : \mathcal{S} \to \mathcal{S}$ as defined in Figure 5.2 (where, as usual, "iff" stands for "if and only if").*

We sometimes write $(\mathcal{K}, s, \beta) \models \varphi$ instead of $val_{\mathcal{K},s,\beta}(\varphi) = tt$. A formula $\varphi \in Fma_\Sigma$ is called logically valid, *in symbols $\models \varphi$, if and only if $(\mathcal{K}, s, \beta) \models \varphi$ for all Kripke structures $\mathcal{K}$, all states $s \in \mathcal{S}$, and all variable assignments β.*

Definition 5.5 is as in JavaDL (without general location symbols, location dependent symbols, and quantified updates). Updates transform one state into another. The meaning of $\{u\}t$, where u is an update and t is a term, formula or update, is that t is evaluated in the state produced by u. Note the *last-win semantics* of parallel updates $u_1 \parallel u_2$: if there is a "clash", where u_1 and u_2 attempt to assign conflicting values to a program variable, then the value written by u_2 prevails.

$$val_{\mathcal{K},s,\beta}(x) = \beta(x)$$

$$val_{\mathcal{K},s,\beta}(\mathsf{a}) = s(\mathsf{a})$$

$$val_{\mathcal{K},s,\beta}(f(t_1,\ldots,t_n)) = I(f)(val_{\mathcal{K},s,\beta}(t_1),\ldots,val_{\mathcal{K},s,\beta}(t_n))$$

$$val_{\mathcal{K},s,\beta}(if(\varphi)then(t_1)else(t_2)) = \begin{cases} val_{\mathcal{K},s,\beta}(t_1) \text{ if } val_{\mathcal{K},s,\beta}(\varphi) = tt \\ val_{\mathcal{K},s,\beta}(t_2) \text{ otherwise} \end{cases}$$

$$val_{\mathcal{K},s,\beta}(\{u\}t) = val_{\mathcal{K},s',\beta}(t), \text{ where } s' = val_{\mathcal{K},s,\beta}(u)(s)$$

$$val_{\mathcal{K},s,\beta}(true) = tt$$

$$val_{\mathcal{K},s,\beta}(false) = ff$$

$$val_{\mathcal{K},s,\beta}(p(t_1,\ldots,t_n)) = tt \text{ iff } (val_{\mathcal{K},s,\beta}(t_1),\ldots,val_{\mathcal{K},s,\beta}(t_n)) \in I(p)$$

$$val_{\mathcal{K},s,\beta}(\neg\varphi) = tt \text{ iff } val_{\mathcal{K},s,\beta}(\varphi) = ff$$

$$val_{\mathcal{K},s,\beta}(\varphi_1 \wedge \varphi_2) = tt \text{ iff } ff \notin \{val_{\mathcal{K},s,\beta}(\varphi_1), val_{\mathcal{K},s,\beta}(\varphi_2)\}$$

$$val_{\mathcal{K},s,\beta}(\varphi_1 \vee \varphi_2) = tt \text{ iff } tt \in \{val_{\mathcal{K},s,\beta}(\varphi_1), val_{\mathcal{K},s,\beta}(\varphi_2)\}$$

$$val_{\mathcal{K},s,\beta}(\varphi_1 \rightarrow \varphi_2) = val_{\mathcal{K},s,\beta}(\neg\varphi_1 \vee \varphi_2)$$

$$val_{\mathcal{K},s,\beta}(\varphi_1 \leftrightarrow \varphi_2) = val_{\mathcal{K},s,\beta}(\varphi_1 \rightarrow \varphi_2 \wedge \varphi_2 \rightarrow \varphi_1)$$

$$val_{\mathcal{K},s,\beta}(\forall A\, x; \varphi) = tt \text{ iff } ff \notin \{val_{\mathcal{K},s,\beta_x^d}(\varphi) \mid d \in \mathcal{D}^A\}$$

$$val_{\mathcal{K},s,\beta}(\exists A\, x; \varphi) = tt \text{ iff } tt \in \{val_{\mathcal{K},s,\beta_x^d}(\varphi) \mid d \in \mathcal{D}^A\}$$

$$val_{\mathcal{K},s,\beta}([\mathsf{p}]\varphi) = tt \text{ iff } ff \notin \{val_{\mathcal{K},s',\beta}(\varphi) \mid (s,s') \in \rho(\mathsf{p})\}$$

$$val_{\mathcal{K},s,\beta}(\langle\mathsf{p}\rangle\varphi) = tt \text{ iff } tt \in \{val_{\mathcal{K},s',\beta}(\varphi) \mid (s,s') \in \rho(\mathsf{p})\}$$

$$val_{\mathcal{K},s,\beta}(\{u\}\varphi) = val_{\mathcal{K},s',\beta}(\varphi), \text{ where } s' = val_{\mathcal{K},s,\beta}(u)(s)$$

$$val_{\mathcal{K},s,\beta}(\mathsf{a} := t)(s')(\mathsf{b}) = \begin{cases} val_{\mathcal{K},s,\beta}(t) & \text{if } \mathsf{b} = \mathsf{a} \\ s'(\mathsf{b}) & \text{otherwise} \end{cases}$$

$$\text{for all } s' \in \mathcal{S}, \mathsf{b} \in \mathcal{PV}$$

$$val_{\mathcal{K},s,\beta}(u_1 \parallel u_2)(s') = val_{\mathcal{K},s,\beta}(u_2)(val_{\mathcal{K},s,\beta}(u_1)(s')) \text{ for all } s' \in \mathcal{S}$$

$$val_{\mathcal{K},s,\beta}(\{u_1\}u_2) = val_{\mathcal{K},s',\beta}(u_2), \text{ where } s' = val_{\mathcal{K},s,\beta}(u_1)(s)$$

Figure 5.2.: Semantics of JavaDL* terms, formulas and updates

5.4. Calculus

We reason about logical validity of JavaDL* formulas using a *sequent calculus* [Gentzen, 1935]. The calculus is a set of *rules*, which allow deriving *sequents* from other sequents.

Definition 5.6 (Sequents). *A sequent is a pair* $(\Gamma, \Delta) \in 2^{Fma_\Sigma} \times 2^{Fma_\Sigma}$, *where* Γ *(called the* antecedent *of the sequent) and* Δ *(called the* succedent *of the sequent) are finite sets of formulas. We denote a sequent* (Γ, Δ) *as* $\Gamma \Rightarrow \Delta$, *and use the notation*

$$\Gamma, \; \varphi_1, \ldots, \varphi_n \; \Rightarrow \; \psi_1, \ldots, \psi_m, \; \Delta$$

to stand for the sequent $\Gamma \cup \{\varphi_1, \ldots, \varphi_n\} \Rightarrow \{\psi_1, \ldots, \psi_m\} \cup \Delta$. *The set of all sequents is denoted as* Seq_Σ.

The semantics *of a sequent* $\Gamma \Rightarrow \Delta$ *is the same as that of the formula* $\bigwedge \Gamma \to \bigvee \Delta$: *we define* $val_{\mathcal{K},s,\beta}(\Gamma \Rightarrow \Delta) = val_{\mathcal{K},s,\beta}(\bigwedge \Gamma \to \bigvee \Delta)$.

The notations $\bigwedge$ and $\bigvee$ have their usual meaning; i.e., $\bigwedge\{\varphi_1, \ldots, \varphi_n\} = \varphi_1 \wedge \cdots \wedge \varphi_n$, and $\bigvee\{\varphi_1, \ldots, \varphi_n\} = \varphi_1 \vee \cdots \vee \varphi_n$, where an empty conjunction is *true* and an empty disjunction is *false*.

Definition 5.7 (Rules). *A* rule *is a binary relation* $r \subseteq Seq_\Sigma^* \times Seq_\Sigma$. *If* $((p_1, \ldots, p_n), c) \in r$, *then we say that the* conclusion $c \in Seq_\Sigma$ *is derivable from the* premises $p_1, \ldots, p_n$ *using* r.

A rule r *is called* sound *if the following holds for all* $((p_1, \ldots, p_n), c) \in r$: *if all premises* $p_1, \ldots, p_n$ *are logically valid, then the conclusion* c *is also logically valid.*

A *proof tree* is constructed by starting with a sequent as its root, and incrementally applying rules to its leaves. *Applying a rule* to a leaf means adding children below the leaf, such that the former leaf is derivable from the children using the rule.

Definition 5.8 (Proof trees). *A* proof tree *is a finite, directed, rooted tree, whose edges are directed away from the root, and which satisfies that*
- *all inner nodes* n *are labelled with a sequent* $seq(n) \in Seq_\Sigma$, *and*
- *all leaves* n *are labelled either with a sequent* $seq(n) \in Seq_\Sigma$ *or with the symbol* $*$ *(in which case they are called* closed*), and*
- *all edges* $(parent \to child_1), \ldots, (parent \to child_n)$ *originating in the same parent node are labelled with the same rule* r, *such that either*
  - *none of the children* $child_1, \ldots, child_n$ *is closed, and* $seq(parent)$ *is derivable from* $seq(child_1), \ldots, seq(child_n)$ *using* r, *or*
  - $n = 1$, $child_1$ *is closed, and* $((), seq(parent)) \in r$.

A proof tree is called closed *if all of its leaves are closed. A closed proof tree whose root is labelled with s is also called a* proof for s.

Provided that all rules of the calculus are sound, the existence of a proof for a sequent s implies that s is logically valid. Conversely, *completeness* of the calculus would mean that there is a proof for every logically valid sequent s. Completeness is impossible to achieve for a logic like JavaDL*, for example because it includes first-order arithmetic, which is itself inherently incomplete. Still, it is possible in principle to establish a notion of *relative completeness*, meaning that the calculus is complete except for the "unavoidable" degree of incompleteness. A relative completeness proof for ODL is given by Platzer [2004].

To represent the typically infinite number of pairs in a rule in a finite way, rules are denoted *schematically*. We define rules with the notation

$$\frac{p_1 \;\cdots\; p_n}{c} \quad \mathsf{ruleName},$$

where $p_1, \ldots, p_n$ and c are *schematic sequents*, i.e., sequents containing placeholders (so-called *schema variables*) for types, variables, terms, formulas and updates. The induced rule $\mathsf{ruleName}$ consists of all pairs $((p'_1, \ldots, p'_n), c') \in Seq_\Sigma^* \times Seq_\Sigma$ that result from instantiating the placeholders in $p_1, \ldots, p_n$ and in c. For example, two classical sequent calculus rules are $\mathsf{notLeft}$ and $\mathsf{notRight}$:

$$\frac{\Gamma \;\Rightarrow\; \varphi,\, \Delta}{\Gamma,\, \neg\varphi \;\Rightarrow\; \Delta} \; \mathsf{notLeft} \qquad\qquad \frac{\Gamma,\, \varphi \;\Rightarrow\; \Delta}{\Gamma \Rightarrow\; \neg\varphi,\, \Delta} \; \mathsf{notRight}$$

Here, Γ and Δ are placeholders for sets of formulas, and φ is a placeholder for a single formula. The two rules below are examples for rules without premisses:

$$\frac{}{\Gamma,\, \mathit{false} \;\Rightarrow\; \Delta} \; \mathsf{closeFalse} \qquad\qquad \frac{}{\Gamma \;\Rightarrow\; \mathit{true},\, \Delta} \; \mathsf{closeTrue}$$

Besides this classical notation for sequent rules, we also define rules with the notation

$$lhs \rightsquigarrow rhs \qquad \mathsf{ruleName},$$

where either (i) *lhs* and *rhs* are schematic terms (i.e., terms possibly containing schema variables) such that the type of *rhs* is a subtype of the type of *lhs*, or (ii) *lhs* and *rhs* are schematic formulas, or (iii) *lhs* and *rhs* are schematic updates. The induced rule consists of all pairs $((p), c) \in Seq_\Sigma^* \times Seq_\Sigma$, where p results from c by replacing an occurrence of an instance of *lhs* with the corresponding instance of *rhs*. We refer to rules defined in this fashion as *rewrite rules*. Rewrite rules are sound if and only if (all instantiations of) *lhs* and *rhs* are equivalent. An example for a rewrite rule is

$$t \doteq t \rightsquigarrow \mathit{true} \qquad \mathsf{equal},$$

where t stands for a term of an arbitrary type. In the KeY system, both rewrite rules and (most) other rules are expressed in the *taclet language* [Beckert et al., 2004].

The remainder of this section provides an overview of the calculus for JavaDL*. Most parts of the JavaDL calculus [Beckert et al., 2007] are not affected by the changes in JavaDL*, and these parts are not covered in detail. In particular, the classical first-order part of the sequent calculus is not covered at all (except for the examples notLeft, notRight, closeFalse and closeTrue above), and neither is the calculus part for handling integer arithmetic [Rümmer, 2007]. Interesting groups of rules, which are either new in JavaDL* or otherwise affected by the changes, are the following: rules capturing properties of the logic's *type system* (Subsection 5.4.1), rules for *unique function symbols* (Subsection 5.4.2), rules for *heap arrays* and the *well-formedness* of heap arrays (Subsections 5.4.3 and 5.4.4), rules for *location sets* (Subsection 5.4.5), rules for *updates* (Subsection 5.4.6), and the *symbolic execution* rules for Java programs (Subsection 5.4.7). Finally, an important individual rule that is significantly affected by the changes in JavaDL* is the *loop invariant rule* (Subsection 5.4.8).

5.4.1. Rules for Types

A selection of four rewrite rules that implement properties guaranteed by the type system of JavaDL* is shown in Figure 5.3. These are almost unchanged over JavaDL. They are covered here mostly to give an intuition of how the type system factors into calculus-level reasoning in both JavaDL and JavaDL*.

The castDel rule allows removing an "upcast", i.e., a cast to a supertype of the casted term's own type, which is sound because—by Definition 5.4—such a cast operation does not have any effect. This rule is for example used to remove the casts implicitly present in the $select_A$ function symbols for reading from heap arrays (Subsection 5.4.3). A detailed example involving this role of castDel is contained in Section 5.5.

The inAbstractType rule captures the fact that interfaces and abstract classes have no direct instances, i.e., no objects not belonging to a proper subtype of the interface or abstract class. The rules disjointTypes and disjointObjTypes allow simplifying away an equality where the domains of the involved subterms are disjoint: if A and B have no common subtype, then $\mathcal{D}^A \cap \mathcal{D}^B$ is the empty set, and thus the equality is equivalent to *false*. For subtypes of *Object*, there is always at least the common subtype *Null*. If there are no *other* common subtypes, then the equality holds if and only if both terms are equal to **null**.

As defined in Figure 5.3, the rule disjointObjTypes is applicable only if a complex side condition holds for the instantiation of A and B. This side condition is *not* necessary for soundness of the rule, and it is not present in JavaDL. In fact,

$$(A)t \rightsquigarrow t \quad \text{where } t \in \mathit{Term}_{\Sigma}^{A'}, \ A' \preceq A \qquad\qquad \text{castDel}$$

$$\mathit{exactInstance}_A(t) \rightsquigarrow \mathit{false} \qquad\qquad \text{inAbstractType}$$
$$\text{where } A \text{ is an interface or an abstract class}$$

$$t_1 \doteq t_2 \rightsquigarrow \mathit{false} \qquad\qquad \text{disjointTypes}$$
$$\text{where } t_1 \in \mathit{Term}_{\Sigma}^{A}, \ t_2 \in \mathit{Term}_{\Sigma}^{B},$$
$$\text{with } \{C \in \mathcal{T} \mid C \preceq A, C \preceq B\} = \emptyset$$

$$t_1 \doteq t_2 \rightsquigarrow t_1 \doteq \mathbf{null} \wedge t_2 \doteq \mathbf{null} \qquad\qquad \text{disjointObjTypes}$$
$$\text{where } t_1 \in \mathit{Term}_{\Sigma}^{A}, \ t_2 \in \mathit{Term}_{\Sigma}^{B}$$
$$\text{with } \{C \in \mathcal{T} \mid C \preceq A, C \preceq B\} = \{\mathit{Null}\}, \text{ and where}$$

- none of A and B is an array type or an interface, or
- at least one of A and B is a **final** class, or
- exactly one of A and B is an array type, or
- A and B are array types of different dimensions, or
- A and B are array types of the same dimension, such that
    - none of their element types is an interface, or
    - at least one of their element types is a **final** class, or
    - one of their element types is not a subtype of *Object*.

Figure 5.3.: Rules for types

this side condition leads to a (deliberate) incompleteness of the calculus. The motivation behind consciously introducing this incompleteness is the desire for modularity of reasoning: proofs created in a signature for a particular program *Prg* should not be invalidated by "expected" changes to *Prg*, such as adding new classes and interfaces. If the side condition is violated, then such an extension of *Prg* with new types may introduce a common subtype of A and B. For example, if A is a class and B an interface, the extension may introduce a subclass of A that implements B. A "modular" proof thus must not rely on there being no common subtype, even if in the current signature there happens to be none. If, on the other hand, the side condition is satisfied, then Java's subtyping rules prevent the addition of a common subtype in all extensions of *Prg*, so the calculus is free to exploit its non-existence.

The need for this (in a sense inelegant) "deliberate incompleteness" is a consequence of modelling the reference types of Java directly as types of the verification logic. An alternative is using a single type *Object* or *Ref* for references to ob-

$$f(t_1, \ldots, t_n) \doteq f(t_1', \ldots, t_n') \rightsquigarrow t_1 \doteq t_1' \wedge \cdots \wedge t_n \doteq t_n' \qquad \text{uniqueSame}$$
$$\text{where } f \in \mathcal{F}^{Unique}$$

$$f(t_1, \ldots, t_m) \doteq g(t_1, \ldots, t_n) \rightsquigarrow \textit{false} \qquad \text{uniqueNotSame}$$
$$\text{where } f, g \in \mathcal{F}^{Unique}, f \neq g$$

Figure 5.4.: Rules for unique function symbols

jects of all Java types, and modelling the reference types as values of a type *RefType* similar to *Field*. The known reference types of *Prg* are then referred to via unique constant symbols of type *RefType*. This kind of approach is used in Spec# [Barnett et al., 2006]. Here, a sound but non-modular rule that depends on knowledge about *all* reference types is not only undesirable, but impossible, because the domain of *RefType* is not fixed.

On the other hand, the advantage of modelling Java types as logical types is that it leads to shorter proof obligations and shorter proofs, because it captures many properties already in the type system that otherwise have to be expressed explicitly via formulas. For example, the absence of a common subtype for certain pairs of types has to be axiomatised as a quantified formula in the *RefType* approach, whereas in disjointObjTypes it occurs as a side-condition that, when applying the rule, is checked on the meta-level in a presumably efficient manner. Modularity can be maintained despite the modelling of Java types as logical types by carefully restricting rules that "enumerate" the reference types of the program, such as disjointObjTypes. These restrictions could be formally captured by defining notions of "modular soundness" and "modular completeness" that deviate from ordinary soundness and completeness [Leino, 1995; Müller, 2002; Roth, 2006].

5.4.2. Rules for Unique Function Symbols

The properties of unique function symbols are captured by the rules in Figure 5.4: two terms that both have unique function symbols as their top level operators are equal if and only if the symbol is the same in both terms, and if all subterms below the symbol are equal. A common application of uniqueNotSame is simplifying $f \doteq g$ to *false*, where f and g are unique constant symbols of type *Field*. An example for an application of uniqueSame is simplifying $arr(i) \doteq arr(j)$ to $i \doteq j$, where i and j are terms of type *Int*.

$$select_A(store(h, o, f, x), o', f') \rightsquigarrow if(o \doteq o' \wedge f \doteq f' \wedge f \not\doteq created) \qquad \text{selectOfStore}$$
$$then((A)x)else(select_A(h, o', f')))$$

$$select_A(create(h, o), o', f) \rightsquigarrow if(o \doteq o' \wedge o \not\doteq \texttt{null} \wedge f \doteq created) \quad \text{selectOfCreate}$$
$$then((A)TRUE)else(select_A(h, o', f)))$$

$$select_A(anon(h, s, h'), o, f) \rightsquigarrow if((o, f) \dot\in s \wedge f \not\doteq created$$
$$\vee (o, f) \dot\in unusedLocs(h)) \qquad \text{selectOfAnon}$$
$$then(select_A(h', o, f))else(select_A(h, o, f)))$$

$$store(\ldots(store(h, o, f, x), \ldots), o, f, y) \qquad\qquad \text{dropStore}$$
$$\rightsquigarrow store(\ldots(h, \ldots), o, f, y)$$

Figure 5.5.: Rules for heap arrays

5.4.3. Rules for Heap Arrays

Rules for the JavaDL* version of the theory of arrays are shown in Figure 5.5. The three rules selectOfStore, selectOfCreate and selectOfAnon correspond directly to the semantics of *store*, *create* and *anon* as fixed in Definition 5.4. Applying these rules means to simplify an application of $select_A$ by propagating $select_A$ inwards to the subterms of *store*, *create* or *anon*. Concrete values are cast to the desired type A with the help of the function symbol $cast_A$. If the static type of the term representing the value is a subtype of A, then the cast can subsequently be removed with the help of the castDel rule (Figure 5.3).

The dropStore rule is an auxiliary rule which is not strictly necessary. Given a cascade of nested applications of *store*, *create* and *anon*, it removes an inner application of *store* which is guaranteed to be overwritten by a more outward application of *store*, because both applications operate on syntactically identical object terms o and field terms f. We have seen an example in Section 5.1, namely simplifying the term $store(store(\texttt{heap}, o, f, 1), o, f, 2)$ to the equivalent term $store(\texttt{heap}, o, f, 2)$.

5.4.4. Rules for Well-formedness of Heap Arrays

Typical proof obligations such as those defined in Chapter 6 contain an assumption stating the initial "well-formedness" of the heap, i.e., the assumption *wellFormed*(heap). Well-formedness of a heap array h implies the property that all objects referenced in it (except *null*) are created in h. This implication of well-formedness can be exploited in proofs with the help of the reflsNullOrCreated rule shown in Figure 5.6.

The reflsNullOrCreated rule is applicable if *wellFormed*(h) is present in the antecedent. The placeholders o and f (standing for an object term and a field term, respectively) do not occur in the conclusion and can be instantiated freely. In practice, application of the rule is triggered by an occurrence of the term $select_A(h, o, f)$ somewhere in the conclusion.

The soundness of reflsNullOrCreated depends on a subtle detail of Definition 5.4. We thus formally state the core observation behind it as a lemma.

Lemma 5.1 (A consequence of well-formedness). *For all types $A \in \mathcal{T}$ with $A \preceq Object$, the following formula is logically valid:*

$$\forall Heap\ h; \forall Object\ o; \forall Field\ f; \big(wellFormed(h)$$
$$\rightarrow select_A(h, o, f) \doteq \mathbf{null}$$
$$\lor select_{Boolean}(h, select_A(h, o, f), created)$$
$$\doteq TRUE \big)$$

Lemma 5.1 is proven in Appendix A.2. The subtlety is that well-formedness of a heap array h guarantees for all objects o and fields f only that $h(o, f)$ is *null* or created, but *not* immediately that the same holds for $I(select_A)(h, o, f)$: if $h(o, f) \notin \mathcal{D}^A$, then $I(select_A)(h, o, f)$ is different from $h(o, f)$, i.e., it is different from the value actually stored in h at the location (o, f). The definition of $I(cast_A)$ in Definition 5.4 solves this problem by demanding that $I(cast_A)(x) = null$ for all $x \notin \mathcal{D}^A$, which implies that $I(select_A)(h, o, f) = null$ if $h(o, f) \notin \mathcal{D}^A$.

An alternative approach would be strengthening the definition of $I(wellFormed)$ such that in a well-formed heap, every location must hold a value in the domain of a particular type, which is determined by the Java type of the corresponding field. However, this would make proving the preservation of well-formedness more complex (see below). In contrast, the chosen solution does not incur a cost during verification, and it is harmless semantically because there is no conflicting expectation towards the value of a "failed" cast; the value would just be unspecified otherwise.

A second property implied by well-formedness of a heap array is that all location sets stored in it contain only locations belonging to created objects or to *null*. This can be made use of in proofs with the help of the elementIsNullOrCreated rule of Figure 5.6. The argument for the soundness of this rule is analogous to the argument for the soundness of reflsNullOrCreated. It relies on the fact that by Definition 5.4, we have $I(cast_{LocSet})(x) = \emptyset$ for all $x \notin \mathcal{D}^{LocSet}$.

Sometimes the well-formedness of a heap array must be proven. Such situations are for example created by the loop invariant rule defined in Subsection 5.4.8.

$$\frac{\begin{array}{l}\Gamma,\ wellFormed(h),\\ select_A(h, o, f) \doteq \texttt{null}\\ \quad \lor\ select_{Boolean}(h, select_A(h, o, f), created) \doteq TRUE\ \Rightarrow\ \Delta\end{array}}{\Gamma,\ wellFormed(h)\ \Rightarrow\ \Delta} \quad \text{reflsNullOrCreated}$$

where $A \preceq Object$

$$\frac{\begin{array}{l}\Gamma,\ wellFormed(h),\ (o', f') \dot{\in} select_{LocSet}(h, o, f),\\ o' \doteq \texttt{null} \lor select_{Boolean}(h, o', created) \doteq TRUE\ \Rightarrow\ \Delta\end{array}}{\Gamma,\ wellFormed(h),\ (o', f') \dot{\in} select_{LocSet}(h, o, f)\ \Rightarrow\ \Delta} \quad \text{elementIsNullOrCreated}$$

$$\frac{\begin{array}{l}\Gamma\ \Rightarrow\ wellFormed(h),\ \Delta\\ \Gamma\ \Rightarrow\ x \doteq \texttt{null},\ select_{Boolean}(h, x, created) = TRUE,\ \Delta\end{array}}{\Gamma\ \Rightarrow\ wellFormed(store(h, o, f, x)),\ \Delta} \quad \text{wellFormedStoreObject}$$

where $x \in Term_{\Sigma}^{A}$, $A \preceq Object$

$$\frac{\begin{array}{l}\Gamma\ \Rightarrow\ wellFormed(h),\ \Delta\\ \Gamma\ \Rightarrow\ disjoint(x, unusedLocs(h)),\ \Delta\end{array}}{\Gamma\ \Rightarrow\ wellFormed(store(h, o, f, x)),\ \Delta} \quad \text{wellFormedStoreLocSet}$$

where $x \in Term_{\Sigma}^{LocSet}$

$$\frac{\Gamma\ \Rightarrow\ wellFormed(h),\ \Delta}{\Gamma\ \Rightarrow\ wellFormed(store(h, o, f, x)),\ \Delta} \quad \text{wellFormedStorePrimitive}$$

where $x \in Term_{\Sigma}^{A}$, $A \npreceq Object$, $A \neq LocSet$

$$\frac{\Gamma\ \Rightarrow\ wellFormed(h),\ \Delta}{\Gamma\ \Rightarrow\ wellFormed(create(h, o)),\ \Delta} \quad \text{wellFormedCreate}$$

$$\frac{\Gamma\ \Rightarrow\ wellFormed(h) \land wellFormed(h'),\ \Delta}{\Gamma\ \Rightarrow\ wellFormed(anon(h, s, h')),\ \Delta} \quad \text{wellFormedAnon}$$

Figure 5.6.: Rules for well-formedness of heap arrays

They are handled with the rules wellFormedStoreObject, wellFormedStoreLocSet, wellFormedStorePrimitive, wellFormedCreate and wellFormedAnon which are shown in Figure 5.6. These rules are applicable if the succedent contains an application of *wellFormed* to *store*, *create* or *anon*.

Proving well-formedness with these rules works incrementally: a heap array constructed with *store*, *create* or *anon* is proven to be well-formed by showing that the "original" heap array is well-formed, and that the change preserves well-formedness. Note that each of these rules is incomplete, in the sense that the conclusion may be valid without the premiss being valid. This happens if the original heap array is ill-formed, but if the application of *store*, *create* or *anon* turns it into a well-formed heap array, for example by overwriting a forbidden reference to a non-created object with a reference to a created object. This incompleteness is irrelevant in practice, because Java programs always *preserve* well-formedness, never establish well-formedness after starting from an ill-formed heap.

Because the JavaDL* definition of $I(store)$ in Definition 5.4 prevents *store* from ever deallocating a created object, applications of *store* can negate well-formedness only by writing a reference to a non-created object, or by writing a location set that contains a location which belongs to a non-created object. The wellFormedStoreObject rule handles the case where *store* is used to write an object reference: we can prove that the resulting heap array is well-formed by proving that the original heap array is well-formed, and that the written object is either *null* or a created object. As this is not entirely obvious, we cast it as a lemma.

Lemma 5.2 (Well-formedness after storing an object)**.** *The following formula is logically valid:*

$$\forall Heap\ h;\ \forall Object\ o, x;\ \forall Field\ f;\ \big(wellFormed(h)$$
$$\wedge\ (x \doteq \mathtt{null}$$
$$\vee\ select_{Boolean}(h, x, created) \doteq TRUE)$$
$$\rightarrow\ wellFormed(store(h, o, f, x)))$$

Lemma 5.2 is proven in Appendix A.3. The proof makes use of the fact that by Definition 5.4, the function $I(cast_{Boolean})$ returns *ff* for arguments not in $\mathcal{D}^{Boolean}$. Without this additional restriction on the behaviour of "failed" casts, the function symbol $select_{Any}$ would have to be used in place of $select_{Boolean}$ for reading the *created* field, which would be possible but out of line with the treatment of other fields.

The wellFormedStoreObject rule is complemented by wellFormedStoreLocSet and wellFormedStorePrimitive, which cover the cases of writing a location set and writing a value which is neither an object nor a location set, respectively. For location sets, one must prove that the original heap array is well-formed, and that the written location set does not contain locations that belong to non-created objects. For other ("primitive") values, the definition of $I(wellFormed)$ does not impose any restriction, so such a write operation always preserves well-formedness. Also, creating an object with *create* always preserves well-formedness, making the wellFormedCreate rule similar to wellFormedStorePrimitive.

The last rule in Figure 5.6 is wellFormedAnon, which reduces the task of proving well-formedness for an "anonymised" heap array to the task of proving well-formedness for the two argument heap arrays. The insight underlying the soundness of wellFormedAnon is formalised in Lemma 5.3 below.

Lemma 5.3 (Well-formedness after anonymisation). *The following formula is logically valid:*

$$\forall Heap\, h, h';\; \forall LocSet\, l;\; \big(wellFormed(h) \wedge wellFormed(h')$$
$$\rightarrow wellFormed(anon(h, l, h')) \big)$$

A proof for Lemma 5.3 is contained in Appendix A.4. The soundness of wellFormedAnon is an obvious consequence of Lemma 5.3.

5.4.5. Rules for Location Sets

Location sets are handled by the (unsurprising) rules in Figure 5.7. Propositions about membership in a set constructed with one of the built-in set constructors $\emptyset$, *allLocs*, *singleton*, $\dot\cup$, $\dot\cap$, $\backslash$, *allFields*, *arrayRange* and *unusedLocs* are simplified using the definition of the respective built-in function symbol. Formulas that compare sets using the predicate symbols $\dot=$, $\dot\subseteq$ and *disjoint* are transformed into equivalent formulas using $\dot\in$.

The rules inArrayRange, setEquality, subset and disjoint introduce quantifiers. The placeholders for the quantified variables (such as x in the rule inArrayRange) may be instantiated with any logical variable not occurring free in terms of the rule's left hand side. The function $fv : Term_\Sigma \cup Fma_\Sigma \cup Upd_\Sigma \rightarrow 2^\mathcal{V}$ returns the set of free variables of a term, formula or update, and is defined as usual. In particular, we have $fv(x) = \{x\}$ for $x \in \mathcal{V}$, and $fv(\mathcal{Q}A\,x; \varphi) = fv(\varphi) \backslash \{x\}$ for $\mathcal{Q} \in \{\forall, \exists\}$.

5.4.6. Rules for Updates

The part of the calculus that deals with updates is shown in Figure 5.8. It is essentially a subset of the update calculus of Rümmer [2006], missing the parts that handle updates to general location symbols, as well as quantified updates.

The dropUpdate$_1$ rule simplifies away an ineffective elementary sub-update of a larger parallel update: if there is an update to the same program variable a further to the right of the parallel composition, then this second elementary

$$(o, f) \mathbin{\dot\in} \dot\emptyset \rightsquigarrow false \qquad\qquad \text{inEmpty}$$

$$(o, f) \mathbin{\dot\in} allLocs \rightsquigarrow true \qquad\qquad \text{inAllLocs}$$

$$(o, f) \mathbin{\dot\in} \{(o', f')\} \rightsquigarrow o \doteq o' \wedge f \doteq f' \qquad\qquad \text{inSingleton}$$

$$(o, f) \mathbin{\dot\in} (s_1 \mathbin{\dot\cup} s_2) \rightsquigarrow (o, f) \mathbin{\dot\in} s_1 \vee (o, f) \mathbin{\dot\in} s_2 \qquad\qquad \text{inUnion}$$

$$(o, f) \mathbin{\dot\in} (s_1 \mathbin{\dot\cap} s_2) \rightsquigarrow (o, f) \mathbin{\dot\in} s_1 \wedge (o, f) \mathbin{\dot\in} s_2 \qquad\qquad \text{inIntersect}$$

$$(o, f) \mathbin{\dot\in} (s_1 \mathbin{\dot\setminus} s_2) \rightsquigarrow (o, f) \mathbin{\dot\in} s_1 \wedge (o, f) \mathbin{\dot\notin} s_2 \qquad\qquad \text{inSetMinus}$$

$$(o, f) \mathbin{\dot\in} allFields(o') \rightsquigarrow o \doteq o' \qquad\qquad \text{inAllFields}$$

$$(o, f) \mathbin{\dot\in} arrayRange(o', i, j) \rightsquigarrow o \doteq o' \qquad\qquad \text{inArrayRange}$$
$$\wedge \exists Int\, x; \big(f \doteq arr(x) \wedge i \le x \wedge x \le j\big)$$
$$\text{where } x \notin fv(f) \cup fv(i) \cup fv(j)$$

$$(o, f) \mathbin{\dot\in} unusedLocs(h) \rightsquigarrow o \not\doteq \mathbf{null} \qquad\qquad \text{inUnusedLocs}$$
$$\wedge\, select_{Boolean}(h, o, created) \doteq FALSE$$

$$s_1 \doteq s_2 \rightsquigarrow \forall Object\, o; \forall Field\, f; \big((o, f) \mathbin{\dot\in} s_1 \qquad\qquad \text{setEquality}$$
$$\leftrightarrow (o, f) \mathbin{\dot\in} s_2\big)$$
$$\text{where } o, f \notin fv(s_1) \cup fv(s_2)$$

$$s_1 \mathbin{\dot\subseteq} s_2 \rightsquigarrow \forall Object\, o; \forall Field\, f; \big((o, f) \mathbin{\dot\in} s_1 \rightarrow (o, f) \mathbin{\dot\in} s_2\big) \qquad \text{subset}$$
$$\text{where } o, f \notin fv(s_1) \cup fv(s_2)$$

$$disjoint(s_1, s_2) \rightsquigarrow \forall Object\, o; \forall Field\, f; \big((o, f) \mathbin{\dot\notin} s_1 \vee (o, f) \mathbin{\dot\notin} s_2\big) \qquad \text{disjoint}$$
$$\text{where } o, f \notin fv(s_1) \cup fv(s_2)$$

Figure 5.7.: Rules for location sets

update overrides the first due to the last-win semantics of parallel updates (Definition 5.5). This is similar to the dropStore rule in Figure 5.5, which performs an analogous simplification on nested *store* terms.

The dropUpdate$_2$ rule allows dropping an elementary update $\mathsf{a} := t'$ where the term, formula or update in scope of the update cannot depend on the value of the program variable a, because it does not contain any free occurrences of a. A *free* occurrence of a program variable is any occurrence, except for an occurrence inside a program fragment p that is bound by a declaration within p. In addition to explicit occurrences, we consider program fragments p to always

$$\{ \dots \parallel \mathsf{a} := t_1 \parallel \dots \parallel \mathsf{a} := t_2 \parallel \dots \}t \qquad\qquad \mathsf{dropUpdate}_1$$
$$\leadsto \{ \dots \parallel \dots \parallel \mathsf{a} := t_2 \parallel \dots \}t$$
$$\text{where } t \in \mathit{Term}_\Sigma \cup \mathit{Fma}_\Sigma \cup \mathit{Upd}_\Sigma$$

$$\{ \dots \parallel \mathsf{a} := t' \parallel \dots \}t \leadsto \{ \dots \parallel \dots \}t \qquad\qquad \mathsf{dropUpdate}_2$$
$$\text{where } t \in \mathit{Term}_\Sigma \cup \mathit{Fma}_\Sigma \cup \mathit{Upd}_\Sigma,\ \mathsf{a} \notin \mathit{fpv}(t)$$

$$\{u\}\{u'\}t \leadsto \{u \parallel \{u\}u'\}t \qquad\qquad \mathsf{seqToPar}$$
$$\text{where } t \in \mathit{Term}_\Sigma \cup \mathit{Fma}_\Sigma \cup \mathit{Upd}_\Sigma$$

$$\{u\}x \leadsto x \quad \text{where } x \in \mathcal{V} \cup \{\mathit{true}, \mathit{false}\} \qquad\qquad \mathsf{applyOnRigid}_1$$

$$\{u\}f(t_1, \dots, t_n) \leadsto f(\{u\}t_1, \dots, \{u\}t_n) \quad \text{where } f \in \mathcal{F} \cup \mathcal{P} \qquad \mathsf{applyOnRigid}_2$$

$$\{u\}\mathit{if}(\varphi)\mathit{then}(t_1)\mathit{else}(t_2) \leadsto \mathit{if}(\{u\}\varphi)\mathit{then}(\{u\}t_1)\mathit{else}(\{u\}t_2) \qquad \mathsf{applyOnRigid}_3$$

$$\{u\}\neg\varphi \leadsto \neg\{u\}\varphi \qquad\qquad \mathsf{applyOnRigid}_4$$

$$\{u\}(\varphi_1 \bullet \varphi_2) \leadsto \{u\}\varphi_1 \bullet \{u\}\varphi_2 \quad \text{where } \bullet \in \{\wedge, \vee, \rightarrow, \leftrightarrow\} \quad \mathsf{applyOnRigid}_5$$

$$\{u\}\mathcal{Q}A\,x; \varphi \leadsto \mathcal{Q}A\,x; \{u\}\varphi \ \text{ where } \mathcal{Q} \in \{\forall, \exists\},\ x \notin \mathit{fv}(u) \quad \mathsf{applyOnRigid}_6$$

$$\{u\}(\mathsf{a} := t) \leadsto \mathsf{a} := \{u\}t \qquad\qquad \mathsf{applyOnRigid}_7$$

$$\{u\}(u_1 \parallel u_2) \leadsto \{u\}u_1 \parallel \{u\}u_2 \qquad\qquad \mathsf{applyOnRigid}_8$$

$$\{\mathsf{a} := t\}\mathsf{a} \leadsto t \qquad\qquad \mathsf{applyOnTarget}$$

Figure 5.8.: Rules for updates

contain an implicit free occurrence of the program variable **heap**. The function $\mathit{fpv} : \mathit{Term}_\Sigma \cup \mathit{Fma}_\Sigma \cup \mathit{Upd}_\Sigma \rightarrow 2^{\mathcal{PV}}$ is defined accordingly. For example, we have $\mathit{fpv}([\mathbf{int}\ \mathsf{a} = \mathsf{b};](\mathsf{b} \doteq \mathsf{c})) = \{\mathsf{b}, \mathsf{c}, \mathbf{heap}\}$. Java's rules for *definite assignment* [Gosling et al., 2000, Chapter 16] ensure that within a program fragment p, a declared program variable (such as a in the example) is always written before being read, and that the behaviour of p thus cannot depend on its initial value. In the border case where the parallel update produced by $\mathsf{dropUpdate}_2$ is empty, the update application $\{\}$ disappears entirely.

The $\mathsf{seqToPar}$ rule converts a cascade of two update applications—which corresponds to sequential execution of the two updates—into application of a single parallel update. Due to the last-win semantics for parallel updates, this is possible by applying the first update to the second, and replacing the sequential composition by parallel composition.

The remaining rules are responsible for applying updates to terms, formulas and (other) updates as substitutions. The various applyOnRigid rules propagate an update to the subterms below a (rigid) operator. Ultimately, the update can either be simplified away with dropUpdate$_2$, or it remains as an elementary update a := t applied to the target program variable a itself. In the latter case, the term t is substituted for a by the applyOnTarget rule.

The only case not covered by the rules in Figure 5.8 is that of applying an update to a modal operator, as in $\{u\}[p]\varphi$ or $\{u\}\langle p\rangle\varphi$. For these formulas, the program p must first be eliminated using the symbolic execution rules discussed in Subsection 5.4.7. Only afterwards can the resulting update be applied to φ.

5.4.7. Rules for Symbolic Execution of Java Programs

Formulas containing programs are handled by rules that perform a *symbolic execution* of the embedded programs [King, 1976]. They turn program level assignments into updates and conditional statements into splits of the proof tree, and they unwind loops and inline method calls. In the resulting proof trees, a path through the tree corresponds to an execution path through the program.

The symbolic execution rules of the JavaDL calculus are a formalisation of the semantics of the Java language. There are many hundreds of these rules in the implementation in KeY. The changes in JavaDL* affect these rules in (i) how side-effect free Java expressions are transformed into logical terms (which happens implicitly as a part of many rules), in (ii) the rules for symbolically executing assignments to heap locations, and in (iii) the rules for symbolically executing object allocation. In the following, we sketch the overall symbolic execution calculus, and highlight these differences.

The rules operate on the *first active statement* in a modality, which is the first statement after a *non-active prefix* π of beginnings "{" of code blocks, beginnings "**try**{" of **try-catch-finally** blocks, beginnings "method-frame(...):{" of method frames (Definition 5.2), and labels. We refer to the rest of the program that follows after the first active statement as the *postfix* ω. The postfix ω in particular contains closing braces matching the opening braces in the prefix π. For example, in the following program fragment, the first active statement is i=1, and π and ω are as indicated:

```
method-frame(...) : { try { i=1;  i=2; } catch(E e) { i=3; } } i=4;
```
$$\underbrace{\hspace{3cm}}_{\pi} \qquad \underbrace{\hspace{4cm}}_{\omega}$$

If the first active statement is a **return**, **throw**, **break** or **continue** statement, its meaning is given by the prefix π. The prefix also gives meaning to (explicit or implicit) occurrences of the keyword **this** in the first active statement: such an occurrence is understood as an occurrence of the term t of the innermost opening method frame "method-frame(result=r, this=t):{" in π.

Besides **this**, we also consider the other *simple expressions* of Java to be logical terms, where a simple expression is one that does not have side effects and does not contain method calls. We assume that the necessary operators are present in the signature. In contrast to JavaDL, a field access expression o.f is seen as the term $select_A(\text{heap}, o, \text{f})$, where A is the declared type of the field f in *Prg*. A **static** field access expression f is modelled as the term $select_A(\text{heap}, \text{null}, \text{f})$. That is, we model **static** fields as fields of the *null* object. This is possible because the fields of *null* are not used otherwise. It conveniently allows handling **static** fields in the same way as instance fields. An array access expression a[i] is represented as the term $select_A(\text{heap}, a, arr(i))$, where A is the static component type of a. An array length expression a.length is modelled as the term $\text{length}(a)$.

Non-simple expressions cannot directly be understood as terms. If the first active statement contains such an expression, it is first reduced to (several) simpler expressions. Temporary variables are introduced to buffer the results of sub-expressions. For example, an assignment j=i++; involving a non-simple expression i++ is first transformed into "**int** tmp=i; i=i+1; j=tmp;", before the three resulting assignments can be turned into updates. The updates that assign to the created temporary variables are themselves temporary: as soon as the variable does not occur in the program any more, the update can be eliminated with the dropUpdate$_2$ rule from Figure 5.8.

A selection of symbolic execution rules is shown Figure 5.9. This selection does not include the rules for reducing non-simple expressions; all occurring expressions must already be simple expressions. In addition, the rules are shown in a simplified form which does not check for exceptions that might be thrown by the occurring expressions, in particular exceptions of type NullPointerException and ArrayIndexOutOfBoundsException. This simplification is for presentation purposes only: the implementation in the KeY system handles such exceptions correctly.

Figure 5.9 shows only rules for the box modality, but all these rules have an otherwise identical twin for the diamond modality. The symbolic execution rules are applicable only if the modal operator appears in a formula of the *succedent*. Programs in the antecedent can be shifted to the succedent by making use of the dual nature of box and diamond: we have $\models [p]\varphi \leftrightarrow \neg\langle p\rangle\neg\varphi$ and $\models \langle p\rangle\varphi \leftrightarrow \neg[p]\neg\varphi$, which allows turning an occurrence of a formula $[p]\varphi$ or a formula $\langle p\rangle\varphi$ in the antecedent into an occurrence of $\neg\langle p\rangle\neg\varphi$ or $\neg[p]\neg\varphi$, respectively, and then moving the program to the succedent with the notLeft rule. In all symbolic execution rules, the update u that precedes the modal operator may also be missing.

$$\frac{\Gamma \;\Rightarrow\; \{u\}\{\mathtt{a} := t\}[\pi\;\omega]\varphi,\;\Delta}{\Gamma \;\Rightarrow\; \{u\}[\pi\;\mathtt{a}\;\mathtt{=}\;t;\;\omega]\varphi,\;\Delta} \qquad \mathsf{assignLocal}$$

$$\frac{\Gamma \;\Rightarrow\; \{u\}\{\mathtt{heap} := store(\mathtt{heap}, o, \mathtt{f}, t)\}[\pi\;\omega]\varphi,\;\Delta}{\Gamma \;\Rightarrow\; \{u\}[\pi\;o.\mathtt{f}\;\mathtt{=}\;t;\;\omega]\varphi,\;\Delta} \qquad \mathsf{assignField}$$

$$\frac{\Gamma \;\Rightarrow\; \{u\}\{\mathtt{heap} := store(\mathtt{heap}, a, arr(i), t)\}[\pi\;\omega]\varphi,\;\Delta}{\Gamma \;\Rightarrow\; \{u\}[\pi\;a\,[i]\;\mathtt{=}\;t;\;\omega]\varphi,\;\Delta} \qquad \mathsf{assignArray}$$

$$\frac{\begin{array}{c}\Gamma,\; o' \not\doteq \mathbf{null},\; exactInstance_A(o'),\\ \{u\}\big(wellFormed(\mathtt{heap}) \to select_{Boolean}(\mathtt{heap}, o', created) \doteq FALSE\big)\\ \Rightarrow \{u\}\{\mathtt{heap} := create(\mathtt{heap}, o')\}\{\mathtt{o} := o'\}[\pi\;\omega]\varphi,\;\Delta\end{array}}{\Gamma \;\Rightarrow\; \{u\}[\pi\;\mathtt{o}\;\mathtt{=}\;\mathtt{A.alloc();}\;\omega]\varphi,\;\Delta} \qquad \mathsf{createObject}$$

where $o' : A \in \mathcal{F}$ is fresh

$$\frac{\Gamma \;\Rightarrow\; \{u\}if(g \doteq TRUE)then([\pi\;p_1\;\omega]\varphi)else([\pi\;p_2\;\omega]\varphi),\;\Delta}{\Gamma \;\Rightarrow\; \{u\}[\pi\;\mathbf{if}(g)\;p_1\;\mathbf{else}\;p_2;\;\omega]\varphi,\;\Delta} \qquad \mathsf{conditional}$$

$$\frac{\Gamma \;\Rightarrow\; \{u\}[\pi\;\mathbf{if}(g)\{p';\;\mathbf{while}(g)p\}\;\omega]\varphi,\;\Delta}{\Gamma \;\Rightarrow\; \{u\}[\pi\;\mathbf{while}(g)p;\;\omega]\varphi,\;\Delta} \qquad \mathsf{unwindLoop}$$

$$\frac{\begin{array}{c}\Gamma \;\Rightarrow\; \{u\}[\pi\;\mathtt{method\text{-}frame(result=r,\;}\mathbf{this}\mathtt{=o)}\;:\\ \{\;body(\mathtt{m}, A)\;\}\;\omega]\varphi,\;\Delta\\ \Gamma \;\Rightarrow\; \{u\}exactInstance_A(o),\;\Delta\end{array}}{\Gamma \;\Rightarrow\; \{u\}[\pi\;\mathtt{r}\;\mathtt{=}\;o.\mathtt{m();}\;\omega]\varphi,\;\Delta} \qquad \mathsf{expandMethod}$$

$$\frac{\Gamma \;\Rightarrow\; \{u\}\varphi,\;\Delta}{\Gamma \;\Rightarrow\; \{u\}[\;]\varphi,\;\Delta} \qquad \mathsf{emptyModality}$$

Figure 5.9.: Rules for symbolic execution of Java programs

The three assignment rules assignLocal, assignField and assignArray convert assignment statements into equivalent updates. An assignment to a local variable $\mathtt{a}$ turns into an update assigning to $\mathtt{a}$, whereas assignments to a field $o.\mathtt{f}$ or to an array component $a\,[i]$ are understood as changing the global program variable $\mathtt{heap}$ at the corresponding location. A complication not shown in Figure 5.9 is that both assignField and assignArray need to introduce a case distinction on whether o or a (respectively) is $\mathbf{null}$: if so, the symbolically executed program continues by throwing a $\mathtt{NullPointerException}$. Also not shown is that the assignArray rule additionally has to cover the possibilities that i might be negative or larger than $a.\texttt{length} - 1$ (leading to an `ArrayIndexOutOfBoundsException`), and that the dynamic type of t might not be a subtype of the dynamic component type of a (leading to an `ArrayStoreException`).

Executing an instance creation expression **new** `A(...)`; in Java means to perform a sequence of steps that includes allocating memory for the new object, initialising the object, and invoking the constructor. The details of how this process is modelled during symbolic execution are documented elsewhere [Beckert et al., 2007]. The createObject rule depicted in Figure 5.9 is responsible only for the core step of the process: the actual allocation of a new object. This step is represented as a call to a special **static** method `A.alloc()` that returns a new object of type A.

The createObject rule introduces a *fresh* constant symbol o' to represent the new object, i.e., a constant symbol not occurring anywhere in the conclusion. The rule adds three assumptions about the otherwise unknown object represented by o': (i) it is different from *null*; (ii) its dynamic type is A; and (iii) if the heap is well-formed, then the object is not yet created. These assumptions are always satisfiable, because by Definition 5.4 there is an infinite reservoir of objects of every type, and because in a well-formed heap only a finite number of them is created. If the object to be created is an array of length l, then $\texttt{length}(o') \doteq l$ is an additional assumption that holds if the heap is well-formed (this is not shown in the figure). The new object is then marked as "created" by setting its *created* field to true with an update that uses the function symbol *create*, and the reference to the newly created object is assigned to the program variable o.

The createObject rule of JavaDL* is significantly different from its counterpart in JavaDL. There, in addition to the *created* field, signatures also contain so-called *repository access functions* $get_A : Int \to A$ for all types $A \preceq Object$. These are interpreted as bijective functions, thereby identifying objects with integers. Additionally, there is a **static** field $\texttt{nextToCreate}_A$ of type *Int* for every $A \preceq Object$. *Java reachable states* (which are similar to well-formed heap arrays in JavaDL*) satisfy that exactly those objects $get_A(i)$ have their *created* field set to true for which $0 \le i \wedge i < \texttt{nextToCreate}_A$ holds. In this approach, allocating a new object of type A means to take the object $get_A(\texttt{nextToCreate}_A)$, to set its *created* field to true, and to increment $\texttt{nextToCreate}_A$ by one.

An advantage of the JavaDL approach is that the JavaDL counterpart of createObject does not need to introduce a new constant symbol o', because the object to be created is uniquely determined and accessible as $get_A(\texttt{nextToCreate}_A)$. On the other hand, an advantage of the JavaDL* approach is that it avoids the redundancy between *created* and $\texttt{nextToCreate}_A$, thereby avoiding to further complicate the notion of well-formed heap arrays (or the analogous notion of *Java reachable states*). More importantly, it simplifies implicitly allowing object creation in modifies clauses (as in JML and JML*). In JavaDL, it is difficult to express an "anonymisation" for a modifies clause that includes the possible allocation of arbitrarily many objects of arbitrary types, because the anonymisation has to affect not only the *created* fields of the fresh objects, but also the nextToCreate$_A$ field of all reference types A. Enumerating the instances of nextToCreate$_A$ for all reference types is possible, but neither practical nor modular. Furthermore, a difficulty is to encode that nextToCreate$_A$ is not affected arbitrarily by the anonymisation, but can only be increased. The JavaDL* solution does not have any of these problems, and we make use of this in the loop invariant rule (Subsection 5.4.8) and in the rule for reasoning about method calls using method contracts (Chapter 6), which in contrast to their counterparts in JavaDL do allow arbitrary object creation.

The conditional rule in Figure 5.9 transforms a conditional statement into a conditional term. If the information in the sequent implies that one of the branches is infeasible, then it may be possible to simplify away the conditional term directly. Otherwise, the proof rules for conditional terms create a split of the proof tree, where one proof branch corresponds to the then-branch and the other to the else-branch of the conditional statement.

The unwindLoop rule allows unwinding a single iteration of a **while** loop (**for** loops are first reduced to **while** loops). The program fragment p' is identical to the loop body p, except that program variables declared in p have been replaced by fresh program variables (which is necessary in order to make the program occurring in the premiss syntactically correct). The rule is shown here for the simple case where the loop body p does not contain **break** or **continue** statements. The unwindLoop rule is sufficient only in the (rare) case where there is a literally known bound on the loop's number of iterations. Otherwise, iterated unwinding does not terminate. General loops can be discharged using some form of induction, such as the *loop invariant rule* presented in Subsection 5.4.8.

The expandMethod rule is intended to be used on method calls where the dynamic type A of the receiver object is known, making the second premiss trivial to prove. The rule replaces the method call by a method frame, whose body $body(\mathrm{m}, A)$ is the implementation of m that must be used for receivers of dynamic type A, according to Java's rules for method binding. All program variables declared in the method body are replaced by fresh program variables in $body(\mathrm{m}, A)$. This hides any changes to these variables performed by the body from its context in the sequent (i.e., from Γ, Δ, $\pi\omega$ and φ). The rule is shown only for method calls without parameters; its more general version also takes care to assign the actual parameter values to the method's formal parameter variables. Also not shown is the check for the case where the receiver object is *null*. The treatment of **void** and **static** methods is analogous.

Dynamically bound method calls where the dynamic type of the receiver object is not known can be symbolically executed by introducing a case split on the possible dynamic types of the receiver, i.e., a case split on the subtypes of its static type. However, this of course amounts to a non-modular and thus undesirable enumeration of types. A more modular alternative is to handle method calls with the help of a *contract* for the called method. This is covered in detail in Chapter 6.

Empty method frames can be removed from a modal operator. Ultimately, symbolic execution leads to empty modal operators from which the programs have disappeared entirely. These can be removed with the emptyModality rule shown in Figure 5.9. The update u at this point represents the termination state of the path to the program that corresponds to the current path through the proof tree. Once the modal operator is gone, u can be applied to the postcondition φ using the rules in Figure 5.8.

5.4.8. Loop Invariant Rule

Loops without a literally known bound on their number of iterations can be handled with a *loop invariant rule*. Such a rule makes use of a *loop invariant*, i.e., a formula that holds at the beginning of each loop iteration at the time of checking whether the loop guard is satisfied. Loop invariants can be given as a part of the specification, or they can be provided interactively at the time of applying the rule. The classical loop invariant rule in dynamic logic with updates looks as follows (for the sake of simplicity, we ignore exceptions as well as **return**, **break** and **continue** statements):

$$
\frac{
\begin{array}{ll}
\Gamma \;\Rightarrow\; \{u\}inv, \; \Delta & \textit{(initially valid)} \\
inv, \; g \doteq TRUE \;\Rightarrow\; [p]inv & \textit{(preserved by body)} \\
inv, \; g \doteq FALSE \;\Rightarrow\; [\pi\;\omega]\varphi & \textit{(use case)}
\end{array}
}{
\Gamma \;\Rightarrow\; \{u\}[\pi\; \texttt{while}(g)p;\; \omega]\varphi, \; \Delta
}
$$

Like the unwindLoop rule from Figure 5.9, the rule is applicable to a program where the first active statement is a **while** loop. Its first premiss expresses that the loop invariant *inv* holds when first entering the loop, i.e., in the initial state described by the update u and by the formulas in Γ and in Δ. The second premiss expresses that *inv* is preserved by the loop body p, and the third demands that if *inv* holds after leaving the loop, then the remaining program $\pi\omega$ establishes the postcondition φ.

A problem with this basic version of the loop invariant rule is that the context information encoded in u, Γ and Δ is completely lost in the second and third premiss. It cannot be kept, because these premisses describe symbolic states where an arbitrary number of loop iterations have already been executed, potentially invalidating all information in the context. This puts a significant burden on the person writing the invariant *inv*, because all information from the context that is needed for the validity of the second and the third premiss must be encoded into *inv*. In particular, *inv* often must contain information about which memory locations the loop does *not* change.

An improved version of the loop invariant rule that alleviates this problem has been introduced by Beckert et al. [2005]; Schlager [2007]. Here, in addition to the loop invariant itself, a *modifies clause* for the loop must be provided, which describes the memory locations (including local variables) that may at most be changed by the loop. In the improved loop invariant rule, an *anonymising update v* is generated out of the modifies clause, which sets all locations in the modifies clause to unknown ("anonymous") values. This simulates the effect of an arbitrary number of loop iterations. It allows keeping u, Γ and Δ in the second and third premiss, separated by the update v from the rest of the sequent:

$$
\begin{array}{lll}
\Gamma & \Rightarrow \{u\}inv,\ \Delta & \textit{(initially valid)} \\
\Gamma & \Rightarrow \{u\}\{v\}(inv \wedge g \doteq \mathit{TRUE} \rightarrow [p]inv),\ \Delta & \textit{(preserved by body)} \\
\Gamma & \Rightarrow \{u\}\{v\}(inv \wedge g \doteq \mathit{FALSE} \rightarrow [\pi\,\omega]\varphi),\ \Delta & \textit{(use case)} \\
\hline
& \Gamma \ \Rightarrow\ \{u\}[\pi\ \texttt{while}(g)p;\ \omega]\varphi,\ \Delta &
\end{array}
$$

Now, the loop invariant *inv* must constrain only the values of locations actually modified by the loop, because all other locations are left unchanged by v anyway.

In the loop invariant rule of Beckert et al. [2005]; Schlager [2007], the correctness of the modifies clause is simply assumed. *Verifying* that the modifies clause is correct, i.e., that an arbitrary number of loop iterations never changes a location not covered by the modifies clause, is left as a separate task. Due to the aliasing problem, this task is non-trivial in Java-like languages.

An approach for verifying modifies clauses in JavaDL has been developed by Roth [2006]; Engel et al. [2009]. The approach uses *location dependent symbols* [Bubel, 2007; Bubel et al., 2008] to construct a formula that depends only on the locations not in the modifies clause. Correctness of a program with respect to the modifies clause is encoded as a proof obligation demanding that the validity of this formula is not affected by running the program. The approach can be built into the improved loop invariant rule, yielding a rule that is sound also if the modifies clause for the loop is not correct [Engel et al., 2009]. This is the version of the loop invariant rule that is currently used in JavaDL, as it is implemented in KeY 1.5.

The JavaDL* version of the loop invariant rule is defined in Definition 5.9 below. It improves over the JavaDL version in several ways. Firstly, the explicit modelling of the heap allows quantification over locations, which in turn enables a more intuitive formulation of modifies clause correctness than the formulation using location dependent symbols: a modifies clause is correct if for all locations not in the modifies clause the post-state value is the same as the pre-state value. This more straightforward formulation may help in interactive proofs, where the human user of the theorem prover must be able to grasp the meaning of the occurring sequents.

Also, the mechanism for expressing modifies clauses in JavaDL (called *location descriptors*) supports no form of data abstraction. In contrast, the modifies clauses of JavaDL* are proper terms (of type *LocSet*). Function symbols can be used to denote sets of locations symbolically (Chapter 6). Furthermore, as discussed in Subsection 5.4.7, the modifies clauses of JavaDL* always implicitly allow creating and initialising objects, whereas such an interpretation of modifies clauses is not easily possible in JavaDL, due to the modelling of object creation via a field $\texttt{nextToCreate}_A$ for every reference type A. Finally, the loop invariant rule in JavaDL* takes care to preserve well-formedness properties such as *wellFormed*($\texttt{heap}$) across the loop, whereas this responsibility is placed on the author of the loop invariant in JavaDL.

For the sake of simplicity, we define the loop invariant rule under the assumption that the loop body does not throw exceptions and does not use **return**, **break** and **continue** statements. The rule can be extended to handle these technicalities in the same way as in JavaDL [Schlager, 2007; Beckert et al., 2007]. We also only define the invariant rule for the box modality. Like in JavaDL, it can be extended to also establish termination of the loop, via a *variant term* whose value strictly decreases in every loop iteration towards a fixed lower bound. All of these extensions are present in the version of the rule that is implemented in the KeY system.

Definition 5.9 (Rule loopInvariant).

$$
\begin{array}{ll}
\Gamma \Rightarrow \{u\}\big(inv \wedge \text{wellFormed}(\texttt{heap}) \wedge \text{reachableIn}\big),\ \Delta & \text{\textit{(initially valid)}} \\[4pt]
\Gamma \Rightarrow \{u\}\{pre\}\{v\}\big(inv \wedge \text{wellFormed}(h) \wedge \text{reachableOut} & \text{\textit{(preserved by body)}} \\
\qquad \wedge\, g \doteq \mathit{TRUE} \rightarrow [p](inv \wedge \mathit{frame})\big),\ \Delta & \\[4pt]
\Gamma \Rightarrow \{u\}\{v\}\big(inv \wedge \text{wellFormed}(h) \wedge \text{reachableOut} & \text{\textit{(use case)}} \\
\qquad \wedge\, g \doteq \mathit{FALSE} \rightarrow [\pi\,\omega]\varphi\big),\ \Delta &
\end{array}
$$

$$\overline{\qquad\qquad \Gamma \Rightarrow \{u\}[\pi\ \texttt{while}(g)p;\ \omega]\varphi,\ \Delta \qquad\qquad}$$

where:

- $inv \in Fma_\Sigma$ *is the loop invariant*
- $mod \in Term_\Sigma^{LocSet}$ *is the modifies clause for the loop*
- $\texttt{a}_1, \ldots, \texttt{a}_m \in \mathcal{PV}$ *are the program variables occurring free in the loop body p, except for* $\texttt{heap}$
- $\texttt{b}_1, \ldots, \texttt{b}_n \in \mathcal{PV}$ *are the program variables potentially modified by the loop body p, except for* $\texttt{heap}$
- $\texttt{heap}^{pre} : Heap,\ \texttt{b}_1^{pre} : \alpha(\texttt{b}_1), \ldots, \texttt{b}_n^{pre} : \alpha(\texttt{b}_n) \in \mathcal{PV}$ *are fresh*
- $h : Heap,\ b_1' : \alpha(\texttt{b}_1), \ldots, b_n' : \alpha(\texttt{b}_n) \in \mathcal{F}$ *are fresh*

- $pre = \left(\mathtt{heap}^{pre} := \mathtt{heap} \parallel \mathtt{b}_1^{pre} := \mathtt{b}_1 \parallel \ldots \parallel \mathtt{b}_n^{pre} := \mathtt{b}_n\right)$
- $pre' = \left(\mathtt{heap} := \mathtt{heap}^{pre} \parallel \mathtt{b}_1 := \mathtt{b}_1^{pre} \parallel \ldots \parallel \mathtt{b}_n := \mathtt{b}_n^{pre}\right)$
- $v = \left(\mathtt{heap} := anon(\mathtt{heap}, mod, h) \parallel \mathtt{b}_1 := b'_1 \parallel \ldots \parallel \mathtt{b}_n := b'_n\right)$
- $frame \in Fma_\Sigma$ is the formula

$$\forall Object\ o; \forall Field\ f; \big((o, f) \mathbin{\dot{\in}} \{pre'\} mod \mathbin{\dot{\cup}} unusedLocs(\mathtt{heap}^{pre})$$
$$\lor select_{Any}(\mathtt{heap}, o, f) \doteq select_{Any}(\mathtt{heap}^{pre}, o, f)\big)$$

- $reachableIn \in Fma_\Sigma$ is the formula

$$\bigwedge_{i \in \{1,\ldots,m\},\ \alpha(\mathtt{a}_i) \preceq Object} (\mathtt{a}_i \doteq \mathbf{null} \lor \mathtt{a}_i.\,created \doteq TRUE)$$
$$\land \bigwedge_{i \in \{1,\ldots,m\},\ \alpha(\mathtt{a}_i) = LocSet} disjoint(\mathtt{a}_i, unusedLocs(\mathtt{heap}))$$

- $reachableOut \in Fma_\Sigma$ is the formula

$$\bigwedge_{i \in \{1,\ldots,n\},\ \alpha(\mathtt{b}_i) \preceq Object} (\mathtt{b}_i \doteq \mathbf{null} \lor \mathtt{b}_i.\,created \doteq TRUE)$$
$$\land \bigwedge_{i \in \{1,\ldots,n\},\ \alpha(\mathtt{b}_i) = LocSet} disjoint(\mathtt{b}_i, unusedLocs(\mathtt{heap}))$$

As in Subsection 5.4.6, the local variables $\mathtt{a}_1, \ldots, \mathtt{a}_m$ "occurring free in the loop body p" are those that occur in p without being bound by a declaration within p itself. The $\mathtt{heap}$ variable is not a member of the set $\{\mathtt{a}_1, \ldots, \mathtt{a}_m\}$; it is handled separately. The local variables $\mathtt{b}_1, \ldots, \mathtt{b}_n$ "potentially modified by the loop body p" are essentially those occurring on the left hand side of an assignment in p. The set $\{\mathtt{b}_1, \ldots, \mathtt{b}_n\}$ can be computed by a simple syntactical analysis of p. Changes to local variables declared within p itself are never observable from outside p, and thus we do not consider such variables to be elements of $\{\mathtt{b}_1, \ldots, \mathtt{b}_n\}$. This implies that $\{\mathtt{b}_1, \ldots, \mathtt{b}_n\} \subseteq \{\mathtt{a}_1, \ldots, \mathtt{a}_m\}$.

The first premiss of loopInvariant demands that the initial state when entering the loop satisfies not only the loop invariant inv, but also $wellFormed(\mathtt{heap})$ and $reachableIn$: the heap must be well-formed, and all "input" variables $\mathtt{a}_1, \ldots, \mathtt{a}_n$ must have "reachable" values, i.e., they must not refer to non-created objects, and they must not hold location sets that contain locations belonging to non-created objects. If this property holds in the initial state of the loop, then the semantics of Java guarantees that it is preserved by arbitrary loop iterations. It may thus be used as an assumption in the second and third premiss.

As an optimisation, the assumption used in the second and third premiss is not the formula $wellFormed(\mathtt{heap}) \land reachableIn$ itself. Rather, we assume $wellFormed(h) \land reachableOut$. The formula $reachableOut$ constrains only the "output" variables $b_1, \ldots, b_n$. Because $\{b_1, \ldots, b_n\} \subseteq \{a_1, \ldots, a_m\}$, we have $\models$ *reachableIn* $\rightarrow$ *reachableOut*. The shorter formula *reachableOut* suffices in the second and third premiss, because the variables in the complementary set $\{a_1, \ldots, a_m\} \setminus \{b_1, \ldots, b_n\}$ are not changed by the loop anyway. For the heap, assuming *wellFormed*(heap) in the scope of the update v would amount to assuming *wellFormed*(*anon*(heap, *mod*, h)). Assuming *wellFormed*(h) is shorter and simpler, in particular because this term does not depend on heap. By Lemma 5.3, well-formedness of h and heap implies well-formedness of *anon*(heap, *mod*, h).

A simpler treatment of well-formedness would be to include the well-formedness properties in the invariant *inv*, perhaps automatically. However, the chosen solution is more efficient during verification: there is no need to prove in the second premiss that any well-formedness properties hold at the end of the loop body p, because this is guaranteed by Java itself.

From a practical point of view, the usefulness of proving well-formedness in the first premiss of loopInvariant is dubious, too. In reality, Java programs can never reach a state that violates well-formedness, so proving well-formedness seems superfluous. Nevertheless, omitting *wellFormed*(heap) $\wedge$ *reachableIn* in the first premiss makes the rule unsound. This is because *in a proof*, it is not guaranteed that well-formedness holds for all occurring symbolic states; it is possible to construct a sequent where it is violated. This does not happen during "typical" proofs for "typical" proof obligations (such as those defined in Chapter 6). One can imagine a "pragmatic" version of the rule that leaves out *wellFormed*(heap) $\wedge$ *reachableIn* in the first premiss, saving a minor amount of time during verification at the cost of accepting an unsoundness that typically does not matter.

The update *pre* in the second premiss buffers the pre-loop values of the program variables heap, $b_1, \ldots, b_n$ in the program variables $\text{heap}^{pre}, b_1^{pre}, \ldots, b_n^{pre}$. These buffer variables must be fresh, i.e., they must not occur anywhere in the conclusion. This in particular guarantees that their values are not changed by the loop body p. Thus, they can be used in scope of the modal operator $[p]$ to refer to the pre-loop values of heap, $b_1, \ldots, b_n$. The inverse update *pre'* resets all of heap, $b_1, \ldots, b_n$ to their original values.

The *anonymising update* v simulates the effect of an arbitrary number of loop iterations by setting all potentially modified variables $b_1, \ldots, b_n$ to unknown values, represented by fresh ("anonymous") constant symbols $b_1', \ldots, b_n'$. In contrast to $b_1, \ldots, b_n$, the heap is not anonymised completely by assigning to heap the value of the fresh constant symbol h. Rather, the function symbol *anon* is used to anonymise only the locations in the modifies clause *mod*. By the definition of $I(anon)$, the anonymisation implicitly affects all unused locations, independently of the choice of *mod* itself.

The formula *frame* in the second premiss ensures that the modifies clause *mod* is respected by the loop: after an arbitrary number of iterations (represented by *v*) and one more execution of the loop body *p*, all locations either (i) belong to the pre-loop interpretation of the modifies clause *mod*, or (ii) belong to an object not yet created when initially entering the loop, or (iii) have the same value in the current heap as in the pre-loop heap.

Instead of defining and using an extension to the theory of arrays like *anon* as we do, another solution is to first anonymise the entire heap, and then use a framing formula like *frame* as an assumption constraining the effect of the anonymisation. A solution along these lines is for example used in the Boogie verifier [Barnett et al., 2006]. The main advantage of our approach is that it directly expresses that only some locations change. It avoids the additional occurrences of *frame* as an assumption in the second and third premiss of loopInvariant, and in particular the universal quantifiers in these occurrences. Note that the single occurrence of *frame* in loopInvariant is on the right hand side of the implication arrow. Here, the universal quantifiers can be eliminated simply by Skolemisation. In contrast, when using *frame* as an *assumption*, the quantifiers occur in positions where they have to be handled by instantiation.

Lemma 5.4 below establishes a formal connection between *frame* and *anon*. This connection is the reason why it is admissible to use *anon* for anonymising the locations in the modifies clause, while using *frame* as the proof obligation for verifying the correctness of the modifies clause in the second premiss.

Lemma 5.4 (Connection between *frame* and *anon*). *Let* $mod \in Term_{\Sigma}^{LocSet}$, $\mathsf{b}_1, \ldots, \mathsf{b}_n \in \mathcal{PV}$, $\mathsf{heap}^{pre} : Heap \in \mathcal{PV}$, $\mathsf{b}_1^{pre} : \alpha(\mathsf{b}_1), \ldots, \mathsf{b}_n^{pre} : \alpha(\mathsf{b}_n) \in \mathcal{PV}$, *and let* $pre' \in Upd_{\Sigma}$ *and* $frame \in Fma_{\Sigma}$ *be as in Definition 5.9. Let furthermore* $noDeallocs \in Fma_{\Sigma}$ *be the formula*

$$unusedLocs(\mathsf{heap}) \mathrel{\dot{\subseteq}} unusedLocs(\mathsf{heap}^{pre})$$
$$\wedge\ select_{Any}(\mathsf{heap}, \mathbf{null}, created) \doteq select_{Any}(\mathsf{heap}^{pre}, \mathbf{null}, created),$$

and let $frame' \in Fma_{\Sigma}$ *be the formula*

$$\mathsf{heap} \doteq anon(\mathsf{heap}^{pre}, \{pre'\}mod, \mathsf{heap}).$$

Then the following holds:

$$\models (frame \wedge noDeallocs) \leftrightarrow frame'.$$

A proof of Lemma 5.4 is contained in Appendix A.5. Intuitively, the lemma states that a heap state can be reached from heap^{pre} by anonymisation via *anon* if and only if it satisfies the formulas *frame* and *noDeallocs*. The latter formula expresses that all objects created in the pre-state heap array are still created in the current heap array (and that createdness of *null* does not change). The impossibility of deallocating created objects is built into the definition of $I(anon)$.

In approaches that anonymise the entire heap and use *frame* as an assumption, a formula like *noDeallocs* must be used as an additional explicit assumption, together with *frame* itself.

Lemma 5.4 is a main ingredient in the proof of Theorem 5.5, which establishes that the loopInvariant rule is sound.

Theorem 5.5 (Soundness of loopInvariant). *Let the formula sets* $\Gamma, \Delta \in 2^{Fma_\Sigma}$, *the update* $u \in Upd_\Sigma$, *the program* "π `while`$(g)p$; ω", *the formulas* $\varphi, inv \in Fma_\Sigma$, *the term mod* $\in Term_\Sigma^{LocSet}$, *the program variables* $a_1, \ldots, a_m, b_1, \ldots, b_n$, $\mathbf{heap}^{pre}, \mathbf{b}_1^{pre}, \ldots, \mathbf{b}_n^{pre} \in \mathcal{PV}$, *the constant symbols* $h, b_1, \ldots, b_n \in \mathcal{F}$, *the updates* $pre, pre', v \in Upd_\Sigma$ *and the formulas* $frame, reachableIn, reachableOut \in Fma_\Sigma$ *all be as in Definition 5.9. If*

$$\models \Gamma \ \Rightarrow \ \{u\}\big(inv \wedge wellFormed(\mathbf{heap}) \wedge reachableIn\big), \ \Delta$$
$$\models \Gamma \ \Rightarrow \ \{u\}\{pre\}\{v\}\big(inv \wedge wellFormed(h) \wedge reachableOut$$
$$\wedge\ g \doteq TRUE \rightarrow [p](inv \wedge frame)\big), \ \Delta$$
$$\models \Gamma \ \Rightarrow \ \{u\}\{v\}\big(inv \wedge wellFormed(h) \wedge reachableOut$$
$$\wedge\ g \doteq FALSE \rightarrow [\pi\ \omega]\varphi\big), \ \Delta$$

then the following holds:

$$\models \Gamma \ \Rightarrow \ \{u\}[\pi\ \mathbf{while}(g)p;\ \omega]\varphi, \ \Delta.$$

Theorem 5.5 is proven in Appendix A.6. As the semantics of Java are not formalised in JavaDL*, the parts of the proof that deal with the behaviour of the loop `while`$(g)p$ are only semi-formal: we assume that the loop—if it terminates—gives rise to a finite sequence of states s_i, which are connected by $(s_i, s_{i+i}) \in \rho(p)$. The first two premises of the rule correspond to the base case and the step case of an inductive argument showing that for all states s_i of the sequence, we can find an interpretation of the fresh constant symbols $h, b_1', \ldots, b_n'$ such that s_i is produced by the anonymising update v for this interpretation, and such that inv, $wellFormed(h)$ and $reachableOut$ all hold in s_i. Together with the third premiss, this implies validity of the conclusion.

An example for the use of the loopInvariant rule is contained in Section 5.5 below.

5.5. Example Proofs

In this section, the functioning of the JavaDL* calculus is illustrated with the help of four examples: a proof demonstrating the basics of accessing the heap (Subsection 5.5.1), a variation of this proof that involves aliasing (Subsection 5.5.2), a proof for a program that creates new objects (Subsection 5.5.3), and a proof for a program that contains loops (Subsection 5.5.4).

5.5.1. Reading and Writing the Heap

Suppose that the program *Prg* contains the following class:

```
class C {
    int f, g;
}
```

Let o be a program variable of type C. Our goal is to prove that after executing the legal program fragment "o.f = 1; o.g = 2;", the Java expression o.f evaluates to 1.

Before getting to the proof in JavaDL*, we first sketch the proof in JavaDL. There, the fields f and g are non-rigid function symbols $f : C \to Int$ and $g : C \to Int$, and the postcondition is the formula $f(o) \doteq 1$. The JavaDL proof tree is depicted in Figure 5.10.

Symbolic execution consecutively turns the two assignments into elementary updates in steps (1) and (2). We ignore the possibility of NullPointerExceptions in order to simplify the presentation. The two sequentially connected updates are combined into a single parallel update via update rewrite rules [Rümmer, 2006]. The intermediate steps of the update calculus are usually not shown, neither in writing nor in the implementation in KeY, where the entire update calculus is implemented as a single *update simplification* rule. Consequently, converting the two updates into a parallel update appears in Figure 5.10 as a single step (3). In the example, the resulting parallel update is simply the parallel composition of the two original updates, because these updates happen to be independent of each other.

The empty modal operator is removed in step (4). Applying the update to the postcondition using the update calculus again appears as a single step (5). The resulting formula is simplified to *true* in step (6), and the proof tree is closed in step (7).

We now shift attention to JavaDL*. Here, the fields f and g are represented as unique constant symbols $f : Field \in \mathcal{F}^{Unique}$ and $g : Field \in \mathcal{F}^{Unique}$, and the postcondition is the formula $select_{Int}(\text{heap}, o, f) \doteq 1$. The JavaDL* proof tree is shown in Figure 5.11.

Steps (1) and (2) are again to symbolically execute the assignments, turning them into updates with the assignField rule. The subsequent simplification of the two updates is shown as a single step (3) in Figure 5.11, in keeping with the presentation in Figure 5.10. Note that nesting *store* terms into each other corresponds to parallel composition of updates; the resulting heap array is that of simultaneously executing the changes, where in case of a clash, the outermost *store* (corresponding to the rightmost parallel update) "wins". One could pretty-print updates of the form "$\text{heap} := store(store(\text{heap}, o_1, f_1, t_1), o_2, f_2, t_2)$" as fake parallel updates "$o_1.f_1 := t_1 \parallel o_2.f_2 := t_2$". Together with the usual

$$\Rightarrow [\texttt{o.f = 1; o.g = 2;}](\texttt{f}(\texttt{o}) \doteq 1)$$
$$\downarrow \text{assignment} \qquad\qquad (1)$$
$$\Rightarrow \{\texttt{f}(\texttt{o}) := 1\}[\texttt{o.g = 2;}](\texttt{f}(\texttt{o}) \doteq 1)$$
$$\downarrow \text{assignment} \qquad\qquad (2)$$
$$\Rightarrow \{\texttt{f}(\texttt{o}) := 1\}\{\texttt{g}(\texttt{o}) := 2\}[\,](\texttt{f}(\texttt{o}) \doteq 1)$$
$$\downarrow \text{update simplification} \qquad (3)$$
$$\Rightarrow \{\texttt{f}(\texttt{o}) := 1 \,\|\, \texttt{g}(\texttt{o}) := 2\}[\,](\texttt{f}(\texttt{o}) \doteq 1)$$
$$\downarrow \text{empty modality} \qquad\qquad (4)$$
$$\Rightarrow \{\texttt{f}(\texttt{o}) := 1 \,\|\, \texttt{g}(\texttt{o}) := 2\}(\texttt{f}(\texttt{o}) \doteq 1)$$
$$\downarrow \text{update simplification} \qquad (5)$$
$$\Rightarrow 1 \doteq 1$$
$$\downarrow \text{equal} \qquad\qquad (6)$$
$$\Rightarrow \textit{true}$$
$$\downarrow \text{close} \qquad\qquad (7)$$
$$*$$

Figure 5.10.: Example for reading and writing the heap in JavaDL

$$\Rightarrow [\texttt{o.f = 1; o.g = 2;}](\mathit{select}_{Int}(\mathsf{heap}, \texttt{o}, \texttt{f}) \doteq 1)$$
$$\downarrow \text{assignField} \qquad\qquad (1)$$
$$\Rightarrow \{\mathsf{heap} := \mathit{store}(\mathsf{heap}, \texttt{o}, \texttt{f}, 1)\}[\texttt{o.g = 2;}](\mathit{select}_{Int}(\mathsf{heap}, \texttt{o}, \texttt{f}) \doteq 1)$$
$$\downarrow \text{assignField} \qquad\qquad (2)$$
$$\Rightarrow \{\mathsf{heap} := \mathit{store}(\mathsf{heap}, \texttt{o}, \texttt{f}, 1)\}\{\mathsf{heap} := \mathit{store}(\mathsf{heap}, \texttt{o}, \texttt{g}, 2)\}[\,](\mathit{select}_{Int}(\mathsf{heap}, \texttt{o}, \texttt{f}) \doteq 1)$$
$$\downarrow \text{simplification} \qquad\qquad (3)$$
$$\Rightarrow \{\mathsf{heap} := \mathit{store}(\mathit{store}(\mathsf{heap}, \texttt{o}, \texttt{f}, 1), \texttt{o}, \texttt{g}, 2)\}[\,](\mathit{select}_{Int}(\mathsf{heap}, \texttt{o}, \texttt{f}) \doteq 1)$$
$$\downarrow \text{emptyModality} \qquad\qquad (4)$$
$$\Rightarrow \{\mathsf{heap} := \mathit{store}(\mathit{store}(\mathsf{heap}, \texttt{o}, \texttt{f}, 1), \texttt{o}, \texttt{g}, 2)\}(\mathit{select}_{Int}(\mathsf{heap}, \texttt{o}, \texttt{f}) \doteq 1)$$
$$\downarrow \text{simplification} \qquad\qquad (5,6)$$
$$\Rightarrow \textit{true}$$
$$\downarrow \text{closeTrue} \qquad\qquad (7)$$
$$*$$

Figure 5.11.: Example for reading and writing the heap in JavaDL*

pretty-printing of $\mathit{select}_A(\mathsf{heap}, o, \texttt{f})$ (in JavaDL*) and $\texttt{f}(o)$ (in JavaDL) as $o.\texttt{f}$, this would make the sequents of Figures 5.10 and 5.11 look identical.

After the simplification, the empty modal operator is removed with the help of emptyModality in step (4). The resulting formula can be simplified to *true* in a combined step (5,6), which allows closing the proof tree with closeTrue in step (7).

The JavaDL* proof in Figure 5.11 closely resembles the JavaDL proof in Figure 5.10. The occurring terms and updates are longer (i.e., they have more subterms); this is an unfortunate but unavoidable consequence of the change in heap modelling. But the structure of both proofs is the same. Pretty-printing can make the individual sequents appear the same, too.

Hiding the application of rewrite rules that simplify updates, formulas or terms inside larger "simplification" steps has two advantages. Firstly, presenting the proof in this way facilitates interactive proving, because it avoids cluttering up the presentation with large numbers of uninteresting simplification steps. And secondly, implementing simplification as a single meta-rule can be advantageous for performance, for example because it allows immediately discarding the intermediate steps from memory, instead of storing them for the duration of the verification process. For fully understanding what is happening, it is however instructive to look inside the "simplification" steps. The expanded version of the JavaDL* proof tree from Figure 5.11 is shown in Figure 5.12.

In the expanded proof, step (3) is split up into six sub-steps (3a) to (3f), where for lack of space step (3f) itself abbreviates three individual rule applications. In (3a), the two updates are parallelised using seqToPar. The first update u is then propagated to the subterms of the second update via the applyOnRigid rules, and ultimately applied to the occurrence of heap with applyOnTarget and simplified away elsewhere with dropUpdate$_2$. The original occurrence of u is discarded in (3c) with the help of dropUpdate$_1$, because it is overwritten by the second update that also assigns to heap.

Step (5), i.e., the simplification process triggered by the disappearance of the modal operator after the application of emptyModality, consists of twelve sub-steps (5a) to (5l) in Figure 5.12, where again for lack of space some of these steps comprise several individual rule applications. In steps (5a) to (5c), the final update u' is applied to the postcondition using the update rules, leading to a cascade of *store* terms occurring below the function symbol *select*$_{Int}$. This term is simplified by twice applying selectOfStore in steps (5d) and (5h), each time followed by simplifying the resulting if-then-else terms. In particular, the uniqueNotSame rule is used to quickly rule out the possibility that o.f and o.g could refer to the same location. The rules andFalse, andTrue, notFalse, ifThenElseFalse and ifThenElseTrue have not been introduced, but behave as expected. Because the type of the written value is compatible with the expected type of *select*$_{Int}$, the cast produced by selectOfStore can be removed with castDel.

As can be seen in Figure 5.12, the *simplification* steps in Figure 5.11 are not exclusively concerned with updates. This is in contrast to the *update simplification* steps in JavaDL, and this is the reason why the second simplification step includes both (5) and (6) in Figure 5.11: step (6) is just one further application of the equal rule that has already been used twice in step (5i).

5.5.2. Aliasing

Let the class C be as in Subsection 5.5.1, and let o and o2 be program variables of type C. This time, we consider the program fragment "o.f = 1; o2.f = 2;".

$$\Rightarrow [\texttt{o.f = 1; o.g = 2;}](select_{Int}(\textbf{heap}, \textbf{o}, \textbf{f}) \doteq 1)$$
$$\downarrow \text{assignField} \tag{1}$$
$$\Rightarrow \underbrace{\{\textbf{heap} := store(\textbf{heap}, \textbf{o}, \textbf{f}, 1)\}}_{u}[\texttt{o.g = 2;}](select_{Int}(\textbf{heap}, \textbf{o}, \textbf{f}) \doteq 1)$$
$$\downarrow \text{assignField} \tag{2}$$
$$\Rightarrow \{u\}\{\textbf{heap} := store(\textbf{heap}, \textbf{o}, \textbf{g}, 2)\}[\,](select_{Int}(\textbf{heap}, \textbf{o}, \textbf{f}) \doteq 1)$$
$$\downarrow \text{seqToPar} \tag{3a}$$
$$\Rightarrow \{u \parallel \{u\}(\textbf{heap} := store(\textbf{heap}, \textbf{o}, \textbf{g}, 2))\}[\,](select_{Int}(\textbf{heap}, \textbf{o}, \textbf{f}) \doteq 1)$$
$$\downarrow \text{applyOnRigid}_7 \tag{3b}$$
$$\Rightarrow \{u \parallel \textbf{heap} := \{u\}store(\textbf{heap}, \textbf{o}, \textbf{g}, 2)\}[\,](select_{Int}(\textbf{heap}, \textbf{o}, \textbf{f}) \doteq 1)$$
$$\downarrow \text{dropUpdate}_1 \tag{3c}$$
$$\Rightarrow \{\textbf{heap} := \{u\}store(\textbf{heap}, \textbf{o}, \textbf{g}, 2)\}[\,](select_{Int}(\textbf{heap}, \textbf{o}, \textbf{f}) \doteq 1)$$
$$\downarrow \text{applyOnRigid}_2 \tag{3d}$$
$$\Rightarrow \{\textbf{heap} := store(\{u\}\textbf{heap}, \{u\}\textbf{o}, \{u\}\textbf{g}, \{u\}2)\}[\,](select_{Int}(\textbf{heap}, \textbf{o}, \textbf{f}) \doteq 1)$$
$$\downarrow \text{applyOnTarget} \tag{3e}$$
$$\Rightarrow \{\textbf{heap} := store(store(\textbf{heap}, \textbf{o}, \textbf{f}, 1), \{u\}\textbf{o}, \{u\}\textbf{g}, \{u\}2)\}[\,](select_{Int}(\textbf{heap}, \textbf{o}, \textbf{f}) \doteq 1)$$
$$\downarrow 3 * \text{dropUpdate}_2 \tag{3f}$$
$$\Rightarrow \underbrace{\{\textbf{heap} := store(store(\textbf{heap}, \textbf{o}, \textbf{f}, 1), \textbf{o}, \textbf{g}, 2)\}}_{u'}[\,](select_{Int}(\textbf{heap}, \textbf{o}, \textbf{f}) \doteq 1)$$
$$\downarrow \text{emptyModality} \tag{4}$$
$$\Rightarrow \{u'\}(select_{Int}(\textbf{heap}, \textbf{o}, \textbf{f}) \doteq 1)$$
$$\downarrow 2 * \text{applyOnRigid}_2 \tag{5a}$$
$$\Rightarrow select_{Int}(\{u'\}\textbf{heap}, \{u'\}\textbf{o}, \{u'\}\textbf{f}) \doteq \{u'\}1$$
$$\downarrow \text{applyOnTarget} \tag{5b}$$
$$\Rightarrow select_{Int}(store(store(\textbf{heap}, \textbf{o}, \textbf{f}, 1), \textbf{o}, \textbf{g}, 2), \{u'\}\textbf{o}, \{u'\}\textbf{f}) \doteq \{u'\}1$$
$$\downarrow 3 * \text{dropUpdate}_2 \tag{5c}$$
$$\Rightarrow select_{Int}(store(store(\textbf{heap}, \textbf{o}, \textbf{f}, 1), \textbf{o}, \textbf{g}, 2), \textbf{o}, \textbf{f}) \doteq 1$$
$$\downarrow \text{selectOfStore} \tag{5d}$$
$$\Rightarrow if(\textbf{o} \doteq \textbf{o} \wedge \textbf{f} \doteq \textbf{g} \wedge \textbf{f} \not\doteq created)then((Int)2)else(select_{Int}(store(\textbf{heap}, \textbf{o}, \textbf{f}, 1), \textbf{o}, \textbf{f})) \doteq 1$$
$$\downarrow \text{uniqueNotSame} \tag{5e}$$
$$\Rightarrow if(\textbf{o} \doteq \textbf{o} \wedge false \wedge \textbf{f} \not\doteq created)then((Int)2)else(select_{Int}(store(\textbf{heap}, \textbf{o}, \textbf{f}, 1), \textbf{o}, \textbf{f})) \doteq 1$$
$$\downarrow \text{andFalse} \tag{5f}$$
$$\Rightarrow if(false)then((Int)2)else(select_{Int}(store(\textbf{heap}, \textbf{o}, \textbf{f}, 1), \textbf{o}, \textbf{f})) \doteq 1$$
$$\downarrow \text{ifThenElseFalse} \tag{5g}$$
$$\Rightarrow select_{Int}(store(\textbf{heap}, \textbf{o}, \textbf{f}, 1), \textbf{o}, \textbf{f}) \doteq 1$$
$$\downarrow \text{selectOfStore} \tag{5h}$$
$$\Rightarrow if(\textbf{o} \doteq \textbf{o} \wedge \textbf{f} \doteq \textbf{f} \wedge \textbf{f} \not\doteq created)then((Int)1)else(select_{Int}(\textbf{heap}, \textbf{o}, \textbf{f})) \doteq 1$$
$$\downarrow 2 * \text{equal, uniqueNotSame} \tag{5i}$$
$$\Rightarrow if(true \wedge true \wedge \neg false)then((Int)1)else(select_{Int}(\textbf{heap}, \textbf{o}, \textbf{f})) \doteq 1$$
$$\downarrow \text{notFalse, andTrue} \tag{5j}$$
$$\Rightarrow if(true)then((Int)1)else(select_{Int}(\textbf{heap}, \textbf{o}, \textbf{f})) \doteq 1$$
$$\downarrow \text{ifThenElseTrue} \tag{5k}$$
$$\Rightarrow (Int)1 \doteq 1$$
$$\downarrow \text{castDel} \tag{5l}$$
$$\Rightarrow 1 \doteq 1$$
$$\downarrow \text{equal} \tag{6}$$
$$\Rightarrow true$$
$$\downarrow \text{closeTrue} \tag{7}$$
$$*$$

Figure 5.12.: Example for reading and writing the heap in JavaDL* (full detail)

$$\Rightarrow [\text{o.f = 1; o2.f = 2;}](\text{o.f} \leq 2)$$

$\downarrow$ assignField

$$\Rightarrow \{\text{heap} := store(\text{heap}, \text{o}, \text{f}, 1)\}[\text{o.g = 2;}](\text{o.f} \leq 2)$$

$\downarrow$ assignField

$$\Rightarrow \{\text{heap} := store(\text{heap}, \text{o}, \text{f}, 1)\}\{\text{heap} := store(\text{heap}, \text{o2}, \text{f}, 2)\}[\,](\text{o.f} \leq 2)$$

$\downarrow$ simplification

$$\Rightarrow \{\text{heap} := store(store(\text{heap}, \text{o}, \text{f}, 1), \text{o2}, \text{f}, 2)\}[\,](\text{o.f} \leq 2)$$

$\downarrow$ emptyModality

$$\Rightarrow \{\text{heap} := store(store(\text{heap}, \text{o}, \text{f}, 1), \text{o2}, \text{f}, 2)\}(\text{o.f} \leq 2)$$

$\downarrow$ simplification

$$\Rightarrow if(\text{o} \doteq \text{o2}) then(2) else(1) \leq 2$$

$\downarrow$ split

$$\text{o} \doteq \text{o2} \Rightarrow 2 \leq 2 \qquad\qquad \Rightarrow \text{o} \doteq \text{o2}, 1 \leq 2$$

$\downarrow \cdots \qquad\qquad\qquad\qquad\qquad \downarrow \cdots$

$* \qquad\qquad\qquad\qquad\qquad\qquad *$

Figure 5.13.: Example for aliasing

This is almost the same program as in Subsection 5.5.1, but here, it is possible that the two assignments write to the same location, namely if o and o2 refer to the same object. A proof for the postcondition o.f $\leq$ 2 is shown in Figure 5.13.

The proof proceeds as in Figure 5.11 up to the second simplification step. Here, the if-then-else term produced by one of the two applications of selectOfStore cannot be simplified away, because it is unknown whether o $\doteq$ o2 holds or not. This leads to splitting the proof tree. As the postcondition holds in both cases, each of the two branches can be closed.

The structure of the proof is again the same as in JavaDL. In particular, in both calculi the aliasing induced case split happens only in the end, after the program has been symbolically executed completely, and after all possibilities for simplifying without splitting (such as dropStore) have been exhausted.

5.5.3. Object Creation

Let the class C and the program variables o and o2 be as before. Suppose we want to show that the following sequent is logically valid:

$$\text{o} \not\doteq \textbf{null}, \ \text{o}.\, created \doteq TRUE, \ wellFormed(\text{heap})$$
$$\Rightarrow [\text{o2 = C.alloc();}](\text{o2}.\, created \doteq TRUE \land \text{o} \not\doteq \text{o2})$$

The sequent states that after allocating an object of class C in a well-formed heap, this object is created and different from an—otherwise unspecified—previously created object. Symbolically executing the call to the **alloc** method with the createObject rule yields the sequent below, where o' is a fresh constant symbol of type C.

$\mathsf{o} \not\doteq \mathbf{null}$, $\mathsf{o}.\,created \doteq TRUE$, $wellFormed(\mathbf{heap})$,
$o' \not\doteq \mathbf{null}$, $exactInstance_{\mathsf{C}}(o')$, $\big(wellFormed(\mathbf{heap}) \to o'.\,created \doteq FALSE\big)$
$\Rightarrow \{\mathbf{heap} := create(\mathbf{heap}, o')\}\{\mathsf{o2} := o'\}[\,]\,(\mathsf{o2}.\,created \doteq TRUE \wedge \mathsf{o} \not\doteq \mathsf{o2})$

Applying emptyModality and simplifying the resulting sequent produces:

$\mathsf{o} \not\doteq \mathbf{null}$, $\mathsf{o}.\,created \doteq TRUE$, $wellFormed(\mathbf{heap})$,
$o' \not\doteq \mathbf{null}$, $exactInstance_{\mathsf{C}}(o')$, $\big(wellFormed(\mathbf{heap}) \to o'.\,created \doteq FALSE\big)$
$\Rightarrow \mathsf{o} \not\doteq o'$

The postcondition $\mathsf{o2}.\,created \doteq TRUE$ has vanished, because the update rules turn it into $select_{Boolean}\big(create(\mathbf{heap}, o'), o', created\big) \doteq TRUE$, which is then simplified to *true* using selectOfCreate, equal and castDel. Because o' cannot be both created and non-created in **heap**, the sequent above can easily be shown to be valid, using rules for first-order logic and equalities.

5.5.4. Loops

A Java class that implements the *selection sort* algorithm is given in Figure 5.14. Let a be a program variable of type **int**[], and suppose we want to prove validity of the following sequent, which states that after running the sorting method on an array, the array is sorted:

$wellFormed(\mathbf{heap})$, $\mathsf{a} \not\doteq \mathbf{null}$, $\mathsf{a}.\,created \doteq TRUE$
$\Rightarrow [\texttt{Sorter.sort(a);}]\forall Int\ x;\,\big(0 < x \wedge x < \texttt{a.length} \to \texttt{a}[x-1] \leq \texttt{a}[x]\big)$

The overall structure of a proof for this property is shown in Figure 5.15. Symbolic execution (indicated as "SE" in the figure) uses a variation of expandMethod for **static** methods to inline the method body of **sort**, enclosed in a method frame. The initial assignment is turned into the update $\mathsf{i} := 0$. Then, the first active statement is the outer loop, and loopInvariant is applied. An adequate choice for the loop invariant *inv* is:

$0 \leq \mathsf{i} \wedge \mathsf{i} \leq \texttt{a.length}$
$\wedge\ \forall Int\ x;\,\big(0 < x \wedge x < \mathsf{i} \to \texttt{a}[x-1] \leq \texttt{a}[x]\big)$
$\wedge\ \forall Int\ x, y;\,\big(0 \leq x \wedge x < \mathsf{i} \wedge \mathsf{i} \leq y \wedge y < \texttt{a.length} \to \texttt{a}[x] \leq \texttt{a}[y]\big)$

This loop invariant states that i remains within the bounds of the array, that the sub-array up to the index i is sorted, and that all elements of this sub-array

```
—— Java ——————————————————————————
class Sorter {
    static void sort(int[] a) {
        int i = 0;
        while(i < a.length) {
            int minIndex = i;
            int j = i + 1;
            while(j < a.length) {
                if(a[j] < a[minIndex]) minIndex = j;
                j++;
            }
            int tmp = a[i];
            a[i] = a[minIndex];
            a[minIndex] = tmp;
            i++;
        }
    }
}
——————————————————————————— Java ——
```

Figure 5.14.: Java implementation of selection sort

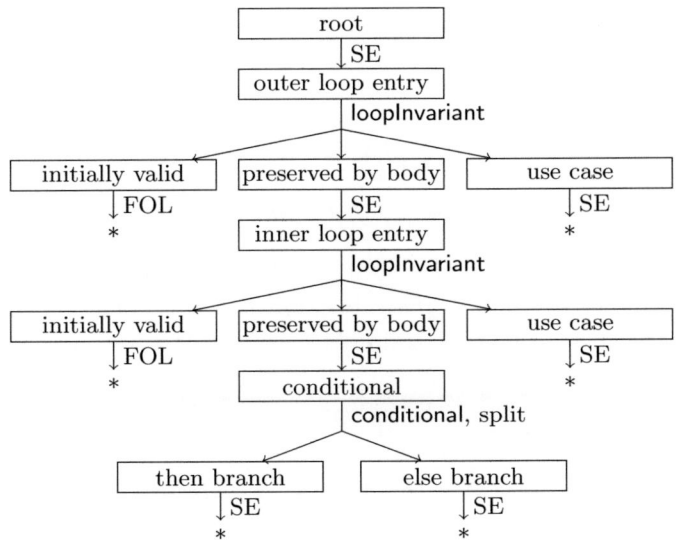

Figure 5.15.: Structure of proof for selection sort

are smaller than the elements of the rest of the array. A correct modifies clause for the loop is *allFields*(a): the only locations changed by the loop are the array components of a. This choice of *mod* gives rise to the following instantiation of the anonymising update v:

$$\texttt{heap} := anon\big(\texttt{heap}, \mathit{allFields}(\texttt{a}), h\big) \,\|\, \texttt{i} := i'$$

It also gives rise to the following instantiation of the formula *frame*:

$$\forall Object\ o;\ \forall Field\ f;\ \big((o, f) \,\dot\in\, \{\texttt{heap} := \texttt{heap}^{pre} \,\|\, \texttt{i} := \texttt{i}^{pre}\}\mathit{allFields}(\texttt{a})$$
$$\dot\cup\ \mathit{unusedLocs}(\texttt{heap}^{pre})$$
$$\vee\ \mathit{select}_{Any}(\texttt{heap}, o, f) \,\dot=\, \mathit{select}_{Any}(\texttt{heap}^{pre}, o, f)\big)$$

Of the local variables occurring in the loop body, only i can potentially be modified, because all others either do not occur on the left hand side of an assignment (a) or are declared within the loop body itself (minIndex, j, tmp). Thus, only i is anonymised by v, and only i must be reset to its pre-loop value by the update *pre'* occurring in *frame*.

The "initially valid" branch created by loopInvariant is:

$$\mathit{wellFormed}(\texttt{heap}),\ \texttt{a} \not\doteq \mathbf{null},\ \texttt{a}.\mathit{created} \doteq \mathit{TRUE}$$
$$\Rightarrow \{\texttt{i} := 0\}\big(\mathit{inv} \wedge \mathit{wellFormed}(\texttt{heap}) \wedge (\texttt{a} \doteq \mathbf{null} \vee \texttt{a}.\mathit{created} \doteq \mathit{TRUE})\big)$$

This branch can be closed using update rules and first-order reasoning with integer arithmetic (indicated as "FOL" in Figure 5.15).

The "use case" branch is:

$$\mathit{wellFormed}(\texttt{heap}),\ \texttt{a} \not\doteq \mathbf{null},\ \texttt{a}.\mathit{created} \doteq \mathit{TRUE}$$
$$\Rightarrow \{\texttt{i} := 0\}\{v\}\big(\mathit{inv} \wedge \mathit{wellFormed}(h) \wedge \texttt{i} \geq \texttt{a.length}$$
$$\rightarrow [\,]\forall Int\ x;\ (0 < x \wedge x < \texttt{a.length} \rightarrow \texttt{a[}x - 1\texttt{]} \leq \texttt{a[}x\texttt{]})\big)$$

Note that the formula *reachableOut* collapses to *true* in this example (and is thus omitted entirely in the sequent above), because the only local variable potentially modified by the loop (namely i) is not of a reference type. Because the chosen loop invariant is strong enough to imply the postcondition, the "use case" branch can be closed by finishing symbolic execution with the emptyModality rule, and by using update rules and first-order reasoning.

The most complex of the three branches is the "preserved by body" branch:

$$\mathit{wellFormed}(\texttt{heap}),\ \texttt{a} \not\doteq \mathbf{null},\ \texttt{a}.\mathit{created} \doteq \mathit{TRUE}$$
$$\Rightarrow \{\texttt{i} := 0\}\{\texttt{heap}^{pre} := \texttt{heap} \,\|\, \texttt{i}^{pre} := \texttt{i}\}\{v\}$$
$$\big(\mathit{inv} \wedge \mathit{wellFormed}(h) \wedge \texttt{i} < \texttt{a.length} \rightarrow [p](\mathit{inv} \wedge \mathit{frame})\big)$$

The body of the outer loop is denoted by p. After simplification and the application of a few first-order rules, the branch becomes:

$wellFormed(\texttt{heap})$, $\texttt{a} \neq \textbf{null}$, $\texttt{a}.\,created \doteq TRUE$

inv', $wellFormed(h)$, $i' < \texttt{a.length}$

$\Rightarrow \{\texttt{heap}^{pre} := \texttt{heap} \,\|\, \texttt{i}^{pre} := 0 \,\|\, \texttt{heap} := anon(\texttt{heap}, allFields(\texttt{a}), h) \,\|\, \texttt{i} := i'\}$

$\qquad [p](inv \wedge frame)$

The formula inv' is the result of replacing in the loop invariant inv the program variable $\texttt{heap}$ by $anon(\texttt{heap}, allFields(\texttt{a}), h)$ and the program variable $\texttt{i}$ by i'.

Symbolic execution continues from the above sequent, until the first active statement is the inner loop. Then, the loopInvariant rule is applied again. A suitable invariant for the inner loop is:

$$\texttt{i} < \texttt{j} \wedge \texttt{j} \leq \texttt{a.length} \wedge \texttt{i} \leq \texttt{minIndex} \wedge \texttt{minIndex} < \texttt{j}$$
$$\wedge \, \forall Int\, x; \left(\texttt{i} \leq x \wedge x < \texttt{j} \rightarrow \texttt{a[minIndex]} \leq \texttt{a}[x] \right)$$

This loop invariant states that $\texttt{j}$ remains between $\texttt{i}$ and the length of the array, that $\texttt{minIndex}$ is always between $\texttt{i}$ and $\texttt{j}$, and that $\texttt{minIndex}$ is the index of the smallest array component within these bounds. Because the inner loop does not modify the heap at all, $\emptyset$ is a correct modifies clause for the inner loop. The corresponding anonymising update is:

$$\texttt{heap} := anon(\texttt{heap}, \dot\emptyset, h') \,\|\, \texttt{j} := j' \,\|\, \texttt{minIndex} := minIndex'$$

All three branches created by this second application of loopInvariant can eventually be closed. On the "initially valid" branch, this requires proving that the heap is well-formed when initially reaching the inner loop, i.e., that $wellFormed\left(anon(\texttt{heap}, allFields(\texttt{a}), h)\right)$ holds in the context of the sequent. This is possible with the help of wellFormedAnon. On the second branch, symbolic execution of the conditional statement splits the proof further. On the "use case" branch, symbolic execution of the outer loop body p continues behind the inner loop.

In practice, other splits of the proof tree occur in addition to those shown in Figure 5.15. During symbolic execution, a side branch is created whenever a statement might throw an exception. As the program in Figure 5.14 does not throw any exceptions if the given precondition holds in the initial state, the corresponding execution paths are infeasible, allowing these proof branches to be closed quickly. Additional proof splitting occurs in the first-order reasoning phase after the end of symbolic execution.

5.6. Conclusion

In this chapter, we have introduced a dynamic logic for verifying Java programs. This logic, called *JavaDL**, is closely based on *JavaDL* [Beckert et al., 2007], but differs in one fundamental aspect, namely in the modelling of heap memory. Representing the heap as a single program variable allows dispensing with general *location functions*, with *location dependent functions* [Bubel et al., 2008] and with *quantified updates* [Rümmer, 2006], although in principle it is of course possible to additionally include any of these concepts anyway. It also allows for quantification over locations, and for terms of a type "set of locations". This simplifies the treatment of *modifies clauses*. An important part of the calculus that is significantly affected by the changes is the *loop invariant rule*. In contrast to its JavaDL counterpart, the loop invariant rule of JavaDL* implicitly allows object creation in its modifies clauses, and it takes care of preserving well-formedness properties across the loop.

Compared with other verification approaches that use an "explicit" heap modelling, a unique feature of JavaDL* (inherited from JavaDL) is the concept of *updates* [Beckert, 2001; Rümmer, 2006]. Updates allow computing weakest preconditions of Java programs by *symbolic execution* of the code. Symbolic execution is closer to human understanding of the code than the backwards procedure usually used for computing weakest preconditions. As a side effect, the use of symbolic execution allows utilising the logical framework of KeY for other applications besides just verification, such as *symbolic debugging* [Hähnle et al., 2010]. In JavaDL*, reasoning about updates is intertwined with reasoning about the arrays used to represent states of the heap. JavaDL* features custom function symbols for constructing such heap arrays, which are specialised towards verifying Java programs, and which thus differ from the classical *theory of arrays* [McCarthy, 1963]. In particular, the function symbol *anon* is tailor-made for reasoning about loops and method calls with the help of modifies clauses.

The JavaDL* calculus is fully implemented in variation of the KeY system, based on KeY version 1.5. An important feature of the implementation is its *one-step simplifier*: a meta rule that eagerly applies as many simplifying rewrite rules as possible, as a single step of the overall proof (like in Figure 5.11, as opposed to Figure 5.12). One-step simplification plays a similar role as the *update simplification* that handles updates in regular KeY. Unlike update simplification, it is independent of the underlying calculus (in particular of the update rules), and it is not limited to simplifying just updates: where the update simplification mechanism is itself an implementation of the update calculus, one-step simplification is a meta-level mechanism that applies given simplification rules. One-step simplification can be switched off, but activating it usually notably improves performance in automatic proofs. This is because it internally uses a more specialised and lightweight machinery for applying rules—and in particular for deciding which rule to apply next—than the general rule application and proof automation machinery of KeY, and because it discards the intermediate sequents immediately, instead of keeping them in memory for the duration of the entire verification process.

In a series of ad-hoc experiments, the KeY version based on JavaDL* verified the selection sort example of Section 5.5 automatically in about 7 seconds (where the loop invariant and the modifies clause for the loop were given as JML* specifications). The proof consisted of roughly 2400 nodes, including 46 leaves. Switching off one-step simplification increased the proving time to about 12 seconds and the number of nodes to about 4900. Normal KeY 1.5 verified the same example in about 9 seconds, the proof consisting of about 3600 nodes with 44 leaves. Verifying 37 valid proof obligations that involve programs from the KeY regression test suite took about 610 seconds with KeY 1.5, and about 700 seconds with the KeY version based on JavaDL* (with one-step simplification activated). This corresponds to a slowdown of about 15%. All these numbers must be taken with a grain of salt, for example because the verification process is not entirely deterministic, and because thus all numbers may vary between runs of the system. Nevertheless, they may be indicative of the order of magnitude of the run-time overhead that comes with the explicit heap model.

The design of JavaDL* has been driven by the goal of enabling the modular verification of dynamic frames style specifications—such as those written in JML* (Chapter 3)—in the framework of dynamic logic with updates. Realising this goal is the topic of the subsequent Chapter 6.

6. Verifying JML Specifications with Dynamic Frames

The dynamic logic defined in Chapter 5 can serve as a foundation for verifying the correctness of Java programs with respect to specifications that use dynamic frames. In particular, it can be used to verify specifications written in JML* (Chapter 3). This chapter describes an approach for doing so. JML* specifications and the corresponding programs are translated into *proof obligations*, i.e., into JavaDL* formulas whose logical validity implies that the program is correct with respect to the specification. This translation into dynamic logic fixes a more formal semantics of the specification language than the JML reference manual [Leavens et al., 2008] and Chapter 3.

Outline   Section 6.1 describes the translation of JML* expressions into JavaDL* terms and formulas. The translation is based on the notion of *observer symbols*, which are function and predicate symbols representing model fields and pure methods. The admissible interpretations of observer symbols are restricted by several classes of axioms, presented in Section 6.2. Besides observer symbols and axioms, a specification is represented on the level of JavaDL* as a set of JavaDL* *contracts*, which are defined in Section 6.3. Contracts give rise to the proof obligations defined in Section 6.4. Conversely, they are used in the proofs of other contracts via two rules defined in Section 6.5 as an extension of the JavaDL* calculus. The verification framework is illustrated with an extended example in Section 6.6. Related work is discussed in Section 6.7, and Section 6.8 contains conclusions.

6.1. Expressions

Because the types of JML* are mostly the types of Java itself, they are mapped to the types of JavaDL* as usual. In particular, reference types are directly represented as elements of $\mathcal{T}$, and integer types are mapped to $Int \in \mathcal{T}$. JML* expressions of type **boolean** are sometimes represented directly as formulas, instead of as terms of type *Boolean*. When necessary for translating an expression, a *Boolean* term b is implicitly converted to the formula $b \doteq TRUE$, and conversely, a formula φ is implicitly converted to the term $if(\varphi)then(TRUE)else(FALSE)$

when needed. The meta-type **\TYPE** is equivalent to the type `java.lang.Class` [Leavens et al., 2008], and could be represented as such. However, the type `java.lang.Class` and the other features of Java's *reflection* facilities are not part of Java Card, and are thus not considered in this thesis. As a consequence, **\TYPE** and the corresponding operators are not supported by the translation defined in this chapter, with one exception mentioned below. The central JML* type **\locset** is mapped to $LocSet \in \mathcal{T}$.

Ghost fields are represented in JavaDL* exactly like ordinary Java fields, i.e., as unique constant symbols of type *Field*. Local *ghost variables* are represented as program variables. Assignments to ghost fields and ghost variables with the **set** keyword are considered to be regular assignments.

Model fields and calls to *pure methods* in specifications are both represented in JavaDL* with the help of so-called *observer symbols*.

Definition 6.1 (Observer symbols). *An* observer symbol *is either a function symbol* $obs : Heap, C, A_1, \ldots, A_m \to A \in \mathcal{F}^{NU}$ *or a predicate symbol* $obs : Heap, C,$ $A_1, \ldots, A_m \in \mathcal{P}$, *where* $C \preceq Object$ *and* $0 \leq m$.

Observer symbols are the JavaDL* counterpart of the *location dependent symbols* of JavaDL [Bubel, 2007; Bubel et al., 2008]. The evaluation of a term $obs(\mathtt{heap}, o, a_1, \ldots, a_m)$ depends on the values of some or all locations in **heap**; intuitively, the observer symbol *obs* "observes" these locations. In JavaDL, location dependent symbols depend on heap locations implicitly, via special treatment in the definition of the logic's semantics. In contrast, here "observer symbols" is merely a name given to function and predicate symbols with certain argument types. Observer symbols depend on the heap explicitly via their first argument.

As syntactic sugar, we sometimes write $o.obs(a_1, \ldots, a_m)$ to denote the term or formula $obs(\mathtt{heap}, o, a_1, \ldots, a_m)$. This deliberately resembles the notation $o.\mathtt{f}$ for field access terms $select_A(\mathtt{heap}, o, \mathtt{f})$, where $\mathtt{f} : Field \in \mathcal{F}^{Unique}$. Nevertheless, observer symbols have different characteristics than field symbols $\mathtt{f}$. This difference mirrors the difference between location dependent symbols and location symbols in JavaDL (Chapter 4), as well as the difference between model fields and ghost fields in JML (Chapter 2), and equally the difference between pure methods and fields in Java. Unlike field symbols, observer symbols do not give rise to memory locations. The value of a term $o.obs(a_1, \ldots, a_m)$ cannot be set directly by an assignment. Rather, it is affected in an unspecified way as a side effect of changing **heap** for one or several locations.

The interpretation of individual observer symbols may be restricted by assumptions that quantify over heap arrays, such as the axioms described in Section 6.2 below. For example, one might want to assume in a proof that for a particular observer function symbol $obs : Heap, Object \to Object \in \mathcal{F}$, the formula

$\forall Heap\, h; \forall Object\, o;\, \big(obs(h, o) \neq \textbf{null}\big)$ holds. This assumption is satisfied by all Kripke structures where the function $I(obs)$ never returns *null*. In contrast, it is inadmissible to assume that a *location* only ever contains certain values in all heap arrays. Doing so is tantamount to assuming *false*: a formula like $\forall Heap\, h; \forall Object\, o;\, \big(select_A(h, o, \textbf{f}) \neq \textbf{null}\big)$ is unsatisfiable, because in every Kripke structure, there is an object $o \in \mathcal{D}^{Object}$ (in fact infinitely many) and a heap array $h \in \mathcal{D}^{Heap}$ such that $h\big(o, I(\textbf{f})\big) = null$. This is because by Definition 5.4, $\mathcal{D}^{Heap}$ contains *all* functions $\mathcal{D}^{Object} \times \mathcal{D}^{Field} \to \mathcal{D}$. This property of Kripke structures ensures that changing a location via *store* always produces a heap array in $\mathcal{D}^{Heap}$, and that thus an assignment $o.\textbf{f} = t$ or an equivalent update $\textbf{heap} := store(\textbf{heap}, o, \textbf{f}, t)$ always produces a state in $\mathcal{S}$.

In the translation from JML* to JavaDL*, a model field $\textbf{m}$ of a JavaDL* type $A \in \mathcal{T}$ which is declared in a class or interface $C \in \mathcal{T}$ is represented as an observer function symbol $\textbf{m}: Heap, C \to A \in \mathcal{F}$. As an exception, for convenience the built-in model field \inv becomes an observer *predicate* symbol $inv : Heap, Object \in \mathcal{P}$. A pure method $\textbf{m}$ declared in $C \in \mathcal{T}$ with argument types $A_1, \ldots, A_m \in \mathcal{T}$ and return type $A \in \mathcal{T}$ becomes an observer function symbol $\textbf{m}: Heap, C, A_1, \ldots, A_m \to A \in \mathcal{F}$. For an observer symbol $\textbf{m}$ representing a pure method without parameters (i.e., $m = 0$), we sometimes write $o.\textbf{m}()$ instead of $o.\textbf{m}$.

The paragraph above applies to non-**static** model fields and pure methods only. In the **static** case, the observer symbol's second parameter representing the receiver object is omitted. In order to simplify the presentation, the **static** case is not covered explicitly in this chapter. Extending the definitions accordingly is straightforward.

The translation of JML* expressions is outlined in Table 6.1. For JML* expressions $\textbf{e}$, the table defines a translation $[\textbf{e}] \in Term_\Sigma \cup Fma_\Sigma$. The translation depends on a context that provides a program variable $\textbf{self} \in \mathcal{PV}$ to be used as the translation of the keyword **this**. For the translation of expressions occurring in postconditions (shown in the lowermost section of the table), the context also provides program variables $\textbf{res}$ and $\textbf{heap}^{pre}$ to be used for translating the keyword \result and for referring to the pre-state of the heap, respectively. For the translation of method specifications, the context furthermore provides program variables to be used for representing the method parameters.

JML* expressions $\textbf{o.f}$, $\textbf{a[i]}$ and $\textbf{a.length}$, where $\textbf{f}: Field \in \mathcal{F}^{Unique}$ is a Java field or a ghost field, are mapped to JavaDL* terms as in Chapter 5. For occurrences of model fields or pure methods $\textbf{m}$, the translation to an occurrence of the corresponding observer symbol is also straightforward. Recall that in JavaDL* (right column of Table 6.1), the notation $[o].\textbf{f}$ stands for $select_A(\textbf{heap}, [o], \textbf{f})$, where $A \in \mathcal{T}$ corresponds to the type of $\textbf{f}$ in *Prg*; that the notation $[o].\textbf{m}$ stands for $\textbf{m}(\textbf{heap}, [o])$; and that the notation $[a].\textbf{length}$ stands for $\textbf{length}([a])$.

JML*	JavaDL*
this	self
o.f	[o].f
a[i]	[a][[i]]
a.length	[a].length
o.m	[o].m
o.m(a1,...,an)	[o].m([a1],...,[an])
(**\forall nullable** T x; b1; b2)	$\dot\forall\,[T]\,x;\,([b1]\rightarrow[b2])$
(**\exists nullable** T x; b1; b2)	$\dot\exists\,[T]\,x;\,([b1]\wedge[b2])$
\typeof(x) == **\type**(T)	$exactInstance_{[T]}([x])$
e1 == e2	$[e1]\doteq[e2]$
\subset(s1, s2)	$[s1]\dot\subseteq[s2]$
\disjoint(s1, s2)	$disjoint([s1],[s2])$
o.f	$\{([o],f)\}$
a[i]	$\{([a],arr([i]))\}$
\singleton(o.f)	$\{([o],f)\}$
\singleton(a[i])	$\{([a],arr([i]))\}$
a[i..j]	$arrayRange([a],[i],[j])$
a[*]	$allFields([a])$
o.*	$allFields([o])$
\nothing	$\dot\emptyset$
\everything	$allLocs\,\dot{\setminus}\,unusedLocs(\text{heap})$
\intersect(s1, s2)	$[s1]\dot\cap[s2]$
\set_minus(s1, s2)	$[s1]\,\dot{\setminus}\,[s2]$
\set_union(s1, s2)	$[s1]\dot\cup[s2]$
\result	res
\old(x)	$\{\text{heap}:=\text{heap}^{pre}\}[x]$
\fresh(o)	$[o]\not\doteq\textbf{null}$
	$\wedge\,select_{Boolean}(\text{heap}^{pre},[o],created)\doteq FALSE$
\fresh(s)	$[s]\dot\subseteq unusedLocs(\text{heap}^{pre})$
\new_elems_fresh(s)	$[s]\dot\subseteq\{\text{heap}:=\text{heap}^{pre}\}[s]$
	$\dot\cup\,unusedLocs(\text{heap}^{pre})$

Table 6.1.: Translation of selected JML* expressions to JavaDL* terms and formulas: heap related expressions, **boolean** expressions, **locset** expressions, and expressions restricted to postconditions

The translation of the JML* quantifiers **\forall** and **\exists** is specified in Table 6.1 with the help of "dotted quantifiers" $\dot{\forall}$ and $\dot{\exists}$, which are defined in Definition 6.2 below.

Definition 6.2 (Dotted quantifier notation). *For $\mathcal{Q} \in \{\forall, \exists\}$, for $A \in \mathcal{T}$, for $x : A \in \mathcal{V}$ and for $\varphi \in Fma_\Sigma$, the notation $\dot{\mathcal{Q}}A\,x; \varphi$ is an abbreviation for a formula which is defined as follows:*

$$\dot{\mathcal{Q}}A\,x; \varphi = \begin{cases} \mathcal{Q}A\,x; \big((x \doteq \textbf{null} \lor x.\,created \doteq \mathit{TRUE}) \bullet \varphi\big) & \text{if } A \preceq \mathit{Object} \\ \mathcal{Q}A\,x; \big(disjoint(x, unusedLocs(\textbf{heap})) \bullet \varphi\big) & \text{if } A = \mathit{LocSet} \\ \mathcal{Q}A\,x; \varphi & \text{otherwise} \end{cases}$$

The symbol $\bullet$ stands for $\to$ if $\mathcal{Q} = \forall$, and for $\land$ if $\mathcal{Q} = \exists$.

The "dotted quantifiers" behave like the ordinary quantifiers, except that the range of quantification is restricted to exclude non-created objects. Note that dotted quantifications over reference types or over *LocSet* thus implicitly depend on **heap**.

JML's default of using **non_null** whenever **nullable** is not given explicitly extends to quantification, too. Thus, the translation of quantifications over reference types that lack the **nullable** keyword has to add an additional guard $x \neq \textbf{null}$ that also excludes *null* from the range of quantification, in addition to excluding non-created objects. This is not shown in Table 6.1. The notation [T] used in the table stands for the JavaDL* counterpart of the JML* type T.

Expressions of the form **\typeof(x) == \type(T)** are the only exception to the rule that the JML type **\TYPE** is not supported by the translation: this is the JML way of expressing that the dynamic type of x is T, which can be stated in JavaDL* as the formula $exactInstance_{[T]}([x])$. Other occurrences of the equality operator == are translated using $\doteq$.

The set predicates **\subset** and **\disjoint** are mapped to the corresponding predicate symbols $\subseteq$ and *disjoint*. Similarly, the location set constructors **\singleton**, **\nothing**, **\intersect**, **\set_minus** and **\set_union** are mapped to their JavaDL* counterparts *singleton*, $\emptyset$, $\dot{\cap}$, $\backslash$ and $\dot{\cup}$. Expressions a[i..j] are translated using *arrayRange*, and both a[*] and o.* are translated with the help of *allFields*. The keyword **\everything** is translated not to *allLocs*, but to *allLocs* $\backslash$ *unusedLocs*(**heap**), i.e., it includes only those locations that belong to created objects (or to *null*). The shorthands o.f and a[i] for **\singleton(o.f)** and **\singleton(a[i])** are translated as such. The syntactical ambiguity between this translation and the translation as a heap access expression [o].f or [a][[i]] (respectively) is resolved by choosing the translation as a heap access expression whenever this is syntactically admissible.

An expression `\old(x)` is translated by substituting the program variable $\texttt{heap}^{pre}$ for all occurrences of `heap` in $[\texttt{x}]$. The substitution can equivalently be expressed with the help of an update $\texttt{heap} := \texttt{heap}^{pre}$, as in Table 6.1. For an expression `o` of a reference type, `\fresh(o)` means that the object which is the value of `o` is different from *null*, and that it is not created in the heap array denoted by $\texttt{heap}^{pre}$. For an expression `s` of type `\locset`, the meaning of `\fresh(s)` is that all locations in the set which is the value of `s` also belong to $unusedLocs(\texttt{heap}^{pre})$. Finally, `\new_elems_fresh(s)` means that all locations in the value of `s` are elements of the pre-state value of `s` or of $unusedLocs(\texttt{heap}^{pre})$.

The issue of *weakly pure* specification expressions, i.e., specification expressions that create and initialise new objects, is resolved here by simply ignoring such side effects. For example, the JavaDL* translation of a JML* expression "`newObject() == newObject()`", where `newObject` is a weakly pure method that creates and returns a fresh object, is the formula $\texttt{newObject}(\texttt{heap}, \texttt{self}) \doteq \texttt{newObject}(\texttt{heap}, \texttt{self})$. This formula is logically valid, even though in Java, the expression "`newObject() == newObject()`" always evaluates to "false".

Other solutions are possible [Darvas and Leino, 2007; Darvas, 2009] and could be combined with JavaDL*. For example, a weakly pure method like `newObject` could be encoded as an observer function symbol $\texttt{newObject}: Heap, Object \rightarrow (Heap, Object)$, where $(Heap, Object)$ is a type whose values are pairs of heap arrays and objects. The "`newObject() == newObject()`" could then be translated to the formula

$$snd\big(\texttt{newObject}(\texttt{heap}, \texttt{self})\big)$$
$$\doteq snd\big(\texttt{newObject}(fst(\texttt{newObject}(\texttt{heap}, \texttt{self})), self)\big),$$

where *fst* and *snd* are pre-defined function symbols that project the first and the second element out of a $(Heap, Object)$ pair, respectively. This translation faithfully models what happens when evaluating the expression in Java, where the second call to `newObject` starts with the heap array that is produced by the first call. Another, simpler solution is to syntactically forbid specification expressions like "`newObject() == newObject()`", where the difference between the possible interpretations of weak purity is observable.

The translation described in this section does not respect JML's *strong validity* semantics of expressions [Chalin, 2007b], which demands that a top-level expression that would throw an exception in Java evaluates to "false" in JML (Chapter 2). Instead, for example, a JML* expression `x/0 == x/0` is translated to the formula $\texttt{x/0} \doteq \texttt{x/0}$. This formula is logically valid: the semantics of the function symbol "/" is underspecified for the case that the second argument is 0, and thus the value of the term `x/0` is unknown; but it is the same value on both sides of the equation. "Good" specifications avoid such issues with well-definedness. It is possible to define first-order proof obligations whose validity for a given specification implies that there are no such problems [Darvas et al., 2008]. These could be integrated into JavaDL* and added to the proof obligations defined in Section 6.4.

6.2. Axioms

When verifying JML* specifications, several kinds of axioms are used as assumptions that constrain the possible interpretations of observer symbols. Firstly, there are axioms expressing that observer symbols never refer to non-created objects, or to location sets containing locations of non-created objects (Subsection 6.2.1). Secondly, there are axioms that connect the observer symbols representing pure methods with the corresponding method implementations (Subsection 6.2.2). Another kind of axioms result from translating the represents clauses of the specification (Subsection 6.2.3). Finally, there are special axioms for the observer symbol *inv* that represents object invariants (Subsection 6.2.4).

6.2.1. Createdness of Observed Objects

Let $obs : Heap, C, A_1, \ldots, A_m \to A \in \mathcal{F}$ be an observer function symbol representing a model field or a pure method. If $A \preceq Object$, then we introduce an axiom

$$\forall Heap\ h; \forall C\ c; \forall A_1\ a_1; \ldots; \forall A_m\ a_m;$$
$$\big(obs(h, c, a_1, \ldots, a_m) \doteq \texttt{null}$$
$$\vee\ select_{Boolean}(h, obs(h, c, a_1, \ldots, a_m), created) \doteq TRUE\big),$$

which expresses that only the *null* object and created objects can be "observed". If $A = LocSet$, then we instead introduce the axiom

$$\forall Heap\ h; \forall C\ c; \forall A_1\ a_1; \ldots; \forall A_m\ a_m; \forall Object\ o; \forall Field\ f;$$
$$\big((o, f) \dot\in obs(h, c, a_1, \ldots, a_m)$$
$$\to o \doteq \texttt{null} \vee select_{Boolean}(h, o, created) \doteq TRUE\big),$$

stating that the "observed" location sets never contain locations of unallocated objects.

Instead of representing such axioms as formulas that are part of the antecedent of the root sequent of a proof, they may also be stated as axiomatic *rules*. In particular, the axioms above can also be represented as the rules obsIsNullOrCreated and elementOfObsIsNullOrCreated:

$$\frac{\begin{array}{l} \Gamma, \ obs(h, c, a_1, \ldots, a_m) \doteq \textbf{null} \\ \quad \vee \ select_{Boolean}(h, obs(h, c, a_1, \ldots, a_m), created) \doteq TRUE \\ \Rightarrow \ \Delta \end{array}}{\Gamma \ \Rightarrow \ \Delta} \quad \text{obsIsNullOrCreated}$$

$$\frac{\begin{array}{l} \Gamma, \ (o, f) \dot{\in} \ obs(h, c, a_1, \ldots, a_m), \\ o \doteq \textbf{null} \vee select_{Boolean}(h, o, created) \doteq TRUE \\ \Rightarrow \ \Delta \end{array}}{\Gamma, \ (o, f) \dot{\in} \ obs(h, c, a_1, \ldots, a_m) \ \Rightarrow \ \Delta} \quad \text{elementOfObsIsNullOrCreated}$$

In practice, the application of the obsIsNullOrCreated rule is triggered by an occurrence of the term $obs(h, c, a_1, \ldots, a_m)$ anywhere in the conclusion of the rule, and the application of the elementOfObsIsNullOrCreated rule is triggered by the occurrence of the formula $(o, f) \dot{\in} obs(h, c, a_1, \ldots, a_m)$ in the antecedent of the conclusion. In both cases, representing the axiom as a rule has the advantage that it avoids cluttering up the sequent, and that it allows for a custom "triggering" for instantiating the universal quantifiers, instead of relying on general quantifier instantiation mechanisms (usually also based on some "triggering" heuristic [Detlefs et al., 2005]).

The obsIsNullOrCreated and elementOfObsIsNullOrCreated rules closely resemble the refIsNullOrCreated and elementIsNullOrCreated rules in Figure 5.6. However, where for observer symbols we are free to assume that the referenced objects are created in *all* heap arrays, the same is guaranteed for locations only in *well-formed* heap arrays. Assuming that all locations have this property in all heap arrays would contradict the definition of $I(store)$, which allows writing an arbitrary value into a location, including a reference to a non-created object.

6.2.2. Pure Methods

Let $\mathtt{m} : Heap, C, A_1, \ldots, A_m \to A \in \mathcal{F}$ be an observer function symbol that represents a pure method $\mathtt{m}$. For every type $D \in \mathcal{T}$ with $D \preceq C$ we introduce an axiom

$$\forall Heap\ h; \forall D\ d; \forall A_1\ a_1; \ldots; \forall A_m\ a_m;$$
$$\big(exactInstance_D(d)$$
$$\to \{\mathtt{heap} := h \,\|\, \mathtt{self} := d \,\|\, \mathtt{a}_1 := a_1 \,\|\, \ldots \,\|\, \mathtt{a}_m := a_m\}$$
$$[\mathtt{res} = \mathtt{self.m(a_1, \ldots, a_m)};]\dot{\forall} A\ r; (\mathtt{res} \doteq r \to r \doteq \mathtt{m}(h, d, a_1, \ldots, a_m)))$$

where $\mathtt{self} : D \in \mathcal{PV}$, $\mathtt{a}_1 : A_1, \ldots, \mathtt{a}_m : A_m \in \mathcal{PV}$ and $\mathtt{res} : A \in \mathcal{PV}$. The axiom uses the box modality to connect the observer symbol $\mathtt{m}$ with a call to the method $\mathtt{m}$ in type D. The method call can subsequently be replaced with the method implementation, using the expandMethod rule of Figure 5.9. This axiom, too, can be expressed as a rule:

$$\Gamma, \; exactInstance_D(d),$$
$$\{\texttt{heap} := h \,\|\, \texttt{self} := d \,\|\, \texttt{a}_1 := a_1 \,\|\, \dots \,\|\, \texttt{a}_m := a_m\}$$
$$[\texttt{res = self.m(a}_1\texttt{,}\dots\texttt{,a}_m\texttt{);}]\dot{\forall} A\, r; (\texttt{res} \doteq r \to r \doteq \texttt{m}(h, d, a_1, \dots, a_m))$$
$$\underline{\Rightarrow \; \Delta} \qquad\qquad\qquad\qquad\qquad\qquad\qquad\qquad\qquad\qquad \text{purelmpl}$$
$$\Gamma, \; exactInstance_D(d) \; \Rightarrow \; \Delta$$

The correctness of the axiom does not rely on m being pure. Potential side effects of the call to m are irrelevant, because they are effective only within the scope of the box modality, and because the formula in scope of the box modality does not depend on **heap** (except for createdness of objects). If the method m does not terminate or if it throws an exception for some or all input values, then the axiom does not state anything on the value of the observer symbol m for these input values.

Furthermore, the purelmpl axiom cannot contradict the obsIsNullOrCreated and elementOfObsIsNullOrCreated axioms of Subsection 6.2.1. This is because of the use of the dotted quantifier $\dot{\forall}$ (Definition 6.2) below the modal operator: the value returned by the method call must be equal to the value of the observer symbol m only if this value is not a non-created object or a location set containing a location of a non-created object; otherwise, the axiom does not demand anything about the value of m.

6.2.3. Represents Clauses

Every represents clause of the specification is translated to a formula $rep \in Fma_\Sigma$. For relational represents clauses "**represents m \such_that b**", this formula is the result of translating the expression b, i.e., $rep = [\texttt{b}]$. Functional represents clauses "**represents m = e**" are considered to be shorthands for relational represents clauses "**represents m \such_that m == e**", and are translated as such.

Let m be an observer function symbol m : $Heap, C \to A \in \mathcal{F}$ or an observer predicate symbol m : $Heap, C \in \mathcal{P}$, for which a represents clause is declared in a type $D \preceq C$, and let $rep \in Fma_\Sigma$ be the translation of this represents clause. The represents clause gives rise to an axiom

$$\forall Heap\, h; \forall D\, d; \left(exactInstance_D(d) \wedge \{\texttt{self} := d \,\|\, \texttt{heap} := h\} sat \right.$$
$$\left. \to \{\texttt{heap} := h \,\|\, \texttt{self} := d\} rep \right),$$

where **self** : $D \in \mathcal{PV}$ is the program variable used for translating **this** in rep. The formula $sat \in Fma_\Sigma$ is defined as

$$sat = \begin{cases} \dot{\exists} A\, a; rep_a & \text{if } \texttt{m} \in \mathcal{F} \\ rep_{true} \vee rep_{false} & \text{if } \texttt{m} \in \mathcal{P} \end{cases}$$

where $rep_a \in Fma_\Sigma$ is the result of replacing in rep all occurrences of `self.m` with $a : A \in \mathcal{V}$, and where rep_{true} and rep_{false} are the results of replacing in rep all occurrences of `self.m` with *true* and with *false*, respectively.

The guard formula *sat* provides some protection against unsatisfiability. Without it, a represents clause like "**represents m \such_that false**" would lead to an unsatisfiable axiom, making all proof obligations hold trivially. Using *sat* as a guard instead means that for a heap array $h \in \mathcal{D}^{Heap}$ and an object $d \in \mathcal{D}^D$, the represents clause constrains the value $I(\mathtt{m})(h, d)$ only if we can find a value $a \in \mathcal{D}^A$ such that h, d and a satisfy the represents clause; otherwise, nothing is said about the value of $I(\mathtt{m})(h, d)$. The dotted quantifier $\dot{\exists}$ additionally demands that the value a must not be an unallocated object or a location set containing a location of an unallocated object. This avoids contradictions with the obsIsNullOrCreated and elementOfObsIsNullOrCreated axioms from Subsection 6.2.1.

For example, for a represents clause "**represents i = i + 1**" the formula *sat* is $\dot{\exists} Int\, a; (a \doteq a + 1)$. As this formula is unsatisfiable, the overall axiom is equivalent to *true*. Similarly, a represents clause "**represents \inv = !\inv**" leads to *sat* being the formula $(true \leftrightarrow \neg true) \vee (false \leftrightarrow \neg false)$, which is again unsatisfiable and thus again makes the overall axiom logically valid. An example for a more meaningful represents clause is "**represents m \such_that x <= m && m <= y**", which demands that the value of `m` is between the values of `x` and `y` when possible (i.e., when `x <= y` holds), and which does not prescribe anything on the value of `m` otherwise.

Note that in spite of these precautions, it is possible that several axioms generated from represents clauses contradict each other. In particular, a contradiction can be the result of mutually recursive represents clauses. Consider for example the two represents clauses "**represents x = y**" and "**represents y = x + 1**": each of them is satisfiable on its own, but their conjunction is not. Systematically preventing such inconsistencies between several represents clauses is beyond the scope of this work. The responsibility for avoiding them is placed on the specifier.

Like the other kinds of axiom, the axioms generated from represents clauses can also be expressed as rules instead of as formulas:

$$\frac{\Gamma,\ exactInstance_D(d) \Rightarrow \{\mathtt{heap} := h \,\|\, \mathtt{self} := d\} sat,\ \Delta \quad \text{(satisfiability)}}{\Gamma,\ exactInstance_D(d) \Rightarrow \Delta} \; \text{rep}$$

The application of the rep rule is triggered by an occurrence of the term or formula $\mathtt{m}(h, d)$ in the conclusion. For functional represents clauses, i.e., represents clauses where $rep = (\mathtt{self.m} \equiv rhs)$, where $\equiv$ stands for $\doteq$ and $rhs \in Term_\Sigma$ if $\mathtt{m} \in \mathcal{F}$, and where $\equiv$ stands for $\leftrightarrow$ and $rhs \in Fma_\Sigma$ if $\mathtt{m} \in \mathcal{P}$, we can also use the rule

$$\cfrac{\begin{array}{ll}\Gamma,\ \mathit{exactInstance}_D(d)\ \Rightarrow\ \{\mathtt{heap}:=h\,\|\,\mathtt{self}:=d\}\mathit{sat},\ \Delta & \text{(satisf.)}\\ \Gamma',\ \mathit{exactInstance}_D(d)\ \Rightarrow\ \Delta' & \text{(use case)}\end{array}}{\Gamma,\ \mathit{exactInstance}_D(d)\ \Rightarrow\ \Delta}\ \text{repSimple}$$

where Γ' and Δ' are the results of replacing in Γ and in Δ all occurrences of $\mathtt{m}(h,d)$ not below an update or a modality with $\{\mathtt{heap}:=h\,\|\,\mathtt{self}:=d\}\mathit{rhs}$. The repSimple rule allows directly replacing model fields by their definition, as given by a functional represents clause. This is more efficient in practice than adding an equation to the antecedent. For represents clauses that are relational or recursive (where the repSimple rule may lead to non-termination of proof search), one can resort to the more general rep rule.

Example 6.1. Consider the represents clause for the dynamic frame `footprint` from the `ArrayList` class in Figure 3.3:

```
//@ represents footprint = array, array[*], size;
```

The formula *rep* that results from translating this represents clause is

$$\mathtt{self.footprint} \doteq \{(\mathtt{self},\mathtt{array})\}\,\dot\cup\,\mathit{allFields}(\mathtt{self.array})\,\dot\cup\,\{(\mathtt{self},\mathtt{size})\},$$

where $\mathtt{footprint}:\mathit{Heap},\mathtt{List}\to\mathit{LocSet}\in\mathcal{F}$, where $\mathtt{self}:\mathtt{ArrayList}\in\mathcal{PV}$, and where $\mathtt{array},\mathtt{size}:\mathit{Field}\in\mathcal{F}^{\mathit{Unique}}$. The guard formula *sat* is

$$\exists\mathit{LocSet}\ a;\ \big(\mathit{disjoint}(a,\mathit{unusedLocs}(\mathtt{heap}))$$
$$\wedge\,a\doteq\{(\mathtt{self},\mathtt{array})\}\,\dot\cup\,\mathit{allFields}(\mathtt{self.array})\,\dot\cup\,\{(\mathtt{self},\mathtt{size})\}\big).$$

Because the represents clause is functional and non-recursive, it can be used in proofs as an instance of the repSimple rule, which replaces occurrences of $\mathtt{footprint}(h,\mathit{list})$ (where $h\in\mathit{Term}_\Sigma^{\mathit{Heap}}$ and $\mathit{list}\in\mathit{Term}_\Sigma^{\mathtt{ArrayList}}$ are arbitrary) with the term

$$\{\mathtt{heap}:=h\,\|\,\mathtt{self}:=\mathit{list}\}(\{(\mathtt{self},\mathtt{array})\}$$
$$\dot\cup\,\mathit{allFields}(\mathtt{self.array})\,\dot\cup\,\{(\mathtt{self},\mathtt{size})\}),$$

which can be simplified to

$$\big\{(\mathit{list},\mathtt{array})\big\}\,\dot\cup\,\mathit{allFields}\big(\mathit{select}_{\mathtt{Object[]}}(h,\mathit{list},\mathtt{array})\big)\,\dot\cup\,\big\{(\mathit{list},\mathtt{size})\big\}.$$

On the "satisfiability" branch of repSimple, it is obvious how to instantiate the existential quantifier in the formula *sat*. The task of closing the branch boils down to proving that the set denoted by the term above does not contain locations of unallocated objects. This can be established if it is known that the object denoted by *list* is created, and that the heap array denoted by h is well-formed.   ∗

135

6.2.4. Object Invariants

Declarations of object invariants are in JML* essentially syntactic sugar for defining the represents clause of the model field \inv. As described in Chapter 3, the entirety of all invariant declarations "**invariant** e_1; ...; **invariant** e_n;" of a given type (including the invariant declarations inherited from its supertypes) stands for a single represents clause "**private represents** \inv = e_1 && ... && e_n". This represents clause defines the exact meaning of \inv (and of its translation $inv \in \mathcal{P}$) for objects of this particular dynamic type. It is used in proofs like any other represents clause (Subsection 6.2.3).

Nevertheless, invariant declarations have two particularities that regular represents clauses do not have: firstly, each invariant declaration has its own visibility level; and secondly, invariant declarations are inherited to subtypes. For doing justice to these particularities, we introduce the following additional axiom for every invariant declaration "**invariant** i" in type C, *not* including declarations inherited from supertypes of C:

$$\forall Heap\ h; \forall C\ c; \big(inv(h, c) \rightarrow \{\mathtt{heap} := h \,\|\, \mathtt{self} := c\}i\big)$$

The formula $i \in Fma_\Sigma$ is the translation of the JML* expression i, i.e., $i = [\mathtt{i}]$. The axiom states that for all objects of type C or any of its subtypes, i is a consequence of inv. It does not need a "satisfiability" guard, because for every $h \in \mathcal{D}^{Heap}$ and every $c \in \mathcal{D}^C$, it is possible to choose $I(inv)(h, c)$ such that the axiom is satisfied (namely, by choosing $I(inv)(h, c) = f\!f$). Note that the axiom is not a corollary of the axioms generated for the represents clauses for \inv, because it constrains the value of inv even if the formula *sat* in the represents clause axiom does not hold, and if thus the represents clause axiom does not prescribe anything on the interpretation of inv at all. The object invariant axiom can also be stated as a rule

$$\frac{\Gamma,\ inv(h, c),\ \{\mathtt{heap} := h \,\|\, \mathtt{self} := c\}i\ \Rightarrow\ \Delta}{\Gamma,\ inv(h, c)\ \Rightarrow\ \Delta}\ \mathtt{inv}$$

where $h \in Term_\Sigma^{Heap}$ and $c \in Term_\Sigma^C$.

Example 6.2. Consider the invariants of the `ArrayList` class from Figure 3.3:

```
//@ public invariant 0 <= size();
/*@ private invariant array != null;
  @ private invariant 0 <= size && size <= array.length;
  @ private invariant (\forall int i; 0 <= i && i < size;
  @                                   array[i] != null);
  @ private invariant \typeof(array) == \type(Object[]);
  @*/
```

The first invariant is inherited from the `List` interface of Figure 3.1, and the others are declared in `ArrayList` itself. Together, the invariants lead to a represents clause axiom where the formula *rep* is:

$$\texttt{self}.inv \leftrightarrow 0 \leq \texttt{self.size}()$$
$$\wedge\, \texttt{self.array} \neq \textbf{null}$$
$$\wedge\, 0 \leq \texttt{self.size} \wedge \texttt{self.size} \leq \texttt{self.array.length}$$
$$\wedge\, \forall Int\, i;\, (0 \leq i \wedge i < \texttt{self.size} \rightarrow \texttt{self.array}[i] \neq \textbf{null})$$
$$\wedge\, exactInstance_{\texttt{Object[]}}(\texttt{self.array})$$

The represents clause axiom can be represented as an instance of the repSimple rule, which defines *inv* for objects of dynamic type `ArrayList`. Additionally, each of the invariant declarations leads to an instance of the inv rule. In particular, the first invariant gives rise to the rule

$$\frac{\Gamma,\; inv(h, list),\; \{\texttt{heap} := h \,\|\, \texttt{self} := list\}\big(0 \leq \texttt{self.size}()\big) \;\Rightarrow\; \Delta}{\Gamma,\; inv(h, list) \;\Rightarrow\; \Delta}$$

where $h \in \mathit{Term}_{\Sigma}^{Heap}$, $list \in \mathit{Term}_{\Sigma}^{\texttt{List}}$. Because the invariant is declared in `List`, the rule applies to all `List` objects, not just `ArrayList` objects. Because of the **public** visibility of the invariant, the rule may be available in proofs where the represents clause axiom for `ArrayList` is not (Section 6.4). ∗

6.3. Contracts

Besides observer symbols and axioms that constrain the interpretation of the observer symbols, the JavaDL* representation of a JML* specification consists of set of *method contracts* that specify the intended behaviour of methods (Subsection 6.3.1), and of a set of *dependency contracts* that specify the intended dependencies of observer symbols (Subsection 6.3.2).

6.3.1. Method Contracts

JavaDL* method contracts are defined in Definition 6.3 below. The definition applies to methods (not including constructors) that are neither **static** nor **void**. Extending it to cover constructors, **static** methods and **void** methods is straightforward.

Definition 6.3 (Method contracts). *A method contract mct is a tuple*

$$mct = \big(\texttt{m}, \texttt{self}, (\texttt{a}_1, \ldots, \texttt{a}_m), \texttt{res}, \texttt{heap}^{pre}, \texttt{exc}, pre, post, mod, \tau\big),$$

where m *is a Java method which is declared in type* $C \in \mathcal{T}$ *with argument types* $A_1, \ldots, A_m \in \mathcal{T}$ $(0 \leq m)$ *and return type* $A \in \mathcal{T}$*; where* self : $D \in \mathcal{PV}$ *for some* $D \preceq C$*; where* $a_1 : A_1, \ldots, a_m : A_m \in \mathcal{PV}$*; where* res : $A \in \mathcal{PV}$*; where* heap^{pre} : *Heap* $\in \mathcal{PV}$*; where* exc : Exception $\in \mathcal{PV}$*; where* pre, post $\in$ Fma$_\Sigma$*; where* mod $\in$ Term$_\Sigma^{LocSet}$*; and where* $\tau \in \{partial, total\}$.

A JavaDL* method contract $\big($m, self, $(a_1, \ldots, a_m)$, res, heap^{pre}, exc, *pre*, *post*, *mod*, $\tau\big)$ with self : D constrains the allowed behaviour of the method m in type D and in all subtypes of D (behavioural subtyping). The program variables self and $a_1, \ldots, a_m$ represent the receiver object of m and the parameters of m (respectively) in the *precondition pre*, in the *postcondition post* and in the *modifies clause mod*. The program variables res and heap^{pre} represent the return value of m and the pre-state heap (respectively) in the postcondition *post*. The program variable exc represents in *post* the exception thrown by the execution of m, or *null* if no exception is thrown. The "termination marker" τ indicates whether the contract demands partial or total correctness.

Every JML* method contract is translated into either one or two JavaDL* method contracts in the sense of Definition 6.3. The **diverges** clause of the JML* contract decides on whether one or two JavaDL* contracts are generated. For contracts with a **diverges** clause of "**diverges true**" or "**diverges false**", we introduce a single contract with $\tau = partial$ or $\tau = total$, respectively. Contracts with an overall **diverges** clause of the general form "**diverges b**", where b is neither **true** nor **false**, lead to one JavaDL* contract with $\tau = partial$, and to a second contract with $\tau = total$ and an additional precondition "**requires !b**".

The precondition *pre* of a generated JavaDL* contract is the conjunction of the formulas that result from translating the individual **requires** clauses. The postcondition *post* is the conjunction of the formulas that result from translating the **ensures** and **signals** clauses, where "**ensures b**" is translated as "exc $\doteq$ **null** $\rightarrow$ [b]", and where "**signals(E e) b**" is translated as "*instance*$_E$(exc) $\rightarrow$ [b]". For every type $A \in \mathcal{T}$, the predicate symbol *instance*$_A$: *Any* $\in \mathcal{P}$ corresponds to Java's **instanceof** operator for this type. In particular, we have $I(instance_A)(null) = f\!f$ for all $A \in \mathcal{T} \setminus \{Null\}$. As described in Chapter 2, both **signals_only** clauses and the two JML keywords **normal_behaviour** and **exceptional_behaviour** are merely syntactic sugar for **ensures** and **signals** clauses, and they are translated as such. Similarly, the **pure** modifier is an abbreviation for "**assignable \nothing**" and "**diverges false**". The modifies clause *mod* is the result of translating the **assignable** clauses of the JML* contract, where multiple clauses are connected by $\dot{\cup}$.

Example 6.3. Consider the specification of method get in the List interface of Figure 3.1:

```
/*@ public normal_behaviour
  @    requires 0 <= index && index < size();
  @    accessible footprint;
  @    ensures \result == get(index);
  @ also public exceptional_behaviour
  @    requires index < 0 || size() <= index;
  @    signals_only IndexOutOfBoundsException;
  @*/
public /*@pure@*/ Object get(int index);
```

The first of the two JML* contracts is translated to a JavaDL* contract

$$\left(\text{get}, \text{self}, (\text{index}), \text{res}, \text{heap}^{pre}, \text{exc}, pre, post, \dot{\emptyset}, total\right),$$

where $\text{self} : \text{List} \in \mathcal{PV}$, where $\text{index} : Int \in \mathcal{PV}$, where $\text{res} : Object \in \mathcal{PV}$, where $\text{heap}^{pre} : Heap \in \mathcal{PV}$, where $\text{exc} : \text{Exception} \in \mathcal{PV}$, and where pre and $post$ are as follows:

$$pre = 0 \leq \text{index} \wedge \text{index} < \text{self.size()} \wedge \text{self}.inv$$
$$post = \left(\text{exc} \doteq \textbf{null} \rightarrow \text{res} \doteq \text{self.get}(\text{index}) \wedge \text{res} \neq \textbf{null} \wedge \text{self}.inv\right)$$
$$\wedge \left(instance_{\text{Exception}}(\text{exc}) \rightarrow false \wedge \text{self}.inv\right)$$

Intuitively, the contract demands that if `get` is called in a state in which the argument `index` is between 0 and `self.size()` and in which the invariants of the receiver object hold, then (i) the call terminates, (ii) the termination is by returning normally, not by throwing an exception, (iii) the returned value is the value of the term `self.get(index)`, (iv) the returned value is not *null*, (v) the invariants of the receiver object hold in the post-state, and (vi) the post-state heap is unchanged over the pre-state heap, except that new objects may have been created and initialised.

The second JML* contract leads to a JavaDL* contract that is identical to the first one, except for the precondition *pre* and the postcondition *post*:

$$pre = \left(\text{index} < 0 \vee \text{self.size()} \leq \text{index}\right) \wedge \text{self}.inv$$
$$post = \left(\text{exc} \doteq \textbf{null} \rightarrow false \wedge \text{self}.inv\right)$$
$$\wedge \left(instance_{\text{Exception}}(\text{exc})\right.$$
$$\left.\rightarrow instance_{\text{IndexOutOfBoundsException}}(\text{exc}) \wedge \text{self}.inv\right)$$

The contract demands that if `get` is called in a state in which the argument `index` is out of bounds and in which the invariants of the receiver object hold, then (i) the call terminates, (ii) the termination is by throwing an exception, (iii) the thrown exception is of type `IndexOutOfBoundsException`, (iv) the invariants of the receiver object hold in the post-state, and (v) the post-state heap is unchanged over the pre-state heap, except that new objects may have been created and initialised.   *

In JML*, method contracts for pure methods can contain depends clauses. For example, the first contract of Example 6.3 contains a depends clause "**accessible footprint**". On the level of JavaDL*, depends clauses are not part of method contracts. Rather, a JML* contract with a depends clause additionally gives rise to a separate *dependency contract*. Dependency contracts are introduced in Subsection 6.3.2 below.

6.3.2. Dependency Contracts

Where a method contract describes the behaviour of a method in a program, a *dependency contract* provides an upper bound on the locations that an observer symbol may depend on.

Definition 6.4 (Dependency contracts). *A dependency contract depct is a tuple*

$$depct = \big(obs, \texttt{self}, (\texttt{a}_1, \ldots, \texttt{a}_m), pre, dep\big),$$

where obs is an observer function symbol $obs : Heap, C, A_1, \ldots, A_m \to A \in \mathcal{F}$ *or an observer predicate symbol* $obs : Heap, C, A_1, \ldots, A_m \in \mathcal{P}$; *where* $\texttt{self} : D \in \mathcal{PV}$ *for some* $D \preceq C$; *where* $\texttt{a}_1 : A_1, \ldots, \texttt{a}_m : A_m \in \mathcal{PV}$; *where* $pre \in Fma_\Sigma$; *and where* $dep \in Term_\Sigma^{LocSet}$.

A dependency contract $\big(obs, \texttt{self}, (\texttt{a}_1, \ldots, \texttt{a}_m), pre, dep\big)$ with $\texttt{self} : D$ constrains the allowed dependencies of the observer symbol *obs* for objects of type D, including subtypes of D (behavioural subtyping). The program variables $\texttt{self}$ and $\texttt{a}_1, \ldots, \texttt{a}_m$ represent the receiver object and the parameters of *obs* (respectively) in the precondition *pre* and in the dependency term *dep*.

Every JML* method contract containing at least one depends clause leads to a JavaDL* dependency contract. The dependency term *dep* of the dependency contract is the result of translating the depends clauses, where multiple clauses are connected by $\dot{\cup}$. The precondition *pre* of the dependency contract is the precondition of the JML* method contract. Dependency contracts are furthermore created from depends clauses for model fields. The precondition *pre* of dependency contracts for model fields is the formula $\texttt{self}.inv$.

Example 6.4. Consider again the JML* method contracts of method **get** in the **List** interface of Figure 3.1, discussed in Example 6.3. The first of the two contracts contains a depends clause "**accessible footprint**", which gives rise to a dependency contract

$$\big(\texttt{m}, \texttt{self}, (\texttt{index}), pre, \texttt{self.footprint}\big),$$

where self : List $\in \mathcal{PV}$, where index : $Int \in \mathcal{PV}$, and where *pre* is the formula

$$0 \leq \text{index} \wedge \text{index} < \text{self.size()} \wedge \text{self}.inv.$$

The contract demands that the value of the term self.get(index) depends at most on the values of the locations in self.footprint, provided that index is within bounds and that the invariants of self hold. *

Example 6.5. The depends clause "**accessible** footprint: footprint" in the List interface of Figure 3.1 is translated to a dependency contract

$$\big(\text{footprint, self, (), self}.inv, \text{self.footprint}\big),$$

which demands that the value of self.footprint should depend only on the values of the locations in self.footprint itself, provided that the invariants of self hold at the time. *

6.4. Proof Obligations

The contracts of Section 6.3 give rise to *proof obligations*, i.e., to JavaDL* formulas whose logical validity must be established in order for the program to be considered correct. For every method contract *mct* of the specification and every subtype E of the type to which the contract belongs (i.e., every subtype of the type of the contract's program variable self), the validity of a proof obligation *CorrectMethodContract(mct, E)* must be proven (Subsection 6.4.1). Analogously, there is a proof obligation *CorrectDependencyContract(depct, E)* for every dependency contract *depct* and every subtype E of the type to which the dependency contract belongs (Subsection 6.4.2).

We consider the overall program to be correct with respect to the specification if and only if all the individual proof obligation formulas are logically valid. The axioms of the specification, as described in Section 6.2, are implicitly assumed. Thus, more precisely, the program is considered correct if and only if all proof obligations are valid for all Kripke structures that satisfy the axioms.

Even though semantically all axioms are assumptions for all proof obligations, in practice it may be undesirable to actually *use* all of them in all proofs. Some of the axioms are implementational secrets of a particular class, and should not be exposed to proofs that belong to other classes if the verification is to be modular. If such secrets are made use of only in "local" proofs, then also the effect that changing them has on previously conducted proofs remains localised. The visibility levels of JML* may be used to determine whether a particular axiom should be available for a particular proof: each axiom has an associated visibility level, and in a proof for a proof obligation *CorrectMethodContract(mct, E)* or

CorrectMethodContract(depct, E), one may want to use only the axioms that are visible in the class or interface *E*, according to Java's visibility rules.

The createdness axioms of Subsection 6.2.1 have the same visibility as the corresponding observer symbols. The pure method axioms of Subsection 6.2.2 have **private** visibility, because they lead to exposing the implementation of the pure method in the particular class. For the represents clause axioms of Subsection 6.2.3 and the object invariant axioms of Subsection 6.2.4, the visibility level is given explicitly as a part of the specification.

6.4.1. Proof Obligations for Method Contracts

The proof obligation formulas for method contracts are defined in Definition 6.5 below. As we are interested in their logical validity, the initial values of the occurring program variables can be seen as being implicitly universally quantified.

Definition 6.5 (Proof obligations for method contracts). *Given a method contract*

$$mct = \big(\texttt{m}, \texttt{self}, (\texttt{a}_1, \ldots, \texttt{a}_m), \texttt{res}, \texttt{heap}^{pre}, \texttt{exc}, pre, post, mod, \tau\big)$$

with $\texttt{self} : D$, *and given a type* $E \in \mathcal{T}$ *with* $E \preceq D$, *the proof obligation formula* *CorrectMethodContract(mct, E)* $\in Fma_\Sigma$ *is defined as*

$pre \wedge wellFormed(\texttt{heap}) \wedge reachableIn$
$\wedge\, \texttt{self} \neq \textbf{null} \wedge \texttt{self}.created \doteq TRUE \wedge exactInstance_E(\texttt{self})$
$\rightarrow \{\texttt{heap}^{pre} := \texttt{heap}\}[\![\texttt{exc} = \textbf{null};$

$$\texttt{try } \{ \texttt{ res } = \texttt{self.m}(\texttt{a}_1, \ldots, \texttt{a}_m); \ \}$$
$$\texttt{catch(Exception e)} \ \{ \ \texttt{exc} = \texttt{e}; \ \}]\!](post \wedge frame)$$

where:
- $[\![\cdot]\!]$ *stands for* $[\cdot]$ *if* $\tau = partial$ *and for* $\langle\cdot\rangle$ *if* $\tau = total$
- *frame* $\in Fma_\Sigma$ *is the formula (as in Definition 5.9 with* $n = 0$*)*

$$\forall Object\ o;\ \forall Field\ f;\ \big((o, f) \dot{\in} \{\texttt{heap} := \texttt{heap}^{pre}\}mod \,\dot{\cup}\, unusedLocs(\texttt{heap}^{pre})$$
$$\vee\ select_{Any}(\texttt{heap}, o, f) \doteq select_{Any}(\texttt{heap}^{pre}, o, f)\big)$$

- *reachableIn* $\in Fma_\Sigma$ *is the formula (as in Definition 5.9)*

$$\bigwedge_{i \in \{1,\ldots,m\},\ \alpha(\texttt{a}_i) \preceq Object} (\texttt{a}_i \doteq \textbf{null} \vee \texttt{a}_i.created \doteq TRUE)$$
$$\wedge \bigwedge_{i \in \{1,\ldots,m\},\ \alpha(\texttt{a}_i) = LocSet} disjoint(\texttt{a}_i, unusedLocs(\texttt{heap}))$$

The proof obligation *CorrectMethodContract*(*mct*, *E*) formalises the meaning of the method contract *mct* for receiver objects of dynamic type *E*, which has been described on an intuitive level in Section 6.3. Besides the precondition *pre*, we assume that the heap is well-formed, that the argument variables $a_1, \ldots, a_n$ hold neither references to non-created objects nor location sets containing locations of non-created objects, and that the receiver object is non-null and created. The **try-catch**-block serves to catch any exception thrown by the method, and to make it available in the variable **exc** of the contract.

The formula *frame* states that the modifies clause *mod* is respected. This is as in the loopInvariant rule of Definition 5.9, except that here, there are no local variables $b_1, \ldots, b_n$ that must be reset to their pre-state values before evaluating *mod*. The method m may assign to its formal parameter variables, but it cannot modify the variables $a_1, \ldots, a_n$ which serve as actual parameters to m. Thus, the only local variables changed within the modality are **res** and **exc**, which are not supposed to occur in *mod*.

Example 6.6. Let $mct_{\texttt{get}}$ be the first of the two method contracts given for the **get** method in Example 6.3. For $E = \texttt{List}$, the proof obligation formula *CorrectMethodContract*($mct_{\texttt{get}}$, List) is trivially valid, because List is an interface type and thus $exactInstance_{\texttt{List}}(\texttt{self})$ is unsatisfiable. Interesting instances of the proof obligation occur if $E \preceq \texttt{List}$ is neither an interface nor an abstract class. For $E = \texttt{ArrayList}$, *CorrectMethodContract*($mct_{\texttt{get}}$, ArrayList) is:

$pre \wedge wellFormed(\texttt{heap})$

$\wedge\, \texttt{self} \neq \textbf{null} \wedge \texttt{self}.created \doteq TRUE \wedge exactInstance_{\texttt{ArrayList}}(\texttt{self})$

$\rightarrow \{\texttt{heap}^{pre} := \texttt{heap}\}\langle\texttt{exc} = \textbf{null};$

$\qquad\qquad\qquad \textbf{try } \{ \texttt{ res = self.get(index); } \}$

$\qquad\qquad\qquad \textbf{catch}(\texttt{Exception e}) \texttt{ \{ exc = e; \}}\rangle(post \wedge frame)$

where *pre* and *post* are as in Example 6.3, and where *frame* is the formula

$\forall Object\; o; \forall Field\; f; \big((o, f) \,\dot{\in}\, \{\texttt{heap} := \texttt{heap}^{pre}\}\,\dot{\emptyset}\,\dot{\cup}\, unusedLocs(\texttt{heap}^{pre})$

$\qquad \vee\, select_{Any}(\texttt{heap}, o, f) \doteq select_{Any}(\texttt{heap}^{pre}, o, f)\big).$

The proof obligation is valid under the assumption of the pureImpl and repSimple axioms that define **size**, **get** and *inv* for objects of dynamic type **ArrayList**. When proving this, one of the first steps is to use the expandMethod rule of Figure 5.9 to inline the body of **get** provided in **ArrayList**. $\qquad\qquad *$

Method contracts attached to *constructors* are not covered by the formal definitions of this chapter, but are nevertheless supported by the implementation in KeY. The proof obligation for such contracts is essentially as in Definition 6.5, except that (i) the statement "**res = self.m($a_1, \ldots, a_m$);**" is replaced by "`self = new C(a`$_1$`,...,a`$_m$`);`", (ii) all assumptions about `self` are omitted, and (iii) there is only one such proof obligation, not one for every E. This reflects the design choice that in JML* constructor contracts apply to whole allocation statements `new C(...)`, not only to the constructor body (Section 3.3).

6.4.2. Proof Obligations for Dependency Contracts

The proof obligations for dependency contracts are defined in Definition 6.6 below.

Definition 6.6 (Proof obligations for dependency contracts). *Given a dependency contract*

$$depct = \big(obs, \texttt{self}, (\texttt{a}_1, \ldots, \texttt{a}_m), pre, dep\big)$$

with `self` $: D$, *and given a type* $E \in \mathcal{T}$ *with* $E \preceq D$, *the proof obligation formula* $CorrectDependencyContract(depct, E) \in Fma_\Sigma$ *is defined as follows:*

$$pre \wedge wellFormed(\texttt{heap}) \wedge wellFormed(h) \wedge reachableIn$$
$$\wedge\, \texttt{self} \not\doteq \textbf{null} \wedge \texttt{self}.created \doteq TRUE \wedge exactInstance_E(\texttt{self})$$
$$\rightarrow \texttt{self}.obs(\texttt{a}_1, \ldots, \texttt{a}_m)$$
$$\equiv \{\texttt{heap} := anon(\texttt{heap}, allLocs \setminus dep, h)\}\big(\texttt{self}.obs(\texttt{a}_1, \ldots, \texttt{a}_m)\big)$$

where:
- $\equiv$ *stands for* $\doteq$ *if* $obs \in \mathcal{F}$ *and for* $\leftrightarrow$ *if* $obs \in \mathcal{P}$
- $h : Heap \in \mathcal{F}$ *is fresh*
- *reachableIn* $\in Fma_\Sigma$ *is the formula (as in Definitions 5.9 and 6.5)*

$$\bigwedge_{i \in \{1,\ldots,m\},\ \alpha(\texttt{a}_i) \preceq Object} (\texttt{a}_i \doteq \textbf{null} \vee \texttt{a}_i.created \doteq TRUE)$$
$$\wedge \bigwedge_{i \in \{1,\ldots,m\},\ \alpha(\texttt{a}_i) = LocSet} disjoint(\texttt{a}_i, unusedLocs(\texttt{heap}))$$

The proof obligation formalises the notion of *obs* "depending" only on the locations in *dep*: if we change the heap array passed to *obs* by modifying all locations except for those in *dep* in an unknown way, then this must not affect the "observed" value.

Example 6.7. Let $depct_{\texttt{get}}$ be the dependency contract for the `get` method of the `List` interface given in Example 6.4. $CorrectDependencyContract(depct_{\texttt{get}}, \texttt{List})$

is trivially valid, because $exactInstance_{\texttt{List}}(\texttt{self})$ is unsatisfiable. More interesting is $CorrectDependencyContract(depct_{\texttt{get}}, \texttt{ArrayList})$:

$0 \leq \texttt{index} \wedge \texttt{index} < \texttt{self.size()} \wedge \texttt{self}.inv \wedge wellFormed(\texttt{heap})$

$\wedge\ wellFormed(h) \wedge \texttt{self} \neq \textbf{null} \wedge \texttt{self}.created \doteq TRUE$

$\wedge\ exactInstance_{\texttt{ArrayList}}(\texttt{self})$

$\rightarrow \texttt{self.get(index)}$

$\qquad \doteq \{\texttt{heap} := anon(\texttt{heap}, allLocs \setminus \texttt{self.footprint}, h)\}(\texttt{self.get(index)})$

The proof obligation is valid under the assumption of the purelmpl axiom for get and the repSimple axiom for footprint (Example 6.1). By the axiom for get, the value of the term $\texttt{self.get(index)}$ is the result of executing the implementation of get in ArrayList. The only two locations read by this implementation (Figure 2.1) are the array field of self and the component at position index of the array pointed to by self.array. By the axiom for footprint, we know that these locations are elements of self.footprint. Thus, they are not affected by the anonymisation.   *

Example 6.8. Let $depct_{\texttt{footprint}}$ be the dependency contract for footprint discussed in Example 6.5. The formula $CorrectDependencyContract(depct_{\texttt{footprint}},$ ArrayList) is:

$\texttt{self}.inv \wedge wellFormed(\texttt{heap}) \wedge wellFormed(h)$

$\wedge\ \texttt{self} \neq \textbf{null} \wedge \texttt{self}.created \doteq TRUE \wedge exactInstance_{\texttt{ArrayList}}(\texttt{self})$

$\rightarrow \texttt{self.footprint}$

$\qquad \doteq \{\texttt{heap} := anon(\texttt{heap}, allLocs \setminus \texttt{self.footprint}, h)\}(\texttt{self.footprint})$

The formula is valid under the assumption of the repSimple axiom for footprint considered in Example 6.1. The axiom reads only the array field of self. Because the axiom defines this location to itself be an element of self.footprint, the location is not affected by the anonymisation.   *

Example 6.9. Suppose that the program *Prg* contains the following class:

```
class C {
    int f;
    //@ public model boolean b;
    //@ private represents b = (\forall C c; 0 < c.f);
    //@ public accessible b: \everything;
}
```

The depends clause gives rise to a dependency contract $depct_{\texttt{b}}$. The proof obligation $CorrectDependencyContract(depct_{\mathtt{b}}, \mathtt{C})$ is:

$\mathtt{self}.inv \wedge wellFormed(\mathtt{heap}) \wedge wellFormed(h)$
$\wedge\, \mathtt{self} \not\doteq \mathbf{null} \wedge \mathtt{self}.created \doteq TRUE \wedge exactInstance_{\mathtt{C}}(\mathtt{self})$
$\rightarrow \mathtt{self.b}$

$\quad\quad\quad \leftrightarrow \big\{\mathtt{heap} := anon(\mathtt{heap}, allLocs \,\dot\setminus\, (allLocs \,\dot\setminus\, unusedLocs(\mathtt{heap})), h)\big\}(\mathtt{self.b})$

The term $allLocs \,\dot\setminus\, (allLocs \,\dot\setminus\, unusedLocs(\mathtt{heap}))$ can be simplified to the term $unusedLocs(\mathtt{heap})$. Furthermore, the definition of $I(anon)$ implies that the term $anon(\mathtt{heap}, unusedLocs(\mathtt{heap}), h)$ is equivalent to $anon(\mathtt{heap}, \dot\emptyset, h)$. Because of this and because of the definition of $\mathtt{b}$ given in the represents clause, the formula above can be reformulated as:

$\quad\quad \mathtt{self}.inv \wedge wellFormed(\mathtt{heap}) \wedge wellFormed(h)$
$\quad\quad\quad \wedge\, \mathtt{self} \not\doteq \mathbf{null} \wedge \mathtt{self}.created \doteq TRUE \wedge exactInstance_{\mathtt{C}}(\mathtt{self})$
$\quad\quad\quad\quad \rightarrow \forall \mathtt{C}\, c; (c.created \doteq TRUE \rightarrow 0 < c.\mathtt{f})$

$\quad\quad\quad\quad\quad \leftrightarrow \big\{\mathtt{heap} := anon(\mathtt{heap}, \dot\emptyset, h)\big\} \forall \mathtt{C}\, c; (c.created \doteq TRUE \rightarrow 0 < c.\mathtt{f})$

After this reformulation it should be evident that the proof obligation is *not* logically valid. The anonymisation may create new objects, and this may change the truth value of the formula $\forall \mathtt{C}\, c; (c.created \doteq TRUE \rightarrow 0 < c.\mathtt{f})$, which demands that some property holds for all created objects of type $\mathtt{C}$. This demonstrates that even a depends clause of **\everything** is meaningful: it is respected only if the constrained model field or pure method is not influenced by creating and initialising new objects. $\quad\quad *$

6.5. Contract Rules

Besides giving rise to proof obligations, the contracts of Section 6.3 can also be used as assumptions in the proofs for other contracts. Method calls can be symbolically executed with the useMethodContract rule (Subsection 6.5.1) instead of the expandMethod rule of Figure 5.9, and dependency contracts can be made use of with the useDependencyContract rule (Subsection 6.5.2).

Using method and dependency contracts leads to dependencies between proofs, where the correctness of one proof relies on the existence of one or more other proofs. Circular dependencies must be avoided: a contract must not be applied if this would lead to cyclic dependencies between proofs. In particular, a contract must not be used in its own proof. This is as in JavaDL [Roth, 2006], and a proof management mechanism that prevents such circularities is implemented in the KeY system. A side effect of entirely forbidding circular contract applications is that (mutually) recursive methods cannot be handled. Extending the contract mechanism to support recursion is possible, but beyond the scope of this work. For JavaDL, such an extension is described by Bubel [2007].

Besides avoiding a contract application if it would lead to circular dependencies between proofs, modularity calls for respecting the *visibility* of the contract to be applied: when proving either *CorrectMethodContract*(*mct*, *E*) or *CorrectDependencyContract*(*depct*, *E*), a contract *c* should be applied only if *c* is visible in *E*.

6.5.1. Rule for Method Contracts

The rule for making use of method contracts is defined in Definition 6.7 below.

Definition 6.7 (Rule useMethodContract).

$$\Gamma \Rightarrow \{u\}\{w\}(pre \wedge wellFormed(\text{heap}) \wedge reachableIn \qquad (pre)$$
$$\wedge\, \texttt{self} \neq \textbf{null} \wedge \texttt{self}.\,created \doteq TRUE), \Delta$$

$$\Gamma \Rightarrow \{u\}\{w\}\{\text{heap}^{pre} := \text{heap}\}\{v\} \qquad\qquad (post)$$
$$(post \wedge wellFormed(h) \wedge reachableOut$$
$$\rightarrow [\![\pi\ \texttt{if(exc\,!=null)\ throw\ exc;}$$
$$\texttt{r\ =\ res;}\ \omega]\!]\varphi), \Delta$$

$$\overline{\Gamma \Rightarrow \{u\}[\![\pi\ \texttt{r\ =\ }o.\texttt{m}(a'_1, \ldots, a'_m);\ \omega]\!]\varphi, \Delta}$$

where:

- $o \in \mathit{Term}_\Sigma^E$ *for some* $E \in \mathcal{T}$ *such that there is a method contract*

$$mct = \big(\texttt{m}, \texttt{self}, (\texttt{a}_1, \ldots, \texttt{a}_m), \texttt{res}, \texttt{heap}^{pre}, \texttt{exc}, pre, post, mod, \tau\big)$$

- $\texttt{self} : D$ *for some* $D \in \mathcal{T}$ *with* $E \preceq D$
- $\tau = total$ *if the modality* $[\![\cdot]\!]$ *is* $\langle\cdot\rangle$*, and where* τ *does not matter otherwise*
- $\texttt{self}, \texttt{a}_1, \ldots, \texttt{a}_m, \texttt{res}, \texttt{heap}^{pre}$ *and* $\texttt{exc}$ *do not occur in the conclusion*
- *reachableIn* $\in \mathit{Fma}_\Sigma$ *is the formula (as in Definitions 5.9, 6.5 and 6.6)*

$$\bigwedge_{i \in \{1, \ldots, m\},\ \alpha(\texttt{a}_i) \preceq Object} (\texttt{a}_i \doteq \textbf{null} \vee \texttt{a}_i.\,created \doteq TRUE)$$

$$\wedge \bigwedge_{i \in \{1, \ldots, m\},\ \alpha(\texttt{a}_i) = LocSet} disjoint(\texttt{a}_i, unusedLocs(\text{heap}))$$

- *reachableOut* $\in \mathit{Fma}_\Sigma$ *is the formula*

$$(\texttt{res} \doteq \textbf{null} \vee \texttt{res}.\,created \doteq TRUE)$$
$$\wedge\,(\texttt{exc} \doteq \textbf{null} \vee \texttt{exc}.\,created \doteq TRUE)$$

if $\alpha(\texttt{res}) \preceq Object$*, and the formula* $\texttt{exc} \doteq \textbf{null} \vee \texttt{exc}.\,created \doteq TRUE$ *otherwise*

- $v = \big(\text{heap} := anon(\text{heap}, mod, h) \,\|\, \text{res} := r \,\|\, \text{exc} := e\big)$
- $w = \big(\text{self} := o \,\|\, \text{a}_1 := a_1' \,\|\, \ldots \,\|\, \text{a}_m := a_m'\big)$
- $h : Heap \in \mathcal{F}, \; r : \alpha(\text{res}) \in \mathcal{F}$ and $e : \text{Exception} \in \mathcal{F}$ are fresh

The formulas *reachableIn* and *reachableOut* have the same roles as in the loopInvariant rule of Definition 5.9. Like in Definition 5.9, the update v anonymises the locations that may be changed by the call to m—namely the members of the modifies clause *mod*—by setting them to unknown values with the help of the fresh constant symbol h. It also sets the variables res and exc to unknown values denoted by the fresh constant symbols r and e, respectively. The update w instantiates the variables used in the contract with the corresponding terms in the method call statement.

In the second premiss of the rule, the method call is replaced by a conditional statement and an assignment. If the call throws an exception (exc != null), then the control flow of the program continues with raising this exception. Otherwise, the returned value is assigned to r, and the control flow continues normally with the next active statement in $\pi \, \omega$.

Theorem 6.1 below states that the useMethodContract rule is sound, provided that for all subtypes $F \preceq E$ of the static receiver type E, the proof obligation formula *CorrectMethodContract*(mct, F) is logically valid.

Theorem 6.1 (Soundness of useMethodContract). *Let the formula sets* $\Gamma, \Delta \in 2^{Fma_\Sigma}$, *the update* $u \in Upd_\Sigma$, *the modal operator* $[\![\cdot]\!] \in \{[\cdot], \langle\cdot\rangle\}$, *the prefix* π, *the postfix* ω, *the program variable* $\text{r} \in \mathcal{PV}$, *the term* $o \in Term_\Sigma^E$, *the method* m, *the terms* $a_1', \ldots, a_m' \in Term_\Sigma$, *the formula* $\varphi \in Fma_\Sigma$, *the method contract* $mct = \big(\text{m}, \text{self}, (\text{a}_1, \ldots, \text{a}_m), \text{res}, \text{heap}^{pre}, \text{exc}, pre, post, mod, \tau\big)$, *the formulas reachableIn, reachableOut* $\in Fma_\Sigma$, *the updates* $v, w \in Upd_\Sigma$, *and the constant symbols* $h, r, e \in \mathcal{F}$ *all be as in Definition 6.7. If*

$$\models \Gamma \;\Rightarrow\; \{u\}\{w\}\big(pre \wedge wellFormed(\text{heap}) \wedge reachableIn$$
$$\wedge \, \text{self} \not\doteq \text{null} \wedge \text{self}.\,created \doteq TRUE\big), \; \Delta$$

$$\models \Gamma \;\Rightarrow\; \{u\}\{w\}\{\text{heap}^{pre} := \text{heap}\}\{v\}$$
$$\big(post \wedge wellFormed(h) \wedge reachableOut$$
$$\rightarrow [\![\pi \; \mathbf{if}(\text{exc} \mathrel{!=} \mathbf{null}) \; \mathbf{throw} \; \text{exc};$$
$$\text{r = res}; \; \omega]\!]\varphi\big), \; \Delta$$

and if for all types $F \in \mathcal{T}$ *with* $F \preceq E$ *we have*

$$\models CorrectMethodContract(mct, F),$$

then the following holds:

$$\models \Gamma \;\Rightarrow\; \{u\}[\![\pi \; \text{r = } o.\text{m}(a_1', \ldots, a_m'); \; \omega]\!]\varphi, \; \Delta.$$

A proof of Theorem 6.1 is contained in Appendix A.7. The proof is similar to the proof of Theorem 5.5 (Appendix A.6) in many respects. In particular, it also makes use of Lemma 5.4.

Using contracts for *constructors* works essentially as in Definition 6.7, except that (i) the first active statement in the conclusion is of the form "$r = \textbf{new } C(a'_1,$ $\ldots, a'_m);$", (ii) the propositions about $\texttt{self}$ in the first premiss are omitted, (iii) in the update w the sub-update $\texttt{self} := o$ is replaced with $\texttt{self} := r$, and (iv) the second premiss contains an additional assumption besides "$post \wedge wellFormed(h) \wedge reachableOut$", namely the formula

$$exactInstance_C(r) \wedge select_{Boolean}(\textbf{heap}^{pre}, r, created) \doteq FALSE$$
$$\wedge \, r.created \doteq TRUE,$$

which states that the dynamic type of the created object is C, that the object was not created previously, and that it is created now.

6.5.2. Rule for Dependency Contracts

Dependency contracts can be used in proofs with the useDependencyContract rule defined in Definition 6.8 below.

Definition 6.8 (Rule useDependencyContract).

$$\frac{\Gamma, \; guard \to equal \; \Rightarrow \; \Delta}{\Gamma \; \Rightarrow \; \Delta}$$

where:
- *the term or formula $obs(h^{post}, o, a'_1, \ldots, a'_m)$ occurs in Γ or in Δ*
- *$h^{post} = f_k(f_{k-1}(\ldots(f_1(h^{pre}, \ldots)))))$ for some $f_1, \ldots, f_k \in \{store, create, anon\}$ with $1 \leq k$ and for some $h^{pre} \in Term_{\Sigma}^{Heap}$*
- *$o \in Term_{\Sigma}^E$ for some $E \in \mathcal{T}$ such that there is a dependency contract*

$$depct = \big(obs, \texttt{self}, (\texttt{a}_1, \ldots, \texttt{a}_m), pre, dep\big)$$

- *$\texttt{self} : D$ for some $D \in \mathcal{T}$ with $E \preceq D$*
- *$\texttt{self}$ and $\texttt{a}_1, \ldots, \texttt{a}_m$ do not occur in the conclusion*
- *$\texttt{heap}^{pre} : Heap \in \mathcal{PV}$ is fresh*
- *$w = (\texttt{self} := o \, \| \, \texttt{a}_1 := a'_1 \, \| \, \ldots \, \| \, \texttt{a}_m := a'_m)$ (as in Definition 6.7)*
- *$mod = allLocs \setminus dep$*
- *$frame \in Fma_{\Sigma}$ is the formula (as in Definitions 5.9 and 6.5)*

$$\forall Object \; o; \forall Field \; f; ((o, f) \,\dot{\in}\, \{\texttt{heap} := \texttt{heap}^{pre}\} mod \;\dot{\cup}\; unusedLocs(\texttt{heap}^{pre})$$
$$\vee \; select_{Any}(\texttt{heap}, o, f) \doteq select_{Any}(\texttt{heap}^{pre}, o, f))$$

- *reachableIn* $\in Fma_\Sigma$ *is the formula (as in Definitions 5.9, 6.5 and 6.6)*

$$\bigwedge_{i \in \{1,\ldots,m\},\ \alpha(\mathtt{a}_i) \preceq Object} (\mathtt{a}_i \doteq \mathbf{null} \lor \mathtt{a}_i.\,created \doteq TRUE)$$

$$\land \bigwedge_{i \in \{1,\ldots,m\},\ \alpha(\mathtt{a}_i) = LocSet} disjoint(\mathtt{a}_i,\, unusedLocs(\mathtt{heap}))$$

- *guard* $\in Fma_\Sigma$ *is the formula*

$$wellFormed(h^{pre}) \land wellFormed(h^{post})$$
$$\land \{w\}\big(\{\mathtt{heap} := h^{pre}\}(pre \land reachableIn \land \mathtt{self} \not\doteq \mathbf{null}$$
$$\land \mathtt{self}.\,created \doteq TRUE) \land \{\mathtt{heap}^{pre} := h^{pre} \,\|\, \mathtt{heap} := h^{post}\}frame\big)$$

- *equal* $\in Fma_\Sigma$ *is the formula*

$$obs(h^{pre}, o, a_1', \ldots, a_m') \equiv obs(h^{post}, o, a_1', \ldots, a_m')$$

where $\equiv$ *stands for* $\doteq$ *if obs* $\in \mathcal{F}$ *and for* $\leftrightarrow$ *if obs* $\in \mathcal{P}$

The useDependencyContract rule adds an assumption *guard* $\to$ *equal* to the sequent, which relates the value of *obs* for the heap arrays denoted by the terms h^{pre} and h^{post}, where h^{post} results from h^{pre} by an arbitrary cascade of applications of the function symbols *store*, *create* and *anon*. Such cascades are created by symbolically executing programs, using the rules of Figure 5.9 as well as the useMethodContractRule of Definition 6.7, and by simplifying the resulting updates.

The formula *guard* corresponds to the left hand side of the implication in the proof obligation of Definition 6.6. Like in Definition 6.7, the update w serves to instantiate the program variables of the contract with the terms occurring as arguments to *obs*. The formula *reachableIn* has its usual role. The formula *frame* must hold if we use h^{pre} for $\mathtt{heap}^{pre}$ and h^{post} for $\mathtt{heap}$; i.e., when going from h^{pre} to h^{post}, the locations in *dep* must not change. If *guard* holds, then the dependency contract guarantees that *obs* has the same value for both heap arrays, as expressed by the formula *equal*.

Besides the property that only certain locations change, the other typically necessary property of a change in the heap is that the change does not deallocate previously created objects; see for example Lemma 5.4. For method calls, this property is guaranteed by Java itself. Similarly, for the state change from h^{pre} to h^{post}, the absence of deallocations is guaranteed by the definitions of the interpretation of the function symbols *store*, *create* and *anon*. This is formalised in Lemma 6.2 below.

Lemma 6.2 (No deallocations). *Let $h^{post} \in Term_\Sigma^{Heap}$ with*

$$h^{post} = f_k(f_{k-1}(\dots(f_1(h^{pre},\dots))))$$

for some $f_1,\dots,f_k \in \{store, create, anon\}$ with $1 \leq k$ and for some $h^{pre} \in Term_\Sigma^{Heap}$. Let furthermore $\mathbf{heap}^{pre} : Heap \in \mathcal{PV}$, and let $noDeallocs \in Fma_\Sigma$ be the formula (as in Lemma 5.4)

$$unusedLocs(\mathbf{heap}) \;\dot{\subseteq}\; unusedLocs(\mathbf{heap}^{pre})$$
$$\wedge\; select_{Any}(\mathbf{heap}, \mathbf{null}, created) \;\dot{=}\; select_{Any}(\mathbf{heap}^{pre}, \mathbf{null}, created).$$

Then the following holds:

$$\models \{\mathbf{heap}^{pre} := h^{pre} \,\|\, \mathbf{heap} := h^{post}\}\,noDeallocs.$$

The proof for Lemma 6.2 in Appendix A.8 is straightforward. The lemma is needed for the proof of Theorem 6.3 below. The theorem states that the useDependencyContract rule is sound, provided that for all subtypes $F \preceq E$ of the static "receiver" type E, the formula $CorrectDependencyContract(depct, F)$ is logically valid.

Theorem 6.3 (Soundness of useDependencyContract). *Let the sets $\Gamma, \Delta \in 2_\Sigma^{Fma}$, the observer symbol $obs \in \mathcal{F} \cup \mathcal{P}$, the term $h^{post} = f_k(f_{k-1}(\dots(f_1(h^{pre},\dots)))) \in Term_\Sigma^{Heap}$, the term $o \in Term_\Sigma^E$, the terms $a_1',\dots,a_m' \in Term_\Sigma$, the dependency contract $depct = (obs, \mathbf{self}, (\mathbf{a}_1,\dots,\mathbf{a}_m), pre, dep)$, the program variable $\mathbf{heap}^{pre} \in \mathcal{PV}$, the update $w \in Upd_\Sigma$, the term $mod = allLocs \setminus dep \in Term_\Sigma^{LocSet}$, and the formulas $frame, reachableIn, guard, equal \in Fma_\Sigma$ all be as in Definition 6.8. If*

$$\models \Gamma,\; guard \to equal \;\Rightarrow\; \Delta$$

and if for all types $F \in \mathcal{T}$ with $F \preceq E$ we have

$$\models CorrectDependencyContract(depct, F),$$

then the following holds:

$$\models \Gamma \;\Rightarrow\; \Delta.$$

The proof of Theorem 6.3 in Appendix A.9 makes use of Lemma 6.2 and of Lemma 5.4.

Automatic application of the useDependencyContract rule is not as straightforward as automatic application of the useMethodContract rule. The problems are that the rule is nondeterministic in the choice of h^{pre}, and that it can be applied repeatedly for the same combination of h^{pre} and h^{post}, which could lead to non-termination of automatic proof search. However, we can prevent non-termination by avoiding duplicate applications of the rule for the same pair of heap terms on any single branch of the proof tree. To avoid a finite, but large number of "unsuccessful" applications where *guard* cannot be proven and where the application thus does not contribute to the proof, a strategy that appears to work well in practice is to apply the rule only lazily (once all other means of advancing the proof have been exhausted), and only for choices of h^{pre} for which the term or formula $obs(h^{pre}, o, a'_1, \ldots, a'_m)$ already occurs in the sequent. This problem area corresponds to the question of how best to instantiate the two universal quantifiers over heap arrays that are explicitly present in the formula on the dependencies of *reach* seen in Subsection 4.2.3, and that are implicitly present in the semantics of JavaDL* dependency contracts.

6.6. Example

This section is a continuation of Section 3.4. We assume that the program *Prg* contains the interface `List` from Figure 3.1, the class `Client` from Figure 3.2, and the class `ArrayList` from Figure 3.3. As an example for the verification of JML specifications with dynamic frames, we consider a proof for the method `m` of the `Client` class:

```
/*@ normal_behaviour
  @    requires list.\inv && \disjoint(list.footprint, this.*);
  @    requires 0 < list.size();
  @*/
void m(List list) {
    x++;
    Object o = list.get(0);
}
```

The JML* method contract is translated to a JavaDL* method contract

$$mct_{\mathtt{m}} = \left(\mathtt{m}, \mathtt{self}, (\mathtt{list}), \mathtt{res}, \mathtt{heap}^{pre}, \mathtt{exc}, pre, post, mod, total\right),$$

where the precondition *pre*, the postcondition *post* and the modifies clause *mod* are:

$$pre = \mathtt{list}.\mathit{inv} \wedge \mathit{disjoint}\left(\mathtt{list}.\mathtt{footprint}, \mathit{allFields}(\mathtt{self})\right)$$
$$\wedge\, 0 < \mathtt{list}.\mathtt{size}() \wedge \mathtt{self}.\mathit{inv} \wedge \mathtt{list} \neq \mathbf{null}$$
$$post = \mathtt{self}.\mathit{inv} \wedge \mathtt{exc} \doteq \mathbf{null}$$
$$mod = \mathit{allLocs} \setminus \mathit{unusedLocs}(\mathtt{heap})$$

The resulting proof obligation $CorrectMethodContract(mct_m, \texttt{Client})$ is:

$$\texttt{list.}\textit{inv} \wedge \textit{disjoint}(\texttt{list.footprint}, \textit{allFields}(\texttt{self}))$$
$$\wedge\, 0 < \texttt{list.size()} \wedge \texttt{self.}\textit{inv} \wedge \texttt{list} \not\doteq \textbf{null}$$
$$\wedge\, \textit{wellFormed}(\texttt{heap}) \wedge (\texttt{list} \doteq \textbf{null} \vee \texttt{list.}\textit{created} \doteq \textit{TRUE})$$
$$\wedge\, \texttt{self} \not\doteq \textbf{null} \wedge \texttt{self.}\textit{created} \doteq \textit{TRUE} \wedge \textit{exactInstance}_{\texttt{Client}}(\texttt{self})$$
$$\rightarrow \{\texttt{heap}^{pre} := \texttt{heap}\}\langle\texttt{exc} = \textbf{null};$$
$$\texttt{try \{ self.m(list); \}}$$
$$\texttt{catch(Exception e) \{ exc = e; \}}\rangle$$
$$\big(\texttt{self.}\textit{inv} \wedge \texttt{exc} \doteq \textbf{null}$$
$$\wedge\, \forall \textit{Object o}; \forall \textit{Field f};$$
$$((o, f) \mathrel{\dot\in} \{\texttt{heap} := \texttt{heap}^{pre}\}(\textit{allLocs} \setminus \textit{unusedLocs}(\texttt{heap}))$$
$$\mathrel{\dot\cup} \textit{unusedLocs}(\texttt{heap}^{pre})$$
$$\vee\, \textit{select}_{Any}(\texttt{heap}, o, f) \doteq \textit{select}_{Any}(\texttt{heap}^{pre}, o, f))))$$

Note that the method does not return a value, and that thus the assignment of the returned value to the program variable `res` is omitted.

The following axioms of Section 6.2 are visible when proving the validity of the formula $CorrectMethodContract(mct_m, \texttt{Client})$:

- The model field `footprint` of `List` has the JavaDL* type *LocSet*. Thus, there is an axiom elementOfObsIsNullOrCreated for `footprint`, as defined in Subsection 6.2.1:

$$\frac{\Gamma, \; (o, f) \mathrel{\dot\in} \textsf{footprint}(h, \textit{list}), \quad o \doteq \textbf{null} \vee \textit{select}_{Boolean}(h, o, \textit{created}) \doteq \textit{TRUE} \;\Rightarrow\; \Delta}{\Gamma, \; (o, f) \mathrel{\dot\in} \textsf{footprint}(h, \textit{list}) \;\Rightarrow\; \Delta}$$

where *list* is a placeholder for a term of type `List` (or of a subtype). The axiom is visible in the context of `Client`, because it adopts the **public** visibility of `footprint` itself.

- The lack of an object invariant declaration in `Client` is equivalent to a single invariant declaration "**private invariant true**". Because `Client` does not inherit any invariant from its supertypes, this means that there is an implicit represents clause "**private represents \inv = true**" in `Client`. This represents clause gives rise to a repSimple axiom for *inv* as defined in Subsection 6.2.3:

$$\frac{\begin{array}{c} \Gamma,\ exactInstance_{\texttt{Client}}(client) \hspace{4cm} \text{(satisfiability)} \\ \Rightarrow \{\texttt{heap} := h \,\|\, \texttt{self} := client\} \\ (true \leftrightarrow true \lor false \leftrightarrow true),\ \Delta \\ \Gamma',\ exactInstance_{\texttt{Client}}(client)\ \Rightarrow\ \Delta' \hspace{2.5cm} \text{(use case)} \end{array}}{\Gamma,\ exactInstance_{\texttt{Client}}(client)\ \Rightarrow\ \Delta}$$

where *client* is a placeholder for a term of type `Client`, and where Γ' and Δ' are the results of replacing in Γ and in Δ all occurrences of $inv(h, client)$ not below an update or a modality with $\{\texttt{heap} := h \,\|\, \texttt{self} := client\}true$.

- The object invariant declaration "**public invariant** 0 <= size()" in `List` gives rise to an inv axiom for *inv* on objects of type `List`, as discussed in Subsection 6.2.4 and in particular in Example 6.2:

$$\frac{\Gamma,\ inv(h, list),\ \{\texttt{heap} := h \,\|\, \texttt{self} := list\}\big(0 \le \texttt{self.size()}\big)\ \Rightarrow\ \Delta}{\Gamma,\ inv(h, list)\ \Rightarrow\ \Delta}$$

where *list* is a placeholder for a term of type `List` (or of a subtype). The axiom is visible in the context of `Client` because of the **public** visibility of the underlying invariant declaration.

Not visible are for example the purelmpl axioms of Subsection 6.2.2 for the `size` and `get` methods in `ArrayList`, and the repSimple axioms of Subsection 6.2.3 for the model fields `\inv` and `footprint` in `ArrayList`.

The structure of a proof for the proof obligation is shown in Figure 6.1. Starting from the root sequent "$\Rightarrow CorrectMethodContract(mct_{\text{m}}, \texttt{Client})$", the first steps are simplifying the sequent and applying non-splitting first-order rules (indicated as "FOL" in the figure), which leads to the following sequent:

$$\left.\begin{array}{l} \texttt{list}.inv, \\[4pt] \forall Field\ f;\, \big((\texttt{self}, f) \,\dot{\notin}\, \texttt{list.footprint}\big), \\[4pt] 0 < \texttt{list.size()}, \\[4pt] \texttt{self}.inv, \\[4pt] wellFormed(\texttt{heap}), \\[4pt] \texttt{list}.created \,\dot{=}\, TRUE, \\[4pt] \texttt{self}.created \,\dot{=}\, TRUE, \\[4pt] exactInstance_{\texttt{Client}}(\texttt{self}) \end{array}\right\} \Gamma$$

$$\Rightarrow$$

$$\texttt{list} \,\dot{=}\, \textbf{null},$$

$$\texttt{self} \,\dot{=}\, \textbf{null},$$

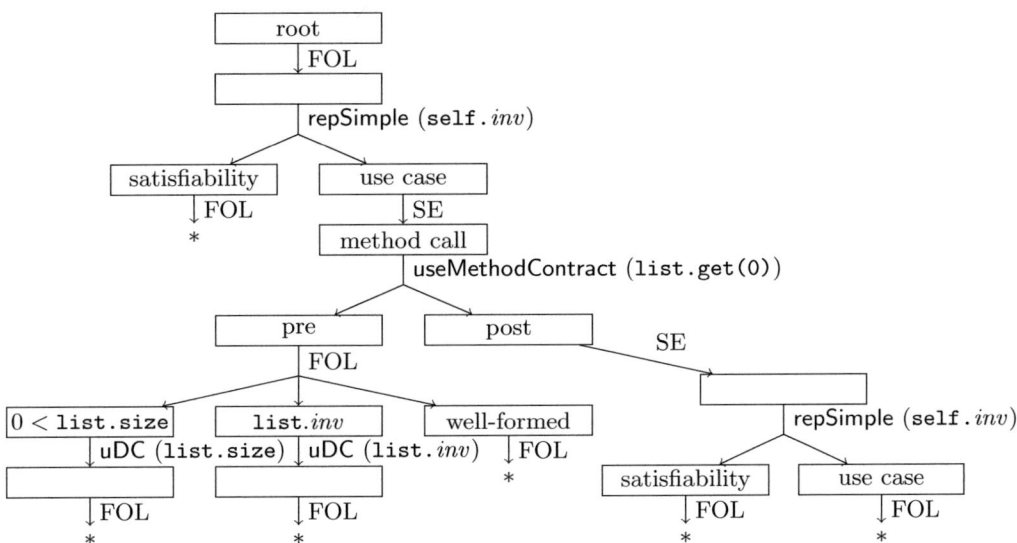

Figure 6.1.: Structure of proof for the method contract of method m in class
        `Client`

$$\langle\texttt{exc = null;}$$
$$\texttt{try \{ self.m(list); \}}$$
$$\texttt{catch(Exception e) \{ exc = e; \}}\rangle(\texttt{self}.\mathit{inv} \wedge \texttt{exc} \doteq \texttt{null})$$

The formula $\mathit{disjoint}(\texttt{list.footprint}, \mathit{allFields}(\texttt{self}))$ has been reduced to
the formula $\forall \mathit{Field}\, f; ((\texttt{self}, f) \notin \texttt{list.footprint})$, using in particular the rules
disjoint and inAllFields of Figure 5.7. The negated occurrences of the formulas
`list` $\doteq$ `null` and `self` $\doteq$ `null` in the antecedent have been replaced by non-
negated occurrences in the succedent via the notLeft rule. The formula *frame*
below the modality has vanished entirely, because it holds trivially due to the
modifies clause being **\everything**. Subsequently, the update $\texttt{heap}^{pre} := \texttt{heap}$
has been eliminated using the dropUpdate$_2$ rule of Figure 5.8, because $\texttt{heap}^{pre}$ no
longer occurred in its scope.

As a next step, we can replace the occurrence of `self.`inv in the antecedent
with its definition, using the repSimple rule for inv in `Client`. The "satisfiability"
branch is trivial to close, because the formula "$\mathit{true} \leftrightarrow \mathit{true} \vee \mathit{false} \leftrightarrow \mathit{true}$" is
logically valid. On the "use case" branch, the formula `self.`inv in the antecedent
is replaced by true (so—because an occurrence of true in the antecedent does not
contribute to the validity of the sequent—the application of repSimple turns out
to be useless in this case).

Next, we start symbolic execution of the program inside the diamond modality, indicated as "SE" in Figure 6.1. As one of the first steps of symbolic execution, the body of the method m being verified is inlined with the expandMethod rule of Figure 5.9. The branch corresponding to the second premiss of expandMethod is trivial to close, and is omitted in the figure. Eventually, symbolic execution reaches the method call "o = list.get(0)" inside m. This call is dispatched using the useMethodContract rule of Subsection 6.5.1. The two method contracts of get are discussed in Example 6.3; here, we use the first of the two contracts, which corresponds to the **normal_behaviour** JML* contract. The application of useMethodContract splits the proof into two branches, called "pre" and "post":

- After applying the update w to the formula below it, the "pre" branch is:

$$\Gamma \Rightarrow$$
$$\texttt{list} \doteq \textbf{null},$$
$$\texttt{self} \doteq \textbf{null},$$
$$\{\texttt{exc} := \textbf{null} \,\|\, \texttt{heap} := store(\texttt{heap}, \texttt{self}, \texttt{x}, \texttt{self.x} + 1)\}$$
$$\big(0 \le 0 \wedge 0 < \texttt{list.size}() \wedge \texttt{list}.\mathit{inv} \wedge \mathit{wellFormed}(\texttt{heap})$$
$$\wedge \texttt{list} \not\doteq \textbf{null} \wedge \texttt{list}.\mathit{created} \doteq \mathit{TRUE}\big)$$

where Γ is the same antecedent as before. Closing the "pre" branch requires showing that the six conjuncts below update hold. The first conjunct $0 \le 0$ holds trivially. For the other conjuncts, we consider a further split of the proof tree into three sub-branches, where the first one corresponds to "$0 < \texttt{list.size}()$", the second one to "$\texttt{list}.\mathit{inv}$", and the third one to "$\mathit{wellFormed}(\texttt{heap}) \wedge \texttt{list} \not\doteq \textbf{null} \wedge \texttt{list}.\mathit{created} \doteq \mathit{TRUE})$":

- "$0 < \texttt{list.size}()$". This branch is:

$$\Gamma \Rightarrow$$
$$\texttt{list} \doteq \textbf{null},$$
$$\texttt{self} \doteq \textbf{null},$$
$$0 < \texttt{size}\big(store(\texttt{heap}, \texttt{self}, \texttt{x}, \texttt{self.x} + 1), \texttt{list}\big)$$

The sequent now contains both the term $\texttt{size}(\texttt{heap}, \texttt{list})$ (inside Γ) and the term $\texttt{size}\big(store(\texttt{heap}, \texttt{self}, \texttt{x}, \texttt{self.x} + 1), \texttt{list}\big)$. This triggers application of the useDependencyContract rule of Subsection 6.5.2 (indicated as uDC in Figure 6.1), where we choose $h^{pre} = \texttt{heap}$ and $h^{post} = store(\texttt{heap}, \texttt{self}, \texttt{x}, \texttt{self.x} + 1)$. The rule uses the dependency contract for $\texttt{size}$ generated out of the JML* depends clause "**accessible footprint**" in line 9 of Figure 3.1. It adds the formula *guard* → *equal* to antecedent, where the subformula *guard* (after some simplification) is:

$$wellFormed(\texttt{heap}) \wedge wellFormed\big(store(\texttt{heap}, \texttt{self}, \texttt{x}, \texttt{self.x} + 1)\big)$$
$$\wedge\ \texttt{list}.inv \wedge \texttt{list} \not\doteq \textbf{null} \wedge \texttt{list}.created \doteq TRUE$$
$$\wedge\ \forall Object\ o; \forall Field\ f;$$
$$\big((o, f) \dot{\in} (allLocs \setminus \texttt{list.footprint}) \dot{\cup} unusedLocs(\texttt{heap})$$
$$\vee\ select_{Any}(store(\texttt{heap}, \texttt{self}, \texttt{x}, \texttt{self.x} + 1), o, f)$$
$$\doteq select_{Any}(\texttt{heap}, o, f)\big)$$

All conjuncts of *guard* follow from the rest of the sequent. In particular, the last conjunct of *guard* is implied by the rest of the sequent, because the only location (o, f) whose value differs between h^{pre} and h^{post} is $(\texttt{self}, \texttt{x})$, which must be an element of $allLocs \setminus \texttt{self.footprint}$ because of the quantified formula in Γ. The formula *equal* is:

$$\texttt{size}(\texttt{heap}, \texttt{list}) \doteq \texttt{size}\big(store(\texttt{heap}, \texttt{self}, \texttt{x}, \texttt{self.x} + 1), o, f), \texttt{list}\big)$$

Because Γ demands that $0 < \texttt{size}(\texttt{heap}, \texttt{list})$, and because the succedent contains the formula $0 < \texttt{size}\big(store(\texttt{heap}, \texttt{self}, \texttt{x}, \texttt{self.x} + 1), o, f), \texttt{list}\big)$, the information given by *equal* is enough to close this branch of the proof.

– "$\texttt{list}.inv$". The branch is:

$$\Gamma \Rightarrow$$
$$\texttt{list} \doteq \textbf{null},$$
$$\texttt{self} \doteq \textbf{null},$$
$$inv\big(store(\texttt{heap}, \texttt{self}, \texttt{x}, \texttt{self.x} + 1), \texttt{list}\big)$$

The sequent now contains both the formula $inv(\texttt{heap}, \texttt{list})$ (inside Γ) and the formula $inv\big(store(\texttt{heap}, \texttt{self}, \texttt{x}, \texttt{self.x}+1), \texttt{list}\big)$. The proof continues as on the "$0 < \texttt{list.size}()$" branch above, except that we apply the useDependencyContract rule for inv instead of for $\texttt{size}$.

– "$wellFormed(\texttt{heap}) \wedge \texttt{list} \not\doteq \textbf{null} \wedge \texttt{list}.created \doteq TRUE$". This branch is easy to close, using propositional reasoning only.

• After some simplification, the "post" branch is:

$$\Gamma \Rightarrow$$
$$\texttt{list} \doteq \textbf{null},$$

$\texttt{self} \doteq \texttt{null},$

$\{\texttt{exc} := \texttt{null} \,\|\, \texttt{heap} := store(\texttt{heap}, \texttt{self}, \texttt{x}, \texttt{self}.\texttt{x} + 1)\}$

$\qquad \{\texttt{heap} := anon(\texttt{heap}, \dot{\emptyset}, h) \,\|\, \textbf{res}' := r \,\|\, \textbf{exc}' := e\}$

$\qquad\qquad ((\textbf{exc}' \doteq \texttt{null} \rightarrow \textbf{res}' \doteq \texttt{list}.\texttt{get}(0) \wedge \textbf{res}' \not\doteq \texttt{null} \wedge \texttt{list}.inv)$

$\qquad\qquad\quad \wedge\, (instance_{\texttt{Exception}}(\textbf{exc}') \rightarrow \mathit{false} \wedge \texttt{list}.\,inv)$

$\qquad\qquad\quad \wedge\, \mathit{wellFormed}(h) \wedge (\textbf{res}' \doteq \texttt{null} \vee \textbf{res}'.\mathit{created} \doteq \mathit{TRUE})$

$\qquad\qquad\quad \rightarrow \langle\textbf{try} \; \{\; \texttt{method-frame}(\textbf{this}=\texttt{self})\texttt{:}\{\; \texttt{if}(\textbf{exc}' \texttt{ != null})$

$\qquad\qquad\qquad\qquad\qquad\qquad\qquad\qquad\qquad\qquad \textbf{throw } \textbf{exc}'\texttt{;}$

$\qquad\qquad\qquad\qquad\qquad\qquad\qquad\qquad \texttt{o = res;} \} \; \}$

$\qquad\qquad\qquad \textbf{catch}\texttt{(Exception e) \{ exc = e; \}}\rangle$

$\qquad\qquad\qquad\quad (\texttt{self}.\,inv \wedge \texttt{exc} \doteq \texttt{null}))$

where $\textbf{res}' : \mathit{Object} \in \mathcal{PV}$ and $\textbf{exc}' : \texttt{Exception} \in \mathcal{PV}$ are the variables used in the applied contract for $\texttt{get}$, and where the constant symbols $r : \mathit{Object} \in \mathcal{F}$ and $e : \texttt{Exception} \in \mathcal{F}$ are fresh.

Because of the type of $\textbf{exc}'$, the formula $instance_{\texttt{Exception}}(\textbf{exc}')$ is equivalent to $\textbf{exc}' \not\doteq \texttt{null}$. The postcondition of the contract, occurring to the left of the implication arrow in the sequent above, thus guarantees that $\textbf{exc}' \doteq \texttt{null}$ holds. During further symbolic execution, the "then" branch of the conditional statement can thus immediately be ruled out. After completely symbolically executing the program, the resulting sequent is:

$\Gamma,$

$\textbf{exc}' \doteq \texttt{null},$

$\textbf{res}' \doteq \texttt{get}\big(anon(store(\texttt{heap}, \texttt{self}, \texttt{x}, \texttt{self}.\texttt{x} + 1), \dot{\emptyset}, h), \texttt{list}, 0\big),$

$inv\big(anon(store(\texttt{heap}, \texttt{self}, \texttt{x}, \texttt{self}.\texttt{x} + 1), \dot{\emptyset}, h), \texttt{list}\big),$

$\mathit{wellFormed}(h),$

$select_{\mathit{Boolean}}\big(anon(store(\texttt{heap}, \texttt{self}, \texttt{x}, \texttt{self}.\texttt{x} + 1), \dot{\emptyset}, h), \textbf{res}', \mathit{created}\big)$

$\qquad \doteq \mathit{TRUE}$

$\Rightarrow$

$\textbf{res}' \doteq \texttt{null},$

$\texttt{list} \doteq \texttt{null},$

$\texttt{self} \doteq \texttt{null},$

$\{\texttt{exc} := \texttt{null} \,\|\, \texttt{heap} := anon(store(\texttt{heap}, \texttt{self}, \texttt{x}, \texttt{self}.\texttt{x} + 1), \dot{\emptyset}, h)\}$

$\qquad \langle\rangle\big(\texttt{self}.\,inv \wedge \texttt{exc} \doteq \texttt{null}\big)$

After applying emptyModality and after further simplification, proving the branch comes down to showing that the formulas $inv(anon(store(\texttt{heap},\texttt{self},\texttt{x},\texttt{self}.\texttt{x}+1)),\texttt{self})$ and $\texttt{null} \doteq \texttt{null}$ are implied by the rest of the sequent. For the latter, this is trivial. For the former, it requires once more applying repSimple for inv in $\texttt{Client}$, which replaces $inv(anon(store(\texttt{heap},\texttt{self},\texttt{x},\texttt{self}.\texttt{x}+1)),\texttt{self})$ with *true*.

This concludes the example proof for the method contract $mct_\texttt{m}$. The proof shows that the implementation of method $\texttt{m}$ in $\texttt{Client}$ satisfies the contract $mct_\texttt{m}$, provided that all implementations of $\texttt{get}$ in subclasses of $\texttt{List}$ satisfy the **normal_behaviour** method contract for $\texttt{get}$, and provided that all implementations of $\texttt{size}$ and inv in subclasses of $\texttt{List}$ satisfy the respective dependency contracts. Note that in this example, the visible axioms obsIsNullOrCreated and inv are not actually needed for the proof. This could be different if the body of $\texttt{m}$ and the postcondition of $mct_\texttt{m}$ were more complex.

6.7. Related Work

Work related to JML* has been discussed in Section 3.6. The discussion is continued here, focusing on aspects related to verification instead of specification.

The verifier of Smans et al. [2008] and the *Dafny* verifier of Leino [2008] also verify (different flavours of) dynamic frames specifications. Both work by encoding the verification problem into the *Boogie* language, which is then processed by the Boogie verifier [Barnett et al., 2006], before the resulting verification condition is fed to an SMT solver such as *Simplify* [Detlefs et al., 2005] or *Z3* [de Moura and Bjørner, 2008]. To the author's knowledge, the approach for verifying dynamic frames specifications presented here is the first that is fully deductive, except for the translation from JML* into JavaDL*, which is a comparatively small step. It is also the first approach based on symbolic execution, if we do not count the verifier of Smans et al. [2009b] for *implicit dynamic frames* [Smans et al., 2009a], which is a significantly different concept than dynamic frames.

The state change caused by a method call is typically encoded in Boogie-based verifiers by first anonymising the entire heap (via Boogie's $\texttt{havoc}$ statement), and by then constraining the change of the heap with the help of quantified assumptions that correspond to the formula *frame* of Definition 6.5 and to the formula *noDeallocs* of Lemma 6.2. The number of quantifiers introduced in this way is reported to have been responsible for performance problems in the *Spec#* system when verifying methods that make many method calls [Barnett et al., 2010]. Using the function symbol *anon* for anonymisation in the useMethodContract rule of Definition 6.7 avoids these quantifiers, just like it avoids such quantifiers in the loopInvariant rule of Definition 5.9.

Both the *pure methods* of Smans et al. [2008] and the *functions* of Dafny consist only of a single return statement. A likely reason is that axiomatising the connection between a function symbol and a general method body is not possible in the Boogie language. The solution in Subsection 6.2.2 uses the ability of dynamic logic to have several modal operators in a single proof obligation.

As far as the use of dynamic logic and of symbolic execution is concerned, the most closely related approach outside of the KeY project itself is the calculus for verifying Java in the *KIV* tool [Stenzel, 2004, 2005]. To the author's knowledge, KIV supports neither dynamic frames nor any other approach for solving the frame problem in abstract specifications.

In JavaDL, the verification of modifies clauses is based on the notion of *location dependent symbols* [Roth, 2006; Engel et al., 2009]. As in the loopInvariant rule, the approach used in this chapter instead uses quantification over locations (in the formula *frame*). Besides supporting dynamic frames and allowing the creation and initialisation of new objects without this being declared in the modifies clause, a secondary advantage of the JavaDL* approach is that it is most probably easier to understand for the user of the verification system than the approach of JavaDL. Boogie-based verifiers typically use yet another approach, where for every assignment statement it is checked separately that the assigned location is covered by the modifies clause. This approach facilitates user feedback in case the modifies clause is violated, because it makes it easy for the verification system to pinpoint the responsible assignment. An advantage of our approach is that it is more liberal, in that it tolerates temporary modifications (see also the discussion in Subsection 2.2.2). An additional, more pragmatic reason for using *frame* instead of performing a separate check for every assignment is that this technique fits more naturally into dynamic logic: classically, dynamic logic supports only a postcondition at the end of the verified program, but not in-program assertions that could be attached to individual assignments. An augmented version of dynamic logic that features in-program assertions has been defined by Ulbrich [2010]. In such a dynamic logic, per-assignment checks for modifies clauses become a viable option.

The proof obligation for verifying dependency contracts in this chapter is similar to the proof obligation of Bubel [2007] for verifying that the axiomatisation of a location dependent symbol respects its declared dependencies. Roughly the same approach is also proposed by Leino and Müller [2008] for verifying that a pure method respects its depends clause: two executions of the pure method's body, starting in states that differ only in the locations not covered by the depends clause, must lead to the same (or equivalent) result values. This kind of approach is sometimes referred to as *self-composition*. A disadvantage of self-composition is that the method body (or represents clause) must be handled twice during verification, which may be cumbersome e.g. if it contains non-trivial loops. Conversely, an advantage is that it is liberal, in the sense that read accesses that do not actually influence the result value are tolerated. Dafny instead checks that every individual read access is covered by the depends clause [Leino, 2008]. These alternatives correspond to the above-mentioned alternatives of checking modifies clauses for every individual assignment, or of checking them at the end of the method via *frame*.

6.8. Conclusion

This chapter has presented a framework for verifying design-by-contract specifications in a dynamic logic for Java with updates, where the heap is modelled as a program variable. The approach supports abstract specifications that use pure methods, model fields and ghost fields, as well as dynamic frames to specify properties of sets of memory locations.

Pure methods and model fields are modelled in the logic as *observer symbols*, which are rigid function symbols that expect a heap array as their first argument and an object as their second argument. The interpretation of observer symbols is constrained by axioms that correspond to method bodies and represents clauses given by the specification.

Besides observer symbols and axioms, a specification consists of a set of method contracts and dependency contracts, which constrain the allowed behaviour of methods and the allowed dependencies of observer symbols, respectively. Both kinds of contracts give rise to proof obligations that must be verified for every subtype of the class or interface in which the contract is defined. Conversely, both kinds of contracts may be used as assumptions in the proofs of other contracts. Special rules are provided for this purpose, and their soundness has been proven.

The verification framework is modular in the sense that every proof obligation belongs to a particular class, and that implementational details not visible in this class are not used in the proof. In particular, **private** object invariants of objects of other classes are treated as a black box, and reasoned about using only what is explicitly stated about them in visible contracts. The same holds for (other) model fields and for pure methods.

The approach has been implemented in the version of the KeY system that is based on JavaDL* (Chapter 5), and it has been used to verify a number of smaller examples. For the example program of Section 3.4, most proof obligations could be verified without user interaction, with proving times on the time scale of seconds to tens of seconds (measured on a 2.4 GHz Core 2 Duo processor). In the remaining proofs (namely, the proofs for the **contains** method of **ArrayList** and for several methods of **Set**), a few interactive rule applications were necessary to guide the prover along, mostly quantifier instantiations. The verification of method `m` of class `Client` discussed in Section 6.6 was fully automatic, with the closed proof consisting of roughly 600 nodes including 37 leaves.

This concludes Part II on *verification*. Part III aims at increasing the degree of automation in dynamic logic based verification, by using abstract interpretation techniques to automatically *generate loop invariants*.

Part III.

Loop Invariant Generation

7. Background on Abstract Interpretation

Deductive verification of imperative programs typically requires hand-crafted *loop invariants*, i.e., assertions about the program states that can possibly occur at the beginning of each iteration of a loop. Finding sufficiently strong loop invariants can be difficult, and today this is often one of only a few human interactions necessary in an otherwise heavily automated verification environment. In particular, the symbolic execution calculus for Java programs described in Chapter 5 can be used automatically, except that the loopInvariant rule for handling general loops requires a manually provided loop invariant.

On the other hand, there are methods that can automatically determine loop invariants. Leaving aside testing-based approaches like the *Daikon* tool of Ernst et al. [2001], such methods are predominantly based on *abstract interpretation* [Cousot and Cousot, 1977], a theoretical framework for automatic static program analysis which can roughly be described as symbolic execution of the program, using an abstract (i.e., approximative) domain for the variable values, together with fixed-point iteration.

The subsequent Chapter 8 presents an approach for integrating a form of abstract interpretation called *predicate abstraction* into the JavaDL* verification framework. The present chapter prepares for Chapter 8 by providing an overview of abstract interpretation theory. It loosely follows the original presentation of Cousot and Cousot [1977], but renders the presented concepts from a JavaDL* perspective (where the differences between JavaDL and JavaDL* are irrelevant in this chapter). The definitions given here are not formally necessary for Chapter 8; instead, the purpose of this chapter is to illuminate on an intuitive level the relationship between verification in dynamic logic on one hand, and abstract interpretation on the other hand.

Outline Section 7.1 sets the stage by defining *control flow graphs*, which are useful for talking about abstract interpretation concepts. At the core of abstract interpretation is the notion of *abstract domains*, which is introduced in Section 7.2. Section 7.3 describes how one abstract domain can be used to approximate another, more concrete abstract domain. An alternative to using one abstract domain to approximate another is to further approximate within a single abstract domain via a so-called *widening*, as described in Section 7.4. Section 7.5 discusses strategies for fixed-point computation. Some abstract domains are described in Section 7.6, and some tools implementing abstract interpretation are mentioned in Section 7.7. The final Section 7.8 provides conclusions.

7.1. Control Flow Graphs

For describing static analysis techniques such as abstract interpretation, it is customary to represent programs as control flow graphs. The advantage of such a representation is that it makes control flow through the program—especially through loops—more explicit than a representation as source code. Definition 7.1 below defines a form of control flow graphs based on sets *Cond* (thought of as side-effect free boolean expressions) and *Asgn* (thought of as assignment statements).

Definition 7.1 (Control flow graphs). *Given sets Cond and Asgn, a control flow graph is a finite, directed, rooted, labelled graph, where the set of nodes is partitioned as follows:*

- *There is exactly one node labelled* `entry`. *It has no predecessors and one successor.*
- *There is exactly one node labelled* `exit`. *It has one predecessor and no successor.*
- *There can be nodes labelled with an element of Cond. They have one predecessor and one successor.*
- *There can be nodes labelled with an element of Asgn. They have one predecessor and one successor.*
- *There can be nodes labelled* `branch`. *They have one predecessor and two successors.*
- *There can be nodes labelled* `junction`. *They have two predecessors and one successor.*

The edges of control flow graphs in the sense of Definition 7.1 represent control states. They are also called *program points*. If we choose *Cond* as the set of all side-effect free **boolean** Java expressions and *Asgn* as the set of all elementary Java assignments, then we can represent a Java program fragment (without method calls) as a control flow graph in a straightforward fashion (made slightly complicated only by the exception facilities of the Java language).

Example 7.1. Figure 7.1 shows a control flow graph representation for the Java implementation of the selection sort algorithm shown in Figure 5.14. Branch and junction nodes are depicted as circles. Note that other control flow graph representations of the same program are possible, and that for simplicity, all exceptional behaviour—such as testing for **null** before dereferencing **a** and throwing `NullPointerExceptions` when applicable—is omitted in the graph. ∗

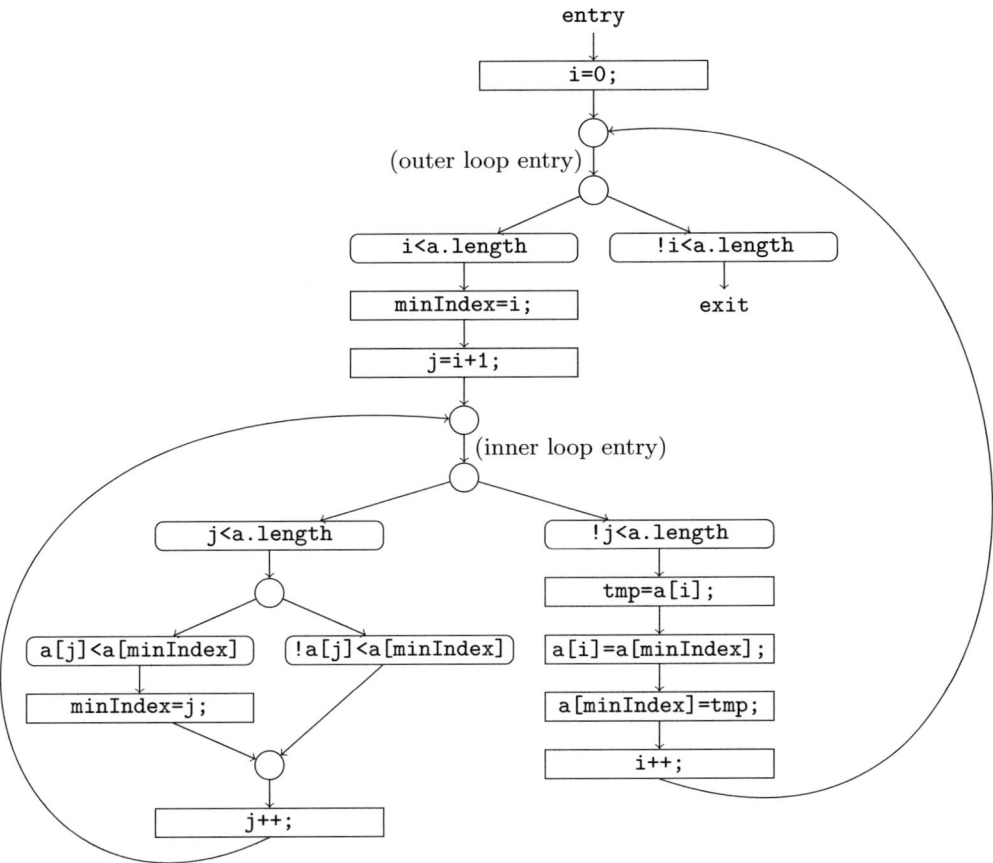

Figure 7.1.: Control flow graph for selection sort

7.2. Abstract Domains

A particular abstract interpretation is defined by fixing a so-called *abstract domain*, whose foundation is a set L of *abstract states* which the program is evaluated in. An abstract state can be thought of as representing a set of concrete states. The set of abstract states is partially ordered by a relation $\sqsubseteq$, where a smaller abstract state is more "precise" than a larger abstract state, in the sense that it stands for a smaller set of concrete states. Formally, $(L, \sqsubseteq)$ is a partially ordered set, and often it is even a lattice or a complete lattice.

Definition 7.2 (Partially ordered sets, lattices, complete lattices).
- *A partially ordered set is a pair* $(L, \sqsubseteq)$ *where* L *is a set and* $\sqsubseteq$ *a partial order or* L, *i.e., a binary relation on* L *which is reflexive, transitive and antisymmetric.*

167

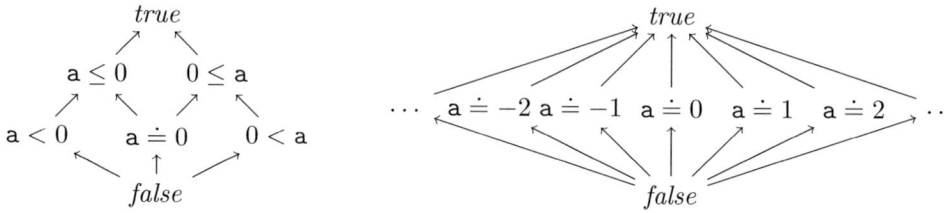

Figure 7.2.: Abstract state lattices for signs analysis (left) and for constant propagation analysis (right), with a single integer program variable a

- A lattice *is a partially ordered set* $(L, \sqsubseteq)$ *where for every pair* $(l_1, l_2) \in L^2$ *there is a greatest lower bound* $l_1 \sqcap l_2$ *and least upper bound* $l_1 \sqcup l_2$.
- A complete lattice *is a lattice where for* all *subsets* $S \subseteq L$ *(not just those with cardinality 2) there is a greatest lower bound* $\sqcap S$ *and a least upper bound* $\sqcup S$.

Example 7.2.
- For every Kripke structure $\mathcal{K}$, the power set of its states together with set inclusion $(2^S, \subseteq)$ is a complete lattice, where for all $T \subseteq 2^S$ the greatest lower bound is $\sqcap T = \bigcap T$, and the least upper bound is $\sqcup T = \bigcup T$. (More generally, $(2^S, \subseteq)$ is a complete lattice for every set S.)
- Let $\Rightarrow$ be the binary relation on Fma_Σ where for all $\varphi_1, \varphi_2 \in Fma_\Sigma$, we have $\varphi_1 \Rightarrow \varphi_2$ if and only if $\models \varphi_1 \rightarrow \varphi_2$. The pair $(Fma_\Sigma, \Rightarrow)$ is not a partially ordered set, because $\Rightarrow$ is not antisymmetric: for example, we have $true \Rightarrow (true \wedge true)$ and $(true \wedge true) \Rightarrow true$, but $true \neq (true \wedge true)$.
- Let $\Leftrightarrow$ be the equivalence relation on Fma_Σ where for all $\varphi_1, \varphi_2 \in Fma_\Sigma$, we have $\varphi_1 \Leftrightarrow \varphi_2$ if and only if $\models \varphi_1 \leftrightarrow \varphi_2$. The quotient set of formulas with respect to $\Leftrightarrow$ $(Fma_\Sigma/\Leftrightarrow, \Rightarrow)$ is a lattice, where for all $\varphi_1, \varphi_2 \in Fma_\Sigma/\Leftrightarrow$, the greatest lower bound is $\varphi_1 \sqcap \varphi_2 = \varphi_1 \wedge \varphi_2$ and the least upper bound is $\varphi_1 \sqcup \varphi_2 = \varphi_1 \vee \varphi_2$. It is not complete, because infinite sets of formulas do not in general have a greatest lower and least upper bound.
- Let $a : Int \in \mathcal{PV}$. Then $\big(\{(a \doteq 0), (a < 0), (0 < a), (a \leq 0), (0 \leq a), false, true\}, \Rightarrow\big)$ is a complete lattice. It is visualised in the left half of Figure 7.2.
- Let $a : Int \in \mathcal{PV}$. Then $\big(\{a \doteq z \mid z \in \mathbb{Z}\} \cup \{false, true\}, \Rightarrow\big)$ is a complete lattice. It is visualised in the right half of Figure 7.2. $\qquad *$

Note that the symbol $\Rightarrow$ is also used for the sequent arrow (Definition 5.6). It should always be clear from the context which of the two meanings of $\Rightarrow$ is intended.

Abstract interpretation involves computing *fixed points* of functions over partially ordered sets. It is often required that the involved functions are *monotonic* or even *continuous*, where continuity implies monotonicity.

Definition 7.3 (Fixed points, monotonicity, continuity).
- *For a set L and a function $f : L \to L$, an element $l \in L$ is called a* fixed point *of f if $f(l) = l$.*
- *For a partially ordered set $(L, \sqsubseteq)$, a function $f : L \to L$ is called* monotonic *if for all $l_1, l_2 \in L$ with $l_1 \sqsubseteq l_2$ we have $f(l_1) \sqsubseteq f(l_2)$.*
- *For a complete lattice $(L, \sqsubseteq)$, a function $f : L \to L$ is called* continuous *if for all $S \subseteq L$ we have $f(\bigsqcup S) = \bigsqcup f(S)$.*

We are now ready to define the core notion of abstract interpretation theory, namely that of an *abstract domain*.

Definition 7.4 (Abstract domains). *Given sets Cond and Asgn, an* abstract domain A *is a tuple*

$$A = (L, \sqsubseteq, \bot, \top, constrain, update, merge),$$

where
- *$(L, \sqsubseteq)$ is a partially ordered set with least element $\bot$ and largest element $\top$,*
- *$constrain : L \times Cond \to L$ is monotonic in its first argument,*
- *$update : L \times Asgn \to L$ is monotonic in its first argument,*
- *$merge : L \times L \to L$ is commutative, and monotonic in both arguments.*

Intuitively, $constrain(l, b)$ is the abstract state obtained by starting in the abstract state l and adding the assumption that the condition b holds. Similarly, $update(l, \mathtt{a} = t)$ is the abstract state where we start in l and then execute the assignment $\mathtt{a} = t$. At junction points in the control flow graph, two abstract states l_1 and l_2 are combined into a single abstract state $merge(l_1, l_2)$. If $(L, \sqsubseteq)$ is a lattice, then *merge* is typically defined to be the lattice join operator, i.e., $merge(l_1, l_2) = l_1 \sqcup l_2$.

For an abstract domain $A = (L, \sqsubseteq, \bot, \top, constrain, update, merge)$ and a control flow graph with program points PP, we are interested in functions $PP \to L$, which map every program point to an element of L. The abstract domain and the control flow graph together give rise to a *transfer function* that transforms one function $PP \to L$ into another.

Definition 7.5 (Transfer function). *For an abstract domain A and a control flow graph with program points PP, the* transfer function $step_A : (PP \to L) \to (PP \to$

L) is defined by

$$
step_A(m)(pp) = \begin{cases} \top & \text{if } label(x) = \texttt{entry} \\ constrain\big(m(in(1,x)), cond\big) & \text{if } label(x) = cond \in Cond \\ update\big(m(in(1,x)), asgn\big) & \text{if } label(x) = asgn \in Asgn \\ m(in(1,x)) & \text{if } label(x) = \texttt{branch} \\ merge\big(m(in(1,x)), m(in(2,x))\big) & \text{if } label(x) = \texttt{junction} \end{cases}
$$

for all $m : PP \to L$ and all $pp = (x \to y) \in PP$, where $label(n)$ denotes the label of node n, and where $in(i,n)$ denotes the ith incoming edge of node n.

This definition corresponds to a *forward analysis* of the program: the abstract state associated with a program point is defined via the abstract states of its predecessors in the control flow graph. A dual definition where the value of a program point is computed from it successors is equally possible (*backward analysis*).

In the following, we are interested in fixed points of $step_A$. Most interesting are *small* fixed points, according to the partial order that results from lifting the relation $\sqsubseteq$ on L to a relation on $PP \to L$ in a pointwise manner: for all $m_1, m_2 : PP \to L$, we define $m_1 \sqsubseteq m_2$ to hold exactly if for all $pp \in PP$ we have $m_1(pp) \sqsubseteq m_2(pp)$. If $(L, \sqsubseteq)$ is a (complete) lattice, then $(PP \to L, \sqsubseteq)$ also is, and the monotonicity of *constrain*, *update* and *merge* implies that the transfer function $step_A$ is monotonic, too. The function $\bar{\top} : PP \to L$ that maps all program points to $\top \in L$ is usually a fixed point of $step_A$, albeit not a very interesting one.

Example 7.3 (Static semantics). Let $Cond$ be the set of side-effect free **boolean** Java expressions, let $Asgn$ be the set of elementary Java assignments, let $\mathcal{K}$ be a Kripke structure $\mathcal{K}$ with states $\mathcal{S}$, and let β be a variable assignment. We consider the abstract domain

$$
(2^{\mathcal{S}}, \subseteq, \emptyset, \mathcal{S}, constrain, update, \cup),
$$

where for all $l \in 2^{\mathcal{S}}$, all $b \in Cond$, and all $(\texttt{a = } t) \in Asgn$:

$$
constrain(l, b) = \{ s \in l \mid (\mathcal{K}, s, \beta) \models b \doteq TRUE \}
$$
$$
update(l, \texttt{a = } t) = \{ s_2 \in \mathcal{S} \mid \text{there is } s_1 \in l \text{ such that } (s_1, s_2) \in \rho(\texttt{a = } t) \}
$$

This abstract domain precisely models the semantics of the considered programming language constructs. Its transfer function $step_A$ has a least fixed point, which associates with every program point the set of states that can possibly occur at the program point. This kind of abstract domain is called the *static semantics* by Cousot and Cousot [1977], and—perhaps more descriptively—the *accumulating semantics* by Jones and Nielson [1995]. In contrast, an *operational semantics* defines the individual *sequences* of states that a program gives rise to. Considering only the sets of states attached to program points is sufficient for many purposes [Floyd, 1967]. In particular, verifying a program with respect to safety assertions such as postconditions amounts to checking whether these assertions are satisfied in all states possible at the program points to which they are attached.

The static semantics cannot be implemented as a program analysis, for example because the abstract states (themselves being arbitrary sets of concrete states) cannot efficiently be represented in computer memory. The abstract domains used in practice are usually approximations of the static semantics, as described in Section 7.3. Example 7.4 below is an example for such a more approximative abstract domain.   *

Example 7.4 (Constant propagation analysis). *Constant propagation* is a program optimisation routinely performed by compilers. It consists in replacing occurrences of program variables that have a statically constant value by the corresponding constant. Which occurrences are guaranteed to have which constant values is detected by a simple data flow analysis, which we can understand as an abstract interpretation.

Let *Cond* and *Assgn* be as in Example 7.3, and let $\mathbf{a} : Int \in \mathcal{PV}$ be the only program variable we are interested in (the generalisation is straightforward). The abstract domain of constant propagation analysis is

$$A = (L, \Rightarrow, false, true, constrain, update, merge),$$

where:

$$L = \{\mathbf{a} \doteq z \mid z \in \mathbb{Z}\} \cup \{false, true\}$$

$$constrain(\varphi, b) = \varphi$$

$$update(\varphi, \mathbf{a} = t) = \begin{cases} false & \text{if } \varphi = false \\ \mathbf{a} \doteq z & \text{if } \varphi \neq false, t = z \in \mathbb{Z} \\ true & \text{otherwise} \end{cases}$$

$$merge(\varphi_1, \varphi_2) = \begin{cases} \varphi_1 & \text{if } \varphi_1 = \varphi_2 \text{ or } \varphi_2 = false \\ \varphi_2 & \text{if } \varphi_1 = false \\ true & \text{otherwise} \end{cases}$$

The complete lattice $(L, \Rightarrow)$ of abstract states is visualised in Figure 7.2. Note that $constrain(\varphi, b)$ overapproximates $\varphi \wedge (b \doteq TRUE)$, and that $merge(\varphi_1, \varphi_2)$

overapproximates $\varphi_1 \vee \varphi_2$: we have $\varphi \wedge (b \doteq TRUE) \Rightarrow constrain(\varphi, b)$ and $\varphi_1 \vee \varphi_2 \Rightarrow merge(\varphi_1, \varphi_2)$. Similarly, *update* overapproximates the result of the assignment on φ: the resulting formula is implied by the strongest postcondition of φ and the assignment. As defined here, the results of *constrain*, *update* and *merge* are not the most precise approximations expressible in L. We could for example sharpen the definition of *constrain* by taking into account the condition b if it is of a representable form (e.g., $a == 3$), instead of ignoring it altogether. $*$

In general, the transfer function $step_A$ does not necessarily have a fixed point, much less a unique *least* fixed point. This is only guaranteed if some further conditions apply. If, for example, the partially ordered set $(L, \sqsubseteq)$ is a complete lattice, then a well-known fixed point theorem (repeated in Proposition 7.1 below) tells us that $step_A$ has a least fixed point. If additionally $step_A$ is continuous, then another fixed point theorem (also in Proposition 7.1) states that additionally, the least fixed point of $step_A$ is the least upper bound of the "Kleene sequence" $\bar{\bot}, step_A(\bar{\bot}), step_A^2(\bar{\bot}), \ldots$, where $\bar{\bot} : PP \to L$ is the function that maps all program points to $\bot \in L$.

Proposition 7.1 (Two fixed-point theorems [Tarski, 1955; Cousot and Cousot, 1977])**.**
- If $(L, \sqsubseteq)$ *is a complete lattice and if* $f : L \to L$ *is monotonic, then the set of fixed points of* f *is also a complete lattice, where the least fixed point is* $\bigsqcap\{l \mid f(l) \sqsubseteq l\}$ *and the largest fixed point is* $\bigsqcup\{l \mid l \sqsubseteq f(l)\}$.
- If $(L, \sqsubseteq)$ *is a complete lattice with least element* $\bot$ *and if* $f : L \to L$ *is continuous, then the least fixed point of* f *is* $\bigsqcup\{f^n(\bot) \mid n \in \mathbb{N}\}$.

These theorems guarantee the existence of the least fixed point for the static semantics discussed in Example 7.3. However, even if the least fixed point of the transfer function $step_A$ exists, this does not imply that it can be computed. This is only possible if the abstract domain satisfies further constraints. In particular, it is helpful if the set of abstract states satisfies the *ascending chain condition*.

Definition 7.6 (Ascending chain condition)**.** *A partially ordered set* $(L, \sqsubseteq)$ *satisfies the* ascending chain condition *if for all ascending chains* $l_1 \sqsubseteq l_2 \sqsubseteq \ldots$ *there is* $n \in \mathbb{N}$ *such that for all* $m \in \mathbb{N}$ *with* $n < m$ *we have* $l_m = l_n$.

If $step_A$ is continuous, if $(L, \sqsubseteq)$ satisfies the ascending chain condition, and if $step_A$ can be computed, then the least fixed point of $step_A$ can also be computed: by Proposition 7.1, the fixed point is the least upper bound of the Kleene sequence $\bar{\bot}, step_A(\bar{\bot}), step_A^2(\bar{\bot}), \ldots$. Because of the monotonicity of $step_A$, the sequence is an ascending chain: $\bar{\bot} \sqsubseteq step_A(\bar{\bot}) \sqsubseteq step_A^2(\bar{\bot}) \sqsubseteq \ldots$. By the ascending chain condition, the sequence stabilises at the least fixed point after finitely many steps. This is the case for constant propagation analysis, which has been introduced in Example 7.4 and which we return to in Example 7.5 below.

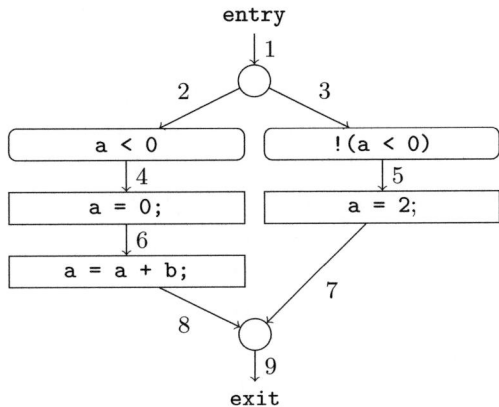

Figure 7.3.: Example program for constant propagation analysis (Example 7.5)

	$\bot$	$step_A(\bot)$	$step_A^2(\bot)$	$step_A^3(\bot)$	$step_A^4(\bot)$	$step_A^5(\bot)$	$step_A^6(\bot)$
1	*false*	*true*	*true*	*true*	*true*	*true*	*true*
2	*false*	*false*	*true*	*true*	*true*	*true*	*true*
3	*false*	*false*	*true*	*true*	*true*	*true*	*true*
4	*false*	*false*	*false*	*true*	*true*	*true*	*true*
5	*false*	*false*	*false*	*true*	*true*	*true*	*true*
6	*false*	*false*	*false*	*false*	$a \doteq 0$	$a \doteq 0$	$a \doteq 0$
7	*false*	*false*	*false*	*false*	$a \doteq 2$	$a \doteq 2$	$a \doteq 2$
8	*false*	*false*	*false*	*false*	*false*	*true*	*true*
9	*false*	*false*	*false*	*false*	*false*	$a \doteq 2$	*true*

Table 7.1.: Results of constant propagation analysis (Example 7.5)

Example 7.5 (Constant propagation analysis, continued). In the constant propagation domain, $(L, \Rightarrow)$ is a complete lattice that satisfies the ascending chain condition, and the fixed point of $step_A$ can effectively be computed. As an example, consider the simple program in Figure 7.3, whose program points are identified with integers between 1 and 9. Table 7.1 shows the Kleene sequence leading to the least fixed point for this program, which is $step_A^6(\bot) = step_A^7(\bot)$. A compiler could derive from this result that it is safe to replace the occurrence of a on the right hand side of the assignment a = a + b by 0. A program verifier could derive that, e.g., an assertion $a \doteq 0$ attached to program point 6 is always satisfied. *

Like we have done for the domain of constant propagation analysis and for the domain of *signs analysis* (which tracks the signs of the occurring variables, Figure 7.2), the base sets of many other domains can also be viewed as subsets of Fma_Σ. The formulas attached to each program point in the fixed point of the transfer function then describe upper limits on the sets of states that can occur there in real executions. For example, *false* means that the program point is unreachable; $0 \leq a$ means that only states where a is evaluated to a non-negative value are possible at the program point; and *true* means that there are no known restrictions on the states possible at the program point. Such formulas are called *invariants* [Floyd, 1967]. The *loop invariants* needed by the loopInvariant rule of JavaDL* are special cases of invariants in this sense, where the program point is a loop entry point (such as the loop entry points marked in Figure 7.1). Loop invariants are the most interesting invariants, because (barring recursion) all others can easily be derived by computing weakest preconditions or strongest postconditions. Thus, we can view abstract interpretation as being all about generating loop invariants.

7.3. Consistency of Abstract Domains

When using an approximative abstract domain, such as the constant propagation domain of Examples 7.4 and 7.5, we may want it to be a "correct" approximation of another abstract domain, such as the static semantics of Example 7.3. The notion of correctness is formalised in Definition 7.7 below.

Definition 7.7 (Consistent abstract domains). *Given two abstract domains*

$$C = (L_C, \sqsubseteq_C, \perp_C, \top_C, constrain_C, update_C, merge_C)$$
$$A = (L_A, \sqsubseteq_A, \perp_A, \top_A, constrain_A, update_A, merge_A),$$

we say that A is consistent with C if there are monotonic functions $\alpha: L_C \to L_A$ and $\gamma: L_A \to L_C$ such that the following holds for every control flow graph with program points PP:
  1. for all $a \in L_A$: $a = \alpha(\gamma(a))$,
  2. for all $c \in L_C$: $c \sqsubseteq_C \gamma(\alpha(c))$, and
  3. for all $m: PP \to PP$: $\bar{\gamma}(step_A(\bar{\alpha}(m))) \sqsubseteq step_C(m)$,
where $\bar{\alpha}: (PP \to L_C) \to (PP \to L_A)$ and $\bar{\gamma}: (PP \to L_A) \to (PP \to L_C)$ are the pointwise extensions of α and γ, i.e., for all $pp \in PP$ we have $\bar{\alpha}(m)(pp) = \alpha(m(pp))$ and $\bar{\gamma}(m)(pp) = \gamma(m(pp))$.

The function α is called an *abstraction function*, and γ is called a *concretisation function*. The first requirement of Definition 7.7 expresses that the composite function $\alpha \circ \gamma$ is the identity function, i.e., that concretising an abstract element and subsequently abstracting again does not have any effect. The second requirement demands that abstracting and subsequently concretising again can make the

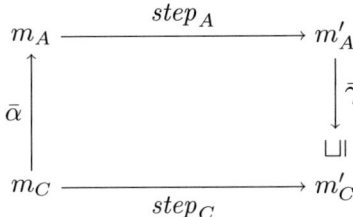

Figure 7.4.: Consistent abstract domains: graphic representation of Definition 7.7 (3)

concrete element larger (i.e., less precise) but never smaller (which would be incorrect). The third requirement is visualised in Figure 7.4. Intuitively, it states that the transfer function of A correctly approximates the transfer function of C.

Example 7.6. The domain of constant propagation analysis (Examples 7.4 and 7.5) is consistent with the static semantics (Example 7.3), where α and γ are as follows:

$$\alpha(l) = \begin{cases} false & \text{if } l = \emptyset \\ \mathsf{a} \doteq z & \text{if } l \neq \emptyset \text{ and if for all } s \in l : s(\mathsf{a}) = z \\ true & \text{otherwise} \end{cases}$$

$$\gamma(\varphi) = \begin{cases} \emptyset & \text{if } \varphi = false \\ \{s \in \mathcal{S} \mid s(\mathsf{a}) = z\} & \text{if } \varphi = \mathsf{a} \doteq z \\ \mathcal{S} & \text{if } \varphi = true \end{cases}$$

for all $l \in 2^{\mathcal{S}}$ and for all $\varphi \in \{\mathsf{a} \doteq z \mid z \in \mathbb{Z}\} \cup \{false, true\}$.

Let for example $l = \{s_1, s_2\} \in 2^{\mathcal{S}}$, where $s_1(\mathsf{a}) = 1$ and $s_2(\mathsf{a}) = 2$. Then $\alpha(l) = true$, and $\gamma(\alpha(l)) = \mathcal{S} \supset l$.   *

Consistency of two abstract domains A and C implies that the results of A are correct approximations of the results of C, in the sense that the concretisation of the least fixed point of $step_A$ is larger or equal than least fixed point of $step_C$.

7.4. Widening

If an abstract domain does not satisfy the ascending chain condition, or if its fixed points cannot practically be computed for some other reason, then one solution is to approximate it with a more abstract domain, as discussed in Section 7.3.

An alternative is to further approximate *within* the abstract domain itself, using a so-called *widening* operator.

Definition 7.8 (Widening operators). *A widening operator for a partially ordered set* $(L, \sqsubseteq)$ *is a function* $widen : L \times L \to L$ *such that*
- *for all* $l_1, l_2 \in L$: $l_1 \sqsubseteq widen(l_1, l_2)$ *and* $l_2 \sqsubseteq widen(l_1, l_2)$
- *for all infinite sequences* $l_0, l_1, l_2 \ldots$ *of elements of* L, *the sequence defined by*

$$s_n = \begin{cases} l_0 & \text{if } n = 0 \\ widen(s_{n-1}, l_n) & \text{otherwise} \end{cases}$$

is not strictly ascending.

Example 7.7 (Intervals analysis). Let *Cond* and *Assgn* be as in Examples 7.3 and 7.4, and let $a : Int \in \mathcal{PV}$ be the only program variable we are interested in (the generalisation is straightforward). Let the notation $t_1 \leq t_2 \leq t_3$ (where $t_1, t_2, t_3 \in Term_\Sigma^{Int}$) be an abbreviation for the formula $t_1 \leq t_2 \wedge t_2 \leq t_3$, and let $-\infty \leq t$ and $t \leq \infty$ (where $t \in Term_\Sigma^{Int}$) be abbreviations for the formula *true*. We use the set $L \subseteq Fma_\Sigma$ defined by

$$L = \{z \leq a \leq z' \mid z \in \mathbb{Z} \cup \{-\infty\}, \; z' \in \mathbb{Z} \cup \{\infty\}, \; z \leq z'\} \cup \{false\}$$

as the set of abstract states of an abstract domain that tracks the intervals in which the value of a must be. This abstract domain is strictly more expressive than the constant propagation domain of Examples 7.4 and 7.5. $(L, \Rightarrow)$ is a complete lattice, but it does not satisfy the ascending chain condition. For example, a strictly ascending chain of infinite length is $(0 \leq a \leq 0) \Rightarrow (0 \leq a \leq 1) \Rightarrow (0 \leq a \leq 2) \Rightarrow \ldots.$

We define a widening operator $widen : L \times L \to L$ as follows:

$$widen(l_1, l_2) = \begin{cases} l_2 & \text{if } l_1 = false \\ l_1 & \text{if } l_2 = false \\ z_1 \leq a \leq z_1' & \text{if } l_1 = (z_1 \leq a \leq z_1'), \, l_2 = (z_2 \leq a \leq z_2'), \\ & \quad z_1 \leq z_2, \, z_2' \leq z_1' \\ -\infty \leq a \leq z_1' & \text{if } l_1 = (z_1 \leq a \leq z_1'), \, l_2 = (z_2 \leq a \leq z_2'), \\ & \quad z_2 < z_1, \, z_2' \leq z_1' \\ z_1 \leq a \leq \infty & \text{if } l_1 = (z_1 \leq a \leq z_1'), l_2 = (z_2 \leq a \leq z_2'), \\ & \quad z_1 \leq z_2, \, z_1' < z_2' \\ -\infty \leq a \leq \infty & \text{otherwise} \end{cases}$$

For the above sequence $(0 \leq a \leq 0), (0 \leq a \leq 1), (0 \leq a \leq 2), \ldots$, the corresponding "widened" sequence

$$s_0 = 0 \leq a \leq 0$$
$$s_1 = widen(0 \leq a \leq 0, \ 0 \leq a \leq 1) = 0 \leq a \leq \infty$$
$$s_2 = widen(0 \leq a \leq \infty, \ 0 \leq a \leq 2) = 0 \leq a \leq \infty$$

$$\ldots$$

stabilises at $0 \leq a \leq \infty$.   *

Definition 7.9 below defines an adapted version of the transfer function of Definition 7.5 that applies a widening operator at pre-selected *widening points* in the control flow graph.

Definition 7.9 (Transfer function with widening). *For an abstract domain A with a widening operator widen, for a control flow graph with program points PP, and for a set $WP \subseteq PP$ of* widening points, *the* transfer function with widening $wstep_A : (PP \to L) \to (PP \to L)$ *is defined by*

$$wstep_A(m)(pp) = \begin{cases} widen\big(m(pp), step_A(m)(pp)\big) & \text{if } pp \in WP \\ step_A(m)(pp) & \text{otherwise} \end{cases}$$

for all $m : PP \to L$ and all $pp \in PP$.

Note that widening operators are not required to be monotonic. For example, the widening operator of Example 7.7 is not monotonic in its first argument: we have $0 \leq a \leq 1 \Rightarrow 0 \leq a \leq 2$, but $widen(0 \leq a \leq 1, \ 0 \leq a \leq 2) = 0 \leq a \leq \infty \not\Rightarrow 0 \leq a \leq 2 = widen(0 \leq a \leq 2, \ 0 \leq a \leq 2)$. As a consequence, $wstep_A$ is also not necessarily monotonic. Nevertheless, Proposition 7.2 below establishes that if the widening points are chosen properly, then the properties of *widen* ensure that iteratively applying it to $\bot$ leads to an ascending chain that even stabilises at a fixed point.

Proposition 7.2 (Stabilisation of $wstep_A$ [Cousot and Cousot, 1977]). *For any abstract domain with widening, any control flow graph, and any choice of WP satisfying that all cycles in the control flow graph contain at least one widening point, there is $m \in \mathbb{N}$ such that the sequence defined by*

$$s_n = wstep_A^n(\bot)$$

(for all $n \in \mathbb{N}$) satisfies

$$s_0 \sqsubseteq \cdots \sqsubseteq s_m = s_{m+1} = \ldots$$

In structured programs, we can choose the loop entry points as the widening points WP. This ensures that every cycle passes through at least one such point.

Example 7.8. (Intervals analysis, continued) We continue with the intervals domain and its widening operator introduced in Example 7.7. Figure 7.5 contains an example program with a simple loop, where the program points are identified with integers 1 to 8. We choose the set of widening points as $WP = \{3\}$. Other valid choices would be $\{4\}$, $\{6\}$, $\{8\}$, or supersets thereof.

The interesting steps of analysing the example program are listed in Table 7.2. We assume canonical interval-arithmetic definitions of the functions *merge*, *update* and *constrain*; for example, we have $merge(z_1 \leq \mathsf{a} \leq z_1', \; z_2 \leq \mathsf{a} \leq z_2') = \big(min(z_1, z_2) \leq \mathsf{a} \leq max(z_1', z_2')\big)$.

In the first two iterations, the abstract state of the widening point 3 is computed as

$$widen\big(false, \; merge(false, \; false)\big) = widen(false, \; false) = false.$$

In the third iteration, this changes to

$$widen\big(false, \; merge(0 \leq \mathsf{a} \leq 0, \; false)\big) = widen(false, \; 0 \leq \mathsf{a} \leq 0) = 0 \leq \mathsf{a} \leq 0.$$

In iterations four to six, the same abstract state for program point 3 is computed as

$$widen\big(0 \leq \mathsf{a} \leq 0, \; merge(0 \leq \mathsf{a} \leq 0, \; false)\big)$$
$$= widen(0 \leq \mathsf{a} \leq 0, \; 0 \leq \mathsf{a} \leq 0) = 0 \leq \mathsf{a} \leq 0.$$

In the seventh iteration, we get a new abstract state, namely

$$widen\big(0 \leq \mathsf{a} \leq 0, \; merge(0 \leq \mathsf{a} \leq 0, \; 1 \leq \mathsf{a} \leq 1)\big)$$
$$= widen(0 \leq \mathsf{a} \leq 0, \; 0 \leq \mathsf{a} \leq 1) = 0 \leq \mathsf{a} \leq \infty.$$

Iterations eight to ten propagate this "widened" abstract state to the successors of program point 3 in the graph. The abstract state of program point 3 itself does not change:

$$widen\big(0 \leq \mathsf{a} \leq \infty, \; merge(0 \leq \mathsf{a} \leq 0, \; 1 \leq \mathsf{a} \leq 1)\big)$$
$$= widen(0 \leq \mathsf{a} \leq \infty, \; 0 \leq \mathsf{a} \leq 1) = 0 \leq \mathsf{a} \leq \infty.$$

In iteration eleven, the abstract state of program point 3 still does not change:

$$widen\big(0 \leq \mathsf{a} \leq \infty, \; merge(0 \leq \mathsf{a} \leq 0, \; 1 \leq \mathsf{a} \leq \infty)\big)$$
$$= widen(0 \leq \mathsf{a} \leq \infty, \; 0 \leq \mathsf{a} \leq \infty) = 0 \leq \mathsf{a} \leq \infty.$$

Because the abstract states of the other program points also do not change, $wstep_A^{10}(\bot) = wstep_A^{11}(\bot)$ is a fixed point of $wstep_A$. It is larger than the least fixed point of $step_A$, where the abstract state of program points 3 to 7 is $0 \leq \mathsf{a} \leq 10$, and where the abstract state of program point 8 is $1 \leq \mathsf{a} \leq 10$. ✳

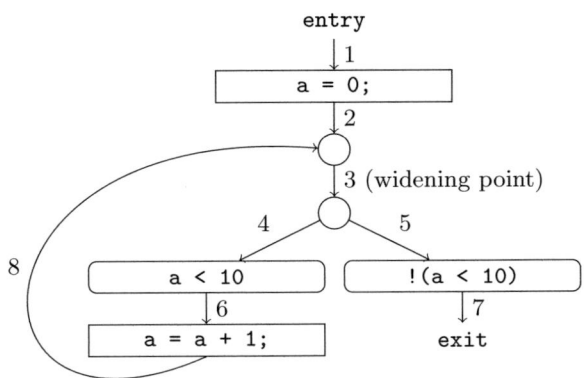

Figure 7.5.: Example program for intervals analysis (Example 7.8)

	$\bot$	$wstep_A^2(\bar{\bot})$	$wstep_A^3(\bar{\bot})$	$wstep_A^6(\bar{\bot})$	$wstep_A^7(\bar{\bot})$	$wstep_A^{10}(\bar{\bot})$
1	*false*	*true*	*true*	*true*	*true*	*true*
2	*false*	$0 \leq a \leq 0$	$0 \leq a \leq 0$	$0 \leq a \leq 0$	$0 \leq a \leq 0$	$0 \leq a \leq 0$
3	*false*	*false*	$0 \leq a \leq 0$	$0 \leq a \leq 0$	$0 \leq a \leq \infty$	$0 \leq a \leq \infty$
4	*false*	*false*	*false*	$0 \leq a \leq 0$	$0 \leq a \leq 0$	$0 \leq a \leq \infty$
5	*false*	*false*	*false*	$0 \leq a \leq 0$	$0 \leq a \leq 0$	$0 \leq a \leq \infty$
6	*false*	*false*	*false*	$0 \leq a \leq 0$	$0 \leq a \leq 0$	$0 \leq a \leq \infty$
7	*false*	*false*	*false*	$0 \leq a \leq 0$	$0 \leq a \leq 0$	$0 \leq a \leq \infty$
8	*false*	*false*	*false*	$1 \leq a \leq 1$	$1 \leq a \leq 1$	$1 \leq a \leq \infty$

Table 7.2.: Results of intervals analysis (Example 7.8)

Cousot and Cousot [1992] show that using widening is in general more powerful than approximating by introducing a consistent abstract domain that satisfies the ascending chain condition. The intuitive reason is that widening allows to approximate dynamically, without limiting the abstract domain in advance. As a complement to widening, Cousot and Cousot [1977] also define the concept of *narrowing*, which serves to retrospectively undo some of the approximation caused by widening. Narrowing is less commonly used than widening and not covered here.

7.5. Iteration Strategies

As we have seen, analysing a program consists in computing the "Kleene sequence" $\bar{\bot}$, $step_A(\bar{\bot})$, $step_A^2(\bar{\bot}),\ldots$ (or with $wstep_A$ instead of $step_A$) until a fixed point is reached. Each application of the transfer function amounts to updating the abstract states of all program points, in parallel. However, implementing the analysis like this is not very efficient, because it does not take into account the control flow of the program. Therefore, as Cousot and Cousot [1977] state: "In practice efficient versions of Kleene's sequence are used. These consist in a symbolic execution of the program which propagates information along paths of the program until stabilization."

Cousot and Cousot [1977] call such versions of the Kleene sequence *chaotic iterations*. They can formally be defined as follows.

Definition 7.10 (Chaotic iterations). *For a control flow graph with program points PP, a partially ordered set $(L, \sqsubseteq)$, and a function $f : (PP \to L) \to (PP \to L)$, a chaotic iteration for f is a sequence of mappings $m_n : PP \to L$ ($n \in \mathbb{N}$) defined by*

$$
m_n(pp) = \begin{cases} \bot & \text{if } n = 0 \\ f(m_{n-1})(pp) & \text{if } 0 < n, \, pp \in J_n \\ m_{n-1}(pp) & \text{otherwise} \end{cases}
$$

where for every $n \in \mathbb{N}$ the set $J_n \subseteq PP$ is arbitrary, except that there must be some $n_0 \in \mathbb{N}$ which satisfies that for all n and all pp, there is a $k \in \{n, \ldots, n+n_0\}$ such that $pp \in J_k$.

The function f can be $step_A$ or $wstep_A$ for some abstract domain A. In the nth step of computing a chaotic iteration, only the abstract states of the program points in the set J_n are updated, while the others are left unchanged over iteration $n - 1$. The restriction on the choice of the sets J_n ensures that no program point is omitted indefinitely. For a loop-free program, the most natural and efficient chaotic iteration is to choose the sets J_n such that the updating process follows the topological order of the control flow graph. The best strategy to handle loops is probably to stabilise each loop by recursively stabilising its subloops [Bourdoncle, 1993]. This corresponds to the intuition of symbolic execution.

7.6. Example Abstract Domains

The abstract interpretation concepts covered so far are independent of the internals of the employed abstract domain. They can be used as a framework for implementing generic abstract interpreters, into which abstract domains can be plugged modularly (see for example the work of Spoto [2005]; Laviron and Logozzo [2009]). The abstract domains then do the core work of the actual program analysis. This section sketches some instances of abstract domains: domains dealing with numerical properties (Subsection 7.6.1), domains dealing with pointer structures (Subsection 7.6.2), and domains dealing with modified or read memory locations (Subsection 7.6.3).

7.6.1. Numerical Domains

We have already looked at the numerical domains of *signs* (Figure 7.2), *constants* (Figure 7.2 and Examples 7.4, 7.5 and 7.6) and *intervals* (Examples 7.7 and 7.8). All these domains are so-called *non-relational* domains: they treat program variables separately, and are not able to consider relationships between them (such as $a < b$, without knowing anything about the absolute values of a and b).

A well-known *relational* numerical domain is the *octagons* domain of Miné [2006]. It derives invariants that are conjunctions of formulas $\pm a \pm b \leq z$, where a and b are program variables, and where $z \in \mathbb{Z}$ (or $\mathbb{R}$). The name comes from the fact that geometrically, formulas of this form correspond to polyhedra with at most eight sides in $\mathbb{Z}^2$.

Another relational domain is the *polyhedra* domain of Cousot and Halbwachs [1978], where the abstract states are conjunctions of formulas $\sum_{i=1}^{n} z_i * a_i \leq z$, where $z_i, z \in \mathbb{Z}$ (or $\mathbb{R}$) and where the a_i are program variables. These linear-arithmetic constraints correspond to geometrical polyhedra in $\mathbb{Z}^n$. Constants, intervals, octagons, and polyhedra are strictly ordered by precision, where constants are least and polyhedra most precise. Accordingly, complexity and computational cost increase from the constants to the polyhedra domain. Devising numerical abstract domains that are close to polyhedra in expressiveness but less computationally expensive is an area of active research [Laviron and Logozzo, 2009].

7.6.2. Pointer Structure Domains

In heap-manipulating programs, a common error symptom is dereferencing the *null* reference. Thus, guaranteeing the absence of such problems is an obvious goal for (lightweight) verification. A popular approach for this are type systems, such as the type system of Fähndrich and Leino [2003]: for each reference type, one introduces a possibly-*null* and a non-*null* version of the type. Attempts to assign a possibly-*null* value to a non-*null* location then show up as type errors. However, statically checking the validity of downcasts from the possibly-*null* to the non-*null* type is beyond the power of (usual) type systems. It is not beyond the power of abstract interpretation, where an abstract domain can be used that tracks properties of the form $a \doteq \textbf{null}$ and $a \neq \textbf{null}$. An analysis of this kind is for example used in the *FindBugs* tool [Hovemeyer et al., 2006].

While such a *null pointer analysis* only cares about references being *null* or not, a *points-to analysis* [Milanova et al., 2002; Sălcianu and Rinard, 2005] more generally attempts to track which reference-type locations may point to which objects. A common abstraction technique in points-to analysis is to identify an object with the allocation statement (in Java, the **new** statement) that creates it. This means that multiple objects created by the same statement, e.g., by an allocation statement in a loop, are not distinguished in the abstraction.

Another name for analyses dealing with pointer structures is *shape analysis* [Wilhelm et al., 2000]. Analyses going under this name tend to be more ambitious (and thus more computationally expensive) than what is commonly called points-to analysis. For example, a shape analysis might attempt to track whether a pointer structure is a cycle-free singly linked list, or similarly complex properties of the heap.

7.6.3. Write and Read Effects, Information Flow

Write effects analysis (or *side effects analysis*) aims at determining which locations can at most be modified by a program. In the design by contract terminology, this means inferring or checking modifies clauses. Similarly, *read effects analysis* tracks which locations are at most read, which corresponds to inferring or checking depends clauses. Such analyses are often built on an underlying points-to analysis [Milanova et al., 2002; Sălcianu and Rinard, 2005; Rakamarić and Hu, 2008]. Spoto and Poll [2003] construct a write effects analysis for checking JML assignable clauses as a stand-alone abstract domain.

The task of read effects analysis can be rephrased as analysing from which input location there is a flow of information to any output location. A natural generalisation is to ask "from which inputs may there be a flow of information to *which* outputs?". Analysis of such questions is known as *information flow analysis* [Sabelfeld and Myers, 2003]. Often, type systems are used for information flow analysis, but abstract interpretation based approaches also exist [Barbuti et al., 2002; Francesco and Martini, 2006].

7.7. Tools

To illustrate current uses of abstract interpretation, this section briefly describes a few exemplary tools, without aiming at completeness.

ASTRÉE [Cousot et al., 2005; Blanchet et al., 2003] is an abstract interpretation based tool that aims at the automatic and sound verification of the absence of program run-time errors, such as array index out of bounds or division by zero errors. In addition, ASTRÉE can verify user-specified assertions. Its target language is a limited form of C; the list of unsupported features includes backwards goto commands, unbounded recursion, and dynamic memory allocation. The intended area of application is embedded safety-critical control software, where the analysed C code is generated automatically from programs in a high-level synchronous language such as *Lustre* [Caspi et al., 1987].

Internally, ASTRÉE uses a combination of several abstract domains, such as octagons and specialised domains to handle floating-point numbers or digital filters. Most of the domains are infinite and do not satisfy the ascending chain condition, and termination is ensured by non-monotonic widening. The abstraction is not the same at every program point; for example, the octagons domain is parametrised by sets of program variables attached to the individual program points, and only these variables are used for abstracting at the corresponding program point.

As is characteristic for abstract interpretation, the analysis process itself is entirely automatic. However, eliminating false alarms is a manual, iterative process, where one needs to fine-tune the analyser to the particular application program [Delmas and Souyris, 2007]. As an indication of the performance of ASTRÉE, Cousot et al. [2005] report that a run on 70 000 lines of code lasted 46 minutes, and one on 400 000 lines took about 12 hours.

PolySpace [PolySpace] is a commercial product of The MathWorks, Inc. Like ASTRÉE, its goal is to soundly prove the absence of run-time errors by abstract interpretation. PolySpace targets embedded software written in C/C++ or Ada, and it internally makes use of the polyhedra domain (and probably others).

The *Boogie verifier* [Barnett et al., 2006] contains an abstract interpretation module for inferring certain loop invariants automatically. It uses several base domains, such as the polyhedra domain, and a coordinating "congruence-closure domain" that deals with heap locations while pretending to the underlying base domains that these locations are ordinary local variables [Chang and Leino, 2005]. Thus, the base domains need not be aware of the heap.

Clousot [Laviron and Logozzo, 2009] is a stand-alone verifier based on abstract interpretation. It is used as the static checker in the *Code Contracts* project at Microsoft Research [Fähndrich et al., 2010].

Besides complete tools that implement abstract interpretation, there are also libraries that provide implementations of abstract domains for use in other tools. Two such libraries, which implement well-known numerical abstract domains, are the *Parma Polyhedra Library* [Bagnara et al., 2006] and the *APRON* library [Jeannet and Miné, 2009].

7.8. Conclusion

This chapter has reviewed abstract interpretation, a generic theoretical framework for static program analysis. A particular analysis is defined in the framework by giving an abstract domain, which provides a set of "abstract states" together with mathematical functions that describe the effect that the elementary constructs of the analysed programming language have on the abstract states. An abstract domain and a particular program induce a transfer function, such that analysing the program means computing a fixed point of the transfer function. The theory furthermore provides notions for soundly approximating a (perhaps uncomputable or inefficient) abstract domain with another (more abstract, less precise) abstract domain, and the concept of widening operators for approximating fixed points in abstract domains whose mathematical characteristics are less than ideal.

Classical abstract domains deal with numerical properties of one or many program variables. One limitation of these domains is that they do not support quantifiers; extending numerical domains to support quantified properties is an area of current research [Gulwani et al., 2008]. Non-numerical domains deal for example with pointer structures on the heap, or with memory locations being modified or read. A general observation is that these different classes of properties can influence each other in a program: for example, whether a reference is *null* or not may depend on numerical properties, and vice versa. Thus, a challenge in practice is to combine several abstract domains in a useful way.

We have seen that the abstract states of abstract domains can be understood as logical formulas, although in implementations they are not typically represented as such. The result of an analysis is a mapping of program points to invariants, where the invariants attached to loop entry points are loop invariants in the sense of Chapter 5. We have also seen that the fixed point computation in an analysis is a form of symbolic execution. The relationship between abstract interpretation and deductive verification in dynamic logic is further explored in Chapter 8, where we see an approach for integrating a form of abstract interpretation into JavaDL*.

8. Predicate Abstraction in Java Dynamic Logic

In Chapter 7, we have reviewed the basics of abstract interpretation theory, and observed similarities between abstract interpretation and deductive verification in dynamic logic. Unlike usual abstract interpretations, the deductive approach can, at least in principle, handle arbitrarily precise properties. This comes at the cost of sometimes needing human interaction for proving the resulting first-order problems, and at the cost of requiring manually specified loop invariants. This chapter aims at alleviating the latter issue by integrating abstract interpretation concepts into the deductive setting. We aim at a *deep* integration, where the logical framework of JavaDL*—in particular its extensive set of symbolic execution rules—is used for performing the invariant generation. In a *shallow* integration, a separate abstract interpretation tool generates loop invariants that are then used in a deductive proof. The advantage of a deep integration is that it avoids the duplication of knowledge that goes along with a shallow integration, where the semantics of the programming language and properties of the involved logical theories are modelled both in the abstract interpreter and in the deductive verifier.

A form of abstract interpretation that is particularly suitable for a deep integration into dynamic logic is *predicate abstraction* [Graf and Saïdi, 1997]. In predicate abstraction, the set of abstract states consists of Boolean combinations of formulas from a predetermined, finite set, called the set of *loop predicates*. Instead of using a transfer function that directly models the approximative effect of program statements on abstract states, in predicate abstraction the program is symbolically executed in a precise fashion, and the necessary approximation is introduced by explicit abstraction steps, where an automated theorem prover is used to determine an abstract state $\alpha(\varphi)$ that correctly approximates the current concrete state represented by the formula φ. Compared with other forms of abstract interpretation, a limitation of predicate abstraction is that it only supports *finite* abstract domains. On the other hand, an advantage is that it allows flexibly adapting the abstract domain by simply changing the set of loop predicates. In the same vein, predicate abstraction can quite easily support complex, quantified invariants [Flanagan and Qadeer, 2002]. It can be extended with an iterative refinement process that automatically adapts the domain to the particular problem [Clarke et al., 2000].

Outline A high level introduction to the approach is contained in Section 8.1. In Section 8.2, new calculus rules are defined, and how these rules are to be used is described in more detail in Section 8.3. Section 8.4 gives details on the predicate abstraction scheme used in a prototypical implementation. The method is further illustrated with the help of an example in Section 8.5, and practical experience with the implementation is reported in Section 8.6. An extension for proofs of dependency contracts is presented in Section 8.7. Section 8.8 gives an overview of related work, and Section 8.9 contains conclusions.

8.1. Approach

We focus on proofs for Hoare-logic like proof obligations $pre \rightarrow [p]post$ in this chapter, such as the proof obligation for method contracts of Chapter 5. We consider only proof obligations where the employed modality is the box modality. Automatically generating the *variant terms* necessary for additionally proving termination is beyond the scope of this work.

Symbolically executing the program p of such a proof obligation in the JavaDL* calculus produces proof nodes labelled with sequents of the form $\Gamma \Rightarrow \{u\}[p']\varphi, \Delta$. Intuitively, these sequents can be read as "we associate with the program point given as the first active statement of p' the pair $\left(\bigwedge(\Gamma \cup \neg\Delta), u \right)$". The formula $\bigwedge(\Gamma \cup \neg\Delta)$ and the update u together describe a set of states which may occur at the program point. In this way, the symbolic execution process is related to an abstract interpretation, where the set of abstract states is $L = \left((Fma_\Sigma \times Upd_\Sigma)/\Leftrightarrow, \Rightarrow \right)$, and where the partial order $\Rightarrow$ is defined such that $(\varphi_1, u_1) \Rightarrow (\varphi_2, u_2)$ holds if and only if for all Kripke structures $\mathcal{K}$ and all variable assignments β we have

$$\left\{ val_{\mathcal{K},s,\beta}(u_1)(s) \mid s \in \mathcal{S}, (\mathcal{K}, s, \beta) \models \varphi_1 \right\}$$
$$\subseteq \left\{ val_{\mathcal{K},s,\beta}(u_2)(s) \mid s \in \mathcal{S}, (\mathcal{K}, s, \beta) \models \varphi_2 \right\}.$$

A difference between the symbolic execution in the calculus and such an abstract interpretation is in the treatment of control flow splits. The calculus handles them by branching the proof tree, where the created branches remain separated permanently. On the other hand, abstract interpretation uses the *merge* function of the abstract domain to combine properties at junction points in the control flow graph (Definition 7.5). This corresponds to accumulating properties for every program point, instead of treating the execution paths separately. For loops, the unbounded number of execution paths makes such an accumulation necessary; deductive verification "cheats" here by assuming to be given a loop invariant, which already is an accumulated description of all paths through the loop.

We can overcome this difference by introducing a rule into the calculus that merges several proof branches into one. For two branches $\Gamma_1 \Rightarrow [p]\varphi, \Delta_1$ and $\Gamma_2 \Rightarrow [p]\varphi, \Delta_2$ (without updates in front of the modal operator), we can simply use logical disjunction to "merge" the sequents into the single sequent $\bigwedge(\Gamma_1 \cup \neg\Delta_1) \vee \bigwedge(\Gamma_2 \cup \neg\Delta_2) \Rightarrow [p]\varphi$. The merged sequent is equivalent to the conjunction of the two original sequents. A rule that performs such a merging has a single premiss and several conclusions. Allowing such rules means to generalise the structure of proofs from trees to directed acyclic graphs which are connected and rooted.

Merging two sequents $\Gamma_1 \Rightarrow \{u_1\}[p]\varphi, \Delta_1$ and $\Gamma_2 \Rightarrow \{u_2\}[p]\varphi, \Delta_2$ (containing updates u_1 and u_2 in front of the modal operator) is slightly more complicated, because there is no disjunction operator on updates. A solution is to convert the updates into formulas in the antecedent, using the strongest postconditions predicate transformer. For example, the sequents $\Rightarrow \{i := 0\}[p]\varphi$ and $\Rightarrow \{i := 1\}[p]\varphi$ can be converted into the equivalent sequents $i \doteq 0 \Rightarrow [p]\varphi$ and $i \doteq 1 \Rightarrow [p]\varphi$, which may then be merged into the sequent $i \doteq 0 \vee i \doteq 1 \Rightarrow [p]\varphi$.

Loops can now be treated in the calculus by applying the unwindLoop and conditional rules of Figure 5.9, symbolically executing the body, and then merging the resulting sequent (where the loop entry is again the first active statement) with the previous such sequent. For example, we might begin with a sequent $\Rightarrow \{i := 0\}[\text{while}(\text{i<j}) \ldots]\varphi$, which says that we have to consider the loop in all states where i has the value 0. After one iteration, we might arrive at the sequent $\Rightarrow \{i := 1\}[\text{while}(\text{i<j}) \ldots]\varphi$, reflecting the fact that after this iteration, i has been incremented by one. "Merging" these sequents yields the sequent $i \doteq 0 \vee i \doteq 1 \Rightarrow [\text{while}(\text{i<j}) \ldots]\varphi$. Thus, we know that after up to one iteration through the loop, the value of i is either 0 or 1.

With every such iteration of unwinding, symbolically executing and merging, the set of states that are deemed possible for the loop entry point becomes larger. In principle, we only have to repeat this iterative process until this set of states stabilises, i.e., until it is a fixed point of the process: once this happens, it covers all states which are possible for the loop entry on any execution path, or in other words, its representation as a formula then is a loop invariant. Having removed the difference in the treatment of control flow splits and added the notion of iterative fixed-point computation, the verification process can now really be seen as an abstract interpretation on the above-mentioned abstract domain, where the abstract states are pairs of formulas and updates. It uses a particular chaotic iteration strategy of "symbolic execution" (Section 7.5).

To make the fixed point iteration in the calculus terminate, we need to introduce approximation. A form of approximation particularly suitable in our context is that of *predicate abstraction* [Graf and Saïdi, 1997; Flanagan and Qadeer, 2002]: we assume that for every loop we are given a finite set P of formulas called *loop predicates.* Then, the abstraction of a formula φ for the entry point of a loop is a Boolean combination $\alpha_P(\varphi)$ of elements of P which is implied by the original formula. That is, the abstraction retains the information from the formula which is expressible by the predicates in P, and approximates away everything else. Similar to how a widening operator can be applied at loop entry points to ensure termination (Section 7.4), we can ensure termination by applying the α_P function to the current formula $\bigwedge(\Gamma \cup \neg\Delta)$ at every loop entry point, before unwinding the loop with unwindLoop. As $\bigwedge(\Gamma \cup \neg\Delta)$ implies $\alpha_P(\bigwedge(\Gamma \cup \neg\Delta))$, replacing the former with the latter is a sound deductive step. Since there are only finitely many Boolean combinations of the predicates, there cannot be an infinite ascending chain of formulas in the range of α_P, so a fixed point must be reached eventually. The found loop invariant can then be used to apply the loopInvariant rule.

With predicate abstraction, the loop predicates P associated with a loop form the building blocks for the invariants which can be found for that loop. Loop predicates can either be specified manually—which is easier than having to specify whole, correct loop invariants—or be generated heuristically based on the particular program and specification being verified.

8.2. Rules

In this section, the calculus of Chapters 5 and 6 is extended with four rules that enable it to perform predicate abstraction based loop invariant inference as described in Section 8.1: a rule for converting updates into formulas (Subsection 8.2.1), a rule for merging proof branches (Subsection 8.2.2), a rule for "resetting" a proof branch to the sequent of an inner node of the proof (Subsection 8.2.3), and a rule performing the predicate abstraction itself (Subsection 8.2.4).

8.2.1. Converting Updates into Formulas

As indicated in Section 8.1, both the rule for merging proof branches (Subsection 8.2.2) and the rule for the abstraction step (Subsection 8.2.4) require that the "current symbolic state" in the sequent is expressed exclusively through formulas. Thus, we need a way to transform sequents of the form $\Gamma \Rightarrow \{u\}[p]\varphi, \Delta$ such that the leading update u is removed from the modality $[p]$. This can be achieved with the shiftUpdate rule defined below.

Definition 8.1 (Rule shiftUpdate).

$$\frac{\{u'\}\Gamma,\ upd \ \Rightarrow\ \varphi,\ \{u'\}\Delta}{\Gamma \ \Rightarrow\ \{u\}\varphi,\ \Delta}$$

where:

- *the function* $targets \colon Upd_\Sigma \to 2^{\mathcal{PV}}$ *is defined by*

$$targets(u) = \begin{cases} \{\mathsf{a}\} & \textit{if } u = \mathsf{a} := t \\ targets(u_1) \cup targets(u_2) & \textit{if } u = u_1 \parallel u_2 \\ targets(u_2) & \textit{if } u = \{u_1\}u_2 \end{cases}$$

- $targets(u) = \{\mathsf{a}_1, \ldots, \mathsf{a}_n\}$ *(where $1 \leq n$)*
- $a_i' \colon \alpha(\mathsf{a}_i) \in \mathcal{F}$ *is a fresh constant symbol for all $i \in \{1, \ldots, n\}$*
- $u' = (\mathsf{a}_1 := a_1' \parallel \ldots \parallel \mathsf{a}_n := a_n')$
- $upd = \bigwedge_{i \in \{1, \ldots, n\}} \mathsf{a}_i \doteq \{u'\}\{u\}\mathsf{a}_i$

Intuitively, the update u' substitutes for each updated program variable a_i a fresh constant symbol a_i' that represents the old, pre-update, value of a. The formula upd links the old instances with the current ones. The new antecedent $(\{u'\}\Gamma,\ upd)$ is the strongest postcondition of Γ under u (see also Section 5.1).

Example 8.1. Applying the shiftUpdate rule to the sequent

$$\mathsf{o.f} \doteq 5 \ \Rightarrow \ \{\mathsf{heap} := store(\mathsf{heap}, \mathsf{o2}, \mathsf{f}, 42)\}[p]\varphi$$

yields the sequent

$$\{\mathsf{heap} := h'\}(\mathsf{o.f} \doteq 5),$$
$$\mathsf{heap} \doteq \{\mathsf{heap} := h'\}\{\mathsf{heap} := store(\mathsf{heap}, \mathsf{o2}, \mathsf{f}, 42)\}\mathsf{heap}$$
$$\Rightarrow [p]\varphi,$$

where $h' \colon Heap \in \mathcal{F}$ is a fresh constant symbol, and where the update u has been "shifted" to the antecedent. Using the update rules of Figure 5.8, the sequent can be simplified to

$$select_{Int}(h', \mathsf{o}, \mathsf{f}) \doteq 5, \ \mathsf{heap} \doteq store(h', \mathsf{o2}, \mathsf{f}, 42) \ \Rightarrow \ [p]\varphi,$$

which does not contain updates any more. $*$

The disadvantages of applying shiftUpdate are that it introduces a new constant h', and that handling an update u is generally more efficient in the JavaDL* calculus than handling a formula upd. This is the motivation for using updates as long as possible, instead of using strongest postconditions for symbolic execution right away.

The shiftUpdate rule benefits from the explicit heap model of JavaDL*. Its JavaDL version [Weiß, 2009, 2011] needs to introduce quantifiers and case distinctions for the possible aliasing situations. These complications are absent in the JavaDL* version of the rule, because—as discussed in Section 5.1—updates in JavaDL* have handed over the responsibility for efficiently dealing with aliasing to the theory of arrays, and thus removing an update with shiftUpdate does not compromise the ability to delay aliasing-related case distinctions as long as possible.

Theorem 8.1 (Soundness of shiftUpdate). *Let the formula sets* $\Gamma, \Delta \in 2_\Sigma^{Fma}$, *the update* $u \in Upd_\Sigma$, *the formula* $\varphi \in Fma_\Sigma$, *the program variables* $\mathsf{a}_1, \ldots, \mathsf{a}_n \in \mathcal{PV}$, *the constant symbols* $a_1, \ldots, a_n \in \mathcal{F}$, *the update* $u' \in Upd_\Sigma$ *and the formula* $upd \in Fma_\Sigma$ *all be as in Definition 8.1. If*

$$\models \{u'\}\Gamma, \ upd \ \Rightarrow \ \varphi, \ \{u'\}\Delta,$$

then the following holds:

$$\models \Gamma \ \Rightarrow \ \{u\}\varphi, \ \Delta.$$

Theorem 8.1 is proven in Appendix A.10.

8.2.2. Merging Proof Branches

Before we can define a rule for merging execution paths at junction points in the control flow graph, we must first generalise the notion of *rules* so that a rule can have more than one conclusion.

Definition 8.2 (Rules, generalisation of Definition 5.7). *A rule is a binary relation* $r \subseteq Seq_\Sigma^* \times Seq_\Sigma^*$. *If* $\big((p_1, \ldots, p_n), (c_1, \ldots, c_m)\big) \in r$, *then we say that the conclusions* $c_1, \ldots, c_m \in Seq_\Sigma$ *are derivable from the premisses* $p_1, \ldots, p_n$ *using* r.

A rule r *is called sound if for all pairs* $\big((p_1, \ldots, p_n), (c_1, \ldots, c_m)\big) \in r$ *the following holds: if all premisses* $p_1, \ldots, p_n$ *are logically valid, then all conclusions* $c_1, \ldots, c_m$ *are also logically valid.*

All rules in the sense of Definition 5.7 are rules also in the sense of Definition 8.2. The notion of *proof trees* (Definition 5.8) is generalised to cover rules with multiple conclusions in Subsection 8.2.3.

Definition 8.3 (Rule merge).

$$\frac{\bigwedge(\Gamma_1 \cup \neg\Delta_1) \vee \cdots \vee \bigwedge(\Gamma_n \cup \neg\Delta_n) \ \Rightarrow \ \varphi}{\Gamma_1 \ \Rightarrow \ \varphi, \ \Delta_1 \qquad \cdots \qquad \Gamma_n \ \Rightarrow \ \varphi, \ \Delta_n}$$

Aside from having multiple conclusions, merge is a simple propositional logic rule, whose soundness is obvious.

Theorem 8.2 (Soundness of merge)**.** *Let the formula sets* $\Gamma_1, \Delta_1, \ldots, \Gamma_n, \Delta_n \in$ 2_Σ^{Fma} *and the formula* $\varphi \in Fma_\Sigma$ *be as in Definition 8.3. If*

$$\models \bigwedge(\Gamma_1 \cup \neg\Delta_1) \vee \cdots \vee \bigwedge(\Gamma_n \cup \neg\Delta_n) \Rightarrow \varphi,$$

then the following holds:

$$\models \Gamma_1 \Rightarrow \varphi, \Delta_1 \qquad \ldots \qquad \Gamma_n \Rightarrow \varphi, \Delta_n.$$

Theorem 8.2 is proven in Appendix A.11. A typical example application of the merge rule is to combine two leaves of the form $\Gamma_1 \Rightarrow [\mathbf{while}(g)p]\varphi$ and $\Gamma_2 \Rightarrow [\mathbf{while}(g)p]\varphi$ into the single new leaf $\bigwedge \Gamma_1 \vee \bigwedge \Gamma_2 \Rightarrow [\mathbf{while}(g)p]\varphi$.

As an aside, the merge rule may be useful beyond the purpose of automatic loop invariant generation. Without it, the splitting of the proof induced by branching in the control flow graph can lead to a duplication of effort, where the same program is handled several times in the verification. For example, symbolically executing the program "$\mathbf{if}(g)\ p_1\ \mathbf{else}\ p_2;\ q$" leads to a split in the proof. All execution paths through the program (except for those throwing exceptions or executing **return** statements) eventually converge on the program fragment q, and thus all proof branches corresponding to these paths eventually deal with q. This duplication can significantly increase the size of the proof if there is a large number of case distinctions in the program. Merging the involved proof branches once they reach q avoids the issue.

8.2.3. Setting Back Proof Branches

Symbolic execution sometimes creates proof branches that do not contribute to the loop invariant, and that we thus do not want to follow up on during the loop invariant generation process. For example, such irrelevant branches occur when the body of the loop throws an uncaught exception: the execution paths where this happens never return to the loop entry, and thus do not affect the loop invariant. Another example is the loop termination branch which is created when applying the unwindLoop and conditional rules and then splitting the proof on the loop guard. Instead of considering these side branches in every iteration, we revert them to the loop entry with a rule setBack.

Even though we refer to setBack as a "rule", strictly speaking it is not a rule in the sense of Definition 8.2. Rather, we build it into the generalised notion of proof graphs, as a second way of extending such a graph besides applying rules in the narrower sense.

Definition 8.4 (Proof graphs, generalisation of Definition 5.8)**.** *A proof graph is a finite, directed, rooted, connected, acyclic graph, whose edges are directed away from the root, and which satisfies that*

- *all inner nodes n are labelled with a sequent seq(n) $\in Seq_\Sigma$, and*
- *all leaves n are labelled either with a sequent seq(n) $\in Seq_\Sigma$ or with the symbol $*$ (in which case they are called* closed*), and*
- *all inner nodes "parent" satisfy that either*
  - *all edges (parent $\rightarrow$ child$_1$),...,(parent $\rightarrow$ child$_n$) originating in this parent node are labelled with the same rule r, such that either*
    - $*$ *none of the children child$_1$,...,child$_n$ is closed, and seq(parent) is derivable from seq(child$_1$),...,seq(child$_n$) using r, or*
    - $*$ *n = 1, child$_1$ is closed, and $\big((),seq(parent)\big) \in r$, or*
  - *there is exactly one edge (parent $\rightarrow$ child) originating in parent, child has no other parents, the edge is labelled with* setBack, *and there is a dominator dom of parent in the graph such that seq(child) = seq(dom).*

A proof tree is called closed *if all of its leaves are closed. A closed proof tree whose root is labelled with s is also called a* proof *for s.*

As usual, a *dominator* of a node n is a node n' with the property that every path from the root to n passes through n'. The setBack operation replaces a leaf in the graph by one of its dominators. This can be seen as a non-destructive form of backtracking. It is not expressible as a sequent calculus rule, but it preserves the overall meaning of the proof: if all leaves are logically valid, then the root must be logically valid.

Theorem 8.3 (Soundness of setBack). *Every proof graph satisfies: if all used rules are sound and if the sequents of all open leaves are logically valid, then the sequent of the root node is also logically valid.*

A proof sketch for Theorem 8.3 is contained in Appendix A.12. An example for a proof graph that uses setBack is shown in Figure 8.1. Instead of continuing on the second of the two branches, it is reverted to the loop entry point with setBack. After the loop body p has been symbolically executed on the other branch, the merge rule of Subsection 8.2.2 is used to reunite the two branches.

8.2.4. Predicate Abstraction

The predicateAbstraction rule defined in Definition 8.5 below is responsible for introducing approximation into the symbolic execution process.

Definition 8.5 (Rule predicateAbstraction).

$$\frac{\alpha_P\big(\bigwedge(\Gamma \cup \neg\Delta)\big) \;\Rightarrow\; [\pi\ \mathtt{while}(g)p;\ \omega]\varphi}{\Gamma \;\Rightarrow\; [\pi\ \mathtt{while}(g)p;\ \omega]\varphi,\ \Delta}$$

where:

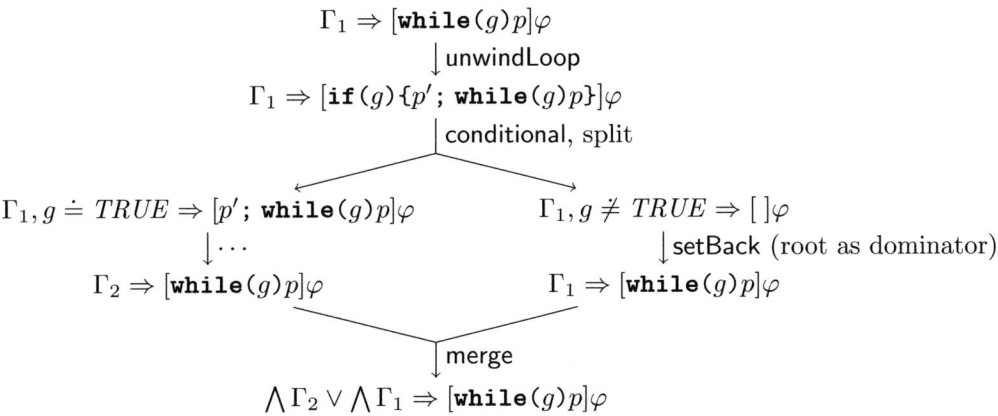

Figure 8.1.: Example proof graph with setBack

- $P \subseteq Fma_\Sigma$ *is the finite set of "loop predicates" associated with the loop*
- $\alpha_P : Fma_\Sigma \to Fma_\Sigma$ *is a function that computes for any formula φ a predicate abstraction using P; i.e., $\alpha_P(\varphi)$ is some Boolean combination of the predicates in P such that $\models \varphi \to \alpha_P(\varphi)$ holds*

Note that the rule uses the loop only as the provider of the set P of loop predicates and is otherwise independent from the form of the program in the sequent. The details of computing $\alpha_P(\varphi)$ depend on the particular predicate abstraction scheme being used (Section 8.4). Usually, this computation itself requires non-trivial first-order reasoning.

The requirement that $\varphi \to \alpha_P(\varphi)$ is logically valid corresponds to the second requirement of Definition 7.7 on the consistency of abstract domains, namely the requirement that the abstraction function α and the concretisation function γ satisfy $c \sqsubseteq_C \gamma(\alpha(c))$ for all c in the set L_C of states of the more concrete domain. Here, L_C is equal to Fma_Σ, the set L_A of states of the more abstract domain is a finite subset of Fma_Σ, the concretisation function $\gamma : L_A \to L_C$ is the identity function, and $\sqsubseteq_C$ is the implication relation $\Rightarrow$ on formulas.

Additionally, α_P is almost a widening operator (Definition 7.8) for an abstract domain whose abstract states are formulas, except that it only takes a single argument. We can see it as a restricted variant of widening, where only the current abstract state is taken into account, instead of both the current abstract state and the previous abstract state.

Theorem 8.4 (Soundness of predicateAbstraction). *Let the formula sets $\Gamma, \Delta \in 2^{Fma_\Sigma}$, the program "$\pi$ while$(g)p$; ω" and the formula $\varphi \in Fma_\Sigma$ be as in*

Definition 8.5. If

$$\models \bigwedge(\Gamma \cup \neg\Delta) \to \alpha_P(\bigwedge(\Gamma \cup \neg\Delta))$$

$$\models \alpha_P(\bigwedge(\Gamma \cup \neg\Delta)) \implies [\pi \,\mathtt{while}(g)p; \,\omega]\varphi$$

then the following holds:

$$\models \Gamma \implies [\pi \,\mathtt{while}(g)p; \,\omega]\varphi, \, \Delta$$

The proof for Theorem 8.4 in Appendix A.13 is simple.

8.3. Proof Search Strategy

Section 8.1 has sketched the overall idea for how to apply the rules defined in Section 8.2. In this section, we concretise this aspect by defining a suitable *proof search strategy*, i.e., an algorithm that automatically chooses the next rule to apply to a given unclosed proof graph. The strategy extends a strategy that is able to do ordinary symbolic execution and first-order reasoning with the capability to infer a loop invariant whenever an invariant-less loop is encountered during proof construction.

The strategy is defined semi-formally in Figures 8.2, 8.3 and 8.4. The functions in Figure 8.2 are assumed to be present by the functions in the other figures; their semantics should be self-explanatory. The functions in Figure 8.3 are helpers for the main function *chooseRuleApplication* in Figure 8.4. This function returns a pair of a set of leaves and a rule, with the meaning that the returned rule should be applied to the returned leaves. The presentation is a bit imprecise in this respect, because in general there may of course be multiple ways to apply a particular rule to a set of leaves. However, for the rules that matter here, the exact application focus is either unique or it is explained in the paragraphs below. We assume that all occurring sequents are of the form $\Gamma \implies \{u\}[p]\varphi, \Delta$, where p is the program being symbolically executed.

We consider a symbolic execution state, as captured by a node of the proof graph, to be "in" a loop when that loop has previously been "entered" by applying the unwindLoop rule but not yet "left" by applying the loopInvariant rule. Accordingly, the *entryNode* function in Figure 8.3 determines the node where a specific loop, passed as a parameter to the function, has last been entered. The *innermostLoop* function returns the loop that has last been entered but not yet left.

The *waiting* function of Figure 8.3 tells whether rules should not currently be applied to the passed node, because operations on other branches have to be performed first. This is the case if the first active statement is a loop, if there

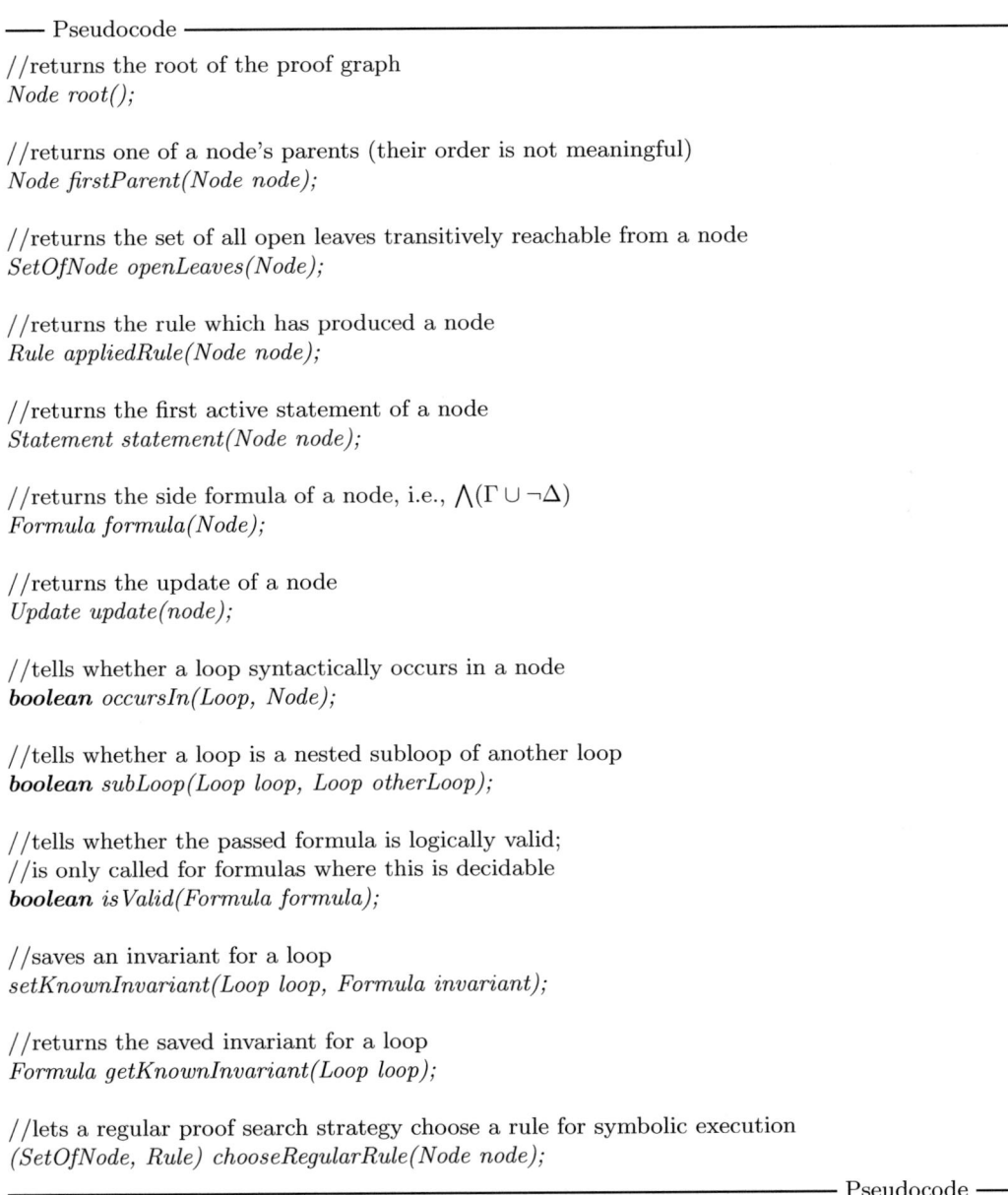

—— Pseudocode ——————————————————————

//returns the root of the proof graph
Node root();

//returns one of a node's parents (their order is not meaningful)
Node firstParent(Node node);

//returns the set of all open leaves transitively reachable from a node
SetOfNode openLeaves(Node);

//returns the rule which has produced a node
Rule appliedRule(Node node);

//returns the first active statement of a node
Statement statement(Node node);

//returns the side formula of a node, i.e., $\bigwedge(\Gamma \cup \neg\Delta)$
Formula formula(Node);

//returns the update of a node
Update update(node);

//tells whether a loop syntactically occurs in a node
boolean *occursIn(Loop, Node);*

//tells whether a loop is a nested subloop of another loop
boolean *subLoop(Loop loop, Loop otherLoop);*

//tells whether the passed formula is logically valid;
//is only called for formulas where this is decidable
boolean *isValid(Formula formula);*

//saves an invariant for a loop
setKnownInvariant(Loop loop, Formula invariant);

//returns the saved invariant for a loop
Formula getKnownInvariant(Loop loop);

//lets a regular proof search strategy choose a rule for symbolic execution
(SetOfNode, Rule) chooseRegularRule(Node node);

—————————————————————————— Pseudocode ——

Figure 8.2.: Proof search strategy for predicate abstraction: assumed functions

```
——— Pseudocode ——————————————————————————————
//returns the node where symbolic execution entered a loop
Node entryNode(Node node, Loop loop)
    if(statement(node) = loop)
        if(appliedRule(node) = unwindLoop) return node;
        else if(appliedRule(node) = loopInvariant) return none;
    if(node = root()) return none;
    else return entryNode(firstParent(node), loop);


//returns the innermost loop that symbolic execution is in
Loop innermostLoop(Node node, SetOfLoop leftLoops)
    if(statement(node) is of type Loop)
        Loop loop := statement(node);
        if(appliedRule(node) = unwindLoop and loop ∉ leftLoops) return loop;
        else if(appliedRule(node) = loopInvariant) leftLoops := leftLoops ∪ {loop};
    if(node = root()) return none;
    else return innermostLoop(firstParent(node), leftLoops);


//tells whether for a leaf another leaf is a merge candidate
boolean isMergeCandidate(Node leaf, Node otherLeaf)
    precondition(statement(leaf) is of type Loop);
    Loop loop := statement(leaf);
    Node entry := entryNode(leaf, loop);
    if(entry ≠ none) return otherLeaf ∈ openLeaves(entry);
    else if(occursIn(loop, otherLeaf))
        if(statement(otherLeaf) is of type Loop and subLoop(loop, statement(otherLeaf)))
            return false;
        else return true;
    return false;


//returns the merge candidates for a leaf (these always include the leaf itself)
SetOfNode mergeCandidates(Node leaf)
    precondition(statement(leaf) is of type Loop);
    SetOfNode result := ∅;
    foreach(otherLeaf ∈ openLeaves(root()))
        if(isMergeCandidate(leaf, otherLeaf)) result := result ∪ {otherLeaf};
    return result;


//tells for a leaf whether there are merge candidates to wait for
boolean waiting(Node leaf)
    if(statement(leaf) is of type Loop and update(leaf) = none)
        Loop loop = statement(leaf);
        foreach(otherLeaf ∈ mergeCandidates(leaf))
            if(statement(otherLeaf) ≠ loop or update(otherLeaf) ≠ none)
                return true;
    return false;
——————————————————————————————————— Pseudocode ———
```

Figure 8.3.: Proof search strategy for predicate abstraction: helper functions

---
—— Pseudocode ——————————————————————————

```
//main: chooses a set of leaves and a rule which should be applied to the leaves
(SetOfNode, Rule) chooseRuleApplication()
    Node leaf := any leaf ∈ openLeaves(root()) such that not waiting(leaf);
    Loop innermostLoop := innermostLoop(leaf, ∅);
    if(innermostLoop ≠ none and not occursIn(innermostLoop, leaf))
        Node entry := entryNode(innermostLoop, leaf);
        return ({leaf}, setBack[dominator=entry]);
    else if(statement(leaf) is of type Loop)
        Loop loop := statement(leaf);
        Node entry := entryNode(leaf, loop);
        Rule lastRule := appliedRule(firstParent(leaf));
        if(knownInvariant(loop) ≠ none and innermostLoop = none)
            return ({leaf}, loopInvariant[inv=knownInvariant(loop)]);
        else if(update(leaf) ≠ none)
            return ({leaf}, shiftUpdate);
        else if(lastRule = shiftUpdate)
            return (mergeCandidates(leaf), merge);
        else if(lastRule = merge)
            return ({leaf}, predicateAbstraction);
        else if(lastRule = predicateAbstraction)
            if(entry ≠ none and isValid(formula(leaf) → formula(entry))
                setKnownInvariant(loop, formula(leaf));
                return ({leaf}, loopInvariant[inv=formula(leaf)])
            else return ({leaf}, loopUnwind);
    else return ({leaf}, chooseRegularRule(leaf));
```

—————————————————————————————— Pseudocode ——

Figure 8.4.: Proof search strategy for predicate abstraction: main function

is no update in front of the modal operator, and if there is at least one "merge candidate" where the first active statement is not that loop or where there is an update in front of the modal operator: in this case, we first want to continue with the merge candidates, before eventually combining all of them with the merge rule.

The set of "merge candidates" needed by the *waiting* function is computed by the *mergeCandidates* function, also shown in Figure 8.3. The *mergeCandidates* in turn uses the *isMergeCandidate* function to filter the merge candidates out of the set of all leaves of the graph. If symbolic execution is currently inside the loop that is the active statement of the leaf being evaluated, then the merge candidates are all leaves below the entry node of this loop. Otherwise, the merge candidates are all leaves in which the loop syntactically occurs, except for those where the active statement is another loop into which the first loop is nested (such that waiting for them would lead to a deadlock).

The main function *chooseRuleApplication* in Figure 8.4 now works as follows. First, it picks an arbitrary open leaf that is not waiting for other branches. Then, it checks whether the innermost loop that symbolic execution is "in" does not occur in the program contained in the modal operator any more. If so, this indicates that the current branch will not return to the loop entry, for example because an exception has been thrown which is not caught within the loop body. The next step is then to revert it to the entry point of the innermost loop with setBack. Otherwise, the choice of the rule depends on whether the first active statement is a loop or not. If not, the strategy chooses a regular applicable symbolic execution rule or a first-order rule. The chosen rule must not destroy the sequent structure $\Gamma \Rightarrow \{u\}[p]\varphi, \Delta$.

If the first active statement is a loop, and if a loop invariant is already known for this loop, the invariant is used to apply loopInvariant. Not shown in the pseudocode is the instantiation of the modifies clause *mod* that is required by loopInvariant. We simply use *allLocs*, unless a more specific modifies clause has been specified. The invariant generation process does not generate modifies clauses. A generated invariant may however contain a formula like *frame* in Definitions 5.9 and 6.5, which semantically has the same effect as a modifies clause.

If no invariant is known, then special rules are applied in a fixed order. First after reaching the loop entry via regular symbolic execution, the shiftUpdate rule is used to get rid of the update preceding the modal operator. Then, merge can be applied to merge the current proof branch with all its merge candidates. The fact that the current leaf is not waiting implies that all merge candidates are ready for merging, i.e., in all these leaves the active statement is the same loop as in the current leaf, and there is no update in front of the modality.

The next step is to abstract with the predicateAbstraction rule. Finally, we check whether the iterative unwinding process has reached a fixed point, i.e., whether the current abstraction implies the previous abstraction for this loop. If so, then the current abstraction is used for applying the loopInvariant rule. Otherwise, one more iteration is initiated with unwindLoop.

Note that the other direction of implication always holds, i.e., the current abstraction is always implied by the previous one. This is because in each iteration, the new abstraction results from disjunctively combining several proof branches, including at least one that corresponds to the previous abstraction. Also note that checking whether the current abstraction implies the previous one is a comparatively simple task: since both formulas are built from the same set P of loop predicates, this check requires propositional reasoning only, not full first-order theorem proving (as in the computation of α_P itself).

8.4. Implementational Details

This section deals with two questions that have been left unanswered so far, namely the question of how to compute the abstraction function α_P (Subsection 8.4.1), and the question of where to get the loop predicates P from (Subsection 8.4.2). There are different possible answers to these questions. The focus of this chapter is on the framework for integrating predicate abstraction into JavaDL*, which is independent of these questions. The present section describes the particular answers that are used in a prototypical implementation of the approach in KeY, which is the basis for the experiments in Section 8.6.

8.4.1. Predicate Abstraction Algorithm

For the predicate abstraction function $\alpha_P : Fma_\Sigma \to Fma_\Sigma$, we have so far only demanded that for all formulas $\varphi \in Fma_\Sigma$ the formula $\varphi \to \alpha_P(\varphi)$ is logically valid, and that $\alpha_P(\varphi)$ is a Boolean combination of the formulas in $P \subseteq Fma_\Sigma$. In practice, computing α_P is non-trivial. Typically it is the most computationally expensive operation of the whole inference/verification process, because it requires many theorem prover queries of the form "does a imply b?", where a and b are first-order formulas.

Several algorithms for computing a predicate abstraction function are available in the literature; see for example the work of Das et al. [1999]; Flanagan and Qadeer [2002]. The implementation in KeY uses a rather simple scheme, where the abstraction of a formula φ is the conjunction of all predicates from P for which we can determine that they are implied by φ, i.e., $\alpha_P(\varphi) = \bigwedge \{p \in P \mid (\varphi \to p)$ is found to be logically valid$\}$. This only allows conjunctions of the predicates, which is less flexible than supporting arbitrary Boolean combinations. On the other hand, it is much cheaper to compute, which allows handling a significantly higher number of predicates.

For efficiency, the implementation uses an external SMT solver instead of KeY itself for checking the validity of the formulas $\varphi \to p$. This is against the general spirit of the approach, which is to integrate everything into a single prover, avoiding duplication of knowledge. The implementational compromise is necessary because KeY is by design not as fast in automatic proving of first-order formulas as specialised SMT solvers are.

In order to keep the number of calls to the SMT solver down, the implementation exploits some known implication relationships between loop predicates: if for two predicates $p_1, p_2 \in P$ it is known a priori that $\models p_1 \to p_2$, and if we have been unsuccessful in proving $\models \varphi \to p_2$, then there is no need to check whether $\models \varphi \to p_1$ holds. Also, predicates that were already found to be not valid in a previous iteration for a loop do not need to be checked again.

8.4.2. Generating Loop Predicates

Besides the computation of α_P, another aspect of practical importance is where to get the loop predicates themselves from. One option is to let them be provided by the user of the verification system. This gives up on full automation, but guessing potentially useful loop predicates is typically easier than specifying an entire, correct loop invariant. Another option, which can complement the first one, is to use heuristics to guess loop predicates automatically.

The implementation in KeY supports both of these possibilities. Loop predicates can be specified manually as JML-style source code annotations, and a large number of other predicates are then added automatically. Manually specified predicates may contain free logical variables. Predicates that contain free variables do not serve directly as elements of P; rather, they are used by the predicate generation heuristics as a basis for generating quantified predicates.

The predicate generation heuristics are run immediately before the first application of the predicateAbstraction rule to a particular loop. Based on the current sequent $\Gamma \Rightarrow [\pi \, \text{while}(g)p; \, \omega]\varphi, \Delta$ and on the loop predicates manually specified by the user (if any), they create in an exhaustive way many typical invariant components. The following paragraphs describe these heuristics in more detail.

As a first step, we identify the program variables that occur both in $\Gamma \cup \Delta$ and in $[\pi \, \text{while}(g)p; \, \omega]\varphi$. These are the only program variables that are interesting at the current program point, because (i) no information is available about those not in $\Gamma \cup \Delta$, and (ii) those not in $[\pi \, \text{while}(g)p; \, \omega]\varphi$ are irrelevant both for the further execution of the program and for the postcondition φ. These program variables, together with the constant symbols 0 and null, are used to form an initial set of terms.

Next, we extend this set by terms $o.\text{f}$ for every term o in the set and every constant symbol $\text{f} : \text{Field} \in \mathcal{F}$ that represents a field defined for o, as well as terms $a[i]$ and $a.\text{length}$ for every term a of an array type and every term i of type Int in the set. The current implementation does exactly one such step of "heap indirection", but in general of course an arbitrary number is possible.

We then generate the following loop predicates for all terms b of type Boolean in the set, for all terms i_1, i_2, i_3, i_4 of type Int in the set, for all terms o_1, o_2 of a reference type in the set, for all arithmetic relations $\lhd_1, \lhd_2, \lhd_3, \lhd_4 \in \{<, \leq\}$, and for all user-specified predicates $p_1(x)$ and $p_2(x, y)$ containing one free variable $x : A \in \mathcal{V}$ or two free variables $x : A \in \mathcal{V}$ and $y : B \in \mathcal{V}$, respectively:

- $b \doteq TRUE$, $b \doteq FALSE$
- $i_1 \lhd_1 i_2$
- $o_1 \doteq o_2$, $o_1 \not\doteq o_2$
- $\forall A \, x; \big(i_1 \lhd_1 x \wedge x \lhd_2 i_2 \rightarrow p_1(x) \big)$
- $\forall A \, x; \forall B \, y; \big(i_1 \lhd_1 x \wedge x \lhd_2 y \wedge y \lhd_3 i_2 \rightarrow p_2(x, y) \big)$

- $\forall A\, x;\, \forall B\, y;\, \big(i_1 \lhd_1 x \wedge x \lhd_2 i_2 \wedge i_3 \lhd_3 y \wedge y \lhd_4 i_4 \to p_2(x, y)\big)$

The last three cases can lead to large numbers of predicates. For example, the number of predicates created by the very last case for each user predicate $p_2(x, y)$ is $2^4 * n^4$, where n is the number of integer terms in the set. Some of these predicates imply others, which is exploited by the predicate abstraction implementation to avoid some validity checks.

In addition to the above predicates, we use each elementary conjunct of the postcondition φ as a loop predicate. For the method contract proof obligations of Chapter 6, one such conjunct is the *frame* formula expressing that the method respects its modifies clause, which typically also is a loop invariant.

Finally, we derive a special predicate from the postcondition in the following common case: frequently, the loop guard is a binary formula such as i < n, while the postcondition contains a guarded quantification such as $\forall Int\, x;\, \big(\varphi_1(x) \wedge x < n \to \varphi_2(x)\big)$, where the quantified variable $x \in \mathcal{V}$ ranges up to the same boundary $n \in Term_\Sigma$ as the variable i $\in \mathcal{PV}$ does in the loop. In this case, we add a loop predicate $\forall Int\, x;\, \big(\varphi_1(x) \wedge x < $ i $\to \varphi_2(x)\big)$, which expresses the likely guess that, in every loop iteration, property $\varphi_2(x)$ has already been established for all x up to i.

Extending and tuning these heuristics to cover more invariant elements is possible quite easily. This flexibility, which enables us to quickly adapt the class of inferable invariants to a new problem domain, is one of the main advantages of predicate abstraction over other forms of abstract interpretation. However, increasing the number of predicates of course has an adverse effect on performance, so one has to trade power against efficiency.

A more ambitious alternative to heuristically generating predicates is attempting to infer the needed predicates systematically from failed proof attempts [Clarke et al., 2000; Beyer et al., 2005]. Combining such a *counterexample-guided abstraction refinement (CEGAR)* technique with the approach of this chapter is a possible line of future work.

8.5. Example

As an extended example, we return to the implementation of *selection sort* discussed in Subsection 5.5.4. The code of Figure 5.14 is repeated in Figure 8.5, enriched with loop predicate annotations. The syntax used for this purpose has been proposed as an extension of JML by Flanagan and Qadeer [2002]: loop annotations starting with **loop_predicate** contain an arbitrary number of user-specified predicates for the loop, and logical variables to be used in loop predicates can be declared with the keyword **skolem_constant**. Figure 8.5 gives exactly those predicates that are minimally necessary to make the implementation arrive

—— Java + JML* ——————————————————————————

```java
class Sorter {
    static void sort(int[] a) {
        int i = 0;
        /*@ skolem_constant int x, y;
          @ loop_predicate a[x] <= a[y];
          @*/
        while(i < a.length) {
            int minIndex = i;
            int j = i + 1;
            /*@ skolem_constant int x;
              @ loop_predicate a[minIndex] <= a[x];
              @*/
            while(j < a.length) {
                if(a[j] < a[minIndex]) minIndex = j;
                j++;
            }
            int tmp = a[i];
            a[i] = a[minIndex];
            a[minIndex] = tmp;
            i++;
        }
    }
}
```

————————————————————————————————————— Java + JML* ——

Figure 8.5.: Java implementation of the selection sort algorithm annotated with
loop predicates

at a loop invariant strong enough for verifying the proof obligation of Subsection 5.5.4, namely:

$$wellFormed(\text{heap}), \ \mathtt{a} \neq \textbf{null}, \ \mathtt{a}.\,created \doteq TRUE$$

$$\Rightarrow [\texttt{Sorter.sort(a);}] \forall Int \, x; \left(0 < x \land x < \mathtt{a.length} \to \mathtt{a}[x-1] \leq \mathtt{a}[x]\right)$$

The user-specified predicates are supplemented by the predicates generated by the heuristics of Subsection 8.4.2. For example, based on the predicate $\mathtt{a[minIndex]} \leq \mathtt{a}[x]$ containing the free variable $x : Int \in \mathcal{V}$, the essential predicate $\forall Int \, x; (\mathtt{i} \leq x \land x < \mathtt{j} \to \mathtt{a[minIndex]} \leq \mathtt{a}[x])$ is generated automatically, together with many similar quantified formulas using different guards. For arriving at the predicate $\mathtt{a[minIndex]} \leq \mathtt{a}[x]$, the user needs the intuition that the array is supposed to contain a value at position $\mathtt{minIndex}$ that is smaller than its values at other indices, and that this may be relevant for the verification of the loop.

Applying the predicate abstraction proof search strategy yields a proof graph whose structure is shown in Figure 8.6. The first step in the construction of the proof is to perform symbolic execution of the program (indicated as "SE" in the figure) until the outer loop becomes the first active statement. We apply shiftUpdate, merge (in this first iteration, to only one predecessor), and finally predicateAbstraction. Since no fixed point has yet been reached, the outer loop is unwound with unwindLoop, creating one branch where the loop body is entered and one where the loop terminates. The latter is immediately cut off with setBack, because it will not return to the loop entry and is therefore irrelevant for the loop invariant. On the former, the body is symbolically executed, which entails dealing with the inner loop (shown in the right half of Figure 8.6) and finally leads to two branches where the outer loop is again the first active statement. After applying shiftUpdate to each of them, these branches can be merged, and predicateAbstraction is applied again. Assuming that the resulting abstraction is not equivalent to the previous one, another identical iteration is performed.

We assume that after this second iteration, a fixed point has been reached: the current antecedent, resulting from applying predicateAbstraction, is logically equivalent to its counterpart in the first iteration, and is thus a loop invariant. In the implementation this inferred invariant is

$$\forall Int\, x; \forall Int\, y; (0 \leq x \wedge x < y \wedge y < \mathtt{i} \rightarrow \mathtt{a}[x] \leq \mathtt{a}[y])$$
$$\wedge\ \forall Int\, x; \forall Int\, y; (0 \leq x < \mathtt{i} \wedge \mathtt{i} \leq y < \mathtt{a.length} \rightarrow \mathtt{a}[x] \leq \mathtt{a}[y])$$
$$\wedge\ 0 \leq \mathtt{a.length}\ \wedge\ \mathtt{i} \leq \mathtt{a.length}\ \wedge\ 0 \leq \mathtt{i}\ \wedge\ \mathtt{a} \neq \mathtt{null}$$

Using this for *inv*, we apply the loopInvariant rule, creating three proof branches. The "initially valid" branch is trivial to close, because the update u is empty and the loop invariant *inv* is identical to the antecedent Γ. Proving the "preserved by body" branch entails applying loopInvariant to the inner loop, using the invariant inferred for that loop in the last iteration. As the inferred invariant is strong enough to imply the postcondition, the "use case" is closable by further symbolic execution of the remaining program and first-order reasoning.

The structure of the subgraph for the inner loop is analogous to the structure of the overall graph. Each time the inner loop is encountered, an invariant is inferred for it by repeated unwindings and abstraction steps. The invariants inferred in the first and the second occurrence of the inner loop are different: they are dependent on the initial states occurring for the inner loop in each iteration for the outer loop. Of the three branches created by loopInvariant, the first one is again trivially closable; the "preserved by body" branch is set back to the outer loop entry, because it does not return to that loop; and the use case is where symbolic execution actually continues back to the outer loop.

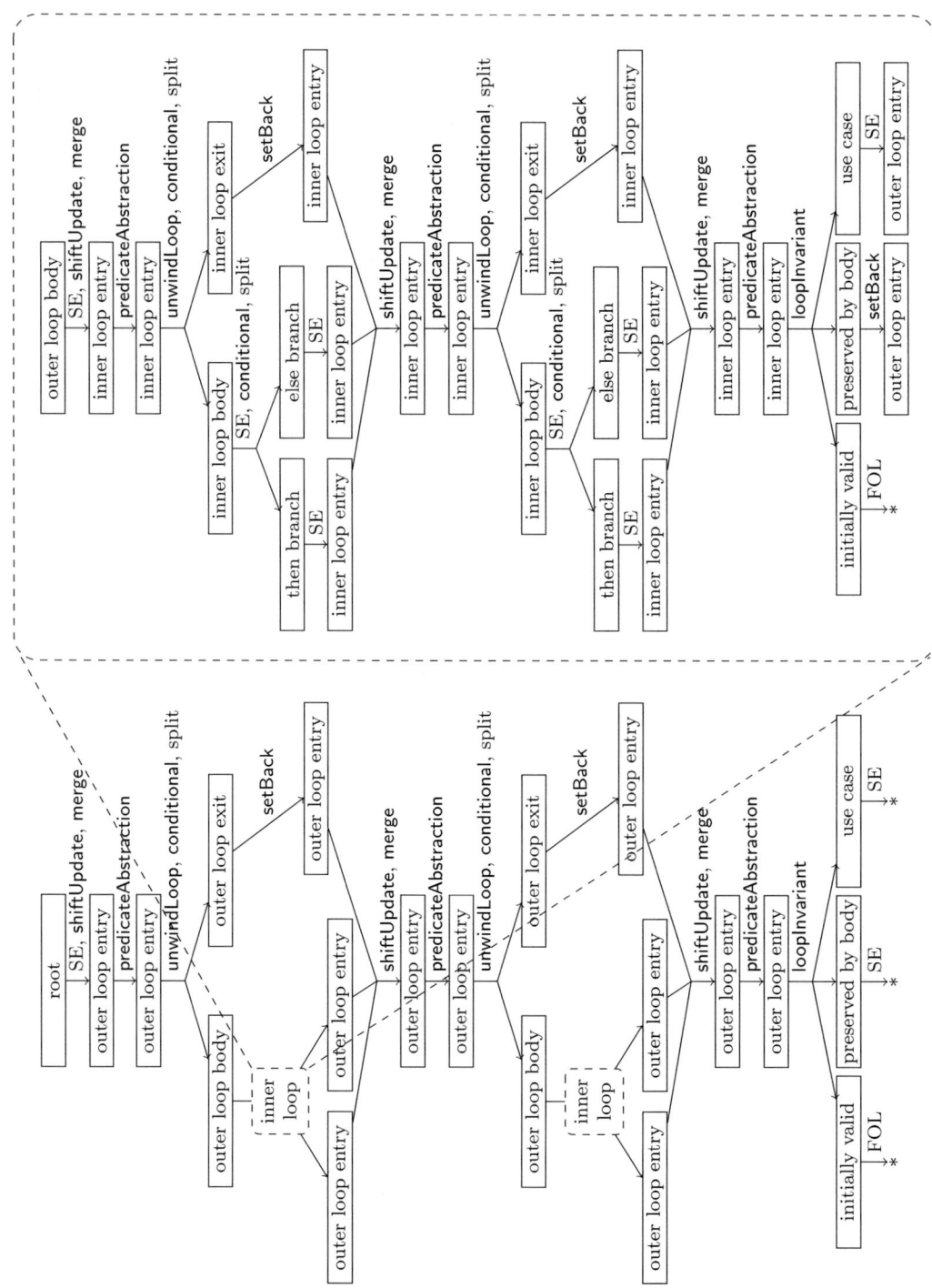

Figure 8.6.: Proof graph for selection sort

	Lines	Predicates	Rule apps.	SMT calls	Time
`LogFile::getMaximumRecord`	22	1 + 30	1362	41	10 s
`Sorter::sort`	22	1 + 1092	4594	431	90 s
`Dispatcher::dispatch`	70	0 + 297	2434	338	85 s
`Dispatcher::removeService`	67	1 + 159	3607	229	55 s
`KeyImpl::clearKey`	74	1 + 105	1777	252	115 s
`KeyImpl::initialize`	69	1 + 104	1746	242	95 s
`IntervalSeq::incSize`	33	2 + 178	3666	231	120 s
`Subject::registerObserver`	36	2 + 185	4431	242	125 s

Table 8.1.: Experimental results for loop invariant generation

In practice, additional proof branches occur, dealing e.g. with the situation where the accessed array `a` is **null**. These are left out in Figure 8.6 for simplicity. In this example, they can always be closed immediately (because the corresponding execution path is obviously infeasible), or cut off with setBack (because the execution path never returns to the respective loop entry).

8.6. Experiments

To give an indication of the feasibility of the approach, the results of applying the implementation to eight Java methods are listed in Table 8.1. For each method, the table shows the number of lines of combined code and specifications; the number of predicates that were given manually; the number of predicates that were generated automatically by the heuristics; the number of rule applications; the total number of SMT solver calls for computing α_P; and an approximate overall running time (measured on a 1.5 GHz Pentium M processor). The *Simplify* prover of Detlefs et al. [2005] was used as the SMT solver.

The `getMaximumRecord` method contains a simple loop that serves to retrieve the "largest" element out of an array of objects. The second example is selection sort, as discussed in Section 8.5. The next four methods are from the Java Card API reference implementation of Mostowski [2007]. These methods are simpler than selection sort algorithmically, but technically more involved. The last two examples are the two methods requiring loop invariants in the KeY tutorial of Ahrendt et al. [2007].

In all cases listed in Table 8.1, the found loop invariant was strong enough to complete the verification task at hand (except for proving termination), without interactive rule applications. Manually specifying the necessary zero to two loop predicates appeared notably easier than having to provide the invariant as a whole, in a similar way as in the selection sort example. On the negative side, there are three additional loops in the code of Mostowski [2007] for which a strong enough invariant could not be inferred. Two of them require invariants of a form (involving, e.g., existentially quantified subformulas) which are not covered by the implemented predicate abstraction scheme. The third contains deeply nested case distinctions in the loop body, which lead to large disjunctive formulas that overwhelmed the Simplify prover.

The implementation underlying the experiments is based on JavaDL, not on JavaDL*. It is to be expected that the impact of the changes from JavaDL to JavaDL* on the invariant generation process is limited. An exception are the heuristics for guessing loop predicates, which should be extended to cover typical propositions about dynamic frames. Another exception are proofs for dependency contracts: the invariant generation process is not made for directly using it with the dependency contract proof obligations of Chapter 6. This incompatibility is the topic of Section 8.7 below.

8.7. Dependency Proofs

The dependency contract proof obligations of Chapter 6 lead to sequents that are not of the conventional form $\Gamma \Rightarrow \{u\}[p]\varphi, \Delta$ used in the present chapter. Nevertheless, proving a dependency contract for a pure method may involve dealing with loops, and may thus require loop invariants. The easiest way to still make use of the loop invariant generation mechanism for this purpose is to generate invariants using a more conventional proof obligation about the same method (such as a method contract proof obligation of Subsection 6.4.1), and to then use the generated loop invariant for verifying the dependency contract in a separate proof. This approach is promising, because often, the same loop invariant is needed for proving a method contract and a dependency contract.

As an example, Figure 8.7 shows an implementation of the `contains` method of the `ArrayList` class of Figure 3.3. The code includes a loop invariant in JML syntax: the variable i remains between 0 and the size of the list, and the object of interest is not an element of the array for an index between 0 and i. Together with a modifies clause of $\dot{\emptyset}$—or together with an equivalent invariant formula *frame* stating that no locations have changed—this loop invariant is suitable for verifying both the method contract and the dependency contract for `contains` given in Figure 3.1:

```
/*@ normal_behaviour
  @   accessible footprint;
  @   ensures \result == (\exists int i; 0 <= i && i < size();
  @                                      get(i) == o);
  @*/
public /*@pure@*/ boolean contains(Object o);
```

—— Java + JML* ——————————————————————————

```
public boolean contains(Object o) {
    int i = 0;
    /*@ loop_invariant 0 <= i && i <= size
      @    && (\forall int x; 0 <= x && x < i; array[i] != o);
      @ assignable \nothing;
      @*/
    while(i < size) {
        if(array[i] == o) {
            return true;
        }
        i++;
    }
    return false;
}
```

—————————————————————————— Java + JML* ——

Figure 8.7.: Implementation of the `contains` method of the `ArrayList` class shown in Figure 3.3

This illustrates that generating loop invariants for dependency proofs is not really a problem that *must* be addressed separately; the present section is thus more of a digression than a necessity.

Still, one may expect that proving dependency contracts should be *easier* than proving method contracts: after all, here one is interested only in which locations influence the method's return value, not in its full functional behaviour. Thus, the required loop invariants should be simpler, and an abstract domain for this purpose should only have to keep track of dependencies, not of actual values.

The present section sketches an alternative encoding of the correctness of dependency contracts for pure methods, which simplifies the necessary loop invariants. In the normal encoding of Subsection 6.4.2, it is not possible to express invariants that only specify dependencies instead of concrete values. Invariants describe a set of states that can occur at a particular program point; in contrast, the set of locations that another location "depends on" at a program point is not a local property of the states occurring at this program point. Rather, it is a joint property of all execution paths passing through the program point.

A solution is to make the program keep track of (an over-approximation of) the dependencies of the occurring locations and variables explicitly [Bubel et al., 2009]. This approach can be seen as adding ghost code to the program, which maintains a set of "dependee" locations for every field and local variable of the original program. Then, the current value of the ghost fields and ghost variables containing the dependees is describable via loop invariants, and it becomes possible to approximate by keeping only information about the ghost fields and ghost variables and dismissing information about the original fields and variables themselves.

In more detail, this means that for every constant symbol $\mathbf{f} : Field \in \mathcal{F}^{Unique}$ representing a Java field or a user-specified ghost field, we introduce another constant symbol $\mathbf{f}^{dep} : Field \in \mathcal{F}^{Unique}$, to be used for storing the "current dependencies" of $\mathbf{f}$. Similarly, we introduce a function symbol $arr^{dep} : Int \rightarrow Field \in \mathcal{F}^{Unique}$ for storing the current dependencies of array components. We also define a constant symbol $\mathbf{res}^{dep} : Field \in \mathcal{F}^{Unique}$ in order to store the dependencies of a method's return value. The correctness of a method with respect to a dependency contract is then expressed by a new proof obligation, which for the example of the `contains` method introduced above looks as follows:

$$\forall Object\ o;\ \big(o.\texttt{array}^{dep} \doteq \{(o, \texttt{array})\}$$
$$\wedge\ o.\texttt{size}^{dep} \doteq \{(o, \texttt{size})\}$$
$$\wedge\ \forall Int\ i;\ o.\texttt{array[}i\texttt{]}^{dep} \doteq \{(o.\texttt{array}, arr(i))\}\big)$$
$$\wedge\ wellFormed(\texttt{heap}) \wedge \texttt{o} \not\doteq \textbf{null} \wedge \texttt{o}.created \doteq TRUE$$
$$\wedge\ \texttt{self} \not\doteq \textbf{null} \wedge \texttt{self}.created \doteq TRUE \wedge exactInstance_{\texttt{ArrayList}}(\texttt{self})$$
$$\rightarrow \{\texttt{heap}^{pre} := \texttt{heap}\}[\texttt{res} = \texttt{self.contains(o);}]$$
$$\big(\mathbf{res}^{dep} \mathrel{\dot{\subseteq}} \texttt{footprint}(\texttt{heap}^{pre}, \texttt{self})\big)$$

Besides the usual assumptions about well-formedness of the heap, about createdness of parameters and about the dynamic type of `self` (Chapter 6), the proof obligation contains the assumption that the locations for the fields `array`, `size` and $arr(i)$ currently "depend exactly on themselves". The postcondition demands that the dependencies of the return value are a subset of the dependencies specified by the contract. Note that without syntactic sugar, the term $o.\texttt{array[}i\texttt{]}^{dep}$ reads as

$$select_{LocSet}\big(\texttt{heap}, select_{\texttt{int[]}}(\texttt{heap}, o, \texttt{array}), arr^{dep}(i)\big),$$

and that $\mathbf{res}^{dep}$ stands for $select_{Object}(\texttt{heap}, null, \mathbf{res}^{dep})$, i.e., for accessing the heap at the "static field" $\mathbf{res}^{dep}$.

The proof obligation mentions the fields `array`, `size` and $arr(i)$ because these are the fields that are mentioned in the method body of `contains`. The method call in the proof obligation refers to a version of the method that is enriched with dependency tracking ghost code, shown in Figure 8.8. The syntax used in the figure is for illustration only, as the ghost code should not be written manually, but rather added automatically in a pre-processing step that is part of generating the proof obligation.

—— Java + JML* ——————————————————————

```
1   public boolean contains(Object o) {
2       //initialisation
3       //@ ghost \locset pc^dep = \nothing;
4       //@ ghost \locset o^dep = \nothing;
5
6       //declaration, assignment
7       //@ ghost \locset i^dep = pc^dep;
8       int i = 0;
9
10      //entering loop
11      //@ set pc^dep = pc^dep, i^dep, size^dep;
12
13      /*@ loop_invariant 0 <= i && i <= size
14        @   && \subset(pc^dep, \old(footprint))
15        @   && \subset(i^dep, \old(footprint));
16        @ assignable \nothing;
17        @*/
18      while(i < size) {
19          //entering conditional
20          //@ set pc^dep = pc^dep, array^dep, i^dep, array[i]^dep,
21          //@               o^dep;
22
23          if(array[i] == o) {
24              //return
25              //@ set \result^dep = pc^dep;
26              return true;
27          }
28
29          //assignment
30          //@ set i^dep = pc^dep, i^dep;
31          i++;
32
33          //entering loop
34          //@ set pc^dep = pc^dep, i^dep, size^dep;
35      }
36
37      //return
38      //@ set \result^dep = pc^dep;
39      return false;
40  }
```

—————————————————————————————— Java + JML* ——

Figure 8.8.: The `contains` method of Figure 8.7 enriched with ghost code for tracking dependencies

The code first introduces a local ghost variable `pc^dep` in line 3, which represents the dependencies of the "program counter", i.e., of the state of control flow. Initially, the program counter does not depend on any location. This changes when reaching a conditional statement or a loop, where the dependencies of the guard are added to the dependencies of the program counter. For example, in line 11 the dependencies of the expression `i < size`, namely the union of `i^dep` and `size^dep` (standing for `self.size`^{dep}), are added to `pc^dep`.

At every declaration of a local variable `x`, the ghost code declares a corresponding ghost variable `x^dep`. At every assignment to a local variable or to a field, the corresponding ghost variable or field is set to the dependencies of the right hand side of the assignment, together with the dependencies of the program counter (which is necessary because control flow determines whether the assignment is executed at all, and thus influences the assigned variable indirectly). For example, line 7 belongs to the declaration and initialisation of the variable `i` in line 8. As `i` is initialised to 0, which is a rigid expression that does not depend on anything, `i^dep` is initialised to the dependencies of the program counter only.

Return statements are treated like assignments to a dedicated result variable. Thus, they are complemented with a **set** statement that assigns to `\result^dep` (standing for **res**^{dep}) the dependencies of the returned expression, together with the dependencies of the program counter. Here, a rigid expression is returned both in line 26 and in line 39, and so the set of locations assigned to `\result^dep` consists only of the dependencies of the program counter in both cases.

Overall, the ghost code ensures that the final contents of the field **res**^{dep} over-approximate the actual dependencies of the returned value. Precision is lost, for example, when determining the **set** statement corresponding to an assignment "`x = y-y;`": the introduced statement is "**set** `x^dep = y^dep, y^dep`", even though in fact the value of `x` after the assignment does not depend on anything at all. This loss of precision already in the proof obligation itself is a disadvantage of this encoding, as opposed to the encoding of Chapter 6. Still, the encoding is more precise than simply forbidding all read accesses that are not covered by the depends clause. Also, it is suitable for performing general *information flow analysis* in dynamic logic [Bubel et al., 2009], where not only the dependencies of the return value are of interest, but the dependencies of any number of locations.

The loop invariant shown in Figure 8.8 is sufficient for verifying the proof obligation for the **contains** method given above. Besides the restriction on the value of `i`, which is necessary to conclude that no `IndexOutOfBoundsException` is thrown, the invariant is concerned with dependencies only. It can be found with the invariant generation technique of this chapter, provided that the two formulas `pc^dep` $\dot{\subseteq}$ `footprint(heap`^{pre}, `self)` and `i^dep` $\dot{\subseteq}$ `footprint(heap`^{pre}, `self)` are present as loop predicates; and heuristically guessing these predicates from the postcondition **res**^{dep} $\dot{\subseteq}$ `footprint(heap`^{pre}, `self)` is easy.

8.8. Related Work

This chapter draws much inspiration from the approach of Flanagan and Qadeer [2002] for using predicate abstraction in program verification. Both in their approach and in ours, a set of loop predicates is associated with each loop in a program, and used to abstract specifically at loop entry points. Quantified loop invariants are supported by allowing the loop predicates to contain free variables which are later quantified over. The main difference is that in the approach of this chapter, the inference is done within a logical calculus, the same that is used for the verification itself. This also distinguishes our technique from the one used in the Boogie verifier [Barnett et al., 2006], where a separate abstract interpretation component is used to infer some loop invariants needed for the verification, leading to a duplication of knowledge between the verifier and the abstract interpreter.

There are several related approaches that also aim at a closer integration between deductive verification and loop invariant generation based on abstract interpretation. In the "loop invariants on demand" technique of Leino and Logozzo [2005], first-order verification conditions are generated from programs, which include placeholder predicates for the loop invariants. These are then passed to a first-order theorem prover. When an invariant is necessary for a sub-proof, the prover tries to infer it by repeatedly invoking an abstract interpreter with successively more precise abstract domains. Still, the verification condition generator, theorem prover and abstract interpreter are all separate components. In later work, Leino and Logozzo [2007] move parts of the invariant generation inside the theorem prover, with the verification condition generation remaining separated. In the approach of this chapter, all three tasks—especially generation of verification conditions and generation of invariants, which are closely related as they both deal with programs—can be performed within one dynamic logic theorem prover. Tiwari and Gulwani [2007] go the other way round by embedding theorem proving techniques in an abstract interpretation framework.

A combination of JavaDL with static analysis based on fixed-point computation is also pursued by Gedell [2005, 2006]. There, the KeY system is used for extracting recursive data-flow equations from the program, which are then solved in a separate step by an external constraint solver. The calculus employed for extracting the equations is not the normal JavaDL calculus, but a custom calculus that is specific to the particular analysis being implemented. The logical meaning of sequents, rules and proofs is dismissed entirely; KeY is used only as an implementational platform, without a semantic integration between its logical foundations and the implemented data-flow analysis.

Gedell [2006]; Gedell and Hähnle [2006] present a technique for automatically handling loops in JavaDL by directly transforming them into quantified updates.

This is possible for loops of a specific form. In particular, the loop iterations must be independent of each other, which is checked by a separate dependency analysis. Other restrictions are that the loop body must not contain nested sub-loops, and that it must not terminate abruptly for any initial state.

The results presented in this chapter evolved out of an earlier technique for invariant generation by combining predicate abstraction and dynamic logic [Weiß, 2007; Schmitt and Weiß, 2007]. Improvements include that the soundness of all rules can now be proven, and has been; that the notion of proofs has been generalised from trees to directed acyclic graphs, which allows for a more natural and robust invariant generation procedure; that the transformation of updates into formulas is now done only at loop entry points, which improves performance; and that exceptions as well as **break** and **continue** statements are now supported.

Another piece of own related work is an approach for integrating abstract interpretation into JavaDL by abstracting on *updates* instead of on formulas [Bubel et al., 2009]. The approach is parametrised by a lattice of abstract values with an associated concretisation function γ mapping abstract values to sets of concrete values. For example, the abstract value lattice might be a signs lattice $\{\bot, <, \leq, \doteq, \geq, >, \top\}$ analogous to the lattice in the left half of Figure 7.2, where, e.g., $\gamma(\leq) = \{z \in \mathbb{Z} \mid z \leq 0\}$ and $\gamma(\geq) = \{z \in \mathbb{Z} \mid z \geq 0\}$.

The core idea of the approach is to introduce a constant symbol $\gamma_{a,z}$ for every abstract value a and every integer z, where the interpretation of these constants is partially fixed: it is required that $I(\gamma_{a,z}) \in \gamma(a)$, i.e., the constant symbol $\gamma_{a,z}$ represents an arbitrary concrete value within the concretisation of the abstract value a. This allows constructing updates like $\mathsf{a} := \gamma_{\geq,0} \parallel \mathsf{b} := \gamma_{\geq,1}$, which assigns to the program variables a and b unknown, non-negative, not necessarily identical integer values. The approach furthermore comprises a loop invariant rule where updates instead of formulas are used as loop invariants, and an iterative process for computing such "invariant updates" by repeated symbolic execution of the loop body, similar to the approach of this chapter. Termination is ensured by proof steps that are a combination of merging and abstracting, where e.g. two updates $\mathsf{a} := 0$ and $\mathsf{a} := 1$ can be simultaneously merged and abstracted to the update $\mathsf{a} := \gamma_{\geq,0}$.

The advantage of abstracting on updates instead of on formulas is that it avoids the need for something like the shiftUpdate rule (Definition 8.1). On the other hand, there are at least two substantial advantages to using formulas. Firstly, for reasoning with the symbols $\gamma_{a,z}$, the update-based approach is dependent on rules capturing the pre-defined semantics of these symbols, which must be provided manually for every choice of the set of abstract values; in contrast, when using a formula like $\mathsf{a} \geq 0 \land \mathsf{b} \geq 0$ instead of an update $\mathsf{a} := \gamma_{\geq,0} \parallel \mathsf{b} := \gamma_{\geq,1}$, there is no need for any abstraction-specific rules. Secondly, the notion of "abstract values" underlying the update-based approach is inherently limited to non-relational abstraction (where the value of every variable and location is handled separately, see also Chapter 7), whereas in the formula-based approach, non-relational properties such as $a \geq 0$ and relational properties such as $a \geq b$ are expressed with equal ease. The update-based approach has so far been elaborated only for a toy language without a heap, and has not yet been implemented.

A main intended application domain for the update-based approach [Bubel et al., 2009] is *information flow analysis*. Information flow properties are made amenable for state-based abstraction by making the program track dependencies explicitly. This idea is transferred to the formula-based approach in Section 8.7. Section 8.7 uses ghost code where in the update-based approach, the semantics of the programming language itself is extended; the effect is the same.

8.9. Conclusion

This chapter has presented an approach for integrating abstract interpretation techniques, in particular predicate abstraction, into the JavaDL* calculus for deductive program verification. This allows us to take advantage of the power of a deductive framework, while selectively introducing the approximation that is characteristic for abstract interpretation to find loop invariants automatically when necessary.

The approach consists of adding a small number of additional rules while generalising the notion of proofs to accommodate these new rules, as well as a dedicated proof search strategy to drive the invariant generation process. As is common for abstract interpretation, this process always finds an invariant for a loop, but the invariant is not in all cases strong enough to prove the intended postcondition. In this case, user intervention is required; the generated invariant, even though too weak, may be helpful in figuring out what to do. The strength of the found invariants heavily depends on the underlying set of loop predicates, whose elements are either generated heuristically or provided manually in place of the loop invariants themselves. Experience with an implementation in the KeY system demonstrates the general feasibility of the approach.

This concludes Part III on generating loop invariants. Conclusions for the thesis as a whole follow.

9. Conclusion

9.1. Summary

This thesis has been concerned with deductively verifying object-oriented programs. We have addressed two major challenges in this area: modularity of the verification on one hand, and automation in the handling of loops on the other hand. Starting from dynamic logic with updates as a verification framework, we have extended this framework with dynamic frames to address the first challenge, and with predicate abstraction to address the second.

Modularity starts already on the level of specification. In the first part of the thesis, we have examined the popular Java specification language JML, and identified several problems that make the language in its current state unsuitable for modular verification. We have solved these issues by replacing some JML concepts (namely data groups and the visible state semantics for object invariants) with core elements of the theory of dynamic frames. The result is a specification language that is more expressive than current JML in several respects, allowing it to be used for modular verification, while at the same time being conceptually simple and avoiding the programming restrictions that come with competing, ownership-based approaches.

In the second part of the thesis, we have adapted dynamic logic with updates so it becomes usable for verifying dynamic frames specifications. The foundation for this adaptation has been to embrace a way of modelling heap memory that makes use of the theory of arrays instead of non-rigid function symbols, thereby turning memory locations into first-class entities that can be talked about in first-order formulas. We have extended the classical theory of arrays with special operators that are useful for modularly verifying Java programs, and we have adapted the verification calculus to the changes in heap modelling. A set of proof obligations captures the correctness of individual program parts as logical validity of dynamic logic formulas, and contract-based rules allow assuming the validity of such proof obligations in other proofs. To the author's knowledge, the defined logic is the first dynamic logic to support dynamic frames, or even to support any approach for handling the interplay between framing and data abstraction, including the older techniques of data groups and ownership.

The final part of the thesis has been about adding abstract interpretation techniques, in particular predicate abstraction, to dynamic logic with updates. This allows generating certain loop invariants automatically when needed during verification. Which invariants can be generated depends on the set of available loop predicates. Because this set can be adapted and extended with relative ease, predicate abstraction is a very flexible, "user-programmable" abstract domain. The integration is a deep integration, where the symbolic execution performed for the verification is at the same time deduction and abstract interpretation. To the author's knowledge, it is the first integration of its kind.

The presented techniques have been implemented in the KeY verification system.

9.2. Future Work

Besides evaluating the presented solutions on larger case studies, several lines of future work for further expanding and improving these solutions suggest themselves.

On the side of specification, one such line of work would be to extend JML with additional abstract data types. These would be primitive types of the language, in the same style as the type "set of memory locations" that we have introduced for supporting dynamic frames. Such types, for example mathematical sets and sequences, are frequently very useful as the types of ghost fields and model fields in abstract specifications. It may be debatable whether adding these types directly to the language is desirable, or whether JML's model classes already adequately fulfil the same role. Points in favour of adding them are that this leads to more concise specifications, and that it elegantly avoids unnecessary complications having to do with (i) the semantical mismatch between mathematical data structures on one hand and Java's reference semantics for objects on the other hand, and (ii) specification expressions that are only weakly pure.

An important area of future work is the verification of recursive data structures, such as linked lists. In principle, the solutions of this thesis are suitable and helpful for verifying such data structures; in particular, dynamic frames solve the modularity problems that arise for multi-object data structures, including recursive data structures. However, it is well known that there are specific difficulties to the verification of recursive data structures, involving a reachability predicate and/or other recursively defined function and predicate symbols, and these have not been explicitly tackled in this thesis (although the implementation can already cope with them to a limited extent).

The calculus defined in this thesis handles propositions about sets of locations (in particular, about dynamic frames) by reducing them to formulas that use only the set-theoretic element-of operator. This approach is simple and, in principle, it works always. But, as the reduction introduces quantifiers and generally enlarges the occurring formulas, it may not be the most efficient approach. It may be possible to improve verification performance by lifting the reasoning about dynamic frames to a higher abstraction level as much as possible, and using the reduction to element-of only as a last resort. The "programming laws" for dynamic frames identified by Kassios [2010] may be useful for this purpose.

In this thesis, object creation is handled by defining the domain of objects to be the same in all states (the "constant domain assumption"), and by distinguishing between created and non-created objects via a ghost field. This approach is relatively common, it is conceptually simple, and in a sense it fits naturally with the reference semantics of Java: the domain of "objects" actually consists of object references, and these (really being addresses) are in fact not newly created when allocating new objects, but taken from the everlasting set of mathematical integers. On the other hand, however, it can be observed in practice that case distinctions on the createdness of objects ("to be or not to be created?") permeate the proofs. Ahrendt et al. [2009] propose an approach where the constant domain assumption is abandoned, promising to avoid such case distinctions and thus to significantly increase the efficiency of the verification. A price for this is that giving up the constant domain assumption leads to complications elsewhere in the logic. At this point in time it is not clear how these complications would affect the solutions proposed in this thesis, and if the advantages would ultimately outweigh the disadvantages or the other way round. Further investigation on this issue is needed.

On the side of loop invariant generation, a promising line of future work would be extending the framework defined in this thesis to support other abstract domains besides predicate abstraction. As we have observed earlier, the predicate abstraction rule essentially plays the role of a widening operator. Extending it to support the widening operators of ordinary abstract domains appears straightforward: one could translate the current context formulas of the sequent to an abstract state of the chosen abstract domain, such that the abstract state over-approximates the set of concrete states described by the formulas, then apply the widening operator of the abstract domain, and finally translate the result back to a formula. An implementation of this approach could make use of the existing library implementations of several classical abstract domains.

A. Proofs

A.1. Preparatory Observations

The propositions below are used as assumptions in the proofs of this appendix. Their validity should be obvious.

Proposition A.1 (Non-occurring program variables). *For all Kripke structures $\mathcal{K}$, all states $s, s' \in \mathcal{S}$, all variable assignments β, and all $t \in Term_\Sigma \cup Fma_\Sigma \cup Upd_\Sigma$: if for all program variables $\mathsf{a} \in fpv(t)$ we have $s(\mathsf{a}) = s'(\mathsf{a})$, then we also have $val_{\mathcal{K},s,\beta}(t) = val_{\mathcal{K},s',\beta}(t)$.*

As described in Subsection 5.4.6, the function $fpv: Term_\Sigma \cup Fma_\Sigma \cup Upd_\Sigma \to 2^{\mathcal{PV}}$ collects all program variables that have *free occurrences* in a term, formula or update. A *free* occurrence of a program variable is any occurrence, except for an occurrence inside a program fragment p that is bound by a declaration within p. A program fragment p always contains an implicit free occurrence of the program variable heap.

Proposition A.2 (Overwritten program variables). *For all Kripke structures $\mathcal{K}$, all states $s, s' \in \mathcal{S}$, all variable assignments β, all updates $(\mathsf{a}_1 := t_1 \parallel \ldots \parallel \mathsf{a}_n := t_n) \in Upd_\Sigma$ where $\mathsf{a}_1, \ldots, \mathsf{a}_n \notin fpv(t_1) \cup \cdots \cup fpv(t_n)$, and all $t \in Term_\Sigma \cup Fma_\Sigma \cup Upd_\Sigma$: if for all program variables $\mathsf{a} \in fpv(t) \setminus \{\mathsf{a}_1, \ldots, \mathsf{a}_n\}$ we have $s(\mathsf{a}) = s'(\mathsf{a})$, then we also have $val_{\mathcal{K},s,\beta}(\{\mathsf{a}_1 := t_1 \parallel \ldots \parallel \mathsf{a}_n := t_n\}t) = val_{\mathcal{K},s',\beta}(\{\mathsf{a}_1 := t_1 \parallel \ldots \parallel \mathsf{a}_n := t_n\}t)$.*

Proposition A.2 holds because the initial values of the program variables $\mathsf{a}_1, \ldots, \mathsf{a}_n$ are overwritten by the update, and thus cannot influence the evaluation of t.

Proposition A.3 (Non-occurring function and predicate symbols). *For all Kripke structures $\mathcal{K} = (\mathcal{D}, \delta, I, \mathcal{S}, \rho)$ and $\mathcal{K}' = (\mathcal{D}, \delta, I', \mathcal{S}, \rho)$ differing only in the interpretation functions I vs. I', all states $s \in \mathcal{S}$, all variable assignments β, and all $t \in Term_\Sigma \cup Fma_\Sigma \cup Upd_\Sigma$: if for all function and predicate symbols $f \in \mathcal{F} \cup \mathcal{P}$ that syntactically occur in t we have $I(f) = I'(f)$, then we also have $val_{\mathcal{K},s,\beta}(t) = val_{\mathcal{K}',s,\beta}(t)$.*

Proposition A.4 (Programs). *Let p be a legal program fragment, $\mathsf{a}_1, \ldots, \mathsf{a}_m \in \mathcal{PV}$ be the program variables occurring free in p (excluding heap), $\mathsf{b}_1, \ldots, \mathsf{b}_m \in$*

$\mathcal{PV}$ be the program variables potentially modified by p (excluding heap), $heap^{pre}$, $b_1^{pre}, \ldots, b_n^{pre} \in \mathcal{PV}$, $pre \in Upd_\Sigma$ and $reachableIn, reachableOut \in Fma_\Sigma$ all as in Definition 5.9, and let the formula $noDeallocs \in Fma_\Sigma$ be as in Lemma 5.4. That is:

$$pre = \mathbf{heap}^{pre} := \mathbf{heap} \parallel b_1^{pre} := b_1 \parallel \ldots \parallel b_n^{pre} := b_n$$

$$reachableIn = \bigwedge_{i \in \{1,\ldots,m\},\ \alpha(a_i) \preceq Object} (a_i \doteq \mathbf{null} \vee a_i.\,created \doteq TRUE)$$

$$\wedge \bigwedge_{i \in \{1,\ldots,m\},\ \alpha(a_i) = LocSet} disjoint(a_i, unusedLocs(\mathbf{heap}))$$

$$reachableOut = \bigwedge_{i \in \{1,\ldots,n\},\ \alpha(b_i) \preceq Object} (b_i \doteq \mathbf{null} \vee b_i.\,created \doteq TRUE)$$

$$\wedge \bigwedge_{i \in \{1,\ldots,n\},\ \alpha(b_i) = LocSet} disjoint(b_i, unusedLocs(\mathbf{heap}))$$

$$noDeallocs = unusedLocs(\mathbf{heap}) \,\dot{\subseteq}\, unusedLocs(\mathbf{heap}^{pre})$$
$$\wedge\ select_{Any}(\mathbf{heap}, \mathbf{null}, created)$$
$$\doteq select_{Any}(\mathbf{heap}^{pre}, \mathbf{null}, created)$$

Then the following holds:

$$\models wellFormed(\mathbf{heap}) \wedge reachableIn$$
$$\to \{pre\}[p]\big(wellFormed(\mathbf{heap}) \wedge reachableOut \wedge noDeallocs\big)$$

Proposition A.4 is guaranteed by the semantics of Java (extended with type \locset): if a program p is executed in a state s where the heap is well-formed and all local input variables have "reachable" values (i.e., values that are neither references to non-created objects nor location sets containing locations that belong to non-created objects), and if it terminates in a state s', then (i) the heap is well-formed in s', (ii) all local output variables hold reachable values in s', and (iii) all objects created in s are still created in s'. Proposition A.5 below is a version of Proposition A.4 specialised towards method calls.

Proposition A.5 (Method calls). *Let p be a legal program fragment of the form*

```
exc = null;
try { res = self.m(a₁,…,aₘ); }
catch(Exception e) { exc = e; }
```

where $exc, res, a_1, \ldots, a_m \in \mathcal{PV}$. *Let furthermore the program variable* $heap^{pre} \in \mathcal{PV}$ *and the formulas* $reachableIn, reachableOut \in Fma_\Sigma$ *be as in Definition 6.7,* and let *noDeallocs* $\in$ *Fma*$_\Sigma$ be as in Lemma 5.4. That is, *reachableIn* and *noDeallocs* are as in Proposition A.4 above, and *reachableOut* is the formula

$$(\texttt{res} \doteq \texttt{null} \vee \texttt{res}.\mathit{created} \doteq \mathit{TRUE}) \wedge (\texttt{exc} \doteq \texttt{null} \vee \texttt{exc}.\mathit{created} \doteq \mathit{TRUE})$$

if $\alpha(\texttt{res}) \preceq \mathit{Object}$, and the formula $\texttt{exc} \doteq \texttt{null} \vee \texttt{exc}.\mathit{created} \doteq \mathit{TRUE}$ otherwise. Then the following holds:

$$\models \mathit{wellFormed}(\texttt{heap}) \wedge \mathit{reachableIn} \wedge \texttt{self} \not\doteq \texttt{null} \wedge \texttt{self}.\mathit{created} \doteq \mathit{TRUE}$$
$$\to \{\texttt{heap}^{\mathit{pre}} := \texttt{heap}\}[p]\big(\mathit{wellFormed}(\texttt{heap}) \wedge \mathit{reachableOut} \wedge \mathit{noDeallocs}\big)$$

A.2. Proof of Lemma 5.1: A Consequence of Well-formedness

Let $\mathcal{K}$ be a Kripke structure, $s \in \mathcal{S}$ be a state, β be a variable assignment, $h \in \mathcal{D}^{\mathit{Heap}}$, $o \in \mathcal{D}^{\mathit{Object}}$, $f \in \mathcal{D}^{\mathit{Field}}$. We assume

$$h \in I(\mathit{wellFormed}) \tag{A.1}$$

and aim to show that at least one of the following holds:

$$I(\mathit{select}_A)(h, o, f) = \mathit{null}$$
$$I(\mathit{select}_{\mathit{Boolean}})\big(h, I(\mathit{select}_A)(h, o, f), \ I(\mathit{created})\big) = tt$$

Using the definition of $I(\mathit{select}_A)$, the proof goals can be simplified to:

$$I(\mathit{cast}_A)\big(h(o, f)\big) = \mathit{null} \tag{lma5.1-goal1}$$
$$I(\mathit{cast}_{\mathit{Boolean}})\big(h(I(\mathit{cast}_A)(h(o, f)), \ I(\mathit{created}))\big) = tt \tag{lma5.1-goal2}$$

One of the following two cases must apply:

- $h(o, f) \in \mathcal{D}^A$. Then (A.1) implies that one of the following two cases applies:
  - $h(o, f) = \mathit{null}$. This and the definition of $I(\mathit{cast}_A)$ together imply (lma5.1-goal1).
  - $h\big(h(o, f), I(\mathit{created})\big) = tt$. Because we know that $h(o, f) \in \mathcal{D}^A$, we also have $I(\mathit{cast}_A)\big(h(o, f)\big) = h(o, f)$. Together, we get

  $$h\big(I(\mathit{cast}_A)(h(o, f)), \ I(\mathit{created})\big) = tt.$$

  This and the definition of $I(\mathit{cast}_{\mathit{Boolean}})$ imply (lma5.1-goal2).

- $h(o, f) \notin \mathcal{D}^A$. Then the definition of $I(\mathit{cast}_A)$ implies (lma5.1-goal1). $\qquad\square$

A.3. Proof of Lemma 5.2: Well-formedness after Storing an Object

Let $\mathcal{K}$ be a Kripke structure, $s \in \mathcal{S}$ be a state, β be a variable assignment, $h \in \mathcal{D}^{Heap}$, $o, x \in \mathcal{D}^{Object}$, and $f \in \mathcal{D}^{Field}$. We assume

$$h \in I(wellFormed) \tag{A.2}$$

$$x = null \ \text{ or } \ I(select_{Boolean})(h, x, I(created)) = tt \tag{A.3}$$

and aim to show that

$$I(store)(h, o, f, x) \in I(wellFormed).$$

By definition of $I(wellFormed)$, we have to show that $I(store)(h, o, f, x)$ has the following three properties:

1. Let $o_1 \in \mathcal{D}^{Object}$, $f_1 \in \mathcal{D}^{Field}$, and $o_2 = I(store)(h, o, f, x)(o_1, f_1)$ be such that $o_2 \in \mathcal{D}^{Object} \setminus \{null\}$. We have to show that

   $$I(store)(h, o, f, x)(o_2, I(created)) = tt,$$

   which by definition of $I(store)$ is the same as showing that

   $$h(o_2, I(created)) = tt. \tag{lma5.2-goal1}$$

   One of the following two cases must apply:

   - $o_1 = o$ and $f_1 = f$. Then by definition of o_2 and the definition of $I(store)$ we have $o_2 = x$. Together with $o_2 \neq null$ and (A.3), we get

     $$I(select_{Boolean})(h, o_2, I(created)) = tt,$$

     which using the definition of $I(select_{Boolean})$ is the same as

     $$I(cast_{Boolean})(h(o_2, I(created))) = tt.$$

     By definition of $I(cast_{Boolean})$, this implies (lma5.2-goal1).

   - $o_1 \neq o$ or $f_1 \neq f$. Then by definition of o_2 and the definition of $I(store)$ we have $o_2 = h(o_1, f_1)$. This and (A.2) imply (lma5.2-goal1).

2. Let $o_1 \in \mathcal{D}^{Object}$, $f_1 \in \mathcal{D}^{Field}$, and $l = I(store)(h, o, f, x)(o_1, f_1)$ be such that $l \in \mathcal{D}^{LocSet}$. We have to show that

   $$l \cap I(unusedLocs)(store(h, o, f, x)) = \emptyset,$$

   which by the definitions of $I(store)$ and $I(unusedLocs)$ is the same as showing that

   $$l \cap I(unusedLocs)(h) = \emptyset. \tag{lma5.2-goal2}$$

   One of the following two cases must apply:

- $o_1 = o$ and $f_1 = f$. Then by definition of l and the definition of $I(store)$ we have $l = x$. Because $x \in \mathcal{D}^{Object}$, $l \in \mathcal{D}^{LocSet}$ and $\mathcal{D}^{Object} \cap \mathcal{D}^{LocSet} = \emptyset$, this case cannot occur.

- $o_1 \neq o$ or $f_1 \neq f$. Then by definition of l and the definition of $I(store)$ we have $l = h(o_1, f_1)$. This and (A.2) imply (lma5.2-goal2).

3. We have to show that

$$\left\{ o' \in \mathcal{D}^{Object} \mid I(store)(h, o, f, x)(o', I(created)) = tt \right\} \text{ is finite.}$$
$$\text{(lma5.2-goal3)}$$

The definition of $I(store)$ guarantees that for all objects $o' \in \mathcal{D}^{Object}$, we have $I(store)(h, o, f, x)(o', I(created)) = h(o', I(created))$. Therefore

$$\left\{ o' \in \mathcal{D}^{Object} \mid I(store)(h, o, f, x)(o', I(created)) = tt \right\}$$
$$= \left\{ o' \in \mathcal{D}^{Object} \mid h(o', I(created)) = tt \right\},$$

and because we know from (A.2) that $\left\{ o' \in \mathcal{D}^{Object} \mid h(o', I(created)) = tt \right\}$ is finite, this implies (lma5.2-goal3). $\qquad \square$

A.4. Proof of Lemma 5.3: Well-formedness after Anonymisation

Let $\mathcal{K}$ be a Kripke structure, $s \in \mathcal{S}$ be a state, β be a variable assignment, $h, h' \in \mathcal{D}^{Heap}$, and $l \in \mathcal{D}^{LocSet}$. We assume

$$h \in I(wellFormed) \qquad\qquad (A.4)$$
$$h' \in I(wellFormed) \qquad\qquad (A.5)$$

and aim to show that

$$I(anon)(h, l, h') \in I(wellFormed).$$

By definition of $I(wellFormed)$, we have to show that $I(anon)(h, l, h')$ has the following three properties:

1. Let $o_1 \in \mathcal{D}^{Object}$, $f_1 \in \mathcal{D}^{Field}$, and $o_2 = I(anon)(h, l, h')(o_1, f_1)$ be such that $o_2 \in \mathcal{D}^{Object} \setminus \{null\}$. We have to show that

$$I(anon)(h, l, h')(o_2, I(created)) = tt. \qquad \text{(lma5.3-goal1)}$$

One of the following two cases must apply:

- $h(o_2, I(created)) = tt$. Then $(o_2, I(created)) \notin I(unusedLocs)(h)$. By definition of $I(anon)$, we get

$$I(anon)(h, l, h')(o_2, I(created)) = h(o_2, I(created)),$$

which together with $h(o_2, I(created)) = tt$ implies (lma5.3-goal1).

- $h(o_2, I(created)) \neq tt$. Then $(o_2, I(created)) \in I(unusedLocs)(h)$. By definition of $I(anon)$, we get

$$I(anon)(h, l, h')(o_2, I(created)) = h'(o_2, I(created)). \qquad (A.6)$$

The definition of o_2 and the definition of $I(anon)$ imply that one of the following two cases must apply:

  - $o_2 = h(o_1, f_1)$. Then (A.4) implies that $h(o_2, I(created)) = tt$, which contradicts the established fact that $h(o_2, I(created)) \neq tt$.
  - $o_2 = h'(o_1, f_1)$. Then (A.5) implies that $h'(o_2, I(created)) = tt$, which together with (A.6) implies (lma5.3-goal1).

2. Let $o_1 \in \mathcal{D}^{Object}$, $f_1 \in \mathcal{D}^{Field}$, and $l' = I(anon)(h, l, h')(o_1, f_1)$ be such that $l' \in \mathcal{D}^{LocSet}$. We have to show that

$$l' \cap I(unusedLocs)(anon(h, l, h')) = \emptyset.$$

Let $o_2 \in \mathcal{D}^{Object} \setminus \{null\}$ and $f_2 \in \mathcal{D}^{Field}$ such that $(o_2, f_2) \in l'$. Our goal is to show

$$I(anon)(h, l, h')(o_2, I(created)) = tt. \qquad (\text{lma5.3-goal2})$$

The proof now proceeds analogously to the proof of property (1) above. One of the following two cases must apply:

- $h(o_2, I(created)) = tt$. Then $(o_2, I(created)) \notin I(unusedLocs)(h)$. By definition of $I(anon)$, we get

$$I(anon)(h, l, h')(o_2, I(created)) = h(o_2, I(created)),$$

which together with $h(o_2, I(created)) = tt$ implies (lma5.3-goal2).

- $h(o_2, I(created)) \neq tt$. Then $(o_2, I(created)) \in I(unusedLocs)(h)$. By definition of $I(anon)$, we get

$$I(anon)(h, l, h')(o_2, I(created)) = h'(o_2, I(created)). \qquad (A.7)$$

The definition of l' and the definition of $I(anon)$ imply that one of the following two cases must apply:

- $l' = h(o_1, f_1)$. Then (A.4) and the definition of o_2 imply that $h(o_2, I(created)) = tt$, which contradicts the established fact that $h(o_2, I(created)) \neq tt$.

- $l' = h'(o_1, f_1)$. Then (A.5) and the definition of o_2 together imply that $h'(o_2, I(created)) = tt$, which together with (A.7) implies (lma5.3-goal2).

3. We have to show that

$$\{o \in \mathcal{D}^{Object} \mid I(anon)(h, l, h')(o, I(created)) = tt\} \text{ is finite.}$$
(lma5.3-goal3)

The definition of $I(anon)$ implies that for all objects $o \in \mathcal{D}^{Object}$, the value of $I(anon)(h, l, h')(o, I(created))$ is either $h(o, I(created))$ or $h'(o, I(created))$. Thus, we have

$$\{o \in \mathcal{D}^{Object} \mid I(anon)(h, l, h')(o, I(created)) = tt\}$$
$$\subseteq \{o \in \mathcal{D}^{Object} \mid h(o, I(created)) = tt\}$$
$$\cup \{o \in \mathcal{D}^{Object} \mid h'(o, I(created)) = tt\}.$$

As (A.4) and (A.5) tell us that the sets $\{o \in \mathcal{D}^{Object} \mid h(o, I(created)) = tt\}$ and $\{o \in \mathcal{D}^{Object} \mid h'(o, I(created)) = tt\}$ are finite, this implies (lma5.3-goal3). □

A.5. Proof of Lemma 5.4: Connection between *frame* and *anon*

Let $\mathcal{K}$ be a Kripke structure, $s \in \mathcal{S}$ be a state, β be a variable assignment, $h = s(\text{heap})$, $h' = val_{\mathcal{K},s,\beta}(anon(\text{heap}^{pre}, \{pre'\}mod, \text{heap}))$, $s^{pre} = val_{\mathcal{K},s,\beta}(pre')(s)$, $h^{pre} = s^{pre}(\text{heap})$, $m^{pre} = val_{\mathcal{K},s^{pre},\beta}(mod)$, $ul = I(unusedLocs)(h)$, and $ul^{pre} = I(unusedLocs)(h^{pre})$. Note that $h^{pre} = s(\text{heap}^{pre})$. By definition of $I(anon)$, we know that the following holds for all $o \in \mathcal{D}^{Object}$, $f \in \mathcal{D}^{Field}$:

$$h'(o, f) = \begin{cases} h(o, f) & \text{if } ((o, f) \in m^{pre} \text{ and } f \neq I(created)) \\ & \text{or } (o, f) \in ul^{pre} \\ h^{pre}(o, f) & \text{otherwise} \end{cases}$$
(A.8)

We first show that $(\mathcal{K}, s, \beta) \models frame \wedge noDeallocs$ implies that $(\mathcal{K}, s, \beta) \models frame'$, and then the other way round.

1. Let $o \in \mathcal{D}^{Object}$, $f \in \mathcal{D}^{Field}$. Using the definitions of *frame*, *noDeallocs* and *frame'*, we assume

$$(o, f) \in m^{pre} \cup ul^{pre} \quad \text{or} \quad h(o, f) = h^{pre}(o, f) \tag{A.9}$$

$$\text{if } (o, f) \in ul, \text{ then } (o, f) \in ul^{pre} \tag{A.10}$$

$$h(null, I(created)) = h^{pre}(null, I(created)) \tag{A.11}$$

and aim to show

$$h'(o, f) = h(o, f). \tag{A.12}$$

From (A.9) we get that one of the following three cases must apply:

- $(o, f) \in m^{pre}$. If $f \neq I(created)$ or $(o, f) \in ul^{pre}$, then (A.12) immediately follows from (A.8). We thus assume

$$f = I(created) \tag{A.13}$$

$$(o, f) \notin ul^{pre}. \tag{A.14}$$

  Now, (A.8) yields

$$h'(o, f) = h^{pre}(o, f). \tag{A.15}$$

  If $o = null$, then we get from (A.11) that $h(o, f) = h^{pre}(o, f)$, which together with (A.15) immediately yields (A.12). Thus we assume

$$o \neq null. \tag{A.16}$$

  From (A.10) and (A.14) we get that

$$(o, f) \notin ul.$$

  This, (A.16), and the definition of $I(unusedLocs)$ together imply that $h(o, I(created)) = tt$. Analogously, combining (A.14) and (A.16) yields $h^{pre}(o, I(created)) = tt$. Altogether, we have $h(o, I(created)) = h^{pre}(o, I(created))$, which because of (A.13) can be written as $h(o, f) = h^{pre}(o, f)$. We combine this with (A.15) to get (A.12).

- $(o, f) \in ul^{pre}$. Then (A.8) immediately yields (A.12).

- $h(o, f) = h^{pre}(o, f)$. If $(o, f) \in m^{pre}$ or $(o, f) \in ul^{pre}$, then the proof proceeds as for the respective case above. Otherwise, (A.8) guarantees that $h'(o, f) = h^{pre}(o, f)$, and thus we have (A.12).

2. Let $o \in \mathcal{D}^{Object}$, $f \in \mathcal{D}^{Field}$. We assume (A.12), and show first (A.9), then (A.10), and finally (A.11).

a) If $(o, f) \in m^{pre}$ or $(o, f) \in ul^{pre}$, then (A.9) holds trivially. Otherwise, (A.12) and (A.8) imply $h(o, f) = h^{pre}(o, f)$, which also implies (A.9).

b) We prove (A.10) by contradiction: we assume that $(o, f) \in ul \setminus ul^{pre}$. By definition of $I(unusedLocs)$, this means that $o \neq null$, that $h(o, I(created)) = f\!f$, and that $h^{pre}(o, I(created)) = tt$. From (A.12) and (A.8) we get that $h(o, I(created)) = h^{pre}(o, I(created))$. Together, we have $f\!f = tt$.

c) The definition of $I(unusedLocs)$ tells us that $(null, I(created)) \notin ul^{pre}$. Thus, (A.12) and (A.8) immediately guarantee (A.11). $\qquad\square$

A.6. Proof of Theorem 5.5: Soundness of loopInvariant

We assume

$$\models \Gamma \Rightarrow \{u\}(inv \wedge wellFormed(\mathtt{heap}) \wedge reachableIn), \Delta \qquad (\text{A.17})$$

$$\models \Gamma \Rightarrow \{u\}\{pre\}\{v\}(inv \wedge wellFormed(h) \wedge reachableOut \qquad (\text{A.18})$$
$$\wedge\, g \doteq TRUE \rightarrow [p](inv \wedge frame)), \Delta$$

$$\models \Gamma \Rightarrow \{u\}\{v\}(inv \wedge wellFormed(h) \wedge reachableOut \qquad (\text{A.19})$$
$$\wedge\, g \doteq FALSE \rightarrow [\pi\,\omega]\varphi), \Delta$$

Let $\mathcal{K} = (\mathcal{D}, \delta, I, \mathcal{S}, \rho)$ be a Kripke structure, $s \in \mathcal{S}$ be a state, and β be a variable assignment. Our goal is to show that

$$(\mathcal{K}, s, \beta) \models \Gamma \Rightarrow \{u\}[\pi\ \mathtt{while}(g)p;\ \omega]\varphi, \Delta.$$

If there is $\gamma \in \Gamma$ with $val_{\mathcal{K},s,\beta}(\gamma) = f\!f$ or if there is $\delta \in \Delta$ with $val_{\mathcal{K},s,\beta}(\delta) = tt$, then this is trivially true. We therefore assume that

$$(\mathcal{K}, s, \beta) \models \bigwedge(\Gamma \cup \neg\Delta), \qquad (\text{A.20})$$

and aim to show that $(\mathcal{K}, s, \beta) \models \{u\}[\pi\ \mathtt{while}(g)p;\ \omega]\varphi$.
Let $s_1 = val_{\mathcal{K},s,\beta}(u)(s)$. We need to show

$$(\mathcal{K}, s_1, \beta) \models [\pi\ \mathtt{while}(g)p;\ \omega]\varphi.$$

Let $s_2 = val_{\mathcal{K},s_1,\beta}(pre)(s_1)$. Because of the definition of pre, we have for all $\mathtt{a} \in \mathcal{PV} \setminus \{\mathtt{heap}^{pre}, \mathtt{b}_1^{pre}, \ldots, \mathtt{b}_n^{pre}\}$ that $s_1(\mathtt{a}) = s_2(\mathtt{a})$. And because $\mathtt{heap}^{pre}, \mathtt{b}_1^{pre}, \ldots, \mathtt{b}_n^{pre}$ do not occur in the above formula, Proposition A.1 tells us that the evaluation of this formula is the same in s_1 and s_2. Thus, it is sufficient if we show

$$(\mathcal{K}, s_2, \beta) \models [\pi\ \mathtt{while}(g)p;\ \omega]\varphi.$$

If the loop does not terminate when started in s_2, then the above holds trivially. We therefore assume that it does terminate. Then—because we ignore exceptions as well as **return**, **break** and **continue** statements—the semantics of Java tells us that there is a finite sequence of states $s_2, \ldots, s_m$ (where $2 \leq m$) such that

$$s_2(\mathsf{a}) = s_i(\mathsf{a}) \qquad \mathsf{a} \in \mathcal{PV} \setminus \{\mathsf{heap}, \mathsf{b}_1, \ldots, \mathsf{b}_n\}, i \in \{2, \ldots, m\} \quad \text{(A.21)}$$

$$(s_i, s_{i+1}) \in \rho(p) \qquad\qquad\qquad i \in \{2, \ldots, m-1\} \quad \text{(A.22)}$$

$$(\mathcal{K}, s_i, \beta) \models g \doteq \mathit{TRUE} \qquad\qquad i \in \{2, \ldots, m-1\} \quad \text{(A.23)}$$

$$(\mathcal{K}, s_m, \beta) \models g \doteq \mathit{FALSE} \qquad\qquad\qquad \text{(A.24)}$$

Our goal is to prove

$$(\mathcal{K}, s_m, \beta) \models [\pi \, \omega]\varphi. \qquad \text{(thm5.5-goal)}$$

We use induction to show that for all $i \in \{2, \ldots, m\}$, there is a Kripke structure $\mathcal{K}_i = (\mathcal{D}, \delta, I_i, \mathcal{S}, \rho)$ identical to $\mathcal{K}$ except in the interpretation of the constant symbols h and $b'_1, \ldots, b'_n$, such that:

$$val_{\mathcal{K}_i, s_2, \beta}(v)(s_2) = s_i \qquad \text{(thm5.5-ind-goal1)}$$

$$(\mathcal{K}_i, s_i, \beta) \models \mathit{inv} \qquad \text{(thm5.5-ind-goal2)}$$

$$(\mathcal{K}_i, s_i, \beta) \models \mathit{wellFormed}(h) \wedge \mathit{reachableOut} \qquad \text{(thm5.5-ind-goal3)}$$

Intuitively, this means that for every s_i we can choose an interpretation of $h, b'_1, \ldots, b'_n$ such that applying the "anonymising update" v to s_2 with this interpretation directly produces s_i, and such that with this interpretation, the state s_i satisfies both the loop invariant *inv* and the formula $\mathit{wellFormed}(h) \wedge \mathit{reachableOut}$. Afterwards, we use this result and (A.19) to show (thm5.5-goal).

- *Base case* ($i = 2$). We choose $\mathcal{K}_2$ such that $I_2(h) = s_2(\mathsf{heap})$ and such that $I_2(b'_1) = s_2(\mathsf{b}_1), \ldots, I_2(b'_n) = s_2(\mathsf{b}_n)$. Using the definitions of v and of $I(anon)$, we know that $val_{\mathcal{K}_2, s_2, \beta}(v)$ is the identity function on states, and thus we have (thm5.5-ind-goal1).

  From (A.20) and (A.17) we get

  $$(\mathcal{K}, s_1, \beta) \models \mathit{inv} \wedge \mathit{wellFormed}(\mathsf{heap}) \wedge \mathit{reachableIn}. \qquad \text{(A.25)}$$

  As $\mathsf{heap}^{pre}, \mathsf{b}_1^{pre}, \ldots, \mathsf{b}_n^{pre}$ do not occur in this formula, and as s_1 and s_2 are otherwise identical, Proposition A.1 tells us that $(\mathcal{K}, s_2, \beta) \models \mathit{inv} \wedge \mathit{wellFormed}(\mathsf{heap}) \wedge \mathit{reachableIn}$. As $h, b'_1, \ldots, b'_n$ also do not occur in the formula, by Proposition A.3 we have $(\mathcal{K}_2, s_2, \beta) \models \mathit{inv} \wedge \mathit{wellFormed}(\mathsf{heap}) \wedge \mathit{reachableIn}$. Because we chose $\mathcal{K}_2$ such that $I_2(h) = s_2(\mathsf{heap})$, this means

  $$(\mathcal{K}_2, s_2, \beta) \models \mathit{inv} \wedge \mathit{wellFormed}(h) \wedge \mathit{reachableIn}.$$

  This implies (thm5.5-ind-goal2). As we have $\{\mathsf{b}_1, \ldots, \mathsf{b}_n\} \subseteq \{\mathsf{a}_1, \ldots, \mathsf{a}_m\}$ and thus $\models \mathit{reachableIn} \rightarrow \mathit{reachableOut}$, it also implies (thm5.5-ind-goal3).

- *Step case ($i \in \{3, \ldots, m\}$).* We assume that properties (thm5.5-ind-goal1), (thm5.5-ind-goal2) and (thm5.5-ind-goal3) hold for $i - 1$:

$$val_{\mathcal{K}_{i-1}, s_2, \beta}(v)(s_2) = s_{i-1} \tag{A.26}$$

$$(\mathcal{K}_{i-1}, s_{i-1}, \beta) \models inv \tag{A.27}$$

$$(\mathcal{K}_{i-1}, s_{i-1}, \beta) \models wellFormed(h) \wedge reachableOut \tag{A.28}$$

We choose $\mathcal{K}_i$ such that $I_i(h) = s_i(\mathsf{heap})$, $I_i(b'_1) = s_i(\mathsf{b}_1), \ldots, I_i(b'_n) = s_i(\mathsf{b}_n)$.

Since $\mathcal{K}_{i-1}$ and $\mathcal{K}$ differ only in the interpretation of $h, b'_1, \ldots, b'_n$, and since these constant symbols do not occur in Γ nor in Δ, (A.20) and Proposition A.3 yield $(\mathcal{K}_{i-1}, s, \beta) \models \bigwedge(\Gamma \cup \neg\Delta)$. Together with (A.18), this implies

$$(\mathcal{K}_{i-1}, s, \beta) \models \{u\}\{pre\}\{v\}\big(inv \wedge wellFormed(h) \wedge reachableOut$$
$$\wedge\, g \doteq TRUE \to [p](inv \wedge frame)\big).$$

As the constant symbols $h, b'_1, \ldots, b'_n$ do not occur in the updates u and pre, Proposition A.3 tells us that $val_{\mathcal{K}_{i-1}, s, \beta}(u)(s) = val_{\mathcal{K}, s, \beta}(u)(s) = s_1$, and furthermore that $val_{\mathcal{K}_{i-1}, s_1, \beta}(pre)(s_1) = val_{\mathcal{K}, s_1, \beta}(pre)(s_1) = s_2$. Thus, the above can be restated as

$$(\mathcal{K}_{i-1}, s_2, \beta) \models \{v\}\big(inv \wedge wellFormed(h) \wedge reachableOut$$
$$\wedge\, g \doteq TRUE \to [p](inv \wedge frame)\big),$$

which we can combine with (A.26) to get

$$(\mathcal{K}_{i-1}, s_{i-1}, \beta) \models inv \wedge wellFormed(h) \wedge reachableOut$$
$$\wedge\, g \doteq TRUE \to [p](inv \wedge frame).$$

Because $h, b'_1, \ldots, b'_n$ do not occur in (A.23), we have $(\mathcal{K}_{i-1}, s_{i-1}, \beta) \models g \doteq TRUE$. Combining this, (A.27), (A.28) and the above yields

$$(\mathcal{K}_{i-1}, s_{i-1}, \beta) \models [p](inv \wedge frame).$$

Because of (A.22), this means $(\mathcal{K}_{i-1}, s_i, \beta) \models inv \wedge frame$. As $h, b'_1, \ldots, b'_n$ do not occur in this formula, we get (thm5.5-ind-goal2) and

$$(\mathcal{K}_i, s_i, \beta) \models frame. \tag{A.29}$$

It remains to show (thm5.5-ind-goal1) and (thm5.5-ind-goal3). Let $p^{i-2} = p; \ldots; p$ be the legal program fragment resulting from concatenating $i - 2$ copies of the loop body p (and performing bound renaming of variables declared in p, such that p^{i-2} is syntactically correct). From Proposition A.4 we know that

$$(\mathcal{K}, s_1, \beta) \models \textit{wellFormed}(\texttt{heap}) \land \textit{reachableIn}$$
$$\rightarrow \{pre\}[p^{i-2}]$$
$$\left(\textit{wellFormed}(\texttt{heap}) \land \textit{reachableOut} \land \textit{noDeallocs}\right).$$

Combining this with (A.25) yields

$$(\mathcal{K}, s_1, \beta) \models \{pre\}[p^{i-2}]\left(\textit{wellFormed}(\texttt{heap}) \land \textit{reachableOut} \land \textit{noDeallocs}\right),$$

which is the same as

$$(\mathcal{K}, s_2, \beta) \models [p^{i-2}]\left(\textit{wellFormed}(\texttt{heap}) \land \textit{reachableOut} \land \textit{noDeallocs}\right).$$

Because of (A.22), this means that

$$(\mathcal{K}, s_i, \beta) \models \textit{wellFormed}(\texttt{heap}) \land \textit{reachableOut} \land \textit{noDeallocs}.$$

As the constant symbols $h, b'_1, \ldots, b'_n$ do not occur in the above formula, we also have

$$(\mathcal{K}_i, s_i, \beta) \models \textit{wellFormed}(\texttt{heap}) \land \textit{reachableOut} \land \textit{noDeallocs}.$$

Because we chose $\mathcal{K}_i$ such that $I_i(h) = s_i(\texttt{heap})$, this can be restated as

$$(\mathcal{K}_i, s_i, \beta) \models \textit{wellFormed}(h) \land \textit{reachableOut} \land \textit{noDeallocs}.$$

Thus, we have (thm5.5-ind-goal3), and

$$(\mathcal{K}_i, s_i, \beta) \models \textit{noDeallocs}. \tag{A.30}$$

It remains to show (thm5.5-ind-goal1). Together, (A.29), (A.30) and Lemma 5.4 tell us that

$$(\mathcal{K}_i, s_i, \beta) \models \texttt{heap} \doteq \textit{anon}(\texttt{heap}^{pre}, \{pre'\}\textit{mod}, \texttt{heap}),$$

which we can also express as

$$s_i(\texttt{heap}) = \textit{val}_{\mathcal{K}_i, s_i, \beta}\left(\textit{anon}(\texttt{heap}^{pre}, \{pre'\}\textit{mod}, \texttt{heap})\right).$$

As we defined $\mathcal{K}_i$ such that $I_i(h) = s_i(\texttt{heap})$, this implies

$$s_i(\texttt{heap}) = \textit{val}_{\mathcal{K}_i, s_i, \beta}\left(\textit{anon}(\texttt{heap}^{pre}, \{pre'\}\textit{mod}, h)\right).$$

By (A.21), we know that s_2 and s_i differ only in the evaluation of the program variables $\mathtt{heap}, \mathtt{b}_1, \ldots, \mathtt{b}_n$. This, the definition of pre', and Proposition A.2 together tell us that $val_{\mathcal{K}_i, s_i, \beta}(\{pre'\}\, mod) = val_{\mathcal{K}_i, s_2, \beta}(\{pre'\}\, mod)$. As $\mathtt{heap}, \mathtt{b}_1, \ldots, \mathtt{b}_n$ do not occur in the other arguments of *anon* above, Proposition A.1 allows us to transform the statement above into

$$s_i(\mathtt{heap}) = val_{\mathcal{K}_i, s_2, \beta}\big(anon(\mathtt{heap}^{pre}, \{pre'\}\, mod, h)\big).$$

The definition of s_2 implies that $val_{\mathcal{K}_i, s_2, \beta}(pre')$ is the identity function. Thus, we can simplify the above into

$$s_i(\mathtt{heap}) = val_{\mathcal{K}_i, s_2, \beta}\big(anon(\mathtt{heap}^{pre}, mod, h)\big).$$

Also, as $s_2(\mathtt{heap}^{pre}) = s_2(\mathtt{heap})$, we can replace $\mathtt{heap}^{pre}$ with $\mathtt{heap}$ to get

$$s_i(\mathtt{heap}) = val_{\mathcal{K}_i, s_2, \beta}\big(anon(\mathtt{heap}, mod, h)\big).$$

This and the fact that by our choice of $\mathcal{K}_i$ we have $I_i(b'_1) = s_i(\mathtt{b}_1)$, $\ldots, I_i(b'_n) = s_i(\mathtt{b}_n)$ imply (thm5.5-ind-goal1).

This finishes the induction. We know now that in particular for $i = m$, there is a Kripke structure $\mathcal{K}_m = (\mathcal{D}, \delta, I_m, \mathcal{S}, \rho)$ identical to $\mathcal{K}$ except in the interpretation of $h, b'_1, \ldots, b'_n$, such that:

$$val_{\mathcal{K}_m, s_2, \beta}(v)(s_2) = s_m \tag{A.31}$$

$$(\mathcal{K}_m, s_m, \beta) \models inv \tag{A.32}$$

$$(\mathcal{K}_m, s_m, \beta) \models wellFormed(h) \wedge reachableOut \tag{A.33}$$

As the constant symbols $h, b'_1, \ldots, b'_n$ do not occur in (A.20), we have $(\mathcal{K}_m, s, \beta) \models \bigwedge(\Gamma \cup \neg\Delta)$. This and (A.19) imply

$$(\mathcal{K}_m, s, \beta) \models \{u\}\{v\}\big(inv \wedge wellFormed(h) \wedge reachableOut$$
$$\wedge\, g \doteq FALSE \to [\pi\, \omega]\varphi\big).$$

As the constant symbols $h, b'_1, \ldots, b'_n$ do not occur in u, this is the same as

$$(\mathcal{K}_m, s_1, \beta) \models \{v\}\big(inv \wedge wellFormed(h) \wedge reachableOut \wedge g \doteq FALSE \to [\pi\, \omega]\varphi\big),$$

and since the program variables $\mathtt{heap}^{pre}, \mathtt{b}_1^{pre}, \ldots, \mathtt{b}_n^{pre}$ do not occur in the above formula, it is also the same as

$$(\mathcal{K}_m, s_2, \beta) \models \{v\}\big(inv \wedge wellFormed(h) \wedge reachableOut \wedge g \doteq FALSE \to [\pi\, \omega]\varphi\big).$$

Combining the above with (A.31) yields

$$(\mathcal{K}_m, s_m, \beta) \models inv \wedge wellFormed(h) \wedge reachableOut \wedge g \doteq FALSE \to [\pi\, \omega]\varphi.$$

Because $h, b'_1, \ldots, b'_n$ do not occur in (A.24), we have $(\mathcal{K}_m, s_m, \beta) \models g \doteq FALSE$. This, (A.32), (A.33), and the above yield (thm5.5-goal). $\qquad\square$

A.7. Proof of Theorem 6.1: Soundness of useMethodContract

We assume

$$\models \Gamma \Rightarrow \{u\}\{w\}(\textit{pre} \wedge \textit{wellFormed}(\texttt{heap}) \wedge \textit{reachableIn} \tag{A.34}$$
$$\wedge\, \texttt{self} \not\doteq \textbf{null} \wedge \texttt{self}.\textit{created} \doteq \textit{TRUE}),\, \Delta$$

$$\models \Gamma \Rightarrow \{u\}\{w\}\{\texttt{heap}^{pre} := \texttt{heap}\}\{v\} \tag{A.35}$$
$$(\textit{post} \wedge \textit{wellFormed}(h) \wedge \textit{reachableOut}$$
$$\rightarrow [\![\pi \ \texttt{if(exc != null) throw exc;}$$
$$\texttt{r = res;}\ \omega]\!]\varphi),\, \Delta$$

Furthermore we assume that for all types $F \in \mathcal{T}$ with $F \preceq E$, we have

$$\models \textit{CorrectMethodContract}(\textit{mct}, F). \tag{A.36}$$

Let $\mathcal{K} = (\mathcal{D}, \delta, I, \mathcal{S}, \rho)$ be a Kripke structure, $s \in \mathcal{S}$ be a state, and β be a variable assignment. Our goal is to show that

$$(\mathcal{K}, s, \beta) \models \Gamma \Rightarrow \{u\}[\![\pi \ \texttt{r = }o.\texttt{m}(a_1', \dots, a_m')\texttt{; }\omega]\!]\varphi,\, \Delta.$$

If there is $\gamma \in \Gamma$ with $\textit{val}_{\mathcal{K},s,\beta}(\gamma) = \textit{ff}$ or if there is $\delta \in \Delta$ with $\textit{val}_{\mathcal{K},s,\beta}(\delta) = \textit{tt}$, then this is trivially true. We therefore assume that

$$(\mathcal{K}, s, \beta) \models \bigwedge(\Gamma \cup \neg\Delta), \tag{A.37}$$

and aim to show that $(\mathcal{K}, s, \beta) \models \{u\}[\![\pi \ \texttt{r = }o.\texttt{m}(a_1', \dots, a_m')\texttt{; }\omega]\!]\varphi$. Let $s_1 = \textit{val}_{\mathcal{K},s,\beta}(u)(s)$. Then our goal is to show

$$(\mathcal{K}, s_1, \beta) \models [\![\pi \ \texttt{r = }o.\texttt{m}(a_1', \dots, a_m')\texttt{; }\omega]\!]\varphi.$$

Let $s_2 = \textit{val}_{\mathcal{K},s_1,\beta}(w)(s_1)$. Because of the definition of w, it holds for all $\texttt{a} \in \mathcal{PV} \setminus \{\texttt{self}, \texttt{a}_1, \dots, \texttt{a}_m\}$ that $s_1(\texttt{a}) = s_2(\texttt{a})$. Since by Definition 6.7 neither $\texttt{self}$ nor $\texttt{a}_1, \dots, \texttt{a}_m$ occur in the above formula, Proposition A.1 tells us that the interpretation of this formula is the same in s_1 and s_2. It is therefore sufficient if we show

$$(\mathcal{K}, s_2, \beta) \models [\![\pi \ \texttt{r = }o.\texttt{m}(a_1', \dots, a_m')\texttt{; }\omega]\!]\varphi.$$

The definition of w and Proposition A.1 ensure that $s_2(\texttt{self}) = \textit{val}_{\mathcal{K},s_2,\beta}(o)$, and that $s_2(\texttt{a}_1) = \textit{val}_{\mathcal{K},s_2,\beta}(a_1')$, ..., $s_2(\texttt{a}_m) = \textit{val}_{\mathcal{K},s_2,\beta}(a_m')$. Thus, we can instead aim to prove:

$$(\mathcal{K}, s_2, \beta) \models [\![\pi \ \texttt{r = self.m}(\texttt{a}_1, \dots, \texttt{a}_m)\texttt{; }\omega]\!]\varphi.$$

Let $s_3 = val_{\mathcal{K},s_2,\beta}(\mathtt{heap}^{pre} := \mathtt{heap})(s_2)$. Since by Definition 6.7 the program variable $\mathtt{heap}^{pre}$ does not occur in the above formula, by Proposition A.1 it is sufficient if we prove

$$(\mathcal{K}, s_3, \beta) \models [\![\pi \; \mathtt{r} \; \mathtt{=} \; \mathtt{self.m(a_1, \ldots, a_m)} ; \omega]\!]\varphi.$$

Since by Definition 6.7 the program variable $\mathtt{res}$ does not occur in the above formula, the semantics of Java allows us to instead show

$$(\mathcal{K}, s_3, \beta) \models [\![\pi \; \mathtt{res} \; \mathtt{=} \; \mathtt{self.m(a_1, \ldots, a_m)} ; \; \mathtt{r} \; \mathtt{=} \; \mathtt{res}; \omega]\!]\varphi.$$

Since by Definition 6.7 the program variable $\mathtt{exc}$ also does not occur in the formula, the semantics of Java furthermore allows us to rewrite the proof goal into:

$$(\mathcal{K}, s_3, \beta) \models [\![\pi \; \mathtt{exc} \; \mathtt{=} \; \mathtt{null}; \quad\quad\quad\quad\quad\quad\quad\quad \text{(thm6.1-goal)}$$
$$\mathtt{try \; \{ \; res \; = \; self.m(a_1, \ldots, a_m); \; \}}$$
$$\mathtt{catch(Exception \; e) \; \{ \; exc \; = \; e; \; \}}$$
$$\mathtt{if(exc \; != \; null) \; throw \; exc;}$$
$$\mathtt{r \; = \; res}; \omega]\!]\varphi$$

We combine (A.37) with (A.34) to get

$$(\mathcal{K}, s, \beta) \models \{u\}\{w\}(pre \wedge wellFormed(\mathtt{heap}) \wedge reachableIn$$
$$\wedge \; \mathtt{self} \not\doteq \mathtt{null} \wedge \mathtt{self}.created \doteq TRUE),$$

which by definition of s_2 is the same as

$$(\mathcal{K}, s_2, \beta) \models pre \wedge wellFormed(\mathtt{heap}) \wedge reachableIn \quad\quad\quad\quad \text{(A.38)}$$
$$\wedge \; \mathtt{self} \not\doteq \mathtt{null} \wedge \mathtt{self}.created \doteq TRUE.$$

Let $F = \delta(val_{\mathcal{K},s_2,\beta}(o))$. Because of the definition of s_2, this means that

$$(\mathcal{K}, s_2, \beta) \models exactInstance_F(\mathtt{self}). \quad\quad\quad\quad\quad\quad \text{(A.39)}$$

Since $o \in Term_\Sigma^E$, we have $F \preceq E$. Instantiating (A.36) with F, $\mathcal{K}$, s_2 and β yields

$$(\mathcal{K}, s_2, \beta) \models pre \wedge wellFormed(\mathtt{heap}) \wedge reachableIn$$
$$\wedge \; \mathtt{self} \not\doteq \mathtt{null} \wedge \mathtt{self}.created \doteq TRUE \wedge exactInstance_F(\mathtt{self})$$
$$\rightarrow \{\mathtt{heap}^{pre} := \mathtt{heap}\}$$
$$[\![\mathtt{exc} \; \mathtt{=} \; \mathtt{null};$$
$$\mathtt{try \; \{ \; res \; = \; self.m(a_1, \ldots, a_m); \; \}}$$
$$\mathtt{catch(Exception \; e) \; \{ \; exc \; = \; e; \; \}}]\!]'(post \wedge frame)$$

where $[\![\cdot]\!]'$ is $\langle\cdot\rangle$ if $[\![\cdot]\!]$ is $\langle\cdot\rangle$, and where $[\![\cdot]\!]'$ is either $\langle\cdot\rangle$ or $[\cdot]$ otherwise. Together with (A.38) and (A.39), this implies:

$$(\mathcal{K}, s_2, \beta) \models \{\mathtt{heap}^{pre} := \mathtt{heap}\}$$
$$[\![\mathtt{exc}\ =\ \mathtt{null};$$
$$\mathtt{try}\ \{\ \mathtt{res}\ =\ \mathtt{self.m(a_1, \ldots, a_m)};\ \}$$
$$\mathtt{catch}(\mathtt{Exception}\ \mathtt{e})\ \{\ \mathtt{exc}\ =\ \mathtt{e};\ \}]\!]'(post \wedge frame)$$

With the definition of s_3, this becomes

$$(\mathcal{K}, s_3, \beta) \models [\![\mathtt{exc}\ =\ \mathtt{null}; \tag{A.40}$$
$$\mathtt{try}\ \{\ \mathtt{res}\ =\ \mathtt{self.m(a_1, \ldots, a_m)};\ \}$$
$$\mathtt{catch}(\mathtt{Exception}\ \mathtt{e})\ \{\ \mathtt{exc}\ =\ \mathtt{e};\ \}]\!]'(post \wedge frame)$$

Let p be the program fragment inside the modal operator $[\![\cdot]\!]'$ above. If there is no state $s_4 \in \mathcal{S}$ such that $(s_3, s_4) \in \rho(p)$ (i.e., if the method call does not terminate when p is started in s_3), then (A.40) implies that $[\![\cdot]\!]'$ must be $[\cdot]$, and thus $[\![\cdot]\!]$ also must be $[\cdot]$. Then, (thm6.1-goal) holds trivially, because there is no final state which would have to satisfy φ.

We thus assume that there is $s_4 \in \mathcal{S}$ such that $(s_3, s_4) \in \rho(p)$. As our programs are deterministic, s_4 is the only such state. Our proof goal (thm6.1-goal) now becomes

$$(\mathcal{K}, s_4, \beta) \models [\![\pi\ \mathtt{if}(\mathtt{exc}\ \mathtt{!=}\ \mathtt{null})\ \mathtt{throw}\ \mathtt{exc}; \tag{thm6.1-goal'}$$
$$\mathtt{r}\ =\ \mathtt{res};\ \omega]\!]\varphi$$

From (A.40) and the definition of s_4 we get

$$(\mathcal{K}, s_4, \beta) \models post \wedge frame. \tag{A.41}$$

Let $noDeallocs \in Fma_\Sigma$ be as in Lemma 5.4. Proposition A.5 tells us that

$$(\mathcal{K}, s_2, \beta) \models wellFormed(\mathtt{heap}) \wedge reachableIn \wedge \mathtt{self} \neq \mathtt{null}$$
$$\wedge\ \mathtt{self}.created \doteq TRUE$$
$$\rightarrow \{\mathtt{heap}^{pre} := \mathtt{heap}\}[p]$$
$$\big(wellFormed(\mathtt{heap}) \wedge reachableOut \wedge noDeallocs\big)$$

Together with (A.38) and the definition of s_4, this turns into

$$(\mathcal{K}, s_4, \beta) \models wellFormed(\mathtt{heap}) \wedge reachableOut \wedge noDeallocs. \tag{A.42}$$

Let $\mathcal{K}' = (\mathcal{D}, \delta, I', \mathcal{S}, \rho)$ be a Kripke structure identical to $\mathcal{K}$, except that $I'(h) = s_4(\mathtt{heap})$, that $I'(r) = s_4(\mathtt{res})$, and that $I'(e) = s_4(\mathtt{exc})$. Since by Definition 6.7

the constant symbols h, r and e occur neither in Γ nor in Δ, we get from (A.37) and Proposition A.3 that $(\mathcal{K}', s, \beta) \models \bigwedge(\Gamma \cup \neg\Delta)$. This and (A.35) imply

$$(\mathcal{K}', s, \beta) \models \{u\}\{w\}\{\mathtt{heap}^{pre} := \mathtt{heap}\}\{v\}\big(post \wedge wellFormed(h) \wedge reachableOut$$
$$\rightarrow \llbracket \pi \text{ if(exc != null) throw exc;}$$
$$\text{r = res; } \omega \rrbracket \varphi\big).$$

As h, r and e do not occur in u, in w or in $\mathtt{heap}^{pre} := \mathtt{heap}$, the above and Proposition A.3 imply that

$$(\mathcal{K}', s_3, \beta) \models \{v\}\big(post \wedge wellFormed(h) \wedge reachableOut$$
$$\rightarrow \llbracket \pi \text{ if(exc != null) throw exc;}$$
$$\text{r = res; } \omega \rrbracket \varphi\big).$$

Let $s_4' = val_{\mathcal{K}', s_3, \beta}(v)(s_3)$. Then the above implies

$$(\mathcal{K}', s_4', \beta) \models post \wedge wellFormed(h) \wedge reachableOut \qquad (A.43)$$
$$\rightarrow \llbracket \pi \text{ if(exc != null) throw exc;}$$
$$\text{r = res; } \omega \rrbracket \varphi.$$

The definition of s_4 and the semantics of Java tell us that for all $\mathtt{a} \in \mathcal{PV} \setminus \{\mathtt{heap}, \mathtt{res}, \mathtt{exc}\}$ we have $s_3(\mathtt{a}) = s_4(\mathtt{a})$. Similarly, the definition of s_4' implies that for all $\mathtt{a} \in \mathcal{PV} \setminus \{\mathtt{heap}, \mathtt{res}, \mathtt{exc}\}$ we have $s_3(\mathtt{a}) = s_4'(\mathtt{a})$. Together, we have

$$\text{for all } \mathtt{a} \in \mathcal{PV} \setminus \{\mathtt{heap}, \mathtt{res}, \mathtt{exc}\} : s_4'(\mathtt{a}) = s_4(\mathtt{a}). \qquad (A.44)$$

The definition of s_4' also guarantees that

$$s_4'(\mathtt{heap}) = val_{\mathcal{K}', s_3, \beta}\big(anon(\mathtt{heap}, mod, h)\big) \qquad (A.45)$$
$$s_4'(\mathtt{res}) = I'(r) = s_4(\mathtt{res}) \qquad (A.46)$$
$$s_4'(\mathtt{exc}) = I'(e) = s_4(\mathtt{exc}) \qquad (A.47)$$

Using (A.41) and (A.42), Lemma 5.4 (with $n = 0$) tells us that

$$(\mathcal{K}, s_4, \beta) \models \mathtt{heap} \doteq anon\big(\mathtt{heap}^{pre}, \{\mathtt{heap} := \mathtt{heap}^{pre}\}mod, \mathtt{heap}\big),$$

which we can also express as

$$s_4(\mathtt{heap}) = val_{\mathcal{K}, s_4, \beta}\big(anon(\mathtt{heap}^{pre}, \{\mathtt{heap} := \mathtt{heap}^{pre}\}mod, \mathtt{heap})\big).$$

Since by Definition 6.7 the constant symbols h, r and e do not occur in the above formula, and since $\mathcal{K}'$ is otherwise identical to $\mathcal{K}$, Proposition A.3 yields

$$s_4(\mathtt{heap}) = val_{\mathcal{K}', s_4, \beta}\big(anon(\mathtt{heap}^{pre}, \{\mathtt{heap} := \mathtt{heap}^{pre}\}mod, \mathtt{heap})\big).$$

As we defined $\mathcal{K}'$ such that $I'(h) = s_4(\mathtt{heap})$, this implies

$$s_4(\mathtt{heap}) = val_{\mathcal{K}',s_4,\beta}\big(anon(\mathtt{heap}^{pre}, \{\mathtt{heap} := \mathtt{heap}^{pre}\}mod, h)\big).$$

Since s_3 and s_4 are identical except for the program variable $\mathtt{heap}$, Proposition A.2 tells us that $val_{\mathcal{K},s_4,\beta}(\{\mathtt{heap} := \mathtt{heap}^{pre}\}mod) = val_{\mathcal{K},s_3,\beta}(\{\mathtt{heap} := \mathtt{heap}^{pre}\}mod)$. As $\mathtt{heap}$ does not occur in the other arguments of *anon*, we can transform the statement above into

$$s_4(\mathtt{heap}) = val_{\mathcal{K}',s_3,\beta}\big(anon(\mathtt{heap}^{pre}, \{\mathtt{heap} := \mathtt{heap}^{pre}\}mod, h)\big).$$

The definition of s_3 implies $s_3(\mathtt{heap}) = s_3(\mathtt{heap}^{pre})$. Thus, the update $\mathtt{heap} := \mathtt{heap}^{pre}$ has no effect in s_3. This allows simplifying the above into

$$s_4(\mathtt{heap}) = val_{\mathcal{K}',s_3,\beta}\big(anon(\mathtt{heap}^{pre}, mod, h)\big),$$

and replacing $\mathtt{heap}^{pre}$ with $\mathtt{heap}$ to get

$$s_4(\mathtt{heap}) = val_{\mathcal{K}',s_3,\beta}\big(anon(\mathtt{heap}, mod, h)\big).$$

This, together with (A.45), implies that $s_4(\mathtt{heap}) = s'_4(\mathtt{heap})$. Combining this result with (A.44), (A.46) and (A.47) yields that $s_4 = s'_4$. Together with (A.43), this means

$$(\mathcal{K}', s_4, \beta) \models post \wedge wellFormed(h) \wedge reachableOut \tag{A.48}$$
$$\rightarrow [\![\pi \; \mathtt{if(exc \; != \; null) \; throw \; exc;}$$
$$\mathtt{r \; = \; res;} \; \omega]\!]\varphi.$$

Since the constant symbols h, r and e do not occur in *post*, in *wellFormed*($\mathtt{heap}$) or in *reachableOut*, (A.41), (A.42) and Proposition A.3 imply

$$(\mathcal{K}', s_4, \beta) \models post \wedge wellFormed(\mathtt{heap}) \wedge reachableOut.$$

Because we defined $\mathcal{K}'$ such that $I'(h) = s_4(\mathtt{heap})$, this is the same as

$$(\mathcal{K}', s_4, \beta) \models post \wedge wellFormed(h) \wedge reachableOut,$$

which can be combined with (A.48) to get

$$(\mathcal{K}', s_4, \beta) \models [\![\pi \; \mathtt{if(exc \; != \; null) \; throw \; exc;}$$
$$\mathtt{r \; = \; res;} \; \omega]\!]\varphi.$$

Because the constant symbols h, r and e do not occur in the above formula, and because $\mathcal{K}$ and $\mathcal{K}'$ are otherwise identical, this implies (thm6.1-goal') by Proposition A.3. $\qquad\square$

A.8. Proof of Lemma 6.2: No Deallocations

Let $\mathcal{K}$ be a Kripke structure, $s \in \mathcal{S}$ be a state, $h^{pre} \in \mathcal{D}^{Heap}$, and

$$h^{post} = I(f_k)(I(f_{k-1})(\ldots(I(f_1)(h^{pre}, \ldots)))) \in \mathcal{D}^{Heap}.$$

Our goal is to show

$$I(unusedLocs)(h^{post}) \subseteq I(unusedLocs)(h^{pre})$$
$$h^{post}(null, I(created)) = h^{pre}(null, I(created))$$

Let $o \in \mathcal{D}^{Object} \setminus \{null\}$ such that $h^{pre}(o, I(created)) = tt$. By definition of $I(unusedLocs)$, what we have to show is

$$h^{post}(o, I(created)) = tt$$
$$h^{post}(null, I(created)) = h^{pre}(null, I(created))$$

Let $h_i = I(f_i)(I(f_{i-1})(\ldots(I(f_1)(h^{pre}, \ldots))))$ for all $i \in \{0, \ldots, k\}$. We use induction to show that for all $i \in \{0, \ldots, k\}$ we have

$$h_i(o, I(created)) = tt \tag{lma6.2-ind-goal1}$$
$$h_i(null, I(created)) = h^{pre}(null, I(created)). \tag{lma6.2-ind-goal2}$$

Because $h_k = h^{post}$, this is sufficient to show our proof goal.

- *Base case ($i = 0$).* Then $h_i = h^{pre}$, and both (lma6.2-ind-goal1) and (lma6.2-ind-goal2) hold trivially.

- *Step case ($i \in \{1, \ldots, k\}$).* We assume that both (lma6.2-ind-goal1) and (lma6.2-ind-goal2) hold for $i - 1$:

$$h_{i-1}(o, I(created)) = tt \tag{A.49}$$
$$h_{i-1}(null, I(created)) = h^{pre}(null, I(created)) \tag{A.50}$$

  One of the following three cases must apply:

  - $f_i = store$. Then there is $o' \in \mathcal{D}^{Object}$, $f \in \mathcal{D}^{Field}$, $x \in \mathcal{D}^{Any}$ such that $h_i = I(store)(h_{i-1}, o', f, x)$. By definition of $I(store)$, this implies that

$$h_i(o, I(created)) = h_{i-1}(o, I(created))$$
$$h_i(null, I(created)) = h_{i-1}(null, I(created))$$

  Together with (A.49) and (A.50), this implies both (lma6.2-ind-goal1) and (lma6.2-ind-goal2).

    – $f_i = create$. Then there is an object $o' \in \mathcal{D}^{Object}$ such that $h_i = I(create)(h_{i-1}, o')$. By definition of $I(create)$, this implies

$$h_i\big(null, I(created)\big) = h_{i-1}\big(null, I(created)\big),$$

which together with (A.50) implies (lma6.2-ind-goal2). One of the following two cases must apply:

       * $o' = o$. Then by definition of $I(create)$ we have (lma6.2-ind-goal1).

       * $o' \neq o$. Then by definition of $I(create)$ we have

$$h_i\big(o, I(created)\big) = h_{i-1}\big(o, I(created)\big),$$

which together with (A.49) implies (lma6.2-ind-goal1).

    – $f_i = anon$. Then there is $s \in \mathcal{D}^{LocSet}$ and $h' \in \mathcal{D}^{Heap}$ such that $h_i = I(anon)(h_{i-1}, s, h')$. By definition of $I(anon)$, this implies

$$h_i\big(null, I(created)\big) = h_{i-1}\big(null, I(created)\big),$$

which together with (A.50) implies (lma6.2-ind-goal2). Because of (A.49), we have $\big(o, I(created)\big) \notin unusedLocs(h_{i-1})$. Thus, the definition of $I(anon)$ also implies

$$h_i\big(o, I(created)\big) = h_{i-1}\big(o, I(created)\big),$$

which together with (A.49) implies (lma6.2-ind-goal1). $\qquad\square$

A.9. Proof of Theorem 6.3: Soundness of useDependencyContract

We assume

$$\models \Gamma, \; guard \rightarrow equal \; \Rightarrow \; \Delta, \qquad\qquad (A.51)$$

and we assume that for all types $F \in \mathcal{T}$ with $F \preceq E$, we have

$$\models \; CorrectDependencyContract(depct, F). \qquad\qquad (A.52)$$

Let $\mathcal{K} = (\mathcal{D}, \delta, I, \mathcal{S}, \rho)$ be a Kripke structure, $s \in \mathcal{S}$ be a state, and β be a variable assignment. Our goal is to show $(\mathcal{K}, s, \beta) \models \Gamma \Rightarrow \Delta$. We do a proof by contradiction and assume that this does *not* hold, or in other words, that $(\mathcal{K}, s, \beta) \models \bigwedge(\Gamma \cup \neg\Delta)$ holds. This and (A.51) imply $(\mathcal{K}, s, \beta) \models \neg(guard \rightarrow equal)$, or equivalently $(\mathcal{K}, s, \beta) \models guard \wedge \neg equal$. If we insert the definitions of *guard* and *equal* and distribute the update w over the conjuncts below it, then this reads as

$$(\mathcal{K}, s, \beta) \models wellFormed(h^{pre}) \wedge wellFormed(h^{post}) \qquad (A.53)$$

$$(\mathcal{K}, s, \beta) \models \{w\}\{\texttt{heap} := h^{pre}\}(pre \wedge reachableIn$$
$$\wedge \, \texttt{self} \neq \textbf{null} \wedge \texttt{self}.created \doteq TRUE)$$

$$(\mathcal{K}, s, \beta) \models \{w\}\{\texttt{heap}^{pre} := h^{pre} \,\|\, \texttt{heap} := h^{post}\}frame$$

$$(\mathcal{K}, s, \beta) \models \neg\big(obs(h^{pre}, o, a'_1, \ldots, a'_m) \equiv obs(h^{post}, o, a'_1, \ldots, a'_n)\big) \qquad (A.54)$$

Let $s_1 = val_{\mathcal{K},s,\beta}(w)(s)$. Then the second and the third of the four statements above become

$$(\mathcal{K}, s_1, \beta) \models \{\texttt{heap} := h^{pre}\}(pre \wedge reachableIn$$
$$\wedge \, \texttt{self} \neq \textbf{null} \wedge \texttt{self}.created \doteq TRUE)$$

$$(\mathcal{K}, s_1, \beta) \models \{\texttt{heap}^{pre} := h^{pre} \,\|\, \texttt{heap} := h^{post}\}frame$$

Let $s_1^{pre} = val_{\mathcal{K},s_1,\beta}(\texttt{heap} := h^{pre})(s_1)$, and let $s_1^{post} = val_{\mathcal{K},s_1,\beta}(\texttt{heap}^{pre} := h^{pre} \,\|\, \texttt{heap} := h^{post})(s_1)$. Then the statements above turn into

$$(\mathcal{K}, s_1^{pre}, \beta) \models pre \wedge reachableIn \wedge \texttt{self} \neq \textbf{null} \wedge \texttt{self}.created \doteq TRUE \qquad (A.55)$$

$$(\mathcal{K}, s_1^{post}, \beta) \models frame \qquad (A.56)$$

As $\texttt{self}, \texttt{a}_1, \ldots, \texttt{a}_m$ do not occur in (A.53) or in (A.54), and as s and s_1 are otherwise identical, we get by Proposition A.1 that

$$(\mathcal{K}, s_1, \beta) \models wellFormed(h^{pre}) \wedge wellFormed(h^{post}) \qquad (A.57)$$

$$(\mathcal{K}, s_1, \beta) \models \neg\big(obs(h^{pre}, o, a'_1, \ldots, a'_m) \equiv obs(h^{post}, o, a'_1, \ldots, a'_m)\big).$$

Because of the definition of s_1, the second of the two statements above implies that

$$(\mathcal{K}, s_1, \beta) \models \neg\big(obs(h^{pre}, \texttt{self}, \texttt{a}_1, \ldots, \texttt{a}_m) \equiv obs(h^{post}, \texttt{self}, \texttt{a}_1, \ldots, \texttt{a}_m)\big). \qquad (A.58)$$

Lemma 6.2 tells us that

$$(\mathcal{K}, s_1, \beta) \models \{\texttt{heap}^{pre} := h^{pre} \,\|\, \texttt{heap} := h^{post}\}noDeallocs,$$

which because of the definition of s_1^{post} implies that

$$(\mathcal{K}, s_1^{post}, \beta) \models noDeallocs.$$

This, (A.56) and Lemma 5.4 (with $n = 0$) tell us that

$$(\mathcal{K}, s_1^{post}, \beta) \models \mathtt{heap} \doteq anon(\mathtt{heap}^{pre}, \{\mathtt{heap} := \mathtt{heap}^{pre}\}mod, \mathtt{heap}),$$

which because of the definition of s_1^{post} is the same as

$$(\mathcal{K}, s_1, \beta) \models h^{post} \doteq anon(h^{pre}, \{\mathtt{heap} := h^{pre}\}mod, h^{post}). \qquad (A.59)$$

Let $F = \delta(val_{\mathcal{K}, s_1, \beta}(o))$. Because of the definition of s_1, this means that

$$(\mathcal{K}, s_1, \beta) \models exactInstance_F(\mathtt{self}),$$

and because $\mathtt{heap}$ does not occur in the formula above, this implies by Proposition A.1 that

$$(\mathcal{K}, s_1^{pre}, \beta) \models exactInstance_F(\mathtt{self}). \qquad (A.60)$$

Let $\mathcal{K}' = (\mathcal{D}, \delta, I', \mathcal{S}, \rho)$ be a Kripke structure that is identical to $\mathcal{K}$, except that $I'(h) = val_{\mathcal{K}, s_1, \beta}(h^{post})$. Because h does not occur in (A.57), Proposition A.3 tells us that

$$(\mathcal{K}', s_1, \beta) \models wellFormed(h^{pre}) \wedge wellFormed(h^{post}).$$

Because h does not occur in h^{post}, we have $val_{\mathcal{K}', s_1, \beta}(h^{post}) = val_{\mathcal{K}, s_1, \beta}(h^{post})$ by Proposition A.3. Because we defined $\mathcal{K}'$ such that $I'(h) = val_{\mathcal{K}, s_1, \beta}(h^{post})$, this implies $I'(h) = val_{\mathcal{K}', s_1, \beta}(h^{post})$. Thus, the statement above implies

$$(\mathcal{K}', s_1, \beta) \models wellFormed(h^{pre}) \wedge wellFormed(h).$$

Using the definition of s_1^{pre} and the fact that $\mathtt{heap}$ does not occur in the formula $wellFormed(h)$, the above can be rewritten as

$$(\mathcal{K}', s_1^{pre}, \beta) \models wellFormed(\mathtt{heap}) \wedge wellFormed(h). \qquad (A.61)$$

Since $o \in Term_{\Sigma}^E$, we have $F \preceq E$. Instantiating (A.52) with F, $\mathcal{K}'$, s_1^{pre} and β yields

$$(\mathcal{K}', s_1^{pre}, \beta) \models pre \wedge wellFormed(\mathtt{heap}) \wedge wellFormed(h) \wedge reachableIn$$
$$\wedge\, \mathtt{self} \not\doteq \mathtt{null} \wedge \mathtt{self}.created \doteq TRUE \wedge exactInstance_F(\mathtt{self})$$
$$\rightarrow \mathtt{self}.obs(\mathtt{a}_1, \ldots, \mathtt{a}_m)$$
$$\equiv \{\mathtt{heap} := anon(\mathtt{heap}, mod, h)\}\big(\mathtt{self}.obs(\mathtt{a}_1, \ldots, \mathtt{a}_m)\big).$$

As h does not occur in (A.55) or in (A.60), by Proposition A.3 they hold also for $\mathcal{K}'$. Thus, we can combine them, (A.61), and the statement above to get

$$(\mathcal{K}', s_1^{pre}, \beta) \models \mathtt{self}.obs(\mathtt{a}_1, \ldots, \mathtt{a}_m)$$
$$\equiv \{\mathtt{heap} := anon(\mathtt{heap}, mod, h)\}\big(\mathtt{self}.obs(\mathtt{a}_1, \ldots, \mathtt{a}_m)\big).$$

Applying the update yields

$$(\mathcal{K}', s_1^{pre}, \beta) \models \texttt{self}.obs(\texttt{a}_1, \ldots, \texttt{a}_m)$$
$$\equiv obs(anon(\texttt{heap}, mod, h), \texttt{self}, \texttt{a}_1, \ldots, \texttt{a}_m).$$

Because of the definition of s_1^{pre}, this is the same as

$$(\mathcal{K}', s_1, \beta) \models obs(h^{pre}, \texttt{self}, \texttt{a}_1, \ldots, \texttt{a}_m)$$
$$\equiv obs(anon(h^{pre}, \{\texttt{heap} := h^{pre}\} mod, h), \texttt{self}, \texttt{a}_1, \ldots, \texttt{a}_m).$$

As we have $I'(h) = val_{\mathcal{K}', s_1, \beta}(h^{post})$, we can write the statement above as

$$(\mathcal{K}', s_1, \beta) \models obs(h^{pre}, \texttt{self}, \texttt{a}_1, \ldots, \texttt{a}_m)$$
$$\equiv obs(anon(h^{pre}, \{\texttt{heap} := h^{pre}\} mod, h^{post}), \texttt{self}, \texttt{a}_1, \ldots, \texttt{a}_m).$$

Because the constant symbol h does not occur in the above formula, and because $\mathcal{K}$ and $\mathcal{K}'$ are otherwise identical, Proposition A.3 tells us that

$$(\mathcal{K}, s_1, \beta) \models obs(h^{pre}, \texttt{self}, \texttt{a}_1, \ldots, \texttt{a}_m)$$
$$\equiv obs(anon(h^{pre}, \{\texttt{heap} := h^{pre}\} mod, h^{post}), \texttt{self}, \texttt{a}_1, \ldots, \texttt{a}_m).$$

We can combine this with (A.59) to get

$$(\mathcal{K}, s_1, \beta) \models obs(h^{pre}, \texttt{self}, \texttt{a}_1, \ldots, \texttt{a}_m) \equiv obs(h^{post}, \texttt{self}, \texttt{a}_1, \ldots, \texttt{a}_m),$$

which contradicts (A.58). □

A.10. Proof of Theorem 8.1: Soundness of shiftUpdate

We assume

$$\models \{u'\}\Gamma, \ upd \ \Rightarrow \ \varphi, \ \{u'\}\Delta. \tag{A.62}$$

Let $\mathcal{K} = (\mathcal{D}, \delta, I, \mathcal{S}, \rho)$ be a Kripke structure, $s \in \mathcal{S}$ be a state, and β be a variable assignment. Our goal is to show that

$$(\mathcal{K}, s, \beta) \models \Gamma \ \Rightarrow \ \{u\}\varphi, \ \Delta.$$

If there is $\gamma \in \Gamma$ with $val_{\mathcal{K}, s, \beta}(\gamma) = f\!f$ or if there is $\delta \in \Delta$ with $val_{\mathcal{K}, s, \beta}(\delta) = tt$, then this is trivially true. We therefore assume that

$$(\mathcal{K}, s, \beta) \models \bigwedge(\Gamma \cup \neg\Delta), \tag{A.63}$$

and aim to show that $(\mathcal{K}, s, \beta) \models \{u\}\varphi$.

Let $\mathcal{K}' = (\mathcal{D}, \delta, I', \mathcal{S}, \rho)$ be a Kripke structure identical to $\mathcal{K}$, except that $I'(a_i') = s(a_i)$ for all $i \in \{1, \ldots, n\}$. Because the constant symbols $a_1', \ldots, a_n'$ do not occur in u or in φ, by Proposition A.3 it is sufficient if we show $(\mathcal{K}', s, \beta) \models \{u\}\varphi$. Let $s_1 = val_{\mathcal{K}', s, \beta}(u)(s)$. Our goal is to show

$$(\mathcal{K}', s_1, \beta) \models \varphi. \tag{thm8.1-goal}$$

Let $s_2 = val_{\mathcal{K}', s_1, \beta}(u')(s_1)$. Because both u and u' assign at most to the program variables $a_1, \ldots, a_n$, the states s and s_2 differ at most in these variables. Furthermore, the definition of u' ensures that for all $i \in \{1, \ldots, n\}$ we have $s_2(a_i) = I'(a_i')$, and because we defined $\mathcal{K}'$ such that $I'(a_i') = s(a_i)$, this implies

$$s_2 = s. \tag{A.64}$$

As the constant symbols $a_1', \ldots, a_n'$ do not occur in Γ or in Δ, Proposition A.3 and (A.63) imply that

$$(\mathcal{K}', s, \beta) \models \bigwedge(\Gamma \cup \neg\Delta),$$

which because of (A.64) is the same as

$$(\mathcal{K}', s, \beta) \models \{u\}\{u'\}\bigwedge(\Gamma \cup \neg\Delta),$$

or in other words

$$(\mathcal{K}', s_1, \beta) \models \{u'\}\bigwedge(\Gamma \cup \neg\Delta). \tag{A.65}$$

Instantiating (A.62) with $\mathcal{K}'$, s_1 and β yields

$$(\mathcal{K}', s_1, \beta) \models \{u'\}\Gamma, \; upd \; \Rightarrow \; \varphi, \{u'\}\Delta.$$

Together with (A.65), this means that

$$(\mathcal{K}', s_1, \beta) \models \; upd \; \Rightarrow \; \varphi. \tag{A.66}$$

Because of (A.64), we have $val_{\mathcal{K}', s_1, \beta}(\{u'\}\{u\}a_i) = val_{\mathcal{K}', s, \beta}(\{u\}a_i)$ for all $i \in \{1, \ldots, n\}$. By definition of s_1, we also have $val_{\mathcal{K}', s, \beta}(\{u\}a_i) = val_{\mathcal{K}', s_1, \beta}(a_i)$. Together we get

$$val_{\mathcal{K}', s_1, \beta}(\{u'\}\{u\}a_i) = val_{\mathcal{K}', s_1, \beta}(a_i),$$

which implies

$$(\mathcal{K}', s_1, \beta) \models upd.$$

This and (A.66) imply (thm8.1-goal). $\qquad\square$

A.11. Proof of Theorem 8.2: Soundness of merge

We assume

$$\models \bigwedge(\Gamma_1 \cup \neg\Delta_1) \vee \cdots \vee \bigwedge(\Gamma_n \cup \neg\Delta_n) \Rightarrow \varphi. \tag{A.67}$$

Let $\mathcal{K}$ be a Kripke structure, $s \in \mathcal{S}$ be a state, β be a variable assignment, and $i \in \{1, \ldots, n\}$. Our goal is to show $(\mathcal{K}, s, \beta) \models (\Gamma_i \Rightarrow \varphi, \Delta_i)$. If there is $\gamma \in \Gamma_i$ with $val_{\mathcal{K},s,\beta}(\gamma) = f\!f$ or if there is $\delta \in \Delta_i$ with $val_{\mathcal{K},s,\beta}(\delta) = tt$, then this is trivially true. We therefore assume that $(\mathcal{K}, s, \beta) \models \bigwedge(\Gamma_i \cup \neg\Delta_i)$, and aim to show that $(\mathcal{K}, s, \beta) \models \varphi$. This follows immediately from (A.67). $\qquad\square$

A.12. Proof of Theorem 8.3: Soundness of setBack

For proof graphs consisting just of a root node, the proposition is trivially satisfied. As an induction hypothesis, assume that we are given a proof graph p with root r and leaves L, where all applied rules are sound and where all sub proof graphs (including p itself) satisfy the proposition. We need to show that a graph p' with leaves L' that results from p by applying setBack again satisfies the proposition, i.e., that logical validity of $seq(l')$ for all open $l' \in L'$ implies logical validity of $seq(r)$. (For graphs p' resulting from applying a rule, this is obvious.) By Definition 8.4, there is a node $parent \in L$ and a node $child \in L'$ such that $L' = (L \setminus \{parent\}) \cup \{child\}$, where $seq(child) = seq(dom)$ for some node dom that dominates $parent$.

Consider the subgraph p_{dom} of p that results from cutting off in p all nodes strictly dominated by dom. For the leaves L_{dom} of p_{dom} we know: $L_{dom} \subseteq (L \setminus \{parent\}) \cup \{dom\}$ (because $parent$ has been cut off, while dom has become a leaf). This implies that $\{seq(l_{dom}) \mid l_{dom} \in L_{dom}, l_{dom} \text{ open}\} \subseteq \{seq(l') \mid l \in L', l' \text{ open}\}$.

By the induction hypothesis, we know that logical validity of $seq(l_{dom})$ for all open $l_{dom} \in L_{dom}$ implies logical validity of $seq(r)$. Because we know that $\{seq(l_{dom}) \mid l_{dom} \in L_{dom}, l_{dom} \text{ open}\} \subseteq \{seq(l') \mid l \in L', l' \text{ open}\}$, this means that also logical validity of $seq(l')$ for all open $l' \in L'$ implies logical validity of $seq(r)$. $\qquad\square$

A.13. Proof of Theorem 8.4: Soundness of predicateAbstraction

We assume

$$\models \bigwedge(\Gamma \cup \neg\Delta) \rightarrow \alpha_P\Big(\bigwedge(\Gamma \cup \neg\Delta)\Big) \tag{A.68}$$

$$\models \alpha_P\Big(\bigwedge(\Gamma \cup \neg\Delta)\Big) \Rightarrow [\pi \; \mathtt{while}(g)p; \; \omega]\varphi \tag{A.69}$$

Let $\mathcal{K} = (\mathcal{D}, \delta, I, \mathcal{S}, \rho)$ be a Kripke structure, $s \in \mathcal{S}$ be a state, and β be a variable assignment. Our goal is to show that

$$(\mathcal{K}, s, \beta) \models \Gamma \Rightarrow [\pi \; \mathbf{while}(g)p; \; \omega]\varphi, \; \Delta.$$

If there is $\gamma \in \Gamma$ with $val_{\mathcal{K},s,\beta}(\gamma) = f\!f$ or if there is $\delta \in \Delta$ with $val_{\mathcal{K},s,\beta}(\delta) = t\!t$, then this is trivially true. We therefore assume that

$$(\mathcal{K}, s, \beta) \models \bigwedge(\Gamma \cup \neg\Delta), \tag{A.70}$$

and aim to show that $(\mathcal{K}, s, \beta) \models [\pi \; \mathbf{while}(g)p; \; \omega]\varphi$.
Combining (A.70) and (A.68) yields

$$(\mathcal{K}, s, \beta) \models \alpha_P\big(\bigwedge(\Gamma \cup \neg\Delta)\big), \tag{A.71}$$

and together with (A.69), implies what we have to show. $\qquad\square$

Bibliography

Jean-Raymond Abrial. *The B-Book: Assigning Programs to Meanings.* Cambridge University Press, 1996. (Cited on pages 1 and 25.)

Wolfgang Ahrendt, Bernhard Beckert, Reiner Hähnle, Philipp Rümmer, and Peter H. Schmitt. Verifying object-oriented programs with KeY: A tutorial. In Frank S. de Boer, Marcello M. Bonsangue, Susanne Graf, and Willem-Paul de Roever, editors, *Revised Lectures, 5th International Symposium on Formal Methods for Components and Objects (FMCO 2006)*, volume 4709 of *LNCS*, pages 70–101. Springer, 2007. (Cited on page 205.)

Wolfgang Ahrendt, Frank S. de Boer, and Immo Grabe. Abstract object creation in dynamic logic - to be or not to be created. In Ana Cavalcanti and Dennis Dams, editors, *Proceedings, Second World Congress on Formal Methods (FM 2009)*, volume 5850 of *LNCS*, pages 612–627. Springer, 2009. (Cited on pages 84 and 217.)

Roberto Bagnara, Patricia M. Hill, and Enea Zaffanella. The Parma Polyhedra Library: Toward a complete set of numerical abstractions for the analysis and verification of hardware and software systems. Technical Report 457, Dipartimento di Matematica, Università di Parma, Italy, 2006. (Cited on page 183.)

Thomas Ball, Ella Bounimova, Byron Cook, Vladimir Levin, Jakob Lichtenberg, Con McGarvey, Bohus Ondrusek, Sriram K. Rajamani, and Abdullah Ustuner. Thorough static analysis of device drivers. In Yolande Berbers and Willy Zwaenepoel, editors, *Proceedings, EuroSys 2006*, pages 73–85. ACM Press, 2006. (Cited on page 3.)

Anindya Banerjee, Mike Barnett, and David A. Naumann. Boogie meets regions: a verification experience report (extended version). Technical Report MSR-TR-2008-79, Microsoft Research, 2008a. (Cited on page 59.)

Anindya Banerjee, David A. Naumann, and Stan Rosenberg. Regional logic for local reasoning about global invariants. In Jan Vitek, editor, *Proceedings, 22nd European Conference on Object-Oriented Programming (ECOOP 2008)*, volume 5142 of *LNCS*, pages 387–411. Springer, 2008b. (Cited on page 59.)

Roberto Barbuti, Cinzia Bernardeschi, and Nicoletta De Francesco. Abstract interpretation of operational semantics for secure information flow. *Information Processing Letters*, 83(2):101–108, 2002. (Cited on page 182.)

John Barnes. *High Integrity Software: The SPARK Approach to Safety and Security*. Addison Wesley, 2003. (Cited on page 13.)

Michael Barnett, Robert DeLine, Manuel Fähndrich, K. Rustan M. Leino, and Wolfram Schulte. Verification of object-oriented programs with invariants. *Journal of Object Technology (JOT)*, 3(6):27–56, 2004. (Cited on pages 23, 39, 58, 59, 62, 70, and 84.)

Mike Barnett, K. Rustan M. Leino, and Wolfram Schulte. The Spec# programming system: An overview. In Gilles Barthe, Lilian Burdy, Marieke Huisman, Jean-Louis Lanet, and Traian Muntean, editors, *Proceedings, International Workshop on Construction and Analysis of Safe, Secure and Interoperable Smart devices (CASSIS 2004)*, volume 3362 of *LNCS*, pages 49–69. Springer, 2005. (Cited on pages 5, 13, and 54.)

Mike Barnett, Bor-Yuh Evan Chang, Robert DeLine, Bart Jacobs, and K. Rustan M. Leino. Boogie: A modular reusable verifier for object-oriented programs. In Frank S. de Boer, Marcello M. Bonsangue, Susanne Graf, and Willem-Paul de Roever, editors, *Revised Lectures, 4th International Symposium on Formal Methods for Components and Objects (FMCO 2005)*, volume 4111 of *LNCS*, pages 364–387. Springer, 2006. (Cited on pages 5, 59, 69, 74, 86, 93, 111, 159, 183, and 211.)

Mike Barnett, Manuel Fähndrich, K. Rustan M. Leino, Peter Müller, Wolfram Schulte, and Herman Venter. Specification and verification: The Spec# experience. *Communications of the ACM*, 2010. To appear. (Cited on pages 5, 58, and 159.)

Gilles Barthe, Lilian Burdy, Julien Charles, Benjamin Grégoire, Marieke Huisman, Jean-Louis Lanet, Mariela Pavlova, and Antoine Requet. JACK: a tool for validation of security and behaviour of Java applications. In Frank S. de Boer, Marcello M. Bonsangue, Susanne Graf, and Willem-Paul de Roever, editors, *Revised Lectures, 5th International Symposium on Formal Methods for Components and Objects (FMCO 2006)*, volume 4709 of *LNCS*, pages 152–174. Springer, 2007. (Cited on page 74.)

Marcus Baum. Debugging by visualizing symbolic execution. Diplomarbeit, Universität Karlsruhe, 2007. (Cited on page 6.)

Bernhard Beckert. A dynamic logic for the formal verification of Java Card programs. In Isabelle Attali and Thomas Jensen, editors, *Revised Papers, International Workshop on Java on Smart Cards: Programming and Security (JavaCard 2000)*, volume 2041 of *LNCS*, pages 6–24. Springer, 2001. (Cited on pages 4, 13, 65, 67, 73, 76, and 122.)

Bernhard Beckert and Christoph Gladisch. White-box testing by combining deduction-based specification extraction and black-box testing. In Bertrand Meyer and Yuri Gurevich, editors, *Revised Papers, First International Conference on Tests and Proofs (TAP 2007)*, volume 4454 of *LNCS*, pages 207–216. Springer, 2007. (Cited on page 6.)

Bernhard Beckert and Vladimir Klebanov. Must program verification systems and calculi be verified? In Serge Autexier and Heiko Mantel, editors, *Proceedings, 3rd International Verification Workshop (VERIFY'06)*, 2006. (Cited on page 3.)

Bernhard Beckert and André Platzer. Dynamic logic with non-rigid functions: A basis for object-oriented program verification. In Ulrich Furbach and Natarajan Shankar, editors, *Proceedings, 3rd International Joint Conference on Automated Reasoning (IJCAR 2006)*, volume 4130 of *LNCS*, pages 266–280. Springer, 2006. (Cited on pages 65, 67, and 73.)

Bernhard Beckert, Martin Giese, Elmar Habermalz, Reiner Hähnle, Andreas Roth, Philipp Rümmer, and Steffen Schlager. Taclets: A new paradigm for constructing interactive theorem provers. *Revista de la Real Academia de Ciencias Exactas, Físicas y Naturales, Serie A: Matemáticas (RACSAM)*, 98(1), 2004. Special Issue on Symbolic Computation in Logic and Artificial Intelligence. (Cited on page 91.)

Bernhard Beckert, Steffen Schlager, and Peter H. Schmitt. An improved rule for while loops in deductive program verification. In Kung-Kiu Lau, editor, *Proceedings, 7th International Conference on Formal Engineering Methods (ICFEM 2005)*, volume 3785 of *LNCS*, pages 315–329. Springer, 2005. (Cited on page 107.)

Bernhard Beckert, Reiner Hähnle, and Peter H. Schmitt, editors. *Verification of Object-Oriented Software: The KeY Approach*, volume 4334 of *LNCS*. Springer, 2007. (Cited on pages 3, 6, 13, 65, 67, 73, 79, 80, 86, 91, 104, 108, and 122.)

Bernhard Beckert, Thorsten Bormer, and Vladimir Klebanov. On essential program annotations and completeness of verifying compilers. In *Proceedings, Workshop on Verified Software: Theory, Tools, and Experiments (VSTTE 2009)*, 2009a. (Cited on page 5.)

Bernhard Beckert, Richard Bubel, Christian Engel, Peter H. Schmitt, Mattias Ulbrich, and Benjamin Weiß. Classification of symbols. Unpublished manuscript, Institut für Theoretische Informatik, Universität Karlsruhe, 2009b. (Cited on page 68.)

Dirk Beyer, Thomas A. Henzinger, Ranjit Jhala, and Rupak Majumdar. Checking memory safety with Blast. In Maura Cerioli, editor, *Proceedings, 8th International Conference on Fundamental Approaches to Software Engineering (FASE 2005)*, volume 3442 of *LNCS*, pages 2–18. Springer, 2005. (Cited on page 201.)

Bruno Blanchet, Patrick Cousot, Radhia Cousot, Jérome Feret, Laurent Mauborgne, Antoine Miné, David Monniaux, and Xavier Rival. A static analyzer for large safety-critical software. In *Proceedings, ACM Conference on Programming Language Design and Implementation (PLDI 2003)*, pages 196–207. ACM Press, 2003. (Cited on page 182.)

Egon Börger and Robert F. Stärk. *Abstract State Machines. A Method for High-Level System Design and Analysis*. Springer, 2003. (Cited on pages 1 and 67.)

Alexander Borgida, John Mylopoulos, and Raymond Reiter. On the frame problem in procedure specifications. *IEEE Transactions on Software Engineering*, 21(10):785–798, 1995. (Cited on page 19.)

François Bourdoncle. Efficient chaotic iteration strategies with widenings. In Dines Bjørner, Manfred Broy, and Igor V. Pottosin, editors, *Proceeedings, International Conference on Formal Methods in Programming and their Applications*, volume 735 of *LNCS*, pages 128–141. Springer, 1993. (Cited on page 180.)

Cees-Bart Breunesse and Erik Poll. Verifying JML specifications with model fields. In *Proceedings, 5th Workshop on Formal Techniques for Java-like Programs (FTfJP 2003)*, 2003. (Cited on page 31.)

Daniel Bruns. Formal semantics for the Java Modeling Language. Diplomarbeit, Universität Karlsruhe, 2009. (Cited on page 13.)

Richard Bubel. *Formal Verification of Recursive Predicates*. PhD thesis, Universität Karlsruhe, 2007. (Cited on pages 68, 107, 126, 147, and 160.)

Richard Bubel, Reiner Hähnle, and Peter H. Schmitt. Specification predicates with explicit dependency information. In Bernhard Beckert, editor, *Proceedings, 5th International Verification Workshop (VERIFY'08)*, volume 372 of *CEUR Workshop Proceedings*, pages 28–43. CEUR-WS.org, 2008. (Cited on pages 68, 107, 122, and 126.)

Richard Bubel, Reiner Hähnle, and Benjamin Weiß. Abstract interpretation of symbolic execution with explicit state updates. In Frank S. de Boer, Marcello M. Bonsangue, and Eric Madeleine, editors, *Revised Lectures, 7th International Symposium on Formal Methods for Components and Objects (FMCO 2008)*, volume 5751 of *LNCS*, pages 247–277. Springer, 2009. (Cited on pages 8, 207, 210, 212, and 213.)

Lilian Burdy, Antoine Requet, and Jean-Louis Lanet. Java applet correctness: A developer-oriented approach. In Keijiro Araki, Stefania Gnesi, and Dino Mandrioli, editors, *Proceedings, International Symposium of Formal Methods Europe (FME 2003)*, volume 2805 of *LNCS*, pages 422–439. Springer, 2003. (Cited on pages 5 and 67.)

Lilian Burdy, Yoonsik Cheon, David R. Cok, Michael D. Ernst, Joseph R. Kiniry, Gary T. Leavens, K. Rustan M. Leino, and Erik Poll. An overview of JML tools and applications. *Software Tools for Technology Transfer*, 7(3):212–232, 2005. (Cited on page 13.)

Paul Caspi, Daniel Pilaud, Nicolas Halbwachs, and John Plaice. Lustre: A declarative language for programming synchronous systems. In *Proceedings, 14th ACM Symposium on Principles of Programming Languages (POPL 1987)*, pages 178–188, 1987. (Cited on page 182.)

Patrice Chalin. Are the logical foundations of verifying compiler prototypes matching user expectations? *Formal Aspects of Computing*, 19(2):139–158, 2007a. (Cited on page 15.)

Patrice Chalin. A sound assertion semantics for the dependable systems evolution verifying compiler. In *Proceedings, 29th International Conference on Software Engineering (ICSE 2007)*, pages 23–33. IEEE Computer Society, 2007b. (Cited on pages 15 and 130.)

Patrice Chalin and Frédéric Rioux. Non-null references by default in the Java Modeling Language. *ACM SIGSOFT Software Engineering Notes*, 31(2), 2006. (Cited on page 19.)

Bor-Yuh Evan Chang and K. Rustan M. Leino. Abstract interpretation with alien expressions and heap structures. In Radhia Cousot, editor, *Proceedings, 6th International Conference on Verification, Model Checking, and Abstract Interpretation (VMCAI 2005)*, volume 3385 of *LNCS*, pages 147–163. Springer, 2005. (Cited on page 183.)

Yoonsik Cheon, Gary T. Leavens, Murali Sitaraman, and Stephen H. Edwards. Model variables: cleanly supporting abstraction in design by contract. *Software—Practice and Experience*, 35(6):583–599, 2005. (Cited on page 28.)

Dave Clarke, John Potter, and James Noble. Ownership types for flexible alias protection. In Craig Chambers, editor, *Proceedings, 13th ACM Conference on Object-Oriented Programming Systems, Languages and Applications (OOPSLA 1998)*, pages 48–64. ACM Press, 1998. (Cited on pages 7, 39, and 56.)

Edmund M. Clarke, Orna Grumberg, Somesh Jha, Yuan Lu, and Helmut Veith. Counterexample-guided abstraction refinement. In E. Allen Emerson and A. Prasad Sistla, editors, *Proceedings, 12th International Conference on Computer Aided Verification (CAV 2000)*, volume 1855 of *LNCS*, pages 154–169. Springer, 2000. (Cited on pages 185 and 201.)

Edmund M. Clarke, Daniel Kroening, and Flavio Lerda. A tool for checking ANSI-C programs. In Kurt Jensen and Andreas Podelski, editors, *10th International Conference on Tools and Algorithms for the Construction and Analysis of Systems (TACAS 2004)*, volume 2988 of *LNCS*, pages 168–176. Springer, 2004. (Cited on page 3.)

Ernie Cohen, Michal Moskal, Wolfram Schulte, and Stephan Tobies. A practical verification methodology for concurrent programs. Technical Report MSR-TR-2009-2019, Microsoft Research, 2009. (Cited on page 58.)

David R. Cok and Joseph R. Kiniry. ESC/Java2: Uniting ESC/Java and JML. In Gilles Barthe, Lilian Burdy, Marieke Huisman, Jean-Louis Lanet, and Traian Muntean, editors, *Proceedings, International Workshop on Construction and Analysis of Safe, Secure and Interoperable Smart devices (CASSIS 2004)*, volume 3362 of *LNCS*, pages 108–128. Springer, 2005. (Cited on pages 5 and 74.)

Patrick Cousot and Radhia Cousot. Abstract interpretation: A unified lattice model for static analysis of programs by construction or approximation of fixpoints. In *Proceedings, 4th ACM Symposium on Principles of Programming Languages (POPL 1977)*, pages 238–252. ACM Press, 1977. (Cited on pages 3, 165, 171, 172, 177, 179, and 180.)

Patrick Cousot and Radhia Cousot. Comparing the Galois connection and widening / narrowing approaches to abstract interpretation. In Maurice Bruynooghe and Martin Wirsing, editors, *Proceedings, 4th International Symposium on Programming Language Implementation and Logic Programming (PLILP 1992)*, volume 631 of *LNCS*, pages 269–295. Springer, 1992. (Cited on page 179.)

Patrick Cousot and Nicolas Halbwachs. Automatic discovery of linear restraints among variables of a program. In *Proceedings, 5th ACM Symposium on Principles of Programming Languages (POPL 1978)*, pages 84–97. ACM Press, 1978. (Cited on page 181.)

Patrick Cousot, Radhia Cousot, Jérôme Feret, Laurent Mauborgne, Antoine Miné, David Monniaux, and Xavier Rival. The ASTRÉE Analyzer. In Mooly Sagiv, editor, *Proceedings, European Symposium on Programming (ESOP 2005)*, volume 3444 of *LNCS*, pages 21–30. Springer, 2005. (Cited on pages 182 and 183.)

Ádám Darvas. *Reasoning About Data Abstraction in Contract Languages*. PhD thesis, ETH Zürich, 2009. (Cited on pages 21 and 130.)

Ádám Darvas and K. Rustan M. Leino. Practical reasoning about invocations and implementations of pure methods. In Matthew B. Dwyer and Antónia Lopes, editors, *Proceedings, 10th International Conference on Fundamental Approaches to Software Engineering (FASE 2007)*, volume 4422 of *LNCS*, pages 336–351. Springer, 2007. (Cited on pages 21 and 130.)

Ádám Darvas and Peter Müller. Faithful mapping of model classes to mathematical structures. In Arnd Poetzsch-Heffter, editor, *Proceedings, Conference on Specification and Verification of Component-Based Systems (SAVCBS 2007)*, pages 31–38. ACM Press, 2007a. (Cited on page 26.)

Ádám Darvas and Peter Müller. Formal encoding of JML Level 0 specifications in Jive. Technical Report 559, ETH Zürich, 2007b. Annual Report of the Chair of Software Engineering. (Cited on page 5.)

Ádám Darvas, Farhad Mehta, and Arsenii Rudich. Efficient well-definedness checking. In Alessandro Armando, Peter Baumgartner, and Gilles Dowek, editors, *Proceedings, 4th International Joint Conference on Automated Reasoning (IJCAR 2008)*, volume 5195 of *LNCS*, pages 100–115. Springer, 2008. (Cited on pages 16 and 131.)

Satyaki Das, David L. Dill, and Seungjoon Park. Experience with predicate abstraction. In Nicolas Halbwachs and Doron Peled, editors, *Proceedings, 11th International Conference on Computer Aided Verification (CAV 1999)*, volume 1633 of *LNCS*, pages 160–171. Springer, 1999. (Cited on page 199.)

Leonardo de Moura and Nikolaj Bjørner. Z3: An efficient SMT solver. In C. R. Ramakrishnan and Jakob Rehof, editors, *Proceedings, 14th International Conference on Tools and Algorithms for the Construction and Analysis of Systems (TACAS 2008)*, volume 4963 of *LNCS*, pages 337–340. Springer, 2008. (Cited on pages 4 and 159.)

David Delmas and Jean Souyris. Astrée: From research to industry. In Hanne Riis Nielson and Gilberto Filé, editors, *Proceedings, 14th International Static Analysis Symposium (SAS 2007)*, volume 4634 of *LNCS*, pages 437–451. Springer, 2007. (Cited on page 183.)

David Detlefs, Greg Nelson, and James B. Saxe. Extended static checking. SRC Research Report 159, Compaq Systems Research Center, 1998. (Cited on page 55.)

David Detlefs, Greg Nelson, and James B. Saxe. Simplify: A theorem prover for program checking. *Journal of the ACM*, 52(3):365–473, 2005. (Cited on pages 4, 132, 159, and 205.)

Edsger W. Dijkstra. Notes on structured programming. 1972. (Cited on page 2.)

Edsger W. Dijkstra. Guarded commands, nondeterminacy and formal derivation of programs. *Communications of the ACM*, 18(8):453–457, 1975. (Cited on pages 66 and 74.)

Dino Distefano and Matthew J. Parkinson. jStar: towards practical verification for Java. In Gail E. Harris, editor, *Proceedings, 23rd Annual ACM SIGPLAN Conference on Object-Oriented Programming, Systems, Languages, and Applications (OOPSLA 2008)*, pages 213–226. ACM Press, 2008. (Cited on page 59.)

Christian Engel and Reiner Hähnle. Generating unit tests from formal proofs. In Bertrand Meyer and Yuri Gurevich, editors, *Revised Papers, First International Conference on Tests and Proofs (TAP 2007)*, volume 4454 of *LNCS*, pages 169–188. Springer, 2007. (Cited on page 6.)

Christian Engel, Andreas Roth, Peter H. Schmitt, and Benjamin Weiß. Verification of modifies clauses in dynamic logic with non-rigid functions. Technical Report 2009-9, Universität Karlsruhe, Department of Computer Science, 2009. (Cited on pages 86, 107, and 160.)

Michael D. Ernst, Jake Cockrell, William G. Griswold, and David Notkin. Dynamically discovering likely program invariants to support program evolution. *IEEE Transactions on Software Engineering*, 27(2):99–123, 2001. (Cited on page 165.)

Manuel Fähndrich and K. Rustan M. Leino. Declaring and checking non-null types in an object-oriented language. *ACM SIGPLAN Notices*, 38(11):302–312, 2003. (Cited on page 181.)

Manuel Fähndrich, Michael Barnett, and Francesco Logozzo. Embedded contract languages. In Sung Y. Shin, Sascha Ossowski, Michael Schumacher, Mathew J. Palakal, and Chih-Cheng Hung, editors, *Proceedings, 2010 ACM Symposium on Applied Computing (SAC 2010)*, pages 2103–2110. ACM Press, 2010. (Cited on page 183.)

Jean-Christophe Filliâtre and Claude Marché. The Why/Krakatoa/Caduceus platform for deductive program verification. In Werner Damm and Holger Hermanns, editors, *Proceedings, 19th International Conference on Computer Aided Verification (CAV 2007)*, volume 4590 of *LNCS*, pages 173–177. Springer, 2007. (Cited on page 74.)

Cormac Flanagan and Shaz Qadeer. Predicate abstraction for software verification. In *Proceedings, 29th ACM Symposium on Principles of Programming Languages (POPL 2002)*, pages 191–202. ACM Press, 2002. (Cited on pages 185, 187, 199, 201, and 211.)

Cormac Flanagan, K. Rustan M. Leino, Mark Lillibridge, Greg Nelson, James B. Saxe, and Raymie Stata. Extended static checking for Java. In *Proceedings, ACM Conference on Programming Language Design and Implementation (PLDI 2002)*, pages 234–245. ACM Press, 2002. (Cited on pages 5 and 55.)

Robert W. Floyd. Assigning meanings to programs. In *Proceedings, 14th Symposium on Applied Mathematics*, pages 19–32. American Mathematical Society, 1967. (Cited on pages 2, 75, 171, and 174.)

Nicoletta De Francesco and Luca Martini. Abstract interpretation to check secure information flow in programs with input-output security annotations. In Theodosis Dimitrakos, Fabio Martinelli, Peter Y. A. Ryan, and Steve A. Schneider, editors, *Proceedings, 3rd International Workshop on Formal Aspects in Security and Trust (FAST 2005)*, volume 3866 of *LNCS*, pages 63–80. Springer, 2006. (Cited on page 182.)

Tobias Gedell. Embedding static analysis into tableaux and sequent based frameworks. In Bernhard Beckert, editor, *Proceedings, International Conference on Automated Reasoning with Analytic Tableaux and Related Methods (Tableaux 2005)*, volume 3702 of *LNCS*, pages 108–122. Springer, 2005. (Cited on page 211.)

Tobias Gedell. Static analysis and deductive verification of programs. Licentiate Thesis, Technical Report 2006–15L, Chalmers University of Technology, Department of Computer Science and Engineering, 2006. (Cited on page 211.)

Tobias Gedell and Reiner Hähnle. Automating verification of loops by parallelization. In Miki Hermann and Andrei Voronkov, editors, *Proceedings, 13th International Conference on Logic for Programming, Artificial Intelligence and Reasoning (LPAR 2006)*, volume 4246 of *LNCS*, pages 332–346. Springer, 2006. (Cited on page 211.)

Gerhard Gentzen. Untersuchungen über das logische Schließen. *Mathematische Zeitschrift*, 39:176–210, 405–431, 1935. (Cited on page 89.)

James Gosling, Bill Joy, Guy Steele, and Gilad Bracha. *The Java Language Specification, Second Edition*. Addison-Wesley, 2000. (Cited on pages 3, 43, 73, 80, 82, and 100.)

Susanne Graf and Hassen Saïdi. Construction of abstract state graphs with PVS. In Orna Grumberg, editor, *Proceedings, 9th International Conference on Computer Aided Verification (CAV 1997)*, volume 1254 of *LNCS*, pages 72–83. Springer, 1997. (Cited on pages 7, 185, and 187.)

David Gries and Fred B. Schneider. Avoiding the undefined by underspecification. In Jan van Leeuwen, editor, *Computer Science Today*, volume 1000 of *LNCS*, pages 366–373. Springer, 1995. (Cited on page 15.)

Sumit Gulwani, Bill McCloskey, and Ashish Tiwari. Lifting abstract interpreters to quantified logical domains. In George C. Necula and Philip Wadler, editors, *Proceedings, 35th ACM symposium on Principles of programming languages (POPL 2008)*, pages 235–246. ACM Press, 2008. (Cited on page 184.)

J. V. Guttag, J. J. Horning, S. J. Garland, K. D. Jones, A. Modet, and J. M. Wing. *Larch: Languages and Tools for Formal Specification*. Springer, 1993. (Cited on pages 13 and 19.)

Christian Haack, Erik Poll, Jan Schäfer, and Aleksy Schubert. Immutable objects for a Java-like language. In Rocco De Nicola, editor, *Proceedings, 16th European Symposium on Programming (ESOP 2007)*, volume 4421 of *LNCS*, pages 347–362. Springer, 2007. (Cited on page 35.)

Reiner Hähnle, Marcus Baum, Richard Bubel, and Marcel Rothe. A visual interactive debugger based on symbolic execution. In Charles Pecheur, Jamie Andrews, and Elisabetta Di Nitto, editors, *Proceedings, 25th IEEE/ACM International Conference on Automated Software Engineering (ASE 2010)*, pages 143–146. ACM Press, 2010. (Cited on pages 6 and 122.)

Stefan Hallerstede. Incremental system modelling in Event-B. In Frank S. de Boer, Marcello M. Bonsangue, and Eric Madelain, editors, *Proceedings, 7th International Symposium on Formal Methods for Components and Objects (FMCO 2008)*, volume 5751 of *LNCS*, pages 139–158. Springer, 2009. (Cited on pages 1, 25, and 28.)

David Harel, Dexter Kozen, and Jerzy Tiuryn. *Dynamic Logic*. MIT Press, 2000. (Cited on pages 4, 66, and 73.)

John Hatcliff, Gary T. Leavens, K. Rustan M. Leino, Peter Müller, and Matthew Parkinson. Behavioral interface specification languages. Technical Report CS-TR-09-01, School of Electrical Engineering and Computer Science, University of Central Florida, 2009. (Cited on page 13.)

Thomas A. Henzinger, Ranjit Jhala, Rupak Majumdar, and Grégoire Sutre. Software verification with BLAST. In Thomas Ball and Sriram K. Rajamani, editors, *Proceedings, 10th International SPIN Workshop on Model Checking Software*, volume 2648 of *LNCS*, pages 235–239. Springer, 2003. (Cited on page 3.)

C. A. R. Hoare. An axiomatic basis for computer programming. *Communications of the ACM*, 12(10):576–580, 1969. (Cited on pages 2, 3, 66, and 74.)

C. A. R. Hoare. Proof of correctness of data representations. *Acta Informatica*, 1:271–281, 1972. (Cited on pages 2, 6, 21, and 25.)

C. A. R. Hoare. Assertions: A personal perspective. *IEEE Annals of the History of Computing*, 25(2):14–25, 2003a. (Cited on page 2.)

C. A. R. Hoare. The verifying compiler: A grand challenge for computing research. *Journal of the ACM*, 50(1):63–69, 2003b. (Cited on page 2.)

C. A. R. Hoare. Towards the verifying compiler. In Bernhard K. Aichernig and T. S. E. Maibaum, editors, *Proceedings, Formal Methods at the Crossroads – From Panacea to Foundational Support: The 10th Anniversary Colloquium of UNU/IIST*, volume 2757 of *LNCS*, pages 151–160. Springer, 2003c. (Cited on page 2.)

David Hovemeyer, Jaime Spacco, and William Pugh. Evaluating and tuning a static analysis to find null pointer bugs. *ACM SIGSOFT Software Engineering Notes*, 31(1):13–19, 2006. (Cited on page 181.)

James J. Hunt, Eric Jenn, Stéphane Leriche, Peter Schmitt, Isabel Tonin, and Claus Wonnemann. A case study of specification and verification using JML in an avionics application. In *Proceedings, 4th International Workshop on Java Technologies for Real-time and Embedded Systems (JTRES 2006)*, pages 107–116. ACM Press, 2006. (Cited on page 6.)

Daniel Jackson. Alloy: a lightweight object modelling notation. *ACM Transactions on Software Engineering and Methodology*, 11(2):256–290, 2002. (Cited on page 1.)

Java Card 2003. Java Card 2.2.1 application programming interface, Java Card 2.2.1 runtime environment specification, Java Card 2.2.1 virtual machine specification. Sun Microsystems, 2003. (Cited on pages 4 and 73.)

Bertrand Jeannet and Antoine Miné. Apron: A library of numerical abstract domains for static analysis. In Ahmed Bouajjani and Oded Maler, editors, *Proceedings, 21st International Conference on Computer Aided Verification (CAV 2009)*, volume 5643 of *LNCS*, pages 661–667. Springer, 2009. (Cited on page 183.)

Neil D. Jones and Flemming Nielson. Abstract interpretation: A semantics-based tool for program analysis. In S. Abramsky, D. M. Gabbay, and T. S. E. Maibaum, editors, *Handbook of Logic in Computer Science*, volume 4, pages 527–636. Oxford University Press, 1995. (Cited on page 171.)

Ioannis T. Kassios. Dynamic frames: Support for framing, dependencies and sharing without restrictions. In Jayadev Misra, Tobias Nipkow, and Emil Sekerinski, editors, *Proceedings, 14th International Symposium on Formal Methods (FM 2006)*, volume 4085 of *LNCS*, pages 268–283. Springer, 2006a. (Cited on pages 7, 37, 40, 41, 42, 59, and 61.)

Ioannis T. Kassios. *A Theory of Object Oriented Refinement*. PhD thesis, University of Toronto, 2006b. (Cited on page 37.)

Ioannis T. Kassios. The dynamic frames theory. *Formal Aspects of Computing*, 2010. To appear. (Cited on pages 37 and 217.)

James C. King. Symbolic execution and program testing. *Communications of the ACM*, 19(7):385–394, 1976. (Cited on pages 76 and 101.)

Vladimir Klebanov. *Extending the Reach and Power of Deductive Program Verification*. PhD thesis, Universität Koblenz-Landau, 2009. (Cited on page 5.)

Roman Krenický. A calculus for data abstraction. Diplomarbeit, Universität Karlsruhe, 2009. (Cited on page 68.)

Vincent Laviron and Francesco Logozzo. Subpolyhedra: A (more) scalable approach to infer linear inequalities. In Neil D. Jones and Markus Müller-Olm, editors, *Proceedings, 10th International Conference on Verification, Model Checking, and Abstract Interpretation (VMCAI 2009)*, volume 5403 of *LNCS*, pages 229–244. Springer, 2009. (Cited on pages 180, 181, and 183.)

Gary T. Leavens. JML's rich, inherited specifications for behavioral subtypes. In Zhiming Liu and Jifeng He, editors, *Proceedings, 8th International Conference on Formal Engineering Methods (ICFEM 2006)*, volume 4260 of *LNCS*, pages 2–34. Springer, 2006. (Cited on page 39.)

Gary T. Leavens, Yoonsik Cheon, Curtis Clifton, Clyde Ruby, and David R. Cok. How the design of JML accommodates both runtime assertion checking and formal verification. *Science of Computer Programming*, 55(1–3):185–208, 2005. (Cited on page 26.)

Gary T. Leavens, Albert L. Baker, and Clyde Ruby. Preliminary design of JML: A behavioral interface specification language for Java. *ACM SIGSOFT Software Engineering Notes*, 31(3):1–38, 2006a. (Cited on pages 4 and 13.)

Gary T. Leavens, David A. Naumann, and Stan Rosenberg. Preliminary definition of core JML. CS Report 2006-07, Stevens Institute of Technology, 2006b. (Cited on page 13.)

Gary T. Leavens, K. Rustan M. Leino, and Peter Müller. Specification and verification challenges for sequential object-oriented programs. *Formal Aspects of Computing*, 19(2):159–189, 2007. (Cited on page 32.)

Gary T. Leavens, Erik Poll, Curtis Clifton, Yoonsik Cheon, Clyde Ruby, David Cok, Peter Müller, Joseph Kiniry, Patrice Chalin, Daniel M. Zimmerman, and Werner Dietl. JML reference manual (draft, revision 1.235), 2008. (Cited on pages 13, 21, 23, 31, 35, 38, 39, 40, 45, 125, and 126.)

K. Rustan M. Leino. *Toward Reliable Modular Programs*. PhD thesis, California Institute of Technology, 1995. (Cited on pages 40 and 93.)

K. Rustan M. Leino. Data groups: Specifying the modification of extended state. In Craig Chambers, editor, *Proceedings, 13th ACM Conference on Object-Oriented Programming Systems, Languages and Applications (OOPSLA 1998)*, pages 144–153. ACM Press, 1998. (Cited on pages 31, 39, and 56.)

K. Rustan M. Leino. Specification and verification of object-oriented software. Lecture Notes, Marktoberdorf International Summer School, 2008. (Cited on pages 5, 31, 42, 55, 61, 70, 159, and 161.)

K. Rustan M. Leino and Francesco Logozzo. Loop invariants on demand. In Kwangkeun Yi, editor, *Proceedings, 3rd Asian Symposium on Programming Languages and Systems (APLAS 2005)*, volume 3780 of *LNCS*, pages 119–134. Springer, 2005. (Cited on page 211.)

K. Rustan M. Leino and Francesco Logozzo. Using widenings to infer loop invariants inside an SMT solver, or: A theorem prover as abstract domain. In *Proceedings, 1st International Workshop on Invariant Generation (WING 2007)*, 2007. (Cited on page 211.)

K. Rustan M. Leino and Peter Müller. Object invariants in dynamic contexts. In Martin Odersky, editor, *Proceedings, 18th European Conference on Object-Oriented Programming (ECOOP 2004)*, volume 3086 of *LNCS*, pages 491–516. Springer, 2004. (Cited on pages 23, 39, and 58.)

K. Rustan M. Leino and Peter Müller. A verification methodology for model fields. In Peter Sestoft, editor, *Proceedings, 15th European Symposium on Programming (ESOP 2006)*, volume 3924 of *LNCS*, pages 115–130. Springer, 2006. (Cited on pages 31 and 58.)

K. Rustan M. Leino and Peter Müller. Verification of equivalent-results methods. In Sophia Drossopoulou, editor, *Proceedings, European Symposium on Programming (ESOP 2008)*, volume 4960 of *LNCS*, pages 307–321. Springer, 2008. (Cited on page 160.)

K. Rustan M. Leino and Greg Nelson. Data abstraction and information hiding. *ACM Transactions on Programming Languages and Systems*, 24(5):491–553, 2002. (Cited on pages 28, 40, 41, 42, 55, and 56.)

K. Rustan M. Leino and Philipp Rümmer. A polymorphic intermediate verification language: Design and logical encoding. In Javier Esparza and Rupak Majumdar, editors, *Proceedings, 16th International Conference on Tools and Algorithms for the Construction and Analysis of Systems (TACAS 2010)*, volume 6015 of *LNCS*, pages 312–327. Springer, 2010. (Cited on pages 69 and 72.)

K. Rustan M. Leino, Arnd Poetzsch-Heffter, and Yunhong Zhou. Using data groups to specify and check side effects. In *Proceedings, ACM Conference on Programming Language Design and Implementation (PLDI 2002)*, pages 246–257. ACM Press, 2002. (Cited on pages 40, 42, and 56.)

Barbara Liskov and Jeannette M. Wing. A behavioral notion of subtyping. *ACM Transactions on Programming Languages and Systems*, 16(6):1811–1841, 1994. (Cited on page 23.)

Claude Marché and Christine Paulin-Mohring. Reasoning about Java programs with aliasing and frame conditions. In Joe Hurd and Tom Melham, editors, *Proceedings, 18th International Conference on Theorem Proving in Higher Order Logics (TPHOLs 2005)*, volume 3603 of *LNCS*, pages 179–194. Springer, 2005. (Cited on page 72.)

Claude Marché, Christine Paulin-Mohring, and Xavier Urbain. The Krakatoa tool for certification of Java/JavaCard programs annotated in JML. *Journal of Logic and Algebraic Programming*, 58(1–2):89–106, 2004. (Cited on pages 5, 70, and 72.)

John McCarthy. Towards a mathematical science of computation. In *Information Processing 1962*, pages 21–28, 1963. (Cited on pages 8, 65, 70, 73, and 122.)

Bertrand Meyer. Applying "design by contract". *Computer*, 25(10):40–51, 1992. (Cited on pages 2 and 13.)

Bertrand Meyer. *Object-Oriented Software Construction*. Prentice Hall, 2000. (Cited on pages 2 and 13.)

Jörg Meyer and Arnd Poetzsch-Heffter. An architecture for interactive program provers. In Susanne Graf and Michael I. Schwartzbach, editors, *Proceedings, 6th International Conference on Tools and Algorithms for Construction and Analysis of Systems (TACAS 2000)*, volume 1785 of *LNCS*, pages 63–77. Springer, 2000. (Cited on page 5.)

Ana Milanova, Atanas Rountev, and Barbara G. Ryder. Parameterized object sensitivity for points-to and side-effect analyses for Java. *ACM SIGSOFT Software Engineering Notes*, 27(4):1–11, 2002. (Cited on pages 181 and 182.)

Antoine Miné. The octagon abstract domain. *Higher-Order and Symbolic Computation*, 19:31–100, 2006. (Cited on page 181.)

Carroll Morgan. *Programming from specifications*. Prentice-Hall, 1990. (Cited on page 25.)

Wojciech Mostowski. *Formal Development of Safe and Secure Java Card Applets*. PhD thesis, Chalmers University of Technology, 2005. (Cited on page 73.)

Wojciech Mostowski. Fully verified Java Card API reference implementation. In Bernhard Beckert, editor, *Proceedings, 4th International Verification Workshop (VERIFY'07)*, volume 259 of *CEUR Workshop Proceedings*, pages 136–151. CEUR-WS.org, 2007. (Cited on pages 6 and 205.)

Peter Müller. *Modular Specification and Verification of Object-Oriented Programs*, volume 2262 of *LNCS*. Springer, 2002. (Cited on pages 7, 39, 56, and 93.)

Peter Müller, Arnd Poetzsch-Heffter, and Gary T. Leavens. Modular specification of frame properties in JML. *Concurrency and Computation: Practice and Experience*, 15(2):117–154, 2003. (Cited on page 56.)

Peter Müller, Arnd Poetzsch-Heffter, and Gary T. Leavens. Modular invariants for layered object structures. *Science of Computer Programming*, 62(3):253–286, 2006. (Cited on pages 23, 39, 57, 58, and 59.)

OCL 2006. Object Constraint Language specification, version 2.0. Object Modeling Group, 2006. (Cited on pages 4 and 13.)

Matthew Parkinson. Class invariants: The end of the road? In Tobias Wrigstad, editor, *Proceedings, 3rd International Workshop on Aliasing, Confinement and Ownership in object-oriented programming (IWACO 2007)*, 2007. (Cited on page 59.)

Matthew J. Parkinson and Gavin M. Bierman. Separation logic and abstraction. In Jens Palsberg and Martín Abadi, editors, *Proceedings, 32nd ACM Symposium on Principles of Programming Languages (POPL 2005)*, pages 247–258. ACM Press, 2005. (Cited on page 59.)

David Lorge Parnas. On the criteria to be used in decomposing systems into modules. *Communications of the ACM*, 15(12), 1972. (Cited on page 25.)

Benjamin C. Pierce. *Types and Programming Languages*. MIT Press, 2002. (Cited on page 1.)

André Platzer. An object-oriented dynamic logic with updates. Diplomarbeit, Universität Karlsruhe, 2004. (Cited on page 90.)

Arnd Poetzsch-Heffter. Specification and verification of object-oriented programs. Habilitationsschrift, Technische Universität München, 1997. (Cited on pages 23 and 70.)

Arnd Poetzsch-Heffter and Peter Müller. A programming logic for sequential Java. In S. Doaitse Swierstra, editor, *Proceedings, 8th European Symposium on Programming (ESOP 1999)*, volume 1576 of *LNCS*, pages 162–176. Springer, 1999. (Cited on pages 70 and 74.)

PolySpace. Code verification and run-time error detection through abstract interpretation. White paper, The MathWorks, Inc. (Cited on page 183.)

Vaughan R. Pratt. Semantical considerations on Floyd-Hoare logic. In *Proceedings, 17th Annual Symposium on Foundations of Computer Science (FOCS 1976)*, pages 109–121. IEEE Press, 1976. (Cited on pages 4, 66, and 73.)

Arun D. Raghavan and Gary T. Leavens. Desugaring JML method specifications. Technical Report 00-03c, Iowa State University, Department of Computer Science, 2000. (Cited on page 24.)

Zvonimir Rakamarić and Alan J. Hu. Automatic inference of frame axioms using static analysis. In *Proceedings, 23rd IEEE/ACM International Conference on Automated Software Engineering (ASE 2008)*, pages 89–98. IEEE Press, 2008. (Cited on page 182.)

Silvio Ranise and Cesare Tinelli. The SMT-LIB standard: Version 1.2. Technical report, University of Iowa, 2006. (Cited on pages 69 and 70.)

Wolfgang Reif. The KIV-approach to software verification. In Manfred Broy and Stefan Jähnichen, editors, *KORSO - Methods, Languages, and Tools for the Construction of Correct Software*, volume 1009 of *LNCS*, pages 339–370. Springer, 1995. (Cited on page 5.)

John C. Reynolds. Separation logic: A logic for shared mutable data structures. In *Proceedings, 17th IEEE Symposium on Logic in Computer Science (LICS 2002)*, pages 55–74. IEEE Press, 2002. (Cited on page 58.)

Andreas Roth. Specification and verification of encapsulation in Java programs. In Martin Steffen and Gianluigi Zavattaro, editors, *Proceedings, 7th International Conference on Formal Methods for Open Object-Based Distributed Systems (FMOODS 2005)*, volume 3535 of *LNCS*, pages 195–210. Springer, 2005. (Cited on page 61.)

Andreas Roth. *Specification and Verification of Object-oriented Software Components*. PhD thesis, Universität Karlsruhe, 2006. (Cited on pages 23, 60, 61, 93, 107, 146, and 160.)

Philipp Rümmer. Sequential, parallel, and quantified updates of first-order structures. In Miki Hermann and Andrei Voronkov, editors, *Proceedings, 13th International Conference on Logic for Programming, Artificial Intelligence and Reasoning (LPAR 2006)*, volume 4246 of *LNCS*, pages 422–436. Springer, 2006. (Cited on pages 4, 73, 76, 82, 98, 113, and 122.)

Philipp Rümmer. A sequent calculus for integer arithmetic with counterexample generation. In Bernhard Beckert, editor, *Proceedings, 4th International Verification Workshop (VERIFY'07)*, volume 259 of *CEUR Workshop Proceedings*, pages 179–194. CEUR-WS.org, 2007. (Cited on page 91.)

Andrei Sabelfeld and Andrew C. Myers. Language-based information-flow security. *IEEE Journal on Selected Areas in Communications*, 21(1):5–19, 2003. (Cited on pages 35 and 182.)

Steffen Schlager. *Symbolic Execution as a Framework for Deductive Verification of Object-Oriented Programs*. PhD thesis, Universität Karlsruhe, 2007. (Cited on pages 79, 107, and 108.)

Peter H. Schmitt and Isabel Tonin. Verifying the Mondex case study. In *Proceedings, 5th IEEE International Conference on Software Engineering and Formal Methods (SEFM 2007)*, pages 47–58. IEEE Press, 2007. (Cited on page 6.)

Peter H. Schmitt and Benjamin Weiß. Inferring invariants by symbolic execution. In Bernhard Beckert, editor, *Proceedings, 4th International Verification Workshop (VERIFY'07)*, volume 259 of *CEUR Workshop Proceedings*, pages 195–210. CEUR-WS.org, 2007. (Cited on page 212.)

Peter H. Schmitt, Mattias Ulbrich, and Benjamin Weiß. Dynamic frames in Java dynamic logic: Formalisation and proofs. Technical Report 2010-11, Karlsruhe Institute of Technology, Department of Computer Science, 2010. (Cited on page 8.)

Peter H. Schmitt, Mattias Ulbrich, and Benjamin Weiß. Dynamic frames in Java dynamic logic. In Bernhard Beckert and Claude Marché, editors, *Proceedings, International Conference on Formal Verification of Object-Oriented Software (FoVeOOS 2010)*, volume 6528 of *LNCS*, pages 138–152. Springer, 2011. To appear. (Cited on page 8.)

Jan Smans, Bart Jacobs, Frank Piessens, and Wolfram Schulte. An automatic verifier for Java-like programs based on dynamic frames. In José Luiz Fiadeiro and Paola Inverardi, editors, *Proceedings, 11th International Conference on Fundamental Approaches to Software Engineering (FASE 2008)*, volume 4961 of *LNCS*, pages 261–275. Springer, 2008. (Cited on pages 5, 42, 54, 55, 60, 61, 70, 159, and 160.)

Jan Smans, Bart Jacobs, and Frank Piessens. Implicit dynamic frames: Combining dynamic frames and separation logic. In Sophia Drossopoulou, editor, *Proceedings, 23rd European Conference on Object-Oriented Programming (ECOOP 2009)*, volume 5653 of *LNCS*, pages 148–172. Springer, 2009a. (Cited on pages 59 and 159.)

Jan Smans, Bart Jacobs, and Frank Piessens. Symbolic execution for implicit dynamic frames. Draft, available at http://www.cs.kuleuven.be/~jans/vericool3/, 2009b. (Cited on pages 59 and 159.)

J. M. Spivey. *The Z notation: a reference manual (2nd Edition)*. Prentice-Hall, 1992. (Cited on page 1.)

Fausto Spoto. Julia: A generic static analyser for the Java bytecode. In *Proceedings, 7th Workshop on Formal Techniques for Java-like Programs (FTfJP 2005)*, 2005. (Cited on page 180.)

Fausto Spoto and Erik Poll. Static analysis for JML's assignable clauses. In Giorgio Ghelli, editor, *Proceedings, 10th International Workshop on Foundations of Object-Oriented Languages (FOOL-10)*, 2003. (Cited on page 182.)

Kurt Stenzel. A formally verified calculus for full Java Card. In Charles Rattray, Savi Maharaj, and Carron Shankland, editors, *Proceedings, 10th International Conference on Algebraic Methodology and Software Technology (AMAST 2004)*, volume 3116 of *LNCS*, pages 491–505. Springer, 2004. (Cited on pages 5, 70, 73, and 160.)

Kurt Stenzel. *Verification of Java Card Programs*. PhD thesis, Universität Augsburg, 2005. (Cited on page 160.)

Alexandru D. Sălcianu and Martin C. Rinard. Purity and side effect analysis for Java programs. In Radhia Cousot, editor, *Proceedings, 6th International Conference on Verification, Model Checking and Abstract Interpretation (VMCAI 2005)*, volume 3385 of *LNCS*, pages 199–215. Springer, 2005. (Cited on pages 181 and 182.)

Alexander J. Summers, Sophia Drossopoulou, and Peter Müller. The need for flexible object invariants. In *Proceedings, International Workshop on Aliasing, Confinement and Ownership in Object-Oriented Programming (IWACO 2009)*, pages 1–9. ACM Press, 2009. (Cited on page 59.)

Alfred Tarski. A lattice-theoretical fixpoint theorem and its applications. *Pacific Journal of Mathematics*, 5:285–309, 1955. (Cited on page 172.)

Ashish Tiwari and Sumit Gulwani. Logical interpretation: Static program analysis using theorem proving. In Frank Pfenning, editor, *Proceedings, 21st International Conference on Automated Deduction (CADE-21)*, volume 4603 of *LNCS*, pages 147–166. Springer, 2007. (Cited on page 211.)

Mattias Ulbrich. A dynamic logic for unstructured programs with embedded assertions. In Bernhard Beckert and Claude Marché, editors, *Proceedings, International Conference on Formal Verification of Object-Oriented Software (FoVeOOS 2010)*, 2010. (Cited on page 160.)

Benjamin Weiß. Inferring invariants by static analysis in KeY. Diplomarbeit, Universität Karlsruhe, 2007. (Cited on page 212.)

Benjamin Weiß. Predicate abstraction in a program logic calculus. In Michael Leuschel and Heike Wehrheim, editors, *Proceedings, 7th International Conference on integrated Formal Methods (iFM 2009)*, volume 5423 of *LNCS*, pages 136–150. Springer, 2009. (Cited on pages 8 and 189.)

Benjamin Weiß. Predicate abstraction in a program logic calculus. *Science of Computer Programming*, 2011. To appear. (Cited on pages 8 and 189.)

Reinhard Wilhelm, Shmuel Sagiv, and Thomas W. Reps. Shape analysis. In David A. Watt, editor, *Proceedings, 9th International Conference on Compiler Construction (CC 2000)*, volume 1781 of *LNCS*, pages 1–17. Springer, 2000. (Cited on page 182.)

Index